D1104686

VANESSA BELL

VANESSA BELL

FRANCES SPALDING

Ticknor & Fields
NEW HAVEN AND NEW YORK

I envy painters, I think they are happy people. The painter lives with his craft the whole time: the visual world, which I adore, is always present, and the artist can always be thinking about his work, being inspired by light and so on. . . . Painting is an image of the spiritual life; the painter really sees, and the veil is taken away.

IRIS MURDOCH
interviewed by John Haffenden

Library of Congress Cataloging in Publication Data

Spalding, Frances.
Vanessa Bell.

Bibliography: p.
Includes index.
1. Bell, Vanessa, 1879–1961.   2. Painters—England—
Biography.   I. Title.
ND497.B44S62   1983   759.2   [B]   83–4967
ISBN 0–89919-205-X

Printed in the United States of America

D 10 9 8 7 6 5 4 3

Contents

Black and White Illustrations

Unless otherwise stated, all paintings illustrated are by Vanessa Bell. These illustrations, when referred to in the text, are marked §.

vii

The line drawings in the text are taken from the *Charleston Bulletin*

Colour Illustrations

Acknowledgements

I am indebted to the following individuals for generous assistance with the writing of this book: Sir Geoffrey Agnew; Dr Francis Ames-Lewis; Lord Annan; Dr and Mrs Igor Anrep; Miss Isabelle Anscombe; Mrs Benita Armstrong; Lady Ashton (Madge Garland); Sir Frederick Ashton; Mr and Mrs Walter Aylen; Mrs Barbara Bagenal; Mr and Mrs Michael Bagenal; Major Michael Heward Bell; Mr Alan Bennett; Madame Y. Berro; Mr Edward Bradbury; Professor Richard Braithwaite; Mr Noel Carrington; Lord Clark; Miss Judith Collins; Signorina Anna Corsini; Mr Raymond Coxon; Mrs Mina Curtiss; Miss Caroline Cuthbert; Mrs Pamela Diamand; Dr Dennis Farr; Mr Tim Fell; Miss Jane Fowles; Viscount Gage; the late David Garnett; Mr and Mrs Richard Garnett; Mr Oliver Garnett; Professor Diane Gillespie; Professor Lawrence Gowing; Miss Anna Greutzner; Mr Nigel Henderson; Mrs P. Heriot (formerly of Shelley's Hotel, Lewes); Mrs Grace Higgens; Mrs Frances Hillier, of Seend; Mr Michael Holroyd; Lord Hutchinson; Mr Sidney C. Hutchison; Mr Paul Hyslop; Mr Richard Jefferies of the Watts Museum, Compton; Lord Kahn; Dr Milo Keynes; Professor Mary Lago; Ling Su-Hua (Mrs Chen); Sir Henry and Lady Lintott; Mrs Bea Lubbock; Dr and Mrs Dermod MacCarthy; Mr Colin Mackenzie; Madame J. Maffei; Miss Jean McKinney of the Royal West of England Academy; Mr Robert Medley; Lord Milford; Mrs Barbara Morrison; Mr Richard Morphet; the late Raymond Mortimer; Mr Nigel Nicolson; Mrs Felicity Nellen; Mrs Trekkie Parsons; Mrs Frances Partridge; Sir Roland Penrose; Mrs Rosemary Peto; Dr Antoinette Pirie; the late Mary Potter; Mrs Lettice Ramsey; Mr David Reed of Clifton College Library; Mr and Mrs Paul Roche; Professor S. P. Rosenbaum; the late Maud Russell; Mr George Rylands; Miss Chattie Salaman; Mr Richard Shone; Professor Robert Skidelsky; Mrs Sylvia Towb; Dame Janet Vaughan; Mrs Julian Vinogradoff; Mr R. W. T. Vint; Mr Simon Watney; Mr John Willett; the late Edward Wolfe.

To the following I am indebted for permission to quote from either documents in their possession or published or unpublished material over

xi

which they own copyright: Dr Igor Anrep for extracts from Helen Anrep's letters; Mrs Pamela Diamand for extracts from Roger Fry's letters; Frances Partridge for extracts from Clive Bell's letters to herself; Henrietta Couper for extracts from documents among Duncan Grant's literary estate; Richard Garnett for extracts from David Garnett's memoirs, diaries and letters; Mrs Angelica Garnett for extracts from Vanessa Bell's letters and memoirs; Professor Quentin Bell for extracts from Clive and Julian Bell's papers; the Provost and Scholars of King's College, Cambridge, for extracts from the Keynes and Forster papers and the Society of Authors on behalf of the estate of E.M. Forster and on behalf of the Strachey Trust for the letters of Lytton Strachey © 1983; the Author's Literary Estate and the Hogarth Press for passages from the edited volumes of Virginia Woolf's letters and diaries; the Author's Literary Estate, the Hogarth Press and the University Press, Sussex, for extracts from Virginia Woolf's *Moments of Being*.

I am grateful to the staff of various institutions for access to material in their possession and for their assistance: Kensington Public Libraries; the University of Sussex Library; the British Library Manuscript Department and the Collingwood Newspaper Library; the Tate Gallery Archives; Mrs Lola Szladits of the Henry W. and Albert A. Berg Collection and the Astor Lenox and Tilden Foundations, New York Public Library; Ellen S. Dunlap and the Humanities Research Center, University of Texas; Dr Michael Halls and the staff at King's College Library, Cambridge; and John Kirby and his staff at the Faculty of Art Library, Sheffield City Polytechnic.

I have a particular debt of gratitude to record to Angelica Garnett for the chapter heading illustrations, and to her and Anthony d'Offay for the financial assistance that made possible the colour illustrations. Throughout the making of this book the artist's family has been uncommonly generous, and to Quentin and Olivier Bell, to Angelica and her daughter Henrietta Couper I wish to express, with affectionate respect, my warmest thanks. I am grateful also for the valuable editorial help and guidance given me by Elizabeth Burke, John Curtis and Tanya Schmoller at Weidenfeld's, and by the American publisher Ticknor and Field. I have again benefited from Mrs Maureen Daly who typed the manuscript, with some assistance from Mrs Virginia Messenger. My thanks go also to my husband Julian for giving me space and time, the stillness and silence in which to write this book.

Preface

Vanessa Bell lived at the very centre of Bloomsbury and, though neither an intellectual nor a writer, held sway with her acuity, integrity, maturity and ironic sense of humour. In addition she had a gift for organization, bringing an element of creative risk to her management of practicalities. 'How much I admire this handling of life,' wrote her sister Virginia Woolf, 'as if it were a thing one could throw about; this handling of circumstance.'⋆ When Vanessa left London for Studland, Asheham, Wittering, Charleston or Cassis, others followed, attracted by the atmosphere of tolerance and freedom which, with her easy control over domestic matters and her scorn of accepted conventions, she helped to create. Her hospitality is one reason why the disparate individuals who composed Bloomsbury continued to meet, to retain a group identity long after the circumstances that had helped shape their homogeneity had vanished. Vanessa remained a powerful, magnetic figure, made enigmatic by the impenetrable privacy that cloaked her deepest feelings; as her life progresses we find that, despite her tenacious belief in the need for honesty, or perhaps because of it, there were things she would not discuss.

As a painter, she also commands attention. Her commitment to art never wavered; it runs like a rod of steel through her life, an unbending central core of conviction. Combined with her talent, it led her to play an important part within the history of English painting during the first thirty years of this century and a less central but still distinguished role as a colourist from the 1930s until her death. As an artist, she invites biography because her work is so intimately associated with her family, friends and surroundings; moreover, these surroundings had often already received the imprint of her personality in the decorations with which she and Duncan Grant transformed many interiors.

In her art, as in her life, she displayed an 'inviolable reticence', as Virginia Woolf observed. In the naturalistic paintings of her mature and late years

⋆ *The Diary of Virginia Woolf. Volume III. 1925–1930*, ed. Anne Olivier Bell (London: Hogarth Press 1980), p. 220.

the world of appearances is reproduced with sympathy and feeling but never exaggerated or underlined in order to make the effect more stylish or dramatic. The mood is always contemplative, the outcome of quiet concentration. Vanessa Bell disliked story-telling in art; she shared the Bloomsbury belief that art only achieves unity and completeness if it is detached; she selected her subjects for the reflections, shapes, colours, patterns, lines and spatial relationships that they presented. Nevertheless her attitude towards her subject matter is, I believe, more complex than this suggests. The recurrence in her *oeuvre* of certain motifs and themes, the prevalence of certain groupings and simple geometric shapes, suggests that they had for her a personal significance, even if this was unconsciously formulated. Vanessa Bell herself would have denied any conscious use of symbolism and argued instead that her subject was 'this painter's world of form and colour'.* It is, therefore, surprising that she quite often turned to 'subject' pictures, large compositions in which the figures are grouped in such a way as to suggest narrative content. Moreover, even her still lifes, interiors and garden scenes rarely deal with 'pure form' but often seem deliberately arranged to arouse associations.

I hope that this book will broaden understanding of the fabric of thought and feeling from which her art sprang. Critical analysis of her work has here been limited, necessarily, so as not to impede the narrative. A monograph on her entire *oeuvre* is needed to establish her full stature as an artist, and a more detailed examination of both her and Duncan Grant's work before any clear account can be given of the two-way exchange between these artists, one which certainly enriched but may also have restricted their developments.

My personal interest in Vanessa Bell grew in tandem with my commitment to Roger Fry. I first saw her paintings in any considerable number at the exhibition of her work put on by Anthony d'Offay at his gallery in 1973. Like many who visited that show, I was stunned by the audacity of her post-impressionist paintings, shorn of all detail or intrusive sentiment, boldly but sensitively composed out of blocks of sheer colour.† Not long after this, I began my research into the life and work of Roger Fry which culminated in the book *Roger Fry: Art and Life* (1980), a study that extended my knowledge of, among other things, his relationship with Vanessa Bell. Though their affair lasted only some two to three years, it was of major

*From a talk given by Vanessa Bell at Leighton Park School in 1925. Typescript in the possession of Mrs Angelica Garnett.

† 'When eventually a Rewald of English Post-Impressionism appears, they will surely emerge as some of the key pictures.' Ronald Pickvance, introduction to *Vanessa Bell*, catalogue to the Arts Council Memorial exhibition, 1964.

importance to them both. Roger, for his part, asserted: 'Nessa I should be a real artist really truly and without doubt if I could draw you often because you have this miracle of rhythm in you and not in your body only but in everything you do. It means ease in all the things around you and in your relations.'* When she withdrew from him, he endured prolonged suffering. She, on the other hand, more attracted, to her lasting benefit and inestimable tragedy, to the homosexual Duncan Grant, never forgot what Roger had taught her, for his magnanimous temperament and energetic pursuit of new ideas broadened her interests and increased her self-confidence. Their coming together marks a turning-point in Vanessa's life, their relationship, though brief, having pivotal importance.

The task of writing on Vanessa Bell has not been easy for she was an exceptional, original and complex woman. Her unusual personality becomes the third reason for writing this book. Judged by its human content alone, the story of her life is compelling and deeply moving, yet also highly unorthodox, even by today's standards. Few women in any age have managed their loyalties so diplomatically, keeping husband, ex-lover and lover all within her orbit and all reconciled to each other. Vanessa was also voraciously maternal, unconsciously possessive, in a way that exposed her to suffering. And she was composed of paradoxes: a prey to vagueness, she could be unusually sharp; chilling formality went hand in hand with a quick sensitivity; she upheld the controlling power of reason yet was a victim of her emotions and intuitions, and was led to subterfuges that denied honesty; she relied on safety pins (as certain photographs confirm), yet always looked distinguished. She impressed others with her beauty which went deeper than appearance. Old age merely increased her inherent nobility, causing Lawrence Gowing to liken her to a cathedral.†

From the feminist viewpoint Vanessa Bell seems at first glance disappointing. She never joined the suffragette movement, despised female exhibiting societies and on the whole preferred the conversation and company of men. She did far less for the women's cause than her sister and yet, judged by the standards of everyday behaviour, Vanessa was far more revolutionary. Whereas Virginia Woolf enjoyed the security of a respectable marriage and took a certain delight in society and the aristocracy, Vanessa lived most of her life in a relationship not recognized by church or state, with the man by whom she had an illegitimate daughter. So deeply ingrained was her distrust of conventional society that immediately on entering a room she could detect whether the decoration reflected a genuine sense of taste or merely a desire for social prestige. Her rejection

* Roger Fry to Vanessa Bell, no date (c. 1914): Tate Gallery Archives.
† In conversation with the author.

of most of those habits and customs which curtailed the lives of other women of her class grew out of her belief in the absolute need for personal freedom. This she pursued courageously, knowing that it encouraged creativity and allowed a person to grow, expand, develop. Among Bloomsbury, moreover, such freedom was, for the most part, economically feasible.

Today the weight of institutionalized privilege in England still makes it difficult to assess Bloomsbury with adequate detachment, as both its critics and apologists reveal. When, however, its contribution to social history is finally clarified, Vanessa Bell's personal achievement may appear the most extreme, the most monumental.

ONE
Always the Eldest
1879-1895

In March 1903 Vanessa Stephen, then a student of painting at the Royal Academy Schools, paid a visit to the Guildford home of the artist G. F. Watts. He was small and frail, and in his eighty-fifth year; she was tall (five foot seven) and only twenty-three. From her mother's side of the family she had inherited exceptional beauty, and her finely-sculpted face was made still more remarkable by her large, deeply-hooded grey-blue eyes and her full, sensuous mouth. 1903 was a relatively uneventful year in her life and a stagnant moment in the history of English art. The twentieth century still lay in the shadow of the nineteenth, and Vanessa, confronted with this eminent Victorian, was curious and attentive but on the whole unimpressed. To her he must have seemed the personification of an age that was past. He had been intimately associated with her grandmother and great aunts and in his paintings and sculptures sought to inspire noble and instructive thought, for he upheld the 'high art' ideals that were a part of Vanessa's inheritance. She listened to all that he said, was polite, demure, somewhat reserved. She was soon to rebel against much that he held dear and had already begun to suspect that art, to be effective, need neither teach nor improve.

Vanessa was not, however, insensible to Watts's immense reputation. 'After breakfast I went into the studio,' begins the conscientious report that she sent her friend and fellow student Margery Snowden:

Mr Watts is painting a huge tree covered with ivy. 'That's going to be sent to the Academy as a protest against Impressionism. You see every leaf is clearly painted ... The great mistake of modern art is that they [sic] try to make things too real ... One doesn't want facts in a picture ... When I paint a picture I want to give a message and I care comparatively little about how good the art is.'[1]

Her detailed account took up another four pages. Watts's thoughts rambled from modern portraiture to Rodin, from the English caricaturists to his recollections of Rossetti and Millais, moving on to education and the future of the British Empire. 'He's a very kind old gentleman,' she concluded mildly, 'and has quite a sense of humour.'

Before two years had passed she had become very much more critical of this painter of moral allegories. Watts died in the summer of 1904, a few months after Sir Leslie Stephen, Vanessa's father. While Vanessa moved herself, her sister and two brothers into 46 Gordon Square, the Royal Academy prepared to honour Watts with a huge memorial exhibition. It opened on 2 January 1905 and ran for two months. Vanessa visited it on more than one occasion and wrote to Margery Snowden: 'It does annoy one to see anyone with real talent and capabilities deliberately neglecting the art of painting and using it only as a half-learned language.'[2] Her irritation partly but not fully explains why this exhibition provoked her to write an article on Watts which she sent, without success, to the *Saturday Review*. This uncharacteristic act suggests that Watts, who had once painted her father's portrait, had become associated in her mind with the repressive past from which she was now determined to escape. In a sudden access of self-confidence, she assessed this Victorian's achievement and found it lacking. Her sister Virginia evidently shared her feelings: 'By the way,' she wrote, 'the Watts show is *atrocious*; my last illusion is gone. Nessa and I walked through the rooms, almost in tears. Some of his work – indeed most of it – is quite childlike.'[3]

They were a little, but not much, in advance of public opinion. During the next ten years Watts's immense reputation collapsed like a punctured tyre and, despite attempts to revive it, it still remains limp today. In the spring of 1915 the *Daily Mirror*, the paper at which Vanessa most often glanced, ran a lengthy correspondence on the statues which, in the opinion of many, marred London's beautiful parks. Watts's equestrian monument, *Physical Energy*, on which he had spent many years of labour and which was now prominently situated in Kensington Gardens, received prolonged abuse. Amidst the accounts of naval expansion and other war news, this correspondence caught Vanessa's eye; the letters deploring this statue, so she told her husband Clive, were 'the delight of my life'.[4]

When Vanessa Bell's great aunt, Mrs Thoby Prinsep, announced in 1850 her need for a house large enough to hold a regular salon, Watts suggested Little Holland House, an old farm dwelling, cluttered with many chimneys, gabled roofs and a small thatched porch. Set in an informal garden, fringed with rose-bushes, and shaded by elms and poplars, the house was surrounded by an ancient wall, part of which still runs down Kensington's Ilchester Place. Despite its rural atmosphere, Little Holland House was only two miles from Hyde Park Corner and some five hundred yards from Kensington High Street, then a highway bordered with large houses and elaborate wrought-iron gates. Since the death of its previous owner, five years earlier, the house had remained empty, its garden silent and unused.

Soon after Thoby Prinsep took over the lease, the house and garden became the scene of his wife Sara's 'at homes', held on Sunday afternoons throughout the summer months. Now the crack of croquet mallet and ball punctuated the talk of the guests as they moved into and out of the house or took strawberries and cream under the elms. Though 'at homes' on Sundays were a Victorian convention, the hospitality offered at Little Holland House was unusually cosmopolitan and liberal in spirit. During the afternoon certain guests were invited to stay on for dinner and as many as forty might sit down at the long tables which, if the weather was warm, were brought outside and set on the lawn. Though conversation was esteemed, a certain bohemian freedom placed guests at their ease; civil servants and army officials – friends of Thoby Prinsep, himself a retired Anglo-Indian administrator – mingled with artists, writers and politicians. Sara Prinsep sought not titles but intellect, and succeeded in attracting, among others, Gladstone, Disraeli, Rossetti, Tennyson, Browning, Carlyle, Ruskin and Thackeray.

The house helped contribute to the charm of these occasions. It was old, rambling and informal, containing long corridors and oddly positioned large, low rooms. These were simply decorated, the walls painted green, the ceilings a dusky blue. Gradually the house filled with art, for shortly after the Prinseps had taken up residence, Watts (needing little encouragement) had moved in too. He inhabited a series of upstairs rooms and painted portraits of all Sara Prinsep's sisters, the daughters of James and Adeline Pattle, who were famous for their beauty. They also posed for the decorations which he painted on the walls of the upstairs dining-room. Visitors might find themselves looking across the table at one sister only to see her likeness rise behind her as Earth with the Infant Humanity, or Time unveiling Truth.

Watts's love of Venetian colour and his tendency to derive poses and drapery from the Elgin Marbles contributed to the rich, cultured atmosphere of the house. He was at once the high priest and the altar at which Sara Prinsep and her sisters could display their worship of creativity. They gushed over him, nicknamed him 'Signor' and would emphasize his role still further by pretending occasionally to tease him for being in a very 'high-art' mood. George du Maurier, the illustrator and novelist, grimly observed that Watts was in danger of being emasculated by such treatment. Nevertheless the Prinseps' genuine interest in art attracted many painters to the house; Rossetti came regularly, and brought Burne-Jones. 'You must know these people, Ned,' he told him as they drove to the house. 'They are remarkable.'[5] Quite how remarkable, Burne-Jones was soon to discover. On learning that he had fallen ill, Sara Prinsep swept into his house at Red Lion Square, where he was living with William Morris, and carried him off to Kensington to recuperate. From then on Burne-Jones addressed her as 'Aunt Sara' and was grateful in addition for the lessons he received from Watts. 'It is a nest of proeraphaelites [sic],' du Maurier wrote of Little Holland House, 'where Hunt, Millais, Rossetti, Watts, Leighton, etc., Tennyson, the Brownings and Thackeray etc., and tutti quanti receive dinners and incense, and cups of tea handed to them by these women almost kneeling.'[6]

Beauty was a quintessential ingredient in late Victorian taste, and Watts, living at Little Holland House, had no lack of it. Sara Prinsep and her six sisters were the grandchildren of the Chevalier de l'Etang, a member of Marie Antoinette's household who had been exiled to Pondicherry. Though brought up in India, the girls completed their education at Versailles where their widowed grandmother then lived. On their return home, they shone in Calcutta society. Their distinguished beauty ('Elgin marbles with dark eyes', wrote Ruskin[7]) was blended with charm and energy; they had a natural gift for intimacy, were sociable, warm-hearted; inclined to silliness but not unintelligent. They knew how to exert pressure graciously and usually got their way; they all married successful, if quiescent, men.

When Sara Prinsep and her sister Virginia heard that Burne-Jones was courting Georgiana Macdonald, they hurriedly called on the girl's family to make a visit of inspection. Georgiana and her sister were in turn invited to call at Little Holland House and must have met with the Pattles' approval as the marriage went ahead and Burne-Jones later described Sara Prinsep as 'the nearest thing to a mother that I ever knew'.[8] Sara's interference did not always meet with such success, and when Ellen Terry became part of her household, her sympathy and understanding snapped.

Ellen first came to Little Holland House in order to pose for Watts. She had already embarked on her acting career and, having spent most of her life in lodging houses, marvelled at the beauty of her new surroundings. They seemed to her a paradise; nor did she find it disturbing when the Pattle sisters, for private conversation, resorted to Hindustani. Meanwhile her gestures and poses satisfied the painter's eye and before two years had passed Watts proposed: he would, he argued, save Ellen from the degradation of the stage. More importantly, Mrs Prinsep wished them wed, though Ellen was not quite seventeen and Watts forty-seven.

Inevitably the marriage was not a success. Watts, old for his age and dressed almost permanently in galoshes to protect him from the damp, was tetchy and impatient; Ellen, impetuous and immature. She posed by the hour for Watts but outside the studio had no real role at Little Holland House. Mrs Prinsep, who had advised Ellen to remain silent in company, was horrified one day when the young girl demonstrated her boredom at one tea party by shaking her head from side to side, until her hairpins flew out and her hair fell down. There followed the famous occasion when Ellen appeared at one of the Prinseps' dinner parties dressed as Cupid in a pair of pink tights. After that she was ignominiously sent home: the marriage, such as it was, had lasted less than a year.

Some sixty years later Virginia Woolf satirized the tale of Ellen Terry and Watts in her play *Freshwater*. When this was first performed in 1935 Vanessa Bell played Mrs Cameron, the famous photographer and the least beautiful of the Pattle sisters. Her grizzled hair and the stink of chemicals that clung to her person added a touch of the bizarre to Little Holland House. All the Pattle characteristics were found in her in stronger vein, making her daunting and despotic. She dragooned her friends, relatives, servants, as well as complete strangers, into posing for her, and if they refused she clenched her fists and spoke of eternal damnation. She did not 'take' photographs: she immortalized her sitters. The arrangement and sentiment dictating the poses in her photographs (some of which Vanessa later hung at 46 Gordon Square) echo the 'high-art' mood of Watts's paintings; but the impersonal nature of the photographic plate brings a realism to the subject that Watts's painting often lacks. The technique she used was the complicated and physically arduous one of wet collodion. It required a tenacity which this forgetful, extravagant, original woman, who draped herself in Indian shawls, did not lack. 'A woman of noble plainness', Watts politely recalled,[9] with, as Leslie Stephen admitted, 'the temperament, at least, of genius'.[10]

Less daunting was Vanessa's grandmother, Maria Pattle. Taller than her sister Sara and more refined than Mrs Cameron, she looked elegant without being obviously wealthy. Maria married John Jackson, a doctor who specialized in tetanus and was a leading physician in Calcutta where he taught at the Medical College. Such was his devotion to his work in India that he did not once, during his first twenty-five years of service, make a return visit to England. Even when his wife was forced by ill health to return to London with her children, he did not rejoin her till his retirement seven years later. What seems heartless behaviour was in fact the result of his complete dedication to the service of others. It may, however, explain why his wife made excessive demands for sympathy on her daughters, particularly on her third and youngest, Julia, who, after the marriage of her two sisters, took it upon herself to care for her mother during her frequent illnesses. The chief insight into their relationship is provided by Mrs Jackson's letters to Julia, which reveal that they flourished in an atmosphere of disease; when not describing in detail her own ill-health Mrs Jackson was obsessed with the illnesses of others. These letters suggest that the relationship between mother and daughter was over-demanding on Mrs Jackson's part and perhaps unhealthily close.

Julia Jackson gave to her father both affection and respect, but because, between the ages of two and nine, she had not known him, her filial love turned more naturally to her Uncle Thoby in whose house she grew up. Thoby Prinsep was grand both in size and mind. Renowned for being well-informed, gentle, sweet-natured and something of a philosopher, he probably had the greatest influence on Julia's education, for her beauty naturally allied her with the Pattles and with the life at Little Holland House. By the age of fourteen her looks had already set her apart; she had a fine bone structure, high cheekbones and wide eyes. She was tall and statuesque and, in the Pattle tradition, avoided fashion.

The main events in her early adult life happened within just three years. While in Venice, visiting her sister Mary and her husband on their honeymoon, Julia met Herbert Duckworth, the perfect English gentleman: handsome, courteous, educated at Eton and Trinity College, Cambridge, and called to the Bar. According to Leslie Stephen, Herbert was 'simple, straight-forward and manly'.[11] Julia fell instantly in love. She was twenty-one when they married in 1867 and the following year she bore him her first child, George Herbert. In 1869 a second child, Stella, was born, and Julia was pregnant again when in September 1870 Herbert stretched up into a tree to pick a fig and burst an unsuspected abscess. He died within a matter of hours. Six weeks later Gerald, their third child, was born.

Widowed at the age of twenty-four, Julia was prevented by the newborn child and by well-meaning friends from giving full expression to her grief and the pain that lay buried within her left its imprint on her character. For the next eight years she remained a widow, wishing often for death and shrinking morbidly from any thought of returning happiness. Then in 1877 her close friend and neighbour, the gaunt intellectual Leslie Stephen, himself a widower, proposed. Julia returned his love and respect but doubted if she had the power within her to start a new life. Over the next year they saw each other daily and when apart corresponded at length. In January 1878 she finally committed herself to him and in March that year they were married.

Vanessa Stephen was born at 22 Hyde Park Gate on 30 May 1879. She shared her birthday with Julia's daughter by her first marriage, Stella, and therefore was christened Vanessa, the second of the two women associated with Swift. Almost as soon as she became aware of the world around her Vanessa was conscious of a person smaller and younger than herself, for her brother Julian Thoby was born the year after her. His arrival occasioned no jealousy but instead aroused her affection. Very soon they were surrounded by others; Virginia was born in 1882, Adrian in 1883. Instinctively Vanessa adopted the caring, maternal role often fostered in the eldest child. She gave Thoby his bottle and later taught him his letters. Aware of others' needs, she retained as her earliest memory the image of the two-year-old Virginia in her high chair, drumming impatiently for breakfast.

One of our first pictures of Vanessa is that of a plump, pretty child trotting beside her father's long legs, with Thoby at her side, as they make their way to see the stuffed animals in the newly-opened Natural History Museum. Further glimpses of her can be found in the letters that Leslie Stephen wrote to his wife when her frequent visits to her mother or her habit of nursing others took her away from home. When Vanessa was only two years old Leslie thought he detected on her face a grave sarcastic expression which reminded him of himself. Her gravity repeatedly enchanted him as he watched her absorbed in making boats or decorating a Christmas tree. She was soon able to form her own opinions and at the age of eight amused her father by volunteering a piece of literary criticism. He had been reading aloud to his children, as he told Julia: 'I have begun *The Rose and the Ring* though they tell me that Nurse has read it to them already. However there is no other decent bit of literature and they seem to like it. Nessa remarks that it is "dikkifult" to distinguish between Bulbo and Giglio, in wh. I think there is some truth.'[12]

Much of Vanessa's early life was spent in the company of Thoby, to whom she was devoted. Her first lessons were shared with him. Leslie tried to teach them about Charles I but they distracted him with questions about the sea and how it was formed. Julia also took a hand in the Latin, French and history lessons, preferring to direct their education herself rather than employ a governess. When the lessons became more serious both parents could be strict, Leslie turning severe as he tried to teach arithmetic and Julia becoming impatient of stupidity. When Julia was away, her daughter

7

by her first marriage, Stella, took charge; it was she who gave Vanessa her first music lesson and taught her the art of letter-writing. Ten years older than Vanessa and the most musical member of the family, she observed her half-sister's love of drawing and gave her some chalks. The young child's creative impulse also led her to grub in the garden for clay to model. But if Vanessa's feeling for shape and line was evident from the start, it must have seemed out of place in the literate and articulate world in which she grew up, even if her father did sometimes fill the margins of his books on philosophy and ethics with minutely-drawn hybrid animals.

Her most intimate relationship as a child was not with her mother but with Thoby. She recalled doing everything with him, easily and affably for they rarely argued. When eventually he was sent away to preparatory school, she cried and consoled herself by taking his monkey Jacko to bed with her. Even before this, however, their intimacy had been dented by Virginia, determined to join their alliance. As Virginia grew increasingly articulate, she threw into their childhood world an element of friction; 'though life was more interesting and exciting, it was also less easy', Vanessa recalled.[13] Her private, inner life, connected with the silent realm of form and colour, was set against Virginia's chatter and love of words. At the age of five the younger sister stood on a windowsill and delivered a monologue about a crow and a book that might have gone on for ever had not her audience coughed her down. In the night nursery, while the embers glowed in the fire, it was Virginia who entertained the other three children with elaborate tales. Vanessa encouraged these stories. But from the start something in Virginia's volatile nature conflicted with her sister's steady temperament. At the same time, as Virginia recalled, 'there was some consciousness between us that the other held possibilities'.[14] Therefore if their relationship was, from childhood, based on an exchange of natural affection and unforced admiration, it was also veined with antagonism and fortified by mutual need.

It was Virginia who nicknamed Vanessa 'The Saint'. This taunt underlined Vanessa's matter-of-factness, her ready assumption of responsibility and above all her tenacious clinging to truth. Virginia's imaginative flights threw into relief Vanessa's monolithic literalness. 'She might not see at all,' Virginia later commented, 'but she would not see what was not there.'[15] The cruel nickname, at once exaggerating her merits and devaluing their worth, caught on, and Vanessa found herself the butt of sarcasm not only in the nursery but also among the grown-ups. In this agnostic, highly intelligent household, 'The Saint' implied a narrowness, a fanatic attention to duty that for the young child must have been hard to bear. When not reduced to impotent misery, Vanessa would, with Thoby, in turn taunt

Virginia until she turned purple with rage. Vanessa was equally affected by Virginia's capacity to create suddenly an atmosphere of tense, thundery gloom.

This world of intense childish emotions was mostly confined to the day and night nurseries at the top of the house. Twice a day, however, the children crossed over the main road at the top of Hyde Park Gate and entered the park gates beyond which the various avenues splayed out in many directions. Certain areas of Hyde Park were wilder then than now and Vanessa never forgot the grip of fascination caused by their discovery of a dog's corpse in the long grass. They sailed boats on the Round Pond with their father who could become as absorbed in the proceedings as his children. Or they would follow at his heels while he strode across the grass declaiming Henry Newbolt's famous sea-song 'Admirals All'.

They could not forget their father's presence even when alone in one of the nurseries at the top of the tall Kensington house. His attic study was directly overhead and as he sat in his rocking-chair, sucking a clay pipe and at work on some article, he occasionally let a book fall with a thud to the ground. Here he continued to pursue his literary career which he had begun in 1865, after a ten-year period as a mathematics don at Trinity Hall, Cambridge. Soon after the start of this second career, he was given the editorship of the *Cornhill Magazine*, which enabled him to do less journalism and devote more of his time to the writing of books, in particular his major work, *The History of English Thought in the Eighteenth Century*, which had appeared in 1876 in two volumes. The previous year his first wife Minny, the daughter of Thackeray, died, leaving him with their one daughter Laura.

With Minny, Leslie Stephen had enjoyed eight happy years, but their domestic tranquillity had brought out the recluse in him. Often he had refused dinner parties; he went rarely to the theatre; and when entertaining, it was his sister-in-law, the novelist Anny Thackeray, who carried on the conversation with blithe indifference to his morose presence. At Minny's request, Anny had shared their home, irritating Leslie with her effervescent talk and profligate spending. Nevertheless it was she who had done much to help him over Minny's death, assisting with the move to Hyde Park Gate where they had taken the house next to Anny's close friend Julia Duckworth, whose kindness and sympathy quickly proved indispensable.

The man Julia had eventually agreed to marry in 1878 was quite unlike her first husband. This 'gaunt and difficult' man, as Thomas Hardy described Stephen, was descended from a long line of energetic, argumentative, high-minded professional men who had left their mark in intellec-

9

tual, literary and legal circles. His father James Stephen and his mother Jane Venn were both connected with the Clapham Sect, and their puritanical astringency coloured his upbringing. His own self-discipline was such that he could write an 8,000-word article at one sitting. His voracious appetite for knowledge contributed to his highly productive literary career and directed his editorship of the first twenty-six volumes of the *Dictionary of National Biography*. A scientific humanist, influenced by his reading of Mill, Comte, Hobbes and the British empiricists, he had abandoned the Christian religion and wrote a series of articles on agnosticism which Julia first read during her widowhood. They confirmed her own thoughts and played no small part in his attraction for her.

Leslie Stephen's children, as they grew up, came to know a man whose best years were behind him. He must have seemed perpetually harassed and often exhausted. He longed for a quiet, regular, harmonious existence which the pile of manuscripts and endless reams of copy awaiting him at Waterloo Place, the home of the *Dictionary*, did not permit. During Vanessa's childhood his health gradually declined. He was frequently racked by headaches and in the summer of 1889 collapsed from overwork. Thereafter he was forced to accept an assistant editor and two years later resigned completely from editorship of the *Dictionary*, but continued an active literary career, contributing five biographies to the 'English Men of Letters' series. He brought to his work a regularity and dedication which set an example that both Vanessa and Virginia were to follow. In many ways he was an excellent father, concerning himself with his children's affairs, taking them to the zoo in Regent's Park, returning affection, and showing integrity in all matters that did not concern himself. The other side of his character was self-pitying and melancholy. He easily became self-absorbed, revealing unsatiated ambition. He made extravagant emotional demands on those close to him, particularly Julia, from whom he hated to be parted. His sensitivity had aged into prickliness, making him frequently nervous, irritable and overwrought. As a young man he had often scaled the Alps, where, as a pioneer mountain climber, he had gone regularly for mental and physical refreshment; now, on his visits, he merely pottered about in the valleys.

One important gift that he gave his children was Cornwall. While on a walking holiday in 1881 he had found Talland House at St Ives and for the next thirteen years the Stephens spent several weeks each summer there. This gave a pattern to their lives, throwing into contrast their more circumscribed existence in London. As a young child Vanessa could not believe that two such different places inhabited the same universe and she asked her father if St Ives and London were two different worlds, each with its own separate sky.[16] Virginia associated St Ives with her first experience of ecstasy. The sound of the sea could be heard in every room at Talland House. It was a little outside the town and sat on a hill like an iced cake, the square, stolid house made fragile and ornate by the thin-pillared balconies and chequerboard patterning around the windows. The garden fell away in terraces, a formal lawn giving way to a tennis court, a kitchen garden, thickets of fruit bushes and a greenhouse with a vine. Near by was a sandy cove where the whole family bathed. In the distance, but dominating the entire scene, was the Godrevy lighthouse, later to reappear in *To the Lighthouse* and in some tile designs Vanessa executed for Virginia and her husband to ornament a fireplace at Monk's House. It was also in Leslie Stephen's mind when in 1890, after receiving an honorary doctorate from Harvard University, he travelled home by ship and wrote to his wife, 'I shall be glad to see the Godrevy lighthouse.'[17]

Each year Talland House accumulated more associations. While there the Stephens received many visitors who travelled down by train and sat overlooking the lawn where the children played cricket, Vanessa meeting every ball with the same straightforward stroke. She and Virginia behaved like tomboys at St Ives, clambering over rocks and up trees or playing on the sands. Their interest in lepidoptera had already begun and they contrived to make nets with which to catch moths. Each year they were measured against a shutter by their father and in 1893 it seemed that Vanessa had stopped growing. 'If so,' he commented to Julia, 'she will be about the right height, that is, her mamma's.'[18] The children did little work at St Ives, but in her spare moments Vanessa read Ruskin's *The Elements of Drawing* and virtuously followed its instructions, filling small squares with hatching until they looked like grey silk. She also painted in watercolour.

St Ives was even then a haunt for painters. In the winter of 1893–4 Whistler stayed several weeks in the town. He painted seascapes and shopfronts and was accompanied by two assistants, Mortimer Menpes and Walter Sickert. The latter already knew the town well and some fifty years later told Vanessa that her father had appeared to him the most impressive personage in the area and that her mother had looked superb. Sickert, then a penniless young painter fresh from the Slade, only knew the Stephens by sight and there was probably no contact between the artists in the town and Talland House. But at this time several of the extensive sail-lofts were being converted into studios, and by 1889, when Vanessa was ten, she was conscious enough of what was going on in the town to speak to her father of a school of artists in St Ives. This was the colony of marine painters that centred around Julius Olsson, famous for his nocturnal seascapes.

Looking back on her childhood, Vanessa reflected that any sense of rivalry between herself and her sister was avoided by the tacit agreement that one was to become an artist and the other a writer. But the very fact that there was such an agreement suggests an awareness of competition; and at intervals throughout their lives each would measure her own achievement against that of her sister. If unspoken rivalry was unavoidable, Vanessa experienced very little jealousy of Virginia, even when her younger sister's chatter proved more stimulating and entertaining than her own. Likewise she seems to have admired Virginia's beauty with unstinted pleasure. Both sisters recognized at an early stage the difference in their temperaments, Vanessa appreciating Virginia's wit and cleverness, Virginia relaxing in the presence of Vanessa's relative maturity and calm good sense. She respected, and was a little awed by, Vanessa's ruthless honesty: when some years later Virginia, Vanessa and Adrian one summer evening pretended not to hear their father calling from inside the house, only Vanessa, when later questioned like the rest, revealed their heartlessness by admitting that they had deliberately ignored his voice.

The age gap between the Duckworth and Stephen children meant that, though they all inhabited the same house, they formed two distinct groups. At Hyde Park Gate, George, Stella and Gerald occupied the second floor, while Laura, Leslie's child by his first marriage, spent most of her time in the care of a nurse. Soon after Minny's death she had begun to show signs of being retarded. By the time she reached her teens in the 1880s she was suffering from nervous tics and speech impediments. On occasion she became violent and would howl wildly. In 1887, when she turned seventeen, a temporary arrangement was made for her to live in the country and in 1891 she was placed permanently in a home, though for the next two summers she still joined the Stephen family at St Ives. So long as she remained at 22 Hyde Park Gate she acted as a source of irritation to Leslie Stephen, who sometimes lacked sympathy in his dealings with her, failing to realize that her 'grotesque waywardness', as he called it, was in fact an irredeemable handicap.

As time went on, Vanessa and Virginia were left more and more in each other's company. The rampageous Thoby had been sent away to school, and in 1894, after failing to win a scholarship to Eton, he passed from Evelyn's preparatory school to Clifton College, near Bristol. At Evelyn's he had succeeded in 1891 in being bottom of the school, but at Clifton he began to show an aptitude for Latin and mathematics and for three successive years won internal college scholarships. His brother Adrian, a less extrovert character, remained at home but went as a day boy to

Westminster School, leaving the two sisters alone together.

Virginia's early dependence on Vanessa is reflected in her habit of fingering her sister's amethyst beads and enumerating with each the name of a friend or relative whose place in Vanessa's affections had aroused her jealousy. In Thoby's absence Vanessa, in turn, became more dependent on Virginia. They spent many hours alone in the small conservatory at the back of the house. Here Vanessa painted or drew while Virginia read aloud or wrote the family newspaper, the *Hyde Park Gate News*. For the rest of her life Vanessa, when reading George Eliot or Thackeray, heard much of their novels in Virginia's voice. The two sisters also had their lessons together at home, but were sent out for piano, singing and dancing classes, none of which they enjoyed. Vanessa's description of their singing mistress and her pupils suggests that even by this stage their agnostic family background had made them different from other girls of their class:

> When one day she asked very seriously if any of us knew the meaning of Good Friday, Virginia began to giggle. Of course we hadn't the slightest idea, being little heathens. But when the prize girl of the class, a serious creature with a hooked nose and a fringe and the astonishing name of Pensa Filly, stepped forward and said something (I suppose accurately) about our Lord being crucified on that day, it was too much and Virginia had to be hurriedly banished, shrieking with laughter.[19]

Vanessa kept pace with her more brilliant sister not by dependence on her wits but through her strength of character. Even as a girl she seems to have had an emotional effect on those nearest to her that invited reverence. Virginia's devotion to her sister later enabled her to evoke Vanessa's likeness as a child: 'You see the soft dreamy and almost melancholy expression of the eyes, and it may not be fanciful to discover some kind of test and rejection in them as though, even then, she considered the thing she saw, and did not always find what she needed in it.' Such probity is unusual in a child and reflected the practical streak in Vanessa's nature: it was she who declared after a disappointing ride at an Earl's Court fun-fair that it had only been worth one of the six pennies they had paid for it. Vanessa, Virginia recalled, was 'outwardly sober and austere, the most trustworthy and always the eldest'. But she could also be coltish and awkward, as yet uncertain of her direction though not of her distant goal, the attainment of which, Virginia thought, would make her character more complete.[20]

Vanessa was nine when Virginia sprang on her an unexpected question: did Nessa prefer Mother or Father? Shocked by this line of thought, Vanessa nevertheless instinctively replied that she preferred her mother.

Both girls had just had whooping-cough and the illness had left Virginia thinner and more provocative. Already she was more willing to engage in self-analysis than her sister, and now, with confused logic, she explained her own preference for their father.

Julia Stephen was perhaps too central, too intimately concerned with all aspects of family life, for her own interests and character to emerge with any distinctness. She had, until Laura was sent away, eight children in her care and as many as seven servants. But her responsibilities did not end there. Her charity and kindness were widely known: not infrequently she received begging letters from strangers; she was always ready to nurse the sick; she attended her Uncle Thoby in his last illness and often abandoned Leslie and her family to look after her mother. Mrs Jackson's continual demands on her irritated Leslie, who thought his mother-in-law unintentionally cruel. Julia, however, readily sacrificed her life to others, the habit becoming ingrained in her character.

She was not without certain definite tastes. She shared her husband's passion for literature, was particularly fond of Scott's Waverley Novels and of the autobiographical recollections found in De Quincey's *Confessions of an English Opium Eater*, which she kept always beside her bed. She herself wrote stories for her children and, fired perhaps by a passage in this book, also composed essays on the 'servant problem'. She published only one book, *Notes for a Sick Room*, in which Noël Annan was the first to discover a tone of voice similar to that found in Virginia Woolf's essays.[21] Sensing that her own education had been unsystematic and inadequate, Julia discussed at length with Leslie what education her daughters should receive.

By the time Vanessa had entered her teens Julia had lost the buoyancy of her youth. Her grey hair was parted at the centre and pulled back in a severe style that she had never altered. She could on occasion be harsh. Eight years of widowhood had imprinted a melancholy into her character and had left her a little austere; in photographs she is never seen smiling. She was tall, thin and grave; quick, definite and upright in manner. Leslie worshipped her and she in turn looked after his every need, soothing away his irritations, warming his intelligence with her sensibility. She brought ease to any social occasion over which she presided, and encouraged music to be played in the house. She gave shape and order to the chaos of family life. She was the pivot, at times an almost invisible presence, around which they all revolved. But the amount of personal attention that she gave each child must have been very limited.

Admittedly she was not free of the Pattle tendency to be despotic. She liked to manage and organize others. When in 1889 the poet Henry Newbolt and his wife had difficulty in finding a house in London that they liked, Julia took them in hand. 'She had heard of our indecision. She carried us off one morning on a tour of inspection among streets we had not thought of before, and by evening we were persuaded that No 14 Victoria Road, W., was the one spot in all London where we could live and flourish.'[22] Like all Pattles, marriage was also her concern: she helped secure Frederic Maitland's marriage to her niece Florence Fisher, advised the elderly Watts to lose no time in marrying the young Mary Fraser Tytler and encouraged W.J. Stillman in his courtship of the artist and beauty, Marie Spartali. As soon as Stella came of age Julia chaperoned her to balls. Had she lived longer, her control of matrimonial affairs might have conflicted with Vanessa's own inclinations; almost certainly Julia would have hurried matters and Vanessa would have married earlier than she did.

Such friction remains hypothetical. The woman whom Vanessa and Virginia retained in their memory was beautiful both in appearance and person; unintentionally triumphant, in her insight, intuition and unexpressed passion, over her husband's mastery of facts. In Kensington one day with her children, walking down Melbury Road which, with its new red-brick houses, had been built over the site of Little Holland House, Julia suddenly sprang forward with a clap of her hands and cried, 'That was where it was!', suggesting that the mood and remembrance of those Sunday afternoons remained with her all her life. When, in 1927, Vanessa wrote to Virginia, thanking her for the re-creation of their mother as Mrs Ramsay in *To the Lighthouse*, she recalled only 'the extraordinary beauty of her character'.[23]

In February 1895 Julia took to her bed for a fortnight with influenza. By mid March she seemed to have recovered and in April the Duckworth children travelled to the continent for a holiday. Before the month was out Stella had returned home, having read between the lines of certain letters that her mother's health had suddenly deteriorated owing to suspected rheumatic fever. On 5 May Julia died, aged forty-nine. Beside the bedhead, where she always kept it, rested Thoby Prinsep's walking-stick. Later that morning, as Dr Seton departed, walking up the street with his hands clasped behind his back, Virginia looked out and saw a chill, blue, spring sky. 'Unquenchable seems to me such a presence', wrote Henry James, in condolence.[24]

TWO

Mrs Young's Evening Dress
1895–1904

When the summer of 1895 arrived its bright, gay colours threw into cruel contrast the black clothes and shrouded gloom of mourning. Immediately after Julia's death the family closed in; Virginia recalled them all sobbing in the drawing-room around her father's chair. George and Gerald Duckworth, on a tide of emotion, sought to establish closer friendships with their half-brothers and -sisters. Friends also gathered round, with careful expressions of grief, and these helped to create a dulled, self-conscious mood, constricting and unreal. The Stephen children, sensitized by their recent tragedy, grew suspicious of a hypocrisy which seemed to disguise the true nature of their loss. For with Julia's death the linchpin of family life had been removed; relationships grew brittle, egotisms became more pronounced, Leslie's grief and self-pity often hard to bear.

The house itself fostered darkness and gloom: it faced west and received little sunlight; even the small back garden was damp and overhung with trees. Though the building was six storeys in height, the rooms were not large and now seemed encumbered with personal mementoes: Watts's portraits, Mrs Jackson's letters, Thackeray manuscripts, Herbert Duckworth's barrister's wig and Leslie's alpine trophies; all provoked reminiscence and gave Virginia the sensation that the house was tangled and matted with emotion. Moreover, the predominant colours in the main living-rooms – red, gold and black – must have increased the stuffy and oppressive atmosphere. Living in a house where the style of decoration was still mid-Victorian, Vanessa may sometimes have wondered if time had stopped.

This impression struck the artist William Rothenstein when he visited the Stephens in the summer of 1903: 'The house unchanged since I first saw it a dozen years ago – full of that quality of serious refinement which comes in a curiously hidden way, for few of the things they have are in themselves beautiful or even tasteful, or particularly well arranged, and yet there is a sense of distinction about the whole of it.'[1] On a previous visit he had been given tea in the basement room. 'George was cheerful and talkative,' he recalled, 'but his sister Stella, and Virginia and Vanessa his half-sisters, in plain black dresses with white lace collars and waistbands, looking as though they had walked straight out of a canvas by Watts or Burne-Jones, were embarrassingly silent. Beautiful as they were, they were not more beautiful than their mother.'[2]

Rothenstein's introduction had come through the Cambridge-educated painter Arthur Studd who occasionally entertained the Stephens in his rooms at Cheyne Walk. Here they would have experienced the more up-to-date 'aesthetic' taste, for Studd owned paintings by Whistler (two nocturnes and the *Little White Girl*, all now in the Tate Gallery) and himself painted delicate evocations of night scenes in the style of the master. He was also familiar with modern French art, having trained at the Académie Julian in Paris and encountered Gauguin and Meyer de Haan on a visit to Le Pouldu. Later, in 1897, he travelled in the steps of Gauguin to Tahiti, nursing a strong (but presumably unreciprocated) affection for Stella Duckworth.

Though her family displayed scant interest in the visual arts, Vanessa did not lack for encouragement. When her passion for drawing became pronounced, her father had employed Ebenezer Cooke to give her lessons. He could not have chosen better, for Cooke was a leading reformer in art education. He had absorbed the ideas of Pestalozzi and Froebel and come under Ruskin's influence at the Working Men's College in the 1850s. Ruskin had announced that he was there to teach his pupils not to draw but to see, and he had unveiled for Cooke the beauties inherent in the natural world. While Ruskin looked at nature for, among other things, a sensation of growth, Cooke adopted a more logical approach and sought scientific principles. He specialized in botany and developed a drawing style that was straightforward and unpretentious. His detachment would have been sympathetic to Vanessa, his advice practical and of use. Almost certainly it was he who directed her towards *The Elements of Drawing* and thus grounded her in Ruskin's method which was based on intense observation. It is not known how long Cooke remained her teacher, but his refreshing approach would have encouraged her to adopt an independent view. Despite his interest in science, he upheld drawing, not as a mimetic exercise, but as primarily a means of expression, and his views anticipated those of certain twentieth-century educational theorists.[3]

It is to Leslie Stephen's credit that his dislike of art did not blind him to Vanessa's needs. He himself when visiting Little Holland House had found it too 'arty' for his taste. When abroad, he studiously avoided galleries and museums for they were 'sights' which by his definition were things not to be seen. No such prejudice was allowed to constrict his attitude to education. Most parents of his class believed that a young girl should develop accomplishments, but should any one of these sprout into a passion it was to be firmly clipped back for fear of its obscuring the path that led ultimately to marriage. Leslie Stephen realized that women needed broader horizons: 'What I chiefly hold', he told Julia before their marriage, 'is that women ought to be as well educated as men, indeed a very great deal better than men are now. ... I hate to see so many women's lives wasted simply because they have not been trained well enough to take an independent interest in any study or to be able to work efficiently at any profession.'[4]

When Vanessa was fifteen he therefore agreed that certain of her drawings should be shown to Arthur Cope who, since 1889, had run an art school at Park Cottage, Pelham Street, in South Kensington. He was the son of the artist C.W. Cope, and a respected portrait painter. Vanessa's drawings met with approval and two years later, in 1896, she began attending classes three days a week at this school which was within easy reach of Hyde Park Gate. She bicycled down Queen's Gate, dodging the small butchers' and bakers' carts that trotted sharply round corners, and sometimes lost her hat as she veered round South Kensington station. Once safely arrived at the shabby studio, she settled down next to an elderly friend of her father's called Victor Marshall and wanted for no other company. She became quickly absorbed in the abstract problems set by shape, line and colour and found this world of concentration and peaceful anonymity entirely sympathetic.

Private art schools had mushroomed in London in recent years. Arthur Cope's was one of the most successful in training students for entrance to the Royal Academy Schools, with which it had close links. Several of Cope's visiting artists (who included interesting figures with considerable reputations – Thomas Faed, Luke Fildes, Andrew C. Gow (nicknamed the English Meissonier), W.Q. Orchardson and Seymour Lucas) also taught at the Academy. In preparation for the Academy's entrance examinations, Cope's pupils were taught by J. Watson Nicol to draw from antique casts and from the nude and dressed model by Cope himself. They also received instruction in drapery painting and composition. Despite the school's seriousness of purpose, it attracted a number of young women from good homes who were merely biding their time until marriage. And though oil painting was taught, much greater emphasis fell on draughtsmanship. 'Line! Line!', Cope was in the habit of bellowing, reducing several of his female pupils to tears.

Cope's school not only provided the starting-point for Vanessa's career, but also a refuge from the stifling emotional atmosphere at 22 Hyde Park Gate. Compared with Leslie's newly-developed habit of weeping or moaning aloud, the studio offered a reparative quiet. Even the dullest academic exercises in observation and technique allowed personal anxieties to dissolve in an atmosphere of intense, disinterested study. An impulsion towards art was already deep-rooted in Vanessa. Kleinian analysts would discover a cause for this in her relationship with her mother. If, as the facts of Julia's life suggest, she was obliged to curtail her intimacy with her children after the first few months of their life, then Vanessa's subsequent turning to art may have grown out of a need to repair a sense of loss, to reconstruct that sense of oneness with the world experienced by infants at the breast. The activity of making is also a way of discovering personal identity. When crushed by the harried atmosphere at home, Vanessa could recuperate inner strength at Cope's, coining self-knowledge through art. Painting, set against a background of emotional disorder, developed from a pleasurable and absorbing occupation into an absolute need.

Leslie's distraught condition meanwhile bound him dumbly to his children, leaving George Duckworth to take over as head of the family. George had an impulsive, emotional nature; he was easily moved to generous acts and displays of affection, and was automatically the most considerate member of the family, carrying out numerous small tasks for others. While Julia had lived, her subtly powerful presence had restrained him, but now, motivated by a strong wave of pity and love, his emotionalism sought fresh outlet. As Quentin Bell has described,[5] basing his account on statements made by Virginia and others, George now developed the habit of fondling his half-sisters, confusing sexual attraction with brotherly affection. Gerald Duckworth was also, on one occasion, guilty of a sexual offence. Evidence that Vanessa also received George's attentions is found in a letter written in 1904 on a visit to Dulverton Park in Devon. 'George embraced me and fondled me in front of the company', Vanessa reported to Virginia, ' – but that was only to be expected.'[6] The fact that this fondling occurred in front of polite society raises the question as to its precise nature. As Virginia is our chief source on this matter it is possible that her accounts of George's behaviour were exaggerated. Her mother's death had left her emotionally and mentally disturbed. George's embraces, when compared with those of Thoby – famed for his reserve – would have seemed excessive. Whether or not they overstepped the bounds of propriety, they were unwanted and the disgust they aroused in Virginia left her deeply affected. On Vanessa they apparently had no lasting effect, but at the time they contributed to her sensation that an incipient emotional chaos was undermining family life, making escape to the studio all the more necessary.

Of all those living at 22 Hyde Park Gate, the one perhaps most hit by Julia's death was Stella. She had observed Julia's failing health and had tried to warn Leslie of this. Her awareness that the tragedy could have been avoided was perhaps why she often broke down when replying to letters of condolence. Yet she had no time for self-pity. She had stepped into Julia's position as housekeeper and chief sympathizer with Leslie's moods. She had to assuage his grief and remorse. She had also to take responsibility for Virginia who now suffered her first bout of mental instability. Not surprisingly, when found alone in a room Stella was often in tears, a fact she tried quickly to hide.

An awful helplessness surrounds the story of her life. Because her father had died when she was only a year old, she had grown up, as Virginia observed, in the shade of her mother's widowhood and at an early age began to imitate Julia's dedication to others. She developed a 'passive, suffering affection' towards her mother, and also a 'complete, unquestioning dependence'.[7] Virginia, in her essay 'A Sketch of the Past'[8], chose the analogy of the sun and the moon to imply that Stella followed where her mother led and merely reflected her light. Julia had tended to treat her harshly and when Leslie criticized her for this, Julia replied that her fault lay in regarding Stella as part of herself. As this suggests, Julia had become as demanding of her daughter as her own mother had been of her. In turn, Stella now drew closer to Vanessa, helping to allay the blow of their mother's death. Stella's selfless concern for others makes her character elusive. She was gentle, sympathetic and apparently utterly devoid of personal ambition. Yet she had inherited her mother's quick discernment between the genuine and false and had a very real charm that left an impression on others. She inspired a respectfully-distanced chivalrous affection for, as Virginia remarked, 'she was too remote for real companionship'.[9] She also had an unusually white skin which during this strained period seemed to grow paler and paler.

During the winter of 1895–6 Jack Hills, a young solicitor and future politician, regularly visited the house. Three years earlier he had proposed to Stella and been refused. Custom had obliged him to keep his distance from the family for a while, but shortly before Julia's death he had reappeared. Now he renewed his suit of Stella, and to further his cause spent much time with her half-brothers and -sisters of whom he became genuinely fond. He proved to have an endless store of knowledge on the commonplaces of life and could discourse at length on bicycles and dogs. He also shared with them his interest in philosophy and lepidoptera, taught them how to sugar trees, and gave them his copy of Morris's *Butterflies and Moths*. He was more honest than George or Gerald and once he became familiar with the Stephen children would reply frankly to questions concerning sex. He was neither handsome nor intellectually distinguished; he lacked finesse and his stammer often gave his speech a forced earnestness; but he was kind, loyal, persistent and devoted. The first time he proposed again after Julia's death, Stella refused him. But when in August 1896 he proposed again, she capitulated. In the period immediately following the announcement of their engagement her radiance unveiled her joy.

Her situation was, however, difficult, for Jack threatened to destroy the compact recently formed between Stella and her stepfather. She had filled too well, too willingly, Julia's place in Leslie's life and he now complained that her marriage would be an irreparable blow. His gloom and depression invaded the engaged couple's happiness. He insisted on a longer engagement than was necessary and tried to argue that after marriage Stella and Jack should live at 22 Hyde Park Gate. He eventually agreed to a compromise when a house was found for them further down the street.

Aware of the complications caused by the engagement, Vanessa was meanwhile occupied with preparations for her entry into society. She visited dressmakers and, under Stella's instructions, learnt how to waltz, Thoby galloping her round the room and landing her on a table. Her life was full and active and as yet untroubled by domestic responsibilities. In November 1896 she accompanied George and her rich, fat aunt, Julia's sister-in-law Minna Duckworth, on a tour of northern France. In London she was frequently invited to plays or other entertainments by friends of the family and she paid regular visits to the National Gallery, the Royal Academy and the South Kensington Museum (subsequently renamed the Victoria and Albert Museum). In March 1897 Gerald Duckworth and Philip Burne-Jones, the sociable son of the famous artist, gave a tea party at the New Gallery. 'It was very dull I thought,' Vanessa told Thoby, 'but there were a good many celebrities there, Mrs Beerbohm Tree, Burne-Jones and Sir E. Poynter [President of the Royal Academy] and a lot of other people ... Aunt Minnie ... spent her time in chasing Mr Henry James about the room.'[10]

On 10 April 1897 Stella and Jack were married. Vanessa and Virginia acted as bridesmaids and were rewarded with pendant gold watches bought from Dent's in Pall Mall. (Vanessa later had hers mounted as a wristwatch and wore it for the rest of her life.) The young couple then went on honeymoon to Florence while the Stephen family took a holiday in Brighton. They lodged with the widow of the poet Roden Noel, in a house cluttered with Byronesque photographs of her late husband. Perhaps it was the soiled gentility of the Regency terraces, but more likely the fact that her mother's self-righteous sister, Aunt Mary Fisher, lived nearby, that contributed to Vanessa's lifelong dislike of Brighton. That April she sat on the beach painting the pier while Virginia, close at hand, read *Barchester Towers*.

Back in London they discovered that the young married couple had already returned from Italy and that Stella was in bed with gastro-enteritis. Her condition grew suddenly critical and peritonitis was suspected. Looking back on the period that followed Vanessa recalled 'a time of horrible suspense, muddle, mismanagement, hopeless fighting against the stupidity of those in power'.[11] While Stella's life was thought to be in danger, Virginia was too distraught even to read and had to sleep with Vanessa. Then, almost as suddenly as it had arrived, the wave of shock receded. Stella began to recover and their lives edged again towards normality. Vanessa returned to her drawing classes, Virginia to her lessons. They attacked the overgrown back garden, planted new beds, gave tea to a Frenchman called Lesage on whom Vanessa practised her French. On 30 May Stella and Vanessa both celebrated their birthdays and so luncheon was had at 24 Hyde Park Gate, the home of Jack and Stella, and dinner at No. 22, the evening ending uproariously. Vanessa was the centre of attention for she had now turned eighteen, the age when a young girl was suddenly transformed into a lady: skirts dropped to the floor, hair was firmly wound up on the head. Vanessa's beauty, which had previously been ignored, became the object of admiration, something to be cultivated and adorned. That year George presented her with an opal necklace, Gerald gave her money and the promise of a dress, Stella produced a gold and blue enamel chain. The rest of the family, realizing that underneath this sudden transformation lay the same individual as before, reflected her own tastes in their gifts of books and paints.

Vanessa 'came out' (though she was never presented at court as the term suggests) at a time when there was a momentary lull in the anxiety caused by Stella's health. In its place was a mood of jubilant excitement. Vanessa told Thoby her opal necklace was so grand that she could hardly believe it belonged to her. She, Virginia and Thoby all drove in a carriage obtained by a friend of their father's, Frederick Gibbs, to St Thomas's Hospital whence they watched the river procession celebrating the Queen's Diamond Jubilee. That summer Stella announced she was pregnant and the

Stephens' cousin Adeline Fisher became engaged to the young composer Ralph Vaughan Williams. Vanessa, looking strikingly beautiful, found herself entering her first dinner party on the arm of a senior wrangler called Mr Cowell. She also attended her first ball, danced until three in the morning and, as Virginia's diary records, was the envy of all the other women present. Stella took a motherly delight in Vanessa's success and outwardly life seemed promising and relaxed. It may have been only the exceptional heat that made the family occasionally listless and on edge. 'Broiling again,' Virginia's diary reads 'Perfectly breezeless day, and the sky blue and misty with the heat – Gerald sits in an arm chair by the open window in his shirt sleeves, Georgie gasps at intervals; Nessa sneezes with hay fever – A. [Adrian] *bicycle rides* and prints photographs, and I growl at everything – the effect of nerves doubtless.'[12]

Suddenly this sultry stillness ended. In mid July Virginia fell ill with a fever while visiting Jack and Stella and was put to bed in their house. The next evening Vanessa, resplendent in her new evening dress, called to see how she was before attending a concert at the Lushingtons'. That night Stella took to her bed in pain. Two days later her condition was so critical Virginia was removed from the house. George carried her back to No. 22, Stella calling out 'goodbye' as they passed her bedroom door. At this point the family doctor, Seton, fell ill with sciatica and others were brought in. After anxious consultation they decided that Stella's condition required an operation. It was performed the next day and at three the following morning George and Vanessa entered Virginia's bedroom to tell her that Stella was dead.

Neither sister attended the brief service at Highgate on 21 July when Stella was buried beside her mother, but three days later they accompanied Jack on a visit to the grave. Vanessa may then have arrived at the conclusion which many years later she told her son Julian: that Stella, who had refused to marry while Julia was alive, had died because she could not live without her. It was perhaps an exaggerated idea, but one that grew from her awareness of Stella's morbid attachment to the memory of her mother. Seated that afternoon near both graves, they talked a long time before returning home. The next day Leslie wrote to his friend Charles Eliot Norton: 'My Vanessa is taking her place as mistress of the house very calmly and will be invaluable.'[13]

Almost certainly that Vanessa's evident maturity owed much to the studio. Painting, unlike the complication of words, requires, at a sensuous level, a simple, direct engagement with the medium. (In 1917 Virginia wrote of her sister and Duncan Grant: 'They are very large in effect, these painters;

very little self-conscious; they have smooth broad spaces in their minds where I am all prickles and promontories.'[14]) At Cope's school Vanessa had deepened her innate reflectiveness. Her calm, allied with her statuesque beauty, gave her a certain monumentality. It also controlled and hid her feelings. Aware of the muddle and mismanagement that had surrounded Stella's death, Vanessa must have been further irritated by the many visitors whom she now had to receive. They arrived intent on sharing in the emotional drama of this family, twice bereaved within only two years. The pent-up frustration both sisters felt later found expression through Mrs Ambrose in Virginia's first novel, *The Voyage Out*: 'Directly anything happens – it may be a marriage, or a birth, or a death – on the whole they prefer it to be death – everyone wants to see you. They insist upon seeing you. They've got nothing to say; they don't care a rap for you; but you've got to go to lunch or to tea or to dinner, and if you don't you're damned.' With some Vanessa risked damnation and openly showed dislike, but her behaviour was more often than not excused and a number of unwanted family friends remained on calling terms for several years.

While Julia had lived, their 'at homes' had attracted many eminent members of the professional middle class whose sons and daughters, it was assumed, would in time become friends of the Stephen children. Several of Leslie's literary acquaintances, including Henry James, also paid regular calls. In addition there was a sprinkling of worthy but rather dull elderly gentlemen, one of whom was Frederick Gibbs, a former tutor to the Prince of Wales. He was neat, bald and double-chinned and had only one asset, an encyclopaedic knowledge. 'Oh Gibbs, what a bore you are,' Leslie would groan aloud in his presence, his want of civility being politely overlooked, for Gibbs remained on visiting terms until the end of his life. He took a particular interest in Vanessa, gave her a picture of the Three Fates on her eighteenth birthday and showed her Retzsch's engravings which half a century earlier had inspired the Pre-Raphaelites.

As children the Stephens had laughed at the elderly gentlemen who would arrive punctually in time for tea and take their place among the Fishers and Vaughans, relatives of the Stephens, and among certain young society women, such as the Stillmans, Montgomerys and Lushingtons. Now Vanessa, at the age of eighteen, found herself thrust into the role of hostess and housekeeper, for the smooth running of this large household and its regular influx of guests depended on her. She was observed in her tasks by Violet Dickinson who, when her own mother had died, had been befriended by Julia Stephen. She now wished to repay this kindness and did all she could to alleviate the gloom that had settled over the Stephen family. Though she quickly became one of their closest friends, her first impression was that Vanessa and Virginia were shy, aloof and silent. She recalled:

> There was a feeling of melancholy always about the house in Hyde Park Gate, perhaps from the long silences, and critical atmosphere.
>
> Mr Stephen had a shy furtive manner with strangers, and he was deaf. Vanessa seemed at once to slip into Stella's place as a mother, sister and daughter combined; at tea-time the family were generally to be found, Vanessa behind the tea-pot, elderly friends coming in at intervals, Henry James, Mr Romer, Sir Alfred Lyall, Lady Ritchie, etc. . . .
>
> Vanessa whenever she had the chance of throwing off the cares of her family, (she was dutiful to a degree,) lived for, and thought of nothing else but her career as an artist.[15]

Vanessa followed the precedent set by Julia and Stella but duty must often have conflicted with her own interests. Virginia, recollecting her sister at this period, perceived that 'so many demands were made on her; it was, in a sense, so easy to be what was expected, with such models before her, but also it was so hard to be herself'.[16]

It is probable therefore that when Vanessa sat down at the tea table at four-thirty every afternoon, she attended to the proceedings, like the fictional Katherine Hilbery in *Night and Day*, with only the surface skin of her mind. The cups were filled and refilled, and the pink china shell that held spiced buns passed between the guests. A visitor looking across at Vanessa might have felt that her beauty, as yet unanimated, was a shade sullen; she was demure in company but not wholly sympathetic. Nevertheless both she and Virginia became adept at tea-table conversation which was informal but polite, intelligent but never allowed to settle for too long on any one topic. It cultivated a certain tone which Virginia later felt crept unwanted into her *Common Reader* essays. It left both sisters very well-mannered, supremely well trained in judging and (if they wished) maintaining limitations beyond which civilized intercourse did not go.

In the evenings the two sisters sat alone with their father, reading by the light of an oil lamp. George, observing this routine, reflected that at neither Hyde Park Gate nor at Cope's school was Vanessa moving in high society, or meeting eligible ex-Etonians. Vanessa's initial entry into society had been abruptly terminated by mourning. Now, without Stella to act as chaperon, the two sisters were largely cut off from the social life of their peers; their circumstances had become melancholy and restricted. 'The whole spring of the household', Vanessa recalled, 'seemed to have snapped.'[17] Therefore when George urged her to re-enter the social world, his enthusiasm met with less resistance than it might otherwise have done. Like a highly-strung thoroughbred led round the ring in the private enclosure, Vanessa would now enter society at George's side.

By 1898, having reached the age of thirty, George Duckworth enjoyed an enviable position. He was well established in his civil service career as private secretary to Austen Chamberlain, and had also inherited a considerable private income. He had dark wavy hair, currant eyes, a handlebar moustache and a handsome appearance. Invariably impeccably dressed, he had an air of brisk authority and was graced with charm, manners and good humour – when things went well. The eldest Duckworth, who had been his mother's favourite, he was more nervous and inflexible than Gerald; when crossed he could become stubborn and childish, often resorting to tears. His lack of intelligence had failed to gain him entry into the diplomatic service, but it had eased his position in the upper echelons of a society whose values he never thought to question. In fact society fascinated him, and having no fiancée or wife to consolidate his position, he nurtured the hope that Vanessa, strikingly beautiful and pitifully motherless, should now accompany him on the social round.

Vanessa quickly came to dread the social occasions to which she was now exposed, but George's character made it difficult for her to refuse them. She had little recourse in an argument with George which ended with him seizing her in his arms and drowning her protests with kisses. To tempt her out of the dark confines of Hyde Park Gate and into the glare of a ballroom, he heaped presents upon her. He gave her an Arab mare which, in keeping with fashion, she rode every morning before breakfast down the Ladies' Mile in Rotten Row; he adorned her with opals, amethysts and a blue enamel butterfly to wear in her hair; she was taken to the dressmaker Mrs Young in South Audley Street who concocted a dress that suggested mourning yet was also fashionable and pretty: transparent black material sewn with tiny silver sequins hung over a white underdress. Finally, if she still balked at an invitation, George was not above resorting to emotional blackmail. He told her that Julia would have wished her to accept; that if she did not contribute to the ease of his social life he would be driven to an action at which he could only hint but which suggested the need for a whore; he would declare that Vanessa was deflecting him from his sacred duty which was to ensure that her femininity flowered within the safe bounds of tradition: to fail in society, he implied, was to be found inadequate, unfeminine and undesirable. Vanessa, therefore, stepped out complete with fan, handkerchief, long white gloves, evening bag and the discreet glitter of jewels. At the last moment a large Malmaison carnation would arrive which she pinned to her dress. It was the last trump in George's strong hand. Yet it would be wrong to suggest Vanessa lost the game: she simply refused to play it.

She entered a society which, as it moved into the Edwardian period, grew ever more extravagent in its pursuit of two goals: pleasure and marriage. The season promised balls, levées, state dinners, garden parties, opera, theatre and concerts. Weekend parties were held in large country houses by the 'smart' set, the term referring not only to their appearance but also to a carefully guarded access to power. For behind this sophisticated machinery lay the primitive urge to keep the upper echelons well stocked. Cynthia Asquith, daughter of the Prime Minister, sensed this underlying cause when in breathless terms she described her own experience of 'coming out': 'By just dancing myself dizzy, looking as nice as I could or exploring myself anew through some fresh pair of eyes, I felt I was furthering some momentous, indeed some almost devout purpose.'[18]

Vanessa experienced no such ecstasy. 'Though I felt all the thrill of putting on such a frock,' she wrote of Mrs Young's evening dress, 'still I came to dread the sight of it, so miserable were the many evenings I spent covered in the filmy black and white and sparkling sequins.'[19] Instead of developing in her the art of social coquetry, George merely succeeded in driving Vanessa in on herself, increasing her distrust of 'society'. For her own safety, she began to rely more and more on a natural obstinacy. To George she appeared wooden and deficient in some important area of feeling, for she made it clear that she found little value in these social occasions. While other young women flowered under these circumstances, Vanessa appeared perplexed, mournful and oppressed. Even her beauty seemed at odds with fashionable taste. She may also have been aware that recent developments in technology were undermining the strict social rules that George upheld; the telephone was replacing the calling-card; motorcars and buses were bringing women much greater freedom of movement. As yet still hemmed in by social pressures, Vanessa felt 'vaguely thwarted and repressed and perhaps tantalized sometimes, by glimpses of a life where one might have been at ease'.[20]

George's mantelpiece, meanwhile, remained an ever-changing gallery of invitation cards addressed to 'Mr Duckworth and Miss Stephen'. On Sunday afternoons they did a round of 'at homes', exchanging one matron's drawing-room filled with blushing marriageable daughters for another, Vanessa listening to Lady Kay Shuttleworth on the beauty of sunsets, or to Mrs Humphry Ward, already adverse to feminism and later to be a vociferous opponent of the Suffragettes. She encountered Mrs W.K. Clifford (author of the best-seller *Mrs Keith's Crime*) and her daughter Ethel who affected the pose and dress of the 'aesthetic' movement but who looked even less like the Burne-Jones ideal than her novelist-mother, whose teeth were awry and who delighted in gossip about the literary world. But the name that caused Vanessa particular dread was that of Lady Arthur Russell. Her ancestry and connections made her a larger than usual star on the social horizon; but the fact that she lived in Mayfair and had the windows of her house washed every week did not blind Vanessa and Virginia to the fact that she was 'a rude tyrannical old woman, with a bloodstained complexion and the manners of a turkey cock'.[21] Her son Gilbert recalled that Vanessa was noticeably devoid of smalltalk at these parties.[22] She herself blamed her failure at Lady Russell's on the fact that people were expected to sit and not stand, which made it impossible for a shy young woman to move unless invited to do so.

One of Lady Arthur's invitations brought Vanessa's relationship with George to an impasse. He insisted that the occasion was not one they could refuse: Vanessa thought otherwise. After George had employed every known tactic in his repertoire, she dressed and entered his carriage in fury. They arrived at the house in South Audley Street but George refused to enter with Vanessa in such a temper. The carriage drove round the park and arrived once more, but this time Vanessa refused to move because George was in tears. Whether or not they made an appearance that night is not known but after this George transferred his attention to Virginia. On some occasions both sisters now sat together in silence throughout an entire evening, speaking only to their hostess on arriving and departing. They felt outsiders; they were aware that they lacked the 'social gift'; 'Seriousness', Virginia observed in her diary, 'is just as much out of place here as an old serge skirt'.[23]

Still more agonizing were the house parties that lasted an entire week-end. When Vanessa was invited with George to the Chamberlains, who lived on the outskirts of Birmingham, they made the *faux-pas* of arriving half a day too early and of mistaking the tradesmen's entrance for the front door. Vanessa had fought hard not to go on this occasion and could not relax in the foreign atmosphere created by rich business people. The interior of the house exuded wealth; there were palms in the lounge, orchids in the greenhouses and Royal Academy 'pictures of the year' on the walls. The daughters treated Vanessa kindly and Neville Chamberlain talked to her about moths. But the scant pleasure derived from this visit was instantly demolished by George's complaint that her untidy hair had made her only a modified success.

With relief Vanessa returned to the dark Kensington house with its innumerable small rooms and familiar inhabitants; to her tall, willowy sister assiduously studying Greek; to the lean schoolboy Adrian in his Eton collar and short jacket; to Thoby, who was now losing his clumsiness and fatness and becoming the assured young man who in 1899 went up to

Cambridge; to a home where intellect took precedence over convention, the exercise of reason over that of money or power.

At the top of the house Leslie Stephen worked at his biographies and articles, becoming scraggier with old age and more and more isolated and unworldly. At breakfast, on the days that he received no post, he would petulantly declare that everyone had forgotten him. He had begun to develop more than the usual old man's foibles. Beneath the surface of his life lay a number of irritants, chief of which was his dissatisfaction with his career, the sense that he had dissipated himself and had not made the contribution to philosophy and ethics of which he believed himself capable. Strenuous thought had atrophied certain of his emotions; what the occupational hazards of his career began, the irritation of deafness and the experience of being twice widowed deepened. Even his devoted biographer admitted that Leslie Stephen playing patience in old age was 'not only a sight to see, but if his luck was bad, a sound to hear'.[24] When every Wednesday Vanessa placed the account books in front of Leslie, his displaced anxiety became fear of bankruptcy. The result was a pyrotechnic display of bad temper.

No consideration of Vanessa's feelings would enter Leslie's histrionic performance. Quite unjustly he declared they were 'shooting Niagara to ruin', heading for bankruptcy and the workhouse. In fact he not only owned his substantial house in Hyde Park Gate but also another in Emperor's Gate and had just sold Talland House in St Ives. He had enough invested capital, quite apart from his income from his books and articles, to maintain his family in comfort. The highest income tax that he ever had to pay was 1s 3d in the pound and, as Leonard Woolf has said, his financial state was as impregnably secure as the Bank of England. Yet he raged mercilessly at his daughter, his face flushed, his body trembling.

To his second wife Leslie had often joked about his tantrums and his nervous, 'skinless' temperament which was aggravated by his tendency to overwork. Ever since childhood, when his poor health and sensitivity had caused his mother Jane Venn to indulge him, he had been used to receiving much care and commiseration from women. As Virginia realized, pity had played no small part in her mother's decision to marry him. As his wife, Julia was able to cope with his bad temper and low spirits; she occasionally upbraided him bluntly or chided him for grumbling, for he in fact enjoyed resistance. When, prior to his second marriage, his sister Caroline Emelia Stephen had acted as his housekeeper, he had complained that she took him too seriously, was too passive and did not scold him. Like a spoilt child, he expected others to control his rampant egotism. After three weeks in her brother's company, Caroline Emelia collapsed from the strain and the housekeeping arrangement was terminated. When Julia's turn came, she often practised small deceptions to rid Leslie of irrational anxieties. Stella too, by the exercise of patience and sympathy, had been able to control his alarming moods. She had been mutable to a degree, assuring him, when he suffered a fit of remorse, that his marriage to Julia could not be compared with that of the Carlyles, though in fact she knew nothing about the latter. Both Julia and Stella, in their different ways, had avoided the rages that Vanessa confronted every week.

To some extent Vanessa may have unintentionally goaded Leslie into this excessive behaviour. Instead of expressing sympathy and understanding or promising impossible economies, she stood silent at his side. It was not in her nature to pretend improvements where none could be made. As it was, the ordering of the groceries was done by the cook, Sophie Farrell, who had been with them many years. Vanessa's youth would have made it difficult for her to assume authority over such an experienced person and all she could do was suggest that whiting might suffice instead of salmon or that it was still too early for strawberries. Leslie, exhibiting that fussiness that made him an attentive biographer but a difficult husband and father, insisted that every expenditure should be marked down under one of various headings. It presented Vanessa with a laborious task each week, but instead of being thanked she received a volley of abuse. She was perhaps bewildered by her father's display of wrath, her integrity and honesty offended by his unreasonableness. 'The Saint's' silence exposed Leslie's pettiness and thereby aggravated the situation. The sad result of this was that his ungoverned temper shrivelled her feelings towards him and unbalanced the view of her father that she gave fifty years later to the historian Noël Annan. These weekly sessions over the accounts left her with a deep distaste for emotional scenes; they made her a rigorously careful housekeeper for the rest of her life; and they developed her self-control. From now on, if she so desired, her outward manner could be decidedly chilling.

Housekeeping apart, Leslie Stephen felt content with the progress his children were making. In December 1900 he wrote to Charles Eliot Norton, 'Thoby enjoying Cambridge immoderately; and Vanessa her studio; and Virginia becoming as literary as her papa.'[25] There was also some expansion of their social horizon. The two sisters attended Trinity College May Ball and met some of Thoby's Cambridge friends. They became familiar with Rezia, Guido and Nerino Rasponi, a long-established Florentine family, who paid regular visits to England. When Rezia married into one of the most illustrious Florentine families, the Corsini, she brought her new husband to meet the Stephens at Fritham House, near Lyndhurst, where they spent the summers of 1899 and 1900. Even when on holiday in rented accommodation the Stephens continued to receive a stream of visitors and the most regular was Jack Hills.

Immediately after Stella's death, Jack had turned up at 22 Hyde Park Gate every evening, in need of company. When the Stephen family disappeared that summer to Painswick, near Stroud, Jack had written to them every day and visited them at weekends. On these occasions Vanessa and Virginia sat with him in the summer-house and listened as he re-examined the past and occasionally burst out against Leslie's harsh treatment of Stella. In September they visited him at his parents' home, Corby Castle, near Carlisle, and for a period after that he lived with the Stephens at Hyde Park Gate while he waited to move into a new house. In his unhappiness and need for compassion he preyed on Vanessa's sympathy. 'He began', Virginia recalled, 'to take a regular and unthinking satisfaction in being with her, without I suppose, for I was sometimes jealous, perceiving a single one of the multitude of fine adjustments that composed her presence.'[26] In Vanessa's character Jack would have found many echoes of Stella. During the two years prior to her death, Stella had grown very close to her half-sister whose looks, honesty and wisdom she admired. The loss of Stella affected Vanessa more directly than the death of her mother; and her increasing fondness for Jack may have corresponded with her desire to hold on to the memory of Stella, to assuage a need for understanding. Virginia first realized how things stood when she ventured a criticism of Jack and Vanessa replied with silence. Then George walked Virginia round the garden at Fritham one summer explaining, somewhat incoherently, that it was illegal in England to marry the brother or sister of one's deceased spouse. Several attempts had been made in recent years to change this law but its reform was successfully blocked by the House of Lords until 1907. Fearful of illegality and social embarrassment, George was anxious to stamp out any relationship that might develop between his half-sister and Jack. Lack of evidence makes it impossible to assess whether Vanessa's love for Jack was passionate or merely fond. But if this was the first time she fell in love, it must have been painful to discover that her feelings placed her outside accepted social behaviour, and the experience would have left her further disaffected with society and its rules. When Virginia, as George requested, warned Vanessa of her position, she replied a shade bitterly, 'So you take their side too.'[27]

Leslie Stephen, to his credit, aware that Holman Hunt had faced the same problem and solved it by marrying abroad, refused to admonish his daughter. His behaviour appalled their religious relations the Fishers. Aunt

Mary Fisher, shocked by Leslie's unconcern, decided to intervene and sent Vanessa a surreptitious letter addressed to Cope's school. Vanessa's isolated position aroused Virginia's sympathy and drew the two sisters still closer together. But the affair with Jack proceeded no further. In April 1900 George arranged a trip to Paris with Vanessa, probably to distract her. She visited the Louvre for the first time and returned home ecstatic about the food she had eaten and still more about what she had seen.

The rumpus caused by Vanessa's intimacy with Jack subtly changed her relationship with Thoby. Outwardly Thoby was everything that, from a girl's point of view, a brother should be. He had superb good looks, blue eyes and a determined, resolute character. He shared Vanessa's gift for drawing and awoke in Virginia her love of Shakespeare. He rarely spoke of his feelings, being deeply reserved. Yet even when he said nothing, he emanated affection, sympathy and respect. Both sisters tended to worship him: for Virginia, he had the air 'of one equipped, unperturbed, knowing his place, relishing his inheritance and his part in life, aware of his competence, scenting the battle'.[28] His equilibrium rested on an aloofness and an acceptance of authority which eventually directed him into the legal profession and which would no doubt have brought him a successful, if conventional, career. At Clifton he had not reacted against the tone of muscular Christianity; at Cambridge he befriended in particular Clive Bell who, like Thoby, combined an interest in the arts with a hearty masculinity. At home Thoby upheld those in authority: he implied that his sisters should sympathize with their father's tyrannical demands; and when Vanessa cut Aunt Mary in the street, after receiving her letter about Jack, Thoby immediately condemned his sister's behaviour.

Thoby, therefore, though still revered, no longer stood in direct relation to Vanessa's inner feelings which were now shared chiefly with Virginia. Their relationship was to some extent reflexive in that Virginia tended to project her own image of her sister on to Vanessa, and failed sometimes to notice when the stencil did not fit. Their fascination with each other heightened their introspection and their conversations often turned either on the past or their hypothetical future, for already their ambition was an important bond between them. Violet Dickinson, evoking this period, wrote that 'Vanessa was always sketching and Virginia wrote and read'.[29] These interests could be easily pursued in the country during the summer months but in London they had to be carefully safeguarded. Virginia recalled:

I always think of those curious long autumn walks with which we ended a summer holiday, talking of what we were going to do – 'autumn plans' we called them. They always had reference to painting and writing and how to arrange social life and domestic life better. Often we thought about changing a room, so as to have somewhere to see our own friends. They were always connected with autumn, leaves falling, the country getting pale and wintry, our minds excited at the prospect of lights and streets and a new season of activity beginning – October the dawn of the year.[30]

In 1901 Vanessa was one of twenty students accepted that year into the Painting School of the Royal Academy. She must therefore have acquired by then considerable mimetic skills and knowledge of anatomy: the entrance examinations required four drawings to be produced, one of an undraped antique sculpture, a life-size drawing of a head and arm done from life, a drawing from an antique figure anatomized to show the bones and the same anatomized to show muscles and tendons, all of which had to be correctly labelled.

The Painting and Sculpture Schools are situated in the heart of the West End, tucked away behind Burlington House and reached by a brick alley to one side of Burlington Arcade. Inside the building a long, stone-flagged, cross-vaulted corridor, flanked by plaster casts and dominated at one end by the Laocoön, opens down one side on to the studios, each with its particular smell of either wet clay and hot plaster or the pungent tang of turpentine. All the studios have high ceilings and tall skylights and are heated by a cumbrous system of ducts and underfloor pipes. The inner sanctum was, and still is, the life-room. Here, for over a hundred years, students have sat in two semicircular tiered rows in front of the model's throne, studying the human figure under a seemingly timeless, steady north light.

Attending the Academy Schools must have seemed to Vanessa much like visiting an elderly relative: it was all very familiar. Earlier that year she had received from her father, for her twenty-second birthday, C.R. Leslie's *The Life and Times of Sir Joshua Reynolds* which would have acquainted her with the origin of the Academy. The teaching methods did not differ noticeably from those used at Cope's and among the painting professors was her mother's cousin Val Prinsep. Classes in drawing, from the antique and from life, were supplemented with lessons on anatomy, perspective, portraiture and composition. Each month a subject was set and criticized by a visiting professor, one of a list of prominent artists whose paintings Vanessa would have seen at the annual Academy exhibitions.

Most of these artists specialized in genre painting. Every summer they would exhibit at least one 'subject' picture which, if its sentiment proved popular, would be engraved, printed and widely distributed. One of these visiting teachers was Marcus Stone, highly esteemed for his courtship scenes, made picturesque by the use of Regency costumes and garden settings. Another was Sir Lawrence Alma-Tadema, famous for his domestic anecdotes set in ancient Greece or Rome and for his skilful rendering of marble, flesh and fur. Edwardian taste encouraged a mood of frivolity and vapid sentimentality, and the elaborate skill used to portray a subject often far outstripped its content.

But the importance formerly given to subject-matter was being undermined in various ways, not least by the growing interest in the effects of light. French Impressionism was still shocking to an English audience, but *plein-air* realism, as found in Bastien-Lepage's paintings of peasants seen under a dull grey sky, had successfully been absorbed into the anecdotal vocabulary of the late Victorians. George Clausen, another visitor to the Academy Schools, had changed his style after meeting Bastien-Lepage and did much to extend the latter's influence in England. Few of the Academicians had been able to withstand this new style totally and late Victorian painting owed much to the refreshing vigour of the modern French school. Even the Keeper of the Academy Schools, Ernest Crofts, had allowed its atmospheric effects to influence his historical reconstructions of battle scenes.

Vanessa's teachers ranged from High Victorians to the animal painter John Macallan Swan, but it is difficult to ascertain the extent of their influence. From the two extant oils painted at around this time – a portrait of her father and a small painting of Jack Hills's niece aged one and a half,[31] no obvious direction with regard to her development can be discerned: these are obviously student essays in Old Master styles. Though she received special praise for her work soon after entering the Schools, she took no prizes while there, nor did any of her friends – Mary Creighton, Sylvia Milman and Margery Snowden – with whom she was cloistered in the life-class, for until 1903 these classes remained segregated. The disciplined system of formal training probably did not allow the personalities and interests of the various teachers to emerge with any strong effect. But one artist did seize Vanessa's imagination and gave direction to her career.

'The young have terribly bad taste it is true,' Vanessa admitted to her sister in 1927, 'but after all so had I – Sargent and Fred Walker still haunt me.'[32] The one was her teacher at the Academy, the other a childhood discovery. Vanessa had been brought up in a house which had an entire bookcase filled with the *Cornhill Magazine* which her father had at one time edited. Certain issues were illustrated by Frederick Walker, of whom she would have heard tales from her Aunt Anny for he had first begun work for the *Cornhill* when Thackeray was editor. He had also produced illustrations for Thackeray's unfinished *Denis Duval*. Anny Thackeray declared that Walker's drawings for her serialized novel *The Village on the Cliff* so perfectly corresponded with her own imagination that she was fired with enthusiasm to complete the tale. Walker's skill lay in his marriage of Pre-Raphaelite sentiment with a more relaxed, realistic style and a subtle sense of design. He had died young, at the age of thirty-five in 1875, and thus, like Bastien-Lepage, had brought himself considerable posthumous fame.

If romantic pathos clung to the name of Fred Walker, John Singer Sargent had more immediate appeal. He charged the life-class at the Academy with a note of drama for he stood at the easel, his drawing arm fully extended, his head flung back, his green eyes staring intently, and with a few sweeps of charcoal executed a *tour de force*. 'Sargent is teaching most extraordinarily well at the RA,' Vanessa wrote to Margery Snowden who was temporarily absent. 'He gives lessons as you said he did, that would apply to any paintings. They're chiefly about tone. He insists upon thick paint and makes one try to get the right tone at once. Apparently the drawing is to be got entirely by painting thickly the different tones, which doesn't sound very clear. He generally tells me that my things are too grey. The one thing he is down upon is when he thinks anyone is trying for an effect regardless of truth.'[33] Vanessa took blatant delight in the way Sargent squashed all conceit: he told Miss Claque that it was quite unnecessary for her to produce a pot-boiler as no one was going to buy her painting; he ridiculed a Miss Everett for using huge ridges of impasto. Vanessa was herself highly receptive to technical advice; she never forgot that it was Ebenezer Cooke who had first taught her to observe colour in highlights. Now she had the opportunity to receive, at first hand, instruction from a devastatingly brilliant technician.

She encountered Sargent at the height of his career. He excelled at portraying the elegance and luxury of the Edwardian plutocracy through a series of marvellous hints: the glint of satin and silk, the shiver of light on silver candelabras, pearls and oriental pots. He often borrowed his choice of pose from the aristocratic portraiture of Reynolds or Van Dyck to give to his sitters that which they lacked by birth. At the start of his career in England he had been regarded with suspicion because of the obvious French influence in his work; trained under Carolus-Duran in Paris, he had learnt to construct volume through tone rather than outline, a method that challenged the linear style of the Pre-Raphaelites which Ruskin had done much to promote. But in 1893 Sargent had taken the Academy by storm with his portrait of Lady Agnew (National Gallery of Scotland) in which his nonchalant, assured handling of paint became the superb vehicle for an expression of aristocratic ease.

Friendship with Monet had contributed to the loosening of Sargent's style. It encouraged him in his method of direct painting, which his admiration for Whistler further confirmed. Sargent taught his pupils to concentrate on tone and to use a large, well-loaded brush. He insisted that the background should be brushed into the underpainting of the figure or head, until the subtle modulations of cool and warm, dark and light colour created the smooth curvature of the flesh. The final select details were to be painted *alla prima* at one sitting, and completely rubbed out afterwards if the result was unsatisfactory. Technique apart, Sargent's chief merit as a teacher was the stress he laid on observation: 'Cultivate an ever continuous power of observation. Wherever you are, be always ready to make slight notes of postures, groups and incidents. Store up in the mind without ceasing a continuous stream of observations from which to make selections later. Above all things get abroad, see the sunlight, and everything that is to be seen, the power of selection will follow.'[34]

Through her friendship with the restless and energetic Madge Vaughan, Vanessa came into contact with another leading artist of the day, Charles Furse, who had married Madge's sister Katherine Symonds. Vanessa acted as bridesmaid at their wedding in 1900 and shortly afterwards was invited to stay at their house, Yockley, on Chobham Ridges near Camberley. Furse took the opportunity to paint Vanessa gazing into a mirror, in a pose reminiscent of Whistler's *Little White Girl*. This portrait hung in a place of honour at the New English Art Club in the spring of 1902 where Vanessa's face was compared, by one reviewer, with the type of charm found in early Millais. Like Sargent, Furse employed artifice and bravura to enliven the society portraits at which he excelled.

Many years later Vanessa recalled that she found Furse a formidable, crushing painter, referring most probably to both his style and character. He was enormous, prematurely bald, and not averse to mocking his own physique, for he appeared at one fancy-dress ball in a white muslin frock with a pink satin bow, dragging in his wake a toy lamb. He had considerable influence within the New English Art Club which had been founded in 1886 as an alternative to the Royal Academy. Though it attracted a wide range of artists it favoured those whose work reflected French influence. Furse sat on the jury, opposing the then antiquarian taste of the young Roger Fry who would eloquently uphold the merits of a sober, brown painting of a barn by Charles Holmes that Furse wanted to reject. Furse was one of the artists who gave Vanessa the impression that 'all members of the NEAC seemed somehow to have the secret of the art universe within their grasp, a secret one was not worthy to learn, especially if one was that terrible low creature, a female painter'.[35]

His immediate influence on Vanessa was to change her taste in interior decoration. Used to the sombre gloom of Hyde Park Gate, she was shocked at Yockley to see faces silhouetted against bare light walls. The house had been built for Furse by the architect Reginald Blomfeld, and the distempered walls, in keeping with the 'artistic' taste of the day, had been deliberately kept uncluttered of everything except for a few carefully chosen paintings and prints. The house seemed airy and expansive. To Vanessa, it was as if someone had lifted a blind in a previously darkened room.

But it was not Furse, with all his painterly *éclat*, who converted Vanessa to modern art, but a small book with poor reproductions. This was Camille Mauclair's *The French Impressionists* which appeared, in translation from the French, in 1903 and was the first volume in English to deal authoritatively with each of the various artists and with the historical background of the movement. For Vanessa it opened a window on to a fresh view of art, suggesting, as she later wrote, 'that after all living painters might be as alive as the dead and that there was something besides the lovely quality of old paint to be aimed at, something fundamental and permanent and as discoverable now as in any other age'.[36] Excited by it, she overcame her usual dislike of lectures and attended one on French Impressionism given by Frank Rutter at the Grafton Gallery in the winter of 1904-5. At around this time she surprised her friend Mary Creighton on a visit to a NEAC exhibition by declaring that Steer, Tonks and Furse would 'do nothing better than they had done, [therefore] one could take no interest in their development',[37] a statement that suggests she had by then considerable confidence in her own.

But this confidence was achieved gradually and in unpropitious circumstances. While still a student at the Royal Academy Schools Vanessa had to be home by four-thirty every afternoon to serve tea to Leslie's visitors. Though the twentieth century had begun, life at 22 Hyde Park Gate was still locked into the mid-Victorian age. The two Duckworth brothers did nothing to challenge Leslie's long-established life-style but upheld, without question, all the accepted conventions. As Virginia later observed: 'The cruel thing was that while we could see the future, we were completely in the power of the past.'[38] The future, of course, lay with Thoby's Cambridge friends, one of whom, Clive Bell, had visited them at Fritham during the summer of 1902. After he departed, he sent a present of some partridges and in return received his first letter from Vanessa:

Dear Mr Bell,

I hope you are able to imagine the excitement and joy that your partridges have caused here, as I am quite unable to describe it. Thank you very much indeed for them. It is most kind of you to have provided both such delicious food and such a splendid topic of conversation. I really ought to thank you too for your Collins [letter of thanks] which was received with great applause and which ought to be shown as a model to all other visitors. I hope you will prove its sincerity by coming here again some day, in spite of death in the pony cart and the certainty of endless discussion of one subject. Thank you again for the partridges.

Yours sincerely
Vanessa Stephen[39]

Despite its brevity, the letter is direct, humorous and assured. It extends the possibility of further acquaintance which Clive did not immediately take up as the following year he left England to pursue some historical research in Paris. We therefore get a hint of the more relaxed kind of friendship that Vanessa would like to pursue, but find her in fact still tied to the tea table at Hyde Park Gate, passing the spiced buns, attending to the teacups and replying politely to the intelligent, formal chatter.

She had first learnt that her father had abdominal cancer while on holiday in Italy with George in the spring of 1902. They returned home immediately, as it was thought that an operation would be performed. This proved a false alarm; Leslie did not undergo surgery until December and in the intervening months family life continued much as before. That year Leslie was offered and after some persuasion accepted a knighthood. In the autumn Adrian left home and went up to Trinity College, Cambridge. As Leslie's strength waned, Vanessa found she had to curtail her attendance at the Academy and instead paint from the model in the day nursery which was now turned into a makeshift studio. Her life became increasingly constricted. Virginia later felt that at this period they 'were always battling for that which was always being interfered with, muffled up, snatched away. The most imminent obstacle and burden was of course father.'[40] In practical terms, it meant that Leslie's illness dominated Vanessa's life, as she recalled:

For two years this meant more than ever a life of seclusion from our generation. Visits from his friends had to be arranged and carefully fitted in so that he had the right number each day. This was difficult and exacting for we had to be prepared to entertain Mrs W.K. Clifford and old C.B. Clarke while they waited to replace Mr Haldane and Sir Alfred Lyall in his room. There was of course no telephone and innumerable arrangements had to be made by letter or otherwise. And so no time or inclination was left for other society had it been

38

possible. One or two friends of our own we had who were also links with the older generation and who in those days were the greatest help to us – Mrs Leo Maxse and Violet Dickinson ... were the most intimate and useful.[41]

Of these two friends Vanessa was closer to Kitty Maxse, the daughter of Julia Stephen's greatest friend Mrs Vernon Lushington. Kitty, now married to Leopold Maxse, the editor of the *National Review*, was pretty, seductive and smart. She was socially at ease and after Stella's death adopted a quasi-maternal attitude to Vanessa, taking her out to concerts and parties. Virginia preferred Violet, for she suspected that Kitty's bright conversation hid a want of sympathy. When Leslie's health declined further, Kitty's visits became less frequent and were replaced by sympathetic notes confessing that she felt she could be of little help. Vanessa was hurt to hear that she had gone on a visit to the North without first calling at Hyde Park Gate. More reliable was Vanessa's old friend Margery Snowden, whose Harrogate background differed greatly from that of the Stephens. Virginia, again critical, thought her a commonplace, tragic creature and felt slightly incredulous that Vanessa should take obvious pleasure in her company.

In 1903 the Stephen family, with great deliberation and considerable strain, moved itself to Netherhampton House near Salisbury for the summer. Leslie had still enough strength to walk round the lawn. The others made visits to Wilton House, Romsey Abbey, Stonehenge and the Wilton carpet factory. Vanessa painted a landscape in which she intended putting an express train. Leslie, meanwhile, enjoyed a visit from Frederic Maitland who assisted him with his biography of Hobbes.

Though he was dying, his passion for literature was not. 'He lay there always *reading*', wrote Henry James after a visit to Leslie Stephen in November 1903, commenting also 'how beautiful Vanessa!'[42] On entering hospital in December 1902, Leslie had taken with him the works of Jane Austen, the one author Vanessa also turned to throughout her life with unfailing satisfaction. During the winter of 1903–4 his health declined rapidly. He felt regret that he would not know how his children's lives developed and wished still to hear about their new friends. He had once declared that his enjoyment of literature had begun and would end with Boswell's *Life of Johnson*. On 22 February 1904, after a period of utter physical debility, he died.

THREE

Changing Places

1904-1906

Leslie Stephen's death released Vanessa from a position that had become almost intolerable. For seven years she had borne the brunt of his demand that, as the daughter of an eminent man of letters, she should tailor her life to his needs. He had continued to work at his articles and books until a few months before he died; Vanessa's career, meanwhile, had suffered from circumstances which blocked any free expression of feelings and ideas. She never forgot the repression she endured during these years and was left determined that her children should not experience the same.

Outwardly the two sisters responded very differently to their father's death. Vanessa was relieved by it, and able over the next few months to absorb new experiences with joyful avidity; Virginia, who had formed a special relationship with her father towards the end of his life, was more deeply shaken. Her mourning for him was mixed with guilt, for she felt they had not given him the affection he demanded. Quentin Bell has argued that Vanessa's apparent indifference aggravated Virginia's grief which culminated a few months later in her first serious breakdown. But Vanessa herself could not easily shake off the memory of her father. She dreamt on more than one occasion that she had murdered him, thereby giving expression to angry frustration and a desire to end a painful and unsatisfactory relationship.

Immediately after the funeral the Stephens and George Duckworth took a holiday at Manorbier on the Pembroke coast. They walked along the cliffs, watched for unusual birds and in their lodgings Vanessa painted a small portrait of Thoby (now lost) which Virginia admired. This short stay was followed by a more leisurely trip to Italy made in April. Nothing could detract from Vanessa's joy at seeing Venice for the first time, and

though they arrived late at night with no rooms booked and had to search
the unfamiliar canals for accommodation, she felt no alarm. 'I thoroughly
enjoyed it,' she told Margery Snowden (who received a running account
of this trip), 'and expected a dark figure to jump out from some doorway
or our gondolier to shoot down a side canal and demand money – but
when one came to think of it Thoby and Adrian would be more than a
match for most gondoliers. We did get a hotel at last.'[1] After two nights
in temporary lodgings they moved into the Grand Hotel, Vanessa and
Virginia having a room on the top floor which looked out over the angular
counterpane of pantiled roofs to the distant Dolomites. Each day was spent
sightseeing, to Vanessa's satisfaction. After a visit to the Scuola di San
Rocco, Thoby, in a letter to Clive Bell, compared Tintoretto with Shakespeare. Vanessa shared his enthusiasm, though a few years later she was to
revise this high opinion and only retrieve it again in old age. The second
volume of Ruskin's *Modern Painters* had prepared her for Tintoretto, but
confronted with the actual paintings she realized how little she agreed with
the great critic's point of view: 'He never cares for anything unless it is a
symbol or has several deep meanings, which doesn't seem to me to be
what one wants.'[2]

From Venice they moved on to Florence where they stayed with Rezia
Corsini in the Rasponi family villa in the nearby hills. Here Vanessa could
relax, admire the view of the city and the colours of the oranges and roses
that grew beside the old walls of the villa. As she watched the darting
lizards and the irregular progress of the butterflies she began to feel that
this Mediterranean life-style suited the rhythm of her nature. But its
tranquillity was soon dispelled by the arrival of Violet Dickinson and a
woman friend of hers who wrote on art. Now Vanessa found herself
studying the various schools of Italian painting, admiring in particular
Botticelli, Filippo Lippi and Ghirlandaio. She herself did no painting on
this trip but it was never far from her mind. She bought some old frames,
drawing books covered with red vellum and some handmade paper. She
visited the home of the writer Vernon Lee (a close friend of the Rasponis)
and was delighted to discover Sargent's alert portrait of the author (now
in the Tate Gallery) hanging on one wall.

If Italy had been, to use a Pattle phrase, 'a dream of beauty', Paris, for
Vanessa, had other attractions, as her letter to Margery Snowden written
soon after arriving reveals: 'Your little friend Bell is here – Thoby is staying
with him, as he lives in rooms here, and he knows a lot of the young
artists.'[3] Clive's ostensible reason for being in Paris was to research into
the British policy at the Congress of Verona, a study he had begun on
coming down from Cambridge in 1902. He had made slow progress at first

and, after a shooting holiday with his father in British Columbia, decided he would do better work in Paris. Three visits to the Archives Nationales had driven the subject from his mind entirely and he settled down to one of the most enjoyable years of his life. As his French was then limited, he made friends with three English-speaking artists resident in Paris. One was the Canadian J.W. Morrice, an acquaintance of Toulouse-Lautrec, who soon fell heavily under the influence of Matisse. Though seldom sober, he had a knack for discovering beauty in unexpected quarters and took Clive to the brazenly modern and overpopulated *zincs* as well as the more old-fashioned *cafés-concerts* and music-halls. More intellectual was Clive's second friend, the swarthy Irishman Roderick O'Conor who had adopted Van Gogh's use of strong colour and expressive handling. He had lived for a while at Pont-Aven and become a close friend of Gauguin immediately before the latter's departure for Tahiti in 1895. Photographs of Gauguin's paintings and drawings by him littered O'Conor's studio. It was he who directed Clive's attention to the Salon d'Automne and the Salon des Indépendants. He also had a deep love of literature and extended Clive's knowledge of French authors by recommending Claudel, Laforgue, Remy de Gourmont, Jules Renard and Charles-Louis Philippe. He presented him with a first edition of Mérimée's *Lettres à une inconnue*, a book that Clive afterwards recommended to Virginia.

Clive's third friend was the twenty-four-year-old Gerald Kelly who had suceeded in getting five of his pictures into the Salon that year. This marked the start of his successful but increasingly orthodox career which brought him a knighthood and the Presidency of the Royal Academy. He agreed to help Clive entertain the Stephens, but on first being introduced to Vanessa was so shy that in his nervousness he mixed extravagant praise of his own work with bad jokes. Vanessa visited the Salon and saw Kelly's five paintings. She immediately observed their debt to Whistler, who was honoured in the Salon by a memorial display, and reserved her chief admiration for Sargent's witty portrait of Lord Ribblesdale. Kelly and Bell also took the Stephens to Rodin's studio and to the bohemian haunt, the Chat Blanc, where they sat talking and smoking until late. 'We have been horrifying George with accounts of our doings at cafés and elsewhere,' Vanessa told Clive on her return home. 'You must be prepared to keep it up and add local colour when you next see him. I hope you and Mr Kelly will some day drag yourselves away from the delights of Paris and will come and see us here and continue those arguments in spite of depressing London surroundings.'[4]

The day after they returned Virginia lost control of her reason and remained ill for the better part of the summer. She developed a hatred and distrust of Vanessa, who had the burden of looking after her. To ease matters Virginia was taken away from Hyde Park Gate to the home of Violet Dickinson where she was placed under constant supervision. According to Quentin Bell, she attempted suicide while there, by throwing herself out of a window, but suffered no serious harm. Despite this anxiety, Vanessa meanwhile went ahead with the plan which had first been mooted before Leslie's death, to move out of Hyde Park Gate into new and more congenial surroundings.

The area she selected was Bloomsbury which, though it adjoined low-class districts, attracted upper-middle-class professional families such as the Marshalls and Protheros. Despite the elegance of its Georgian squares, it was not popular with London 'society' and for this reason her relatives thought the choice unfortunate and eccentric. Her friend Kitty Maxse (suitably housed in fashionable Knightsbridge) screamed against it, but Vanessa was undeterred. It was as if she needed to put a certain distance between herself and the area associated with her past. Apart from its proximity to the Slade School of Art, there was little to attach her to Bloomsbury, except the fact that none of her relatives or old family friends lived there. At this date she had only a hazy knowledge of it. She recalled:

> My first memory of Bloomsbury as a district is of a remote, melancholy, foggy, square-ridden quarter and of myself in evening dress in a hansom cab being trotted through square after square in a nightmarish attempt to find No. 24 Bedford Square. I was going to dine with the Protheros, Fanny Prothero ... an impish monkey faced little Irish lady, said never to have been seen without a hat – and her husband, dull and pussy like, who collected Adam mantelpieces and filled the house with them; perhaps they are still there. They were thought eccentric for living in Bloomsbury: at least by our friends who all inhabited Kensington or Bayswater, or possibly Chelsea, Westminster or Mayfair. My Kensington cabman did not know the way and I was very late.
>
> In spite of this first rather dream-like and agitating vision I cannot have been repelled by Bloomsbury. For in 1904, after my father's death ... we resisted strong pressure put upon us by family and old friends to live as they did in one of the recognized districts and insisted on inspecting houses in Bloomsbury. We went to see great houses in Russell Square with immense rambling basements seeming untouched since the 18th century – attractive but impracticable. We nearly took a house in Upper Montagu Place. Finally we settle upon 46 Gordon Square and in the autumn of 1904 we moved in.[5]

When this move was first proposed, it was understood that only the Stephens would take up occupancy of the new house. Gerald was quite content to find bachelor quarters elsewhere but George protested that he must and would remain a part of the family household. Fortunately for the Stephens he was unable to fulfil his intent because that summer he became engaged to the stepdaughter of the Dowager Countess of Carnarvon, Lady Margaret Herbert, whom he married in September. The Stephens were on holiday at Teversal Manor in Nottinghamshire and from there Vanessa and Adrian made the long trek down to Pixton Park, Dulverton, in Somerset, in order to attend the wedding at which Vanessa was to act as bridesmaid. From the start of their long and complicated train journey they maintained only a distant relationship with their luggage, leaving it unattended on the platform at Nottingham while they sat for an hour in the waiting-room reading and playing cards. At one point it vanished altogether only to reappear in the care of a porter. They changed trains again at Derby, Bristol and Exeter and were approaching the completion of their journey when Adrian sprang to his feet and announced, to the amusement of the rest of the carriage, that their luggage had been left behind at Bristol. 'Any luggage, sir?' asked the coachman at Dulverton station. 'It's lost,' replied Adrian nonchalantly, climbing into the carriage. As they drove through the park they kept up their spirits by singing the wedding and funeral marches simultaneously. Their cacophonous arrival cloaked, on Vanessa's part, pure terror because, still dressed in her travelling clothes, she had then to join the rest of the party who had already gone in to dinner. In between clusters of earls and countesses, she discerned two bishops, General Hastings and Mr Luxmoore, George's housemaster from Eton. The conversation was simpler than she expected and she was able to report back to Virginia, 'Dinner was uneventful.'[6] Nor was she too daunted by her future sister-in-law with whom she was closeted alone after dinner. The luggage eventually arrived and Vanessa and the other bridesmaids, following the fashion of the moment, were attired to look like eighteenth-century portraits by Romney and Reynolds. It was a relief when the wedding was over.

Though George's marriage was a stroke of luck for the Stephens, his hold over Vanessa did not instantly cease. He still sent out calling-cards on which her name was appended to that of himself and his wife. Only after Vanessa protested to Margaret, who was none too eager to carry Vanessa in her wake, did George cease his habit. If Vanessa's initial feelings towards her sister-in-law had been phlegmatic, they soon warmed into quick dislike. Their incompatibility surfaced during the few formalities exchanged soon after the marriage; Vanessa invited her sister-in-law to lunch and served pheasant hot, which prompted Margaret to declare that she preferred her game cold.

In October the move to Gordon Square took place. The organization fell chiefly on Vanessa for Thoby had begun to read for the Bar, Adrian returned to Cambridge, and Virginia, who was still recuperating her health, also went to Cambridge to stay with her aunt, Caroline Emelia Stephen. All the objects and furniture that over the years had encrusted the six storeys at Hyde Park Gate had to be dislodged, sorted, packed, disposed of or sold. Amidst the physical and mental disruption caused by a move, Vanessa received news of two tragedies: the artist Charles Furse, who had been ill with tuberculosis, died, and Margaret Hills, the wife of Jack's brother Eustace, was killed when her bicycle collided with a bus. On the day that the Stephens moved into 46 Gordon Square, Vanessa attended Margaret's funeral at Holy Trinity, Sloane Street, and observed how forlorn both Jack and Eustace now looked.

In size and plan 46 Gordon Square was similar to 22 Hyde Park Gate. The practical advantages of the new house were few and slight: there was an additional storey and generally slightly more space; and the kitchen in the basement had access to storage vaults situated under the pavement in front of the house. As at Hyde Park Gate, the rooms were tall and elegant, decorated with cornices and elaborate ceiling rosettes. On the first floor the two main living-rooms were divided by folding doors which could be thrown open to make an L-shaped room. The house was lighter than 22 Hyde Park Gate and on fine days sunlight filled the front rooms; but it was also noisier, for outside cabs ground their way round the square. The greater number of rooms, however, did mean that Vanessa and Virginia could now each have their own sitting-rooms, while Thoby made the large ground-floor library his study. A visitor waiting in the hall while the maid went in search of the relevant member of the family would have felt that the house, with its restrained dignity, well suited the children of Sir Leslie Stephen. And to him or her there probably seemed very little difference between 46 Gordon Square and 22 Hyde Park Gate other than a slight alteration in geographical position.

To the Stephens, however, the two houses represented twin polarities: 46 Gordon Square came to symbolize freedom and independence precisely because life at 22 Hyde Park Gate had been hidebound and restricting. Gordon Square was deliberately kept free of clutter, both material and emotional. Vanessa had sold much of their old furniture to Harrods and let the few remaining pieces stand out against the walls which were distempered a plain white. Nor was there any member of the older generation to impede their lives with outdated rules or formality. Vanessa, however, did still enjoy the services of Sophie Farrell who upheld authoritarian methods and ran the new household on much the same lines as the old. But essentially the weight of an older generation, under which they had lived for so long, had been removed, giving them greater freedom to follow their own inclinations.

Thus on the day of the move we find Vanessa taking tea with Margery Snowden and outlining her plans for the winter. Despite the close proximity of the Slade School of Art, she decided to ask the Academy Schools if she might return for one session, to make up for time lost the previous year, as she had heard that Sargent would be teaching for a month that autumn. Her request was refused and she went instead to the Slade for a few weeks during November and December. Like other female students, she lived in terror of Professor Tonks's hooded gaze and derogatory comments. She made no friends and did not return to the school after the Christmas break. The Slade emphasis on draughtsmanship had, perhaps, little interest for her at a time when she was concentrating on becoming a painter.

The chief outlet for her creativity that autumn was the decoration of the new house. Influenced by Charles Furse, she deliberately strove for a more 'aesthetic' arrangement. She bought green and white chintzes and resurrected some Indian shawls (probably left over from Little Holland House days, as they were often worn by her great aunts) and draped them over chairs and tables. Their colours took on a barbaric richness when seen against the white walls. She bought a new desk and sofa for Virginia, anticipating her return, and a table and red carpet for the dining-room. She re-hung the Watts portraits of her parents and in the hall displayed photographs of Herschel, Lowell, Darwin, Tennyson, Browning and Meredith opposite a whole row of Mrs Cameron's best photographs of her mother. Meanwhile unpacked books and cooking vessels cluttered the house and added to the small irritations and discomforts which they endured for many months. It was not until Thoby went away that she was able to attend to the business of lining the walls of the study with books. 'I have been most virtuous today,' she wrote to Virginia who was still in Cambridge. 'I spent the morning struggling with the study. Certainly books are wonderful things. Even I – though you may hook your learned nose at me in disdain – after spending some time grubbing amongst them – get to feel a great affection for the scrubbiest and most backless volume. I suppose it's from living in a book-loving family. I feel happy and content sitting on the floor in an ocean of calf.'[7] Slowly the tall, rather frigid rooms, heated only by coal fires, took shape. Vanessa recalled looking at the white walls and large windows opening on to trees and lawns and feeling exhilarated that so much gloom and depression had been dispelled.

A family dispute faintly ruffled these hopeful months. Jack Hills advised Vanessa that Leslie Stephen's more intimate letters should not be used in the biography being prepared by Frederic Maitland. His interference infuriated Virginia who was assisting Maitland with his task. Vanessa, against her will, was drawn into the debate and obliged to reveal her own attitude to the writing of biography. She came down, very guardedly, on Virginia's side: 'I don't at all fear that you and Fred will say too much though I own that I was a little alarmed by his wanting to have so many family letters. However it's you who read them first and of course it's necessary for him to know everything even if he makes no use of it. I'm glad that I shall never be celebrated enough to have my life written. It wouldn't matter to oneself though. But there's something horrible to me, which I expect the true literary mind does not feel any sympathy with, in any third person's reading what was meant to be only between two. I shall burn all my letters some day.'[8]*

Virginia, meanwhile, was anxious to return to London and start life in the new house. Sir George Savage, her doctor, advised against it, as he felt her health was not yet strong enough to cope with noise and bustle. Savage was a proponent of the George Beard and Weir Mitchell school of thought which, in this pre-Freudian era, thought that nervous conditions resulted from physical disorder. He advised Virginia to build up her strength by eating well, resting and avoiding work. Vanessa had to uphold his opinion though she suspected that her sister's illness had other causes than fatigue and poor diet. Moreover since Stella's death she had begun to distrust doctors. But in letter after letter, like a mother cajoling a child, she urged Virginia to be patient, to eat and sleep well, to take her medicine and hot drinks at night. From these letters one can infer something of the strain Virginia caused Vanessa. Over the next two years the anxiety she created was to be unremitting.

In order to prolong her convalescence she was sent to Giggleswick School in Yorkshire to stay with her cousin Will Vaughan and his wife Madge, who was the daughter of Leslie Stephen's friend John Addington Symonds. Though brought up in Switzerland, at a remove from the Victorian social mores which her father hated, Madge had finished her education in London where she stayed with the Stephens. Like her father she had taken to writing and in 1892 had published *Days Spent on the Doge's Farm* in which could be observed the note of melancholy that was to vitiate her life. She had suffered greatly when her father died in 1893 and five years later, still on the rebound, married William Wyamar

---

* She did not hold this view all her life. On 28 April 1957 she wrote to her granddaughter Henrietta Garnett: 'Also to tell you that I always keep your letters and not only yours but all from every member of your family – so you will have a good supply of material for your autobiography when you want it. I advise you to keep letters – you can never tell when you won't be very glad you have done so – only keep them in good order and a safe place.'

Vaughan, a schoolmaster whose conventional manner was diametrically opposed to her father's bohemianism. Madge herself often found her impulsive, vivacious character in conflict with the puritan conscience which she had inherited from her mother. Confined to Yorkshire, she missed the company of artists and writers, and when Virginia arrived was pathetically eager to talk books and show her the novel she had written. Her husband did little to encourage her writing and Virginia felt that Madge's talents had been wasted in marriage and child-bearing. She figured prominently in Virginia's letters to Vanessa, who was anxious for news of her friend. Vanessa refused, however, to accept Virginia's strictures and, taking a more domestic view, argued that Madge got much pleasure from her children and should be able to make an interesting life for herself in Yorkshire.

While Virginia was away Vanessa found she had more time to paint than ever before. Her disappointment at not being allowed back into the Academy Schools was mitigated when Kitty Maxse announced that she had encountered Sargent in Harrods and asked if she might bring Vanessa to his studio. The visit did not, however, take place until the spring of 1905 and then nothing came of it, probably because Vanessa was by that time looking around for new mentors. When Virginia returned to 46 Gordon Square that first winter, she was struck by the creativity that the house promised. It seemed to her 'the most beautiful, the most exciting, the most romantic place in the world', for it had a vitality that 22 Hyde Park Gate had lacked; instead of dwelling on the past, it confronted the future. 'We were full of experiments and reforms,' Virginia recalled. 'We were going to do without table napkins ... we were going to paint; to write; to have coffee after dinner instead of tea at nine o'clock. Everything was going to be new, everything was going to be different. Everything was on trial.'[9]

Their optimism can be related to a widespread belief, held by many intellectuals at this time, that nineteenth-century progress would continue and that positive improvements in the conditions of life would be made. Their confidence also rested on financial security. Leslie Stephen had left the substantial sum of £15,000 to his children (this would be, in 1983 terms, roughly equivalent to £350,000) and Jack Hills had generously decided to share with them the income from Stella's marriage settlement. Moreover they hoped to pay for the lease of 46 Gordon Square with the income received from the letting of 22 Hyde Park Gate, but their old house remained obstinately empty due to (so Vanessa thought) Duckworth mismanagement. As a result Vanessa was occasionally worried by their financial situation, for none of the Stephen children was currently earning any income. The servants took it for granted that things should proceed as before, as did the rest of the family. 'Sometimes I had vague suspicions that we were heading for bankruptcy,' Vanessa recalled,

> but all my life I had heard my father say gloomily that we should soon be in the workhouse and I had got used to not taking it seriously. If I was sometimes uneasy, being supposed to be in control of the family finances, yet on the whole all that seemed to matter was that at last we were free, had rooms of our own and space in which to be alone or to work or to see our friends. Such things may come naturally to many of the present generation but to me at least in 1904 it was as if one had stepped suddenly into daylight from darkness.[10]

Soon after the Stephens moved into Gordon Square, Thoby's Cambridge friends began to call. While Virginia stayed for a week in London, in between her rest cures at Cambridge and Giggleswick, Leonard Woolf came to dinner immediately before leaving England to take up an administrative post in Ceylon. In December 1904 Lytton Strachey wrote to Woolf: 'On Sunday I called at the Gothic mansion [i.e. home of Thoby, nicknamed 'the Goth'] and had tea with Vanessa and Virginia. The latter is rather wonderful – quite witty, full of things to say and absolutely out of rapport with reality. The poor Vanessa has to keep her three [sic] mad brothers and sister in control. She looks wan and sad. I don't wonder.'[11] A third Cambridge graduate who began to pay regular visits to the house was Saxon Sydney-Turner, whose reputation for erudition had been enhanced by his enormous capacity for silence. He would pick up a Greek author, translating a passage as he read it aloud without pause. He was fond of acrostics and would pepper his curt, elliptical letters, written in a tight, neat hand, with erudite jokes. Rarely seen without a rolled umbrella, he had a tendency to pirouette and exhibited a feline composure. He was also a little mysterious and unknowable. He composed sonatas and was a fanatical devotee of opera, making regular pilgrimages to Bayreuth. It was hoped he might become a famous composer or the author of some profound tome. He never did either, but buried his talents in the Civil Service, his brilliance proving ultimately sterile.

One aspect of Thoby Stephen's nature was his generous admiration and genuine liking for his friends. He had already told his half-brother Gerald, who had gone into publishing, that Strachey and Bell might one day write something good. In January 1905, anxious to retain regular contact with his Cambridge friends, he began holding 'at homes' on Thursday evenings. These played a crucial role in the formation of the Bloomsbury group which, without Thoby, might never have come into existence. If, as

Quentin Bell has said, Bloomsbury had 'a common attitude to life and was united by friendships',[12] then the Group did not effectively come into being until the winter of 1906-7 when this common attitude became pronounced. However, its roots went back to Cambridge where these friends first met, and the Thursday 'at homes' became its seedbed. They brought Vanessa and Virginia into closer contact with Thoby's friends for, though he may not have intended this, his sisters were present from the start. So were many others now not normally associated with Bloomsbury – Charles Tennyson, Hilton Young (later Lord Kennet), Theodore Llewelyn-Davies and Robin Mayor. Old family friends as well as younger ones of their own generation occasionally looked in, as did George and Gerald and, as Vanessa recalled, 'plenty of odd creatures' who would have been horrified by the idea of Bloomsbury.[13] As these occasions did not begin until nine o'clock in the evening very little food or drink was offered. The sole entertainment was talk which went on until late into the night. It is therefore hardly surprising that the more conventional visitors present were surprised by the absence of social niceties and found the atmosphere a little farouche. The Stephens' 'at homes' became the subject of gossip and laughter. And as a small group of regulars began to form, shock and amusement solidified into antagonism, for the atmosphere of a clique will make even those who are ready to approve, feel excluded.

At the start these occasions were not always a success. There could be awkward silences or conversations that obsessed two people in one corner of the room which made it difficult for talk to flourish elsewhere. Without Thoby's friendliness and composure it is possible that the 'at homes' might have petered out. But he, and Clive Bell, contributed a vital geniality. Clive, especially, had a talent for starting good subjects of conversation and encouraging others to pursue them, as Vanessa observed.

The odd mixture that made up Clive's character caused Thoby to describe him as a cross between Shelley and a country squire. An excellent sportsman (he had kept two or three hunters while up at Cambridge), Clive combined hunting and shooting with a love of poetry and art. He came from a *nouveau riche* Wiltshire family whose fortune was based on coal. Though his brothers and sisters were well educated and were acquainted with the names of all the characters in good, solid English literature (they excelled each year at *The Times* Christmas crossword), the arts on the whole were banished from the house. At Marlborough School Clive had developed a passion for reading which made him precocious and at odds with his family. His cleverness (and his parents' wealth) took him to Cambridge where he became convinced that art and learning were two of the highest achievements: the chief drawback to his attaining either was his immense enjoyment of life.

The sybaritic element in Clive's nature weakened his character and strengthened his attraction. He could not enjoy happiness unless those around him shared his mood and in later years, when he entertained regularly at the Ivy restaurant and elsewhere, this made him an excellent host. His appetite for gaiety drew from David Garnett the comment, 'He is an almost perfect example of James Mill's Utilitarian theory that a man cannot become rich without enriching his neighbours.'[14] Clive pursued conversation with a vivacity that might alternately enchant or exasperate but which was never dull. He exuded a love of good things, as one of his poems admits:

> I was made for airy thinking
> Nimble sallies, champagne-drinking,
> Badinage and argument,
> Reading's infinite content,
> Ill-considered merriment,
> Friendship, anything but love
> ...
> A loiterer in life's pleasant places,
> A well of receptivity.[15]

If Clive was an essential ingredient in the success of the Stephens' Thursday evenings, he was less discerning than Lytton Strachey, Leonard Woolf or Saxon Sydney-Turner. Like them, he had been a member of the 'Midnight' play-reading society at Cambridge, but he had never been invited (as they were) into the more elect, secret conversazione society known as the Apostles. Yet from Thoby's letters to him, we can judge that he must have been a stimulating talker on art. He provoked Thoby to uphold the Greeks against the paintings in the Louvre, to discuss his visits to the National Gallery, the Academy and the Burlington Fine Arts Club. An additional attraction was Clive's shock of russet curls which amused his friends, but which thinned prematurely revealing an intellectual's tall forehead. He also dressed well and shone in society where his ebullience and alert sympathy made him invaluable.

Perhaps one of the most significant influences upon his education had been not his school but a certain Mrs Raven-Hill. She was the wife of the *Punch* illustrator and a neighbour of the Bell family, a weak character with a resolute taste for pleasure and a determination to remain respectable. In the summer of 1899, when Clive was eighteen and about to go up to Trinity College, Cambridge, Mrs Raven-Hill, employing finesse, tact, strategy and great deliberation, seduced him. She paused by the tennis-court at one of the garden parties given by the Bells and, as Clive approached the corner to pick up a ball, she remarked on the beauty of his curls. On this and another occasion Clive inferred that, given propitious conditions, an affair could proceed, and later that summer Mrs Raven-Hill, dressed in lilac silk and black patent high-heeled shoes, and having on hand a bottle of sparkling Moselle, took his virginity, keeping up a conversational tone to ease the proceedings until the moment of his departure.

It was an education, not of the mind, but of the senses. For though the Raven-Hills had lived for a time in Paris, which left its mark on her taste in dress and which may have been the reason why at Cambridge Clive hung a reproduction of Degas in his rooms and before 1904 owned some Lautrec lithographs, her chief lesson to Clive was 'la grande volupté'. She aroused his sensuality; he recalled that 'she could strike a rich note of provocation', that 'sensuality emanated from her like a fine scent'. But in the final assessment she lacked intellect and culture:

> For, as a glance at history will prove to any doubter, in the wardrobe of 'une grande amoureuse', a bluish stocking is the indispensable garment. Only a cultivated and rather intellectual woman can possibly possess that shameless self-consciousness which gives the finest sting of pleasure to our most elaborate encounters. .... It was not that she was too much of a whore, but that she was not sufficiently aware of being a fine lady who was making herself one.[16]

The affair, which had begun in 1899, had proceeded intermittently until 1904 when on his return from France Clive took rooms in King's Bench Walk, which facilitated regular meetings. He recalled how on one occasion, after taking her to see the paintings at the Guildhall, they returned to his rooms for the afternoon, ignored the hammering given to his door by Thoby and Saxon Sydney-Turner in search of tea, and after six hours of 'unflagging, reciprocated sensuality' emerged to dine at the Savoy before driving on to insalubrious Clapham where Mrs Raven-Hill was respectably deposited with friends. Clive, left alone in the hansom with his cigar, reflected that, as near as possible, he had had the experience most men desire.

Arriving, perhaps the next day, at Gordon Square, Clive found himself increasingly attracted to Vanessa. She, too, exuded sensuality, but unlike Mrs Raven-Hill, with whom Clive was not in the least in love, she had a mind and character that intrigued him because they were so unlike those of other women of her class. In Clive's conversation and manner Vanessa, in turn, must have caught a hint of his taste for women. At Cambridge he would almost certainly have let drop, in his conversations with Thoby, allusions to his conquests, and though Thoby would not have repeated these to Vanessa, he may have hinted at the many layers to Bell's character which were best summed up by Lytton Strachey:

> There is the country gentleman layer, which makes him retire to the depths of Wiltshire to shoot partridges. There is the Paris decadent layer, which takes him to the *quartier latin* where he discusses painting and vice with American artists and French models. There is the eighteenth-century layer, which adores Thoby Stephen. There is the layer of innocence which adores Thoby's sister. There is the layer of prostitution, which shows itself in an amazing head of crimped straw-coloured hair. And there is the layer of stupidity, which runs transversely through all the other layers.[17]

As the months progressed Vanessa grew familiar with Clive's good-humoured character. She observed his ability to enter into studio talk and would have admired his familiarity with Parisian art and artists. A great many of his opinions corresponded with her own: he disparaged the Watts memorial exhibition, had a high regard for the works of Jane Austen and a low one for Christianity. On this last subject we can catch a glimpse of his mocking eloquence in a letter to Lytton Strachey: 'Now the lads are singing Onward Christian Soldiers which ought to be the Anglo-Saxons' anthem, and their epitaph. Onward, never stay to ask where you are going, that implies decadence, intellectualization, reason, logic, refine-ment, meditation, all the things that Englishmen and Americans justly abhor.'[18] His attitude was entirely sympathetic to the Stephens who laughed as freely at the absurdities of religious practice as they would at some idiosyncrasy in daily life. Vanessa herself recalled: 'Having been brought up to believe nothing in particular I was converted to Christianity (of a rather vague kind I admit) when I was about 12 by some well-brought-up children of the same age. It lasted 2 or 3 years, then one day walking through Kensington Gardens and enjoying the sight of the trees, suddenly I knew quite certainly that religion meant nothing to me and that never again need I bother about it.'[19]

Vanessa's independence must have played no small part in attracting Clive to her. By July 1905 he was heavily in love, for he wrote to Lytton: 'My chamber is litterary [literally] heavy with the scent of deep red roses; Vanessa dined here last night and it occurred to me that red roses would suggest the appropriate setting; I found armfuls at Covent Garden. I was absolutely justified. The something of duskiness which clings to her was more limpid and translucent than ever before.'[20] Vanessa, now twenty-six years old, was ripe for marriage but as yet showed no desire to make any match. She was content with the new freedom brought about by their recent move and in March 1905 wrote to Madge Vaughan, 'I only wish we could always go on like this, but after all we may for a long time yet. I dread every day to hear that Thoby is in love.'[21] When in August Clive proposed, Vanessa refused him. He was plunged into despair and disappeared to the Highlands where he joined his family for their annual massacre of stags. In the autumn he took himself off to France, lodging at St-Symphorien, a small hamlet across the river from Tours. Still recuperating from his disappointment, he led a quiet life, reading and writing, and in the evenings played chess in a local café with a naval officer. He paid visits to Paris but found he had outgrown the Latin quarter, and the artists and journalists he met now seemed to him slightly stupid and degraded. Throughout this period he remained dreadfully unhappy, wrote to Thoby and Lytton in the hope of news, and meanwhile pondered the state of Vanessa's true feelings.

Immediately after the proposal Vanessa had disappeared on a holiday to Cornwall with her brothers and sister. She did not tell Thoby what had happened until they arrived at Carbis Bay, though he had already surmised the truth. She appears to have shrugged off any pity she may have had for Clive and generally treated the matter lightly. However the letter that she wrote to Margery Snowden has a disingenuous tone, for it rationalizes the situation with very little real regard for her own feelings or those of Clive. She begins with the improbable assertion that she had not flirted with Clive:

> also, unless this particular man is unlike every other, it is highly probable that by this time next year he will have turned to fresh diversions. I can't bring myself to take his unhappiness very seriously – for *I have* had some experience of men! I think that really my being worried was chiefly because of the selfish reason that a comfortable and easy and friendly state of things had to come to an end. Also when one is actually asked by a man to marry him, even though one has no feeling at all of that kind oneself, one is obliged to think rather more seriously about it than one has done before. It really seems to matter so very little to oneself what one does. I should be quite happy living with anyone whom I didn't dislike ... if I could paint and lead the kind of life I like. Yet for some mysterious reason one has to do what someone else very much wants one to. It seems absurd. But absurd or not I could no more marry him than I could fly – so there's an end of it. ... I am ashamed of the length of this letter ... really I am becoming almost as tiresome as a man![22]

As this was the Stephens' first visit to Cornwall for eleven years, there was much to distract her. She and Virginia expected to find many aspects of their past preserved in this far corner of England and were not wholly disappointed. On the first night of their arrival they crept up the dark lane to Talland House and peered through the escallonia hedge at the house but went no further, fearing that its new reality might pierce the film of remembrance through which they saw it. Many of the old St Ives folk remembered them and had followed the fortunes of their family in the newspapers. But it was the sea that dominated this holiday, for not only did it turn silver with the long-expected arrival of the pilchards in the bay, but the sight of porpoises cutting through the water also gave Virginia her first sight of the fin rising above the waves, an image that returned to her mind in hallucinatory form after the completion of *To the Lighthouse*, and when her mind again raced and she arrived at the conception of *The Waves*. Vanessa, in Cornwall, painted several small seascapes, employing Whistler's method, using a red or brown base to deepen the blues of sea and sky.

Throughout this period she was attempting to place her painting on a more professional basis. She began to take an interest in portraiture and early in 1905 had gone down to the home of Lord Robert Cecil at Chelwood Gate in Sussex in order to paint a portrait of his wife Nelly[§], who had been introduced to the Stephens by Violet Dickinson. She had married Lord Robert in 1889, was childless and since 1894 had suffered the tormenting isolation caused by deafness. Vanessa, perhaps unintentionally, conveys her solitariness by accentuating the contained pose and the sharp, bird-like gaze of her sitter. Following Sargent's example, she has emphasized select details but arranges these across the entire composition so that, unlike most of Sargent's portraits, the picture forms a decorative whole. The handling, however, has none of her teacher's panache, but is tentative and in places awkward. Nevertheless this was the first painting Vanessa exhibited. When shown at the New Gallery in April 1905 it brought the artist her first portrait commission from a stranger.

Vanessa's new willingness to exhibit and accept commissions may reflect a desire to keep up with Virginia who had begun to write reviews for the *Women's Supplement*, the *Guardian* and the *Times Literary Supplement*, and whose exceptional talents were becoming evident. In December 1904 Vanessa sent Virginia some praise from Violet Dickinson: 'She thought you would undoubtedly be a great writer one day. Your things are so well thought out, fresh and original and interesting. You always have something to say on any subject. Your writing is so living. Is that enough for you? She really thinks you a genius. Isn't it strange?'[23] Even if she felt no jealousy of Virginia's brilliance in a medium other than her own, such praise would probably have caused a reflex examination of her own talents and position. She now realized that her circle of friends, both old and new, was not conducive to painting. Therefore in the summer of 1905 she founded the Friday Club.

In starting this club Vanessa hoped to create a cultural milieu not unlike that she had observed in certain Parisian cafés. She drew upon her friends from the Royal Academy Schools (Margery Snowden, Mary Creighton and Sylvia Milman) and also tapped contacts made during her brief period at the Slade. During the first few years of the club's history the Slade contingent included J.D. Innes, Derwent Lees, Maxwell Lightfoot, John Currie, Edna Clarke Hall and Claire Atwood. The young painter Henry Lamb, who had trained at William Orpen's and Augustus John's school in Chelsea, also joined, as did certain of Vanessa's friends and relatives – Thoby and Adrian, Saxon Sydney-Turner, Katherine Cox, Marjorie Strachey and Beatrice Mayor – all of whom were allowed in as lay members. Soon after the club was formed, Vanessa looked round for rooms to rent where they could put on regular exhibitions. As most of these plans began to unfold in July 1905, the month before Clive's proposal, Vanessa felt free to turn to him for advice, which he gave willingly. He lectured to the club and, perhaps in order to win Vanessa's affection, himself painted and sent two paintings to its first exhibition in November of that year. Richard Shone has argued that the Friday Club was 'one of the liveliest exhibiting groups before the First World War'.[24] But though this accurately describes the exhibitions put on between 1910 and 1914, which received considerable attention from the press, it does not apply to the first five years of the club's existence. Lacking any dominant style, the odd mixture of artists (many of them still students) and the more dilettante members would have given the exhibitions an amateurish look. Moreover, the artistic debate that split the committee, as Virginia observed ('one half of the committee shriek Whistler and French impressionists, and the other are stalwart British'[25]), was several years out of date.

Whatever the Friday Club achieved, its existence is a testimony to Vanessa's organizational prowess. It was she who, through the exercise of diplomacy, united disparate artists, arranged for talks to be given and kept a healthily argumentative society under control. 'Old Nessa goes ahead, and slashes about her,' Virginia observed, seven months after the club had begun, 'and manages all the business, and rejects all her friends' pictures, and don't mind a bit. She is said to have a genius for organization, and it all seems to interest her – it would bore me to death.'[26] Elsewhere Virginia commented on her sister's talent for stating unpleasant truths in a matter-of-fact voice, for Vanessa's honesty could make her ruthless. Nevertheless, her matter-of-fact approach often benefited others, not least Virginia. When the latter left for a holiday in Spain in March 1905, she forgot her sponge bag. Vanessa, discovering this, found time before departing herself for a tour of northern France with Margery Snowden, to send Virginia instructions to buy another.

During the first two years of their existence at 46 Gordon Square the Stephen sisters hovered between the old world and the new. They had banished from their lives most of the customs that had constricted their previous existence, but they still received visits from old friends such as the Freshfields and accepted invitations from such eminent families as the Balfours. Moreover, the rules governing the conduct of women of their class were rigorously strict. When one afternoon Vanessa took tea alone with Henry Lamb in the King's Road, she was risking her reputation, for it was considered scandalous for a young woman, before marriage, to be seen alone in company with a man not old enough to be her grandfather. When Stella had come of age she had been obliged to take one of her half-brothers or -sisters with her as a chaperon when she crossed London. The lack of social etiquette at the Stephens' Thursday evenings made them seem shockingly informal to both Henry James and George Duckworth who were more accustomed to the Edwardian standards of behaviour which Sir Charles Petrie has described: 'When a man paid a call he took his hat, stick and gloves into the drawing-room, for to do otherwise was for him to lay himself open to the charge of behaving as if he were at a hotel. . . . Informality of any sort was frowned upon – behaviour was either correct or it was not.'[27]

Surrounded still on many sides by conservative opinion, Vanessa and Virginia were delighted when, after the Balfour government resigned in December 1905, the ascendancy of the Liberals seriously discomforted George and Gerald. At this election Jack Hills and Lord Robert Cecil both achieved the remarkable feat of winning seats for the Conservative party. When in April 1906 Vanessa returned to Chelwood Gate in Sussex to paint a portrait of Lord Robert for his wife, she felt unforgivably ignorant of politics at a time when subjects like tariff reform were being discussed. An old Tory, a moderate free trader and, like his father, a supporter of the enfranchisement of women, Lord Robert was at this time in a quandary as to which side of the house he should be on because, in particular, he disliked the new imperialism of Joseph Chamberlain. At Chelwood his wife's deafness left much of the conversation to Vanessa. 'I wish I weren't such an ignoramus,' she complained to Virginia. 'I've come to the conclusion that staying away is a very severe test for one's general intelligence, and it's appalling to find how little I've got. If I were to do it often I should try to get educated.'[28] She formed a high opinion of Lord Robert, and perhaps tried to convey this in her portrait; but he sat badly, at his paper-strewn desk, for only short periods of time, and all she could achieve was a characteristic sketch (present whereabouts unknown).

In May 1906 Vanessa turned twenty-seven. Though still unmarried, there is no indication that she wished her state otherwise. For most women of her class, marriage, in an age when contraception was still little practised, brought ties and social obligations that put an end to any thought of a career. Among certain Fabians in the preceding generation this problem had been solved by celibate marriage which had allowed both partners to get on with their work. This would have been no solution for Vanessa and much therefore depended on her finding a partner who would understand and sympathize with her need to paint. Yet though she had several admirers, she had no more proposals, perhaps because her sense of purpose detached her from the more superficial aspects of daily life and made her difficult to approach. Inevitably she aroused in others much speculation: Aunt Mary Fisher, when she found six drawings of Austen Chamberlain in Vanessa's sketchbook, immediately presumed a romance was afoot; George thought Charles Trevelyan was enamoured of his half-sister. But Vanessa, living happily at Gordon Square with the magnificent Thoby on hand, in whom was blended warmth and reserve, tolerance and natural authority, as yet felt no great need for a husband. And when in July 1906 Clive Bell once more proposed, she again refused him.

This time, however, she did so in such a way as to leave room for doubt. She told him that if marriage were just a question of being good friends and caring for the same things, she would have accepted his offer; she liked him, she added (significantly), better than any other man – outside of her family; she could not marry him but she did not want to banish him completely from her life, as custom demanded: in effect she could not reject him outright. This left the problem as to whether or not they should go on seeing each other. The matter had not been decided when in August she and Virginia took themselves off to Norfolk where they rented Blo' Norton Hall. Thoby and Adrian joined them at intervals and there they made plans for a visit to Greece in the autumn. Thus while writing at length to Clive about her feelings for him, Vanessa was also studying Greek sculpture and making preparations for their trip. She then had to take her farewell of Thoby who, with Adrian, went on ahead in order to travel down the Dalmatian coast on horseback. Vanessa and Virginia, accompanied by Violet Dickinson, set out for Greece in mid September, travelling by boat from Brindisi to Patras. Due to Vanessa's forethought and organization, they were dressed in grey felt hats, white linen suits and white boots and carried green-lined white parasols. Vanessa told Margery Snowden that she was certain the trip would be important for her and that she would return ready to enter a new stage in her artistic development.

While she crossed the Mediterranean, Clive bided his time in the Highlands. He lay in a boat reading and occasionally joined in the shoot, first of grouse, then game. Before long, letters arrived telling him that the two parties had been united and had made their way to Athens. From there they decided to make a trip to the Peloponnese. They set off by boat and during the course of their journey Vanessa began to feel unwell. On their return it was necessary to stop at Corinth so that she might gain strength, and by the time they reached Athens she was seriously ill.

Her illness may have been caused by nervous strain. Over the last three years the fear that Virginia might again lose control of her reason had given Vanessa unremitting anxiety. Her responsibility for her sister had sometimes troubled their relationship and, as Vanessa felt, brought out the worst in her. In addition to this, Clive's recent proposal had tested her loyalties, by offering a new kind of life that would oblige her to break with family ties. Psychologically taxed, she now suffered a physical breakdown, as her London doctor later confirmed. In Athens it took a fortnight's rest and four tumblers of champagne each day before she was well enough to be carried on a litter to the boat bound for Constantinople where they caught the Orient Express.

Thoby had returned to England ahead of the rest. On reaching 46 Gordon Square Vanessa was shocked to discover that her elder brother was in bed and seriously ill. As she herself was obliged to go straight to bed, there was little she could do and in her helplessness she turned to Clive. Shortly before leaving Constantinople she had written to him firmly declaring that they should not see each other that winter. Now, unsettled by Thoby's illness, she revoked this decision:

Dear Mr Bell,

Thank you so much for your letter. I feel as if I had been very brutal to you. I really didn't mean to be. . . . It was horrible to come back and find Thoby in bed and be sent to bed myself and not allowed to look after him. However he seems to be better and I hope the worst is over. . . . As for myself, I am forced to obey this doctor – though I haven't much faith in doctors, and he won't let me see anyone except family . . . I know much better than he does what is good for me and I am quite sure that a visit from you would do me a lot of good (does that sound very like Mrs Gaskell?) but I must wait. I hope you won't find me either sentimental or too proper . . . I will write and ask you to come as soon as I am allowed to see you.

Yours very sincerely,
Vanessa Stephen

Thank you for making Thoby go to bed. I think you just prevented him from getting really bad.[29]

If this letter aroused Clive's hopes, they were dashed by that which he received six days later. In the intervening period Margery Snowden had arrived to supervise the nursing of Vanessa and Thoby, both of whom were thought to be over the worst. Now more confident in herself and of her family, Vanessa told Clive that her feelings were still unclear and that she felt opposed to marriage in the abstract; moreover if he remained in her vicinity on an easy footing nothing would change. She therefore advised him to go away for a year and then review the situation. She could not resist adding a piece of advice:

> I wish that if you decide to go away, you would work at something. I don't mean that I in the least want you to go in for any particular profession, in fact I can't imagine you being a successful barrister or man of business! – but I do think you would be happier and would most likely think less of the Stephen family if you were producing some kind of work and not only adding to your knowledge. Besides I think brains are so badly wanted that people who possess them haven't the right to let them be of no use. I haven't the courage to go on being impertinent.[30]

Margery Snowden stayed only a week. A day or two after she left, and some ten days after their return home, Thoby's illness was found to be not malaria as the doctors had said, but typhoid fever. His condition became suddenly critical; he suffered much pain and was frequently delirious. Clive, now in and out of the house, was in a frenzy of anxiety. 'I'm afraid I have no other sort of news,' he reported to Sydney-Turner. 'At present, you will readily understand that, saving 46 Gordon Square, I am not greatly interested in "external reality".'[31] The next day Thoby was operated on and three days afterwards he died, peacefully and without pain. Two days after his death Clive again proposed and this time was accepted.

To some extent Clive had stepped into Thoby's place in Vanessa's life. Just as after Stella's death Vanessa had clung to her memory by growing closer to Jack, so now she gave her affection to Thoby's greatest friend. Clive had, however, prepared the ground for his new role and to some extent Vanessa's former indifference to marriage is now exposed as bluff. Virginia later recalled that during the summer of 1905 Vanessa, 'stretching her arms above her head with a gesture that was at once reluctant and yielding' had said: 'Of course, I can see that we shall all marry. It's bound to happen.'[32] Virginia resented the suggestion at the time and even after the engagement was announced sometimes grumbled that Clive was not good enough for her sister. But seeing Vanessa lying back against the pillows, happy and contented, with a rose tucked rakishly behind her ear, she could not doubt that the engagement was inevitable. Margery Snowden, to whom Vanessa had once made the promise that she would not marry without love, also approved the news. She wrote to Clive: 'No one knows better than I do how much she has felt the want of an unselfish affection during the last few years; and no one can be more truly glad than I am that she now has it.'[33]

The happiness aroused in Vanessa by the engagement enabled her to look on Thoby's death with surprising benevolence. 'I do feel', she told Madge Vaughan, 'that Thoby's life was not wasted. He was so splendidly happy, in these last two years especially, with everything ahead of him full of the best possibilities and able to see constantly all the people he most cared for, that sorrow does seem selfish and out of place, more than with most people. But I as yet can hardly understand anything but the fact that I am happier than I ever thought people could be, and it goes on getting better every day.'[34] Even a visit to Clive's parents' home in Wiltshire, about which she was to complain voluminously in future years, did not quell her euphoria. 'Have any other engaged couple ever seen each other in the way we have I wonder? We must have talked hard to each other for 7 or 8 hours a day for the last 3 weeks and yet we never seem to have time enough. I get morbid sometimes and think I must be boring him or that it is all too wonderful to be true and that some awful catastrophe must happen.'[35]

What fears and doubts remained seemed ungrounded. Clive, with his vitality, good humour and social sense, was her passport to a new kind of life, to greater maturity and a more natural existence, for she had suddenly developed a ferocious appetite for happiness. Meanwhile arrangements for the marriage proceeded smoothly; George charmed Clive's father and obtained from him financial settlements that would benefit Vanessa and any children she might have; £20,000 was immediately made over to Clive on the condition that if he died the interest from it would go to Vanessa. For the wedding George obtained from his wife's family the use of the Carnarvon carriage emblazoned with arms and driven by a liveried coachman. More accustomed to driving to the Brompton Oratory for such occasions, he had difficulty in finding St Pancras Register Office and the delay later caused Clive and Vanessa and her sheepdog Gurth (who accompanied them on their honeymoon to Manorbier) to arrive at Paddington station after their train had left. Amused by this minor disaster, Vanessa took herself off to the waiting-room and there spent the first hour of her married life writing to the sister she had only just left.

FOUR

Mr and Mrs Clive Bell

1907–1909

Without any doubt Vanessa's marriage was sexually a great success: Clive, instructed by Mrs Raven-Hill, was not lacking in experience; Vanessa, though previously confined to vague, half-conscious desires, was highly sensual. Their compatibility is affirmed by Vanessa's comment to Clive, made four years later, when Virginia's marital relationship came under review: 'Apparently she still gets no pleasure at all from the act, which I think is curious. They were anxious to know when I first had an orgasm. I couldn't remember. Do you? But no doubt I sympathized with such things if I didn't have them from the time I was 2.'[1]

Marriage also encouraged her to take her bearings afresh. It brought a new framework of existence for it was agreed that she and Clive would take over the whole of 46 Gordon Square. Virginia and Adrian looked round for alternative accommodation and found 29 Fitzroy Square. This left Vanessa free to reorganize her house. 'I have great ideas for the studio,' she announced. 'Mauve curtains with yellow linings is one of them. All is to be rather dim and neutral. However one's practice never comes up to one's theories.'[2]

Their honeymoon at Manorbier was immediately followed by a visit to Paris. Clive and Vanessa arrived on Easter Sunday, lodged in the Hôtel du Quai Voltaire, dined with Arthur Studd and made excursions to concerts and galleries. Presently Virginia and Adrian arrived, put up in a different hotel but spent much time in their company. On more than one occasion the two parties dined with a cousin of Lytton Strachey, the young Duncan Grant, currently living in Paris on some money given him for his twenty-first birthday by one of his aunts, and studying at Jacques-Emile Blanche's studio 'La Palette'. Clive and Vanessa both enjoyed his company and expressed the hope that they would see more of him on his return to London. In turn, Duncan was enchanted with his new acquaintances. 'What a quartet!' he wrote to Lytton, reserving his strongest admiration for Virginia, his affection for Adrian, admitting that he and Clive would probably soon bore each other, and making least mention of Vanessa.

Soon after Clive and Vanessa had returned to Gordon Square and begun their life together they received a stream of callers, among them the Booths, Fishers, George Duckworth and Aunt Anny, Leslie Stephen's sister-in-law by his first marriage, the novelist Anny Thackeray, now Lady Ritchie. Their visits sometimes clashed with those of Lytton Strachey or Saxon Sydney-Turner and it became evident that the inner circle which had begun to form during the course of the Thursday evenings did not mix easily with old friends of the Stephen family. In order to rid themselves of unwanted visitors so that they could devote more time to those for whom they genuinely cared, Clive and Vanessa developed a social ruthlessness. Clive let it be known that he thought Violet Dickinson and her brother second-rate; at some point over the next few months the Maxses, Cecils, Booths and Protheros were all irretrievably shocked; Aunt Anny's husband Richmond Ritchie was seriously offended; Mrs Humphry Ward repelled. This created more space in which that 'small concentrated world dwelling inside the much larger and looser world of dances and dinners' could expand.[3] As it was, Thoby's death had brought Vanessa and Virginia closer to his Cambridge friends, whom they now addressed by their Christian names.

Two other factors enhanced the greater intimacy which now developed: one was the absence of Thoby, who had compelled admiration but also upheld a reserved and constricting attitude towards convention; the other was Vanessa's sexual awakening through marriage. Sex, no longer kept off-stage, had become part of everyday life. Lytton Strachey, on one of his visits to Gordon Square, was received by the young couple lying side by side in bed. Only a year before Lytton had been 'Mr Strachey', the bedroom out of bounds. The breakdown in formality happened almost overnight. It was aided by their formation of a Play Reading Society which first met on 27 December 1907 to hear John Vanbrugh's *The Relapse*. Its rollicking bawdiness, mocking wit and anti-clericalism perfectly suited their mood. It presented an intoxicating antidote to Victorian puritanism, and among these friends helped unleash, like a river suddenly breaking its dam, a clamorous exchange of sexual innuendo. By the summer of 1908 Lytton felt able to circulate some of his poems. 'Lytton seems to carry on a good deal with his females,' his friend Maynard Keynes noted. 'He has let Vanessa see his most indecent poems – she is filled with delight, has them by heart, and has made typewritten copies for Virginia and others.'[4]

It was a most unorthodox start to married life, contradicting the whole ethos of the British middle class. A wife in Vanessa's position was expected at this date to be a monument of virtue and chastity, denied a profession, devoid even of those minor domestic talents that in earlier times had been cultivated as crafts, a conspicuous consumer of her husband's wealth. She was expected to be largely ignorant not only of the sources of that wealth but also of the baser male instincts. If her husband read a French novel (as one *Punch* cartoon shows), she, from her protected position, would praise his avid concentration, being completely ignorant of the kind of subject-matter it contained. Vanessa, therefore, by her behaviour was making social history. Not only was she using words that her mother would have pretended not to understand, but she was doing so in conversation with men, thereby insisting on an equality rare even among feminists. Whereas certain socialists and 'new-lifers' had believed that emancipated women would bring a new chastity to the home, Vanessa, in her radicalism, had stepped in another direction, had in effect entered the smoking-room and joined in the all-male chat. Moreover, as Keynes's letter reveals, it was she and not Virginia who took the lead.

She began to produce bawdy words with all the glee of a spoilt child who knows she or he does wrong. Behind this lay an element of bravado but also a desire to be deliberately subversive. Bawdiness pierced through the formality and hypocrisy that, ever since her mother had died, had surrounded their lives. It offered release, provided amusement, banished pretence. It enabled Vanessa to proclaim her new-won independence. Her freedom of speech was also partly a reaction against the tedium of tea-table conversation which she had endured for many years. There a great many words had been used to say very little; much could not be mentioned because it was taboo. How ideologically disruptive, therefore, was Lytton's famous entry into their room when, using just one word, he pointed at a stain on Vanessa's dress and enquired 'Semen?'.

Lytton had become an important figure in Vanessa's life immediately after Thoby's death. 'He came', she later recalled, 'and was such an inex-pressible help and made one think of the things most worth thinking of ... he seemed to see further into things than anyone else could.'[5] Apart from his intelligence and learning, he had a gift for observing the hilarious and could employ his wit in a subtly anarchical fashion, spreading dissatis-faction with much that is prized in the eyes of the world. He affirmed that detachment and integrity which the Stephens had inherited through Leslie from the Clapham Sect and which was later strengthened by the influence of Roger Fry. He also released Vanessa from guilt and the need to conform. 'Only those just getting to know him well in those days when complete freedom of mind and expression were almost unknown', she later wrote, '... can understand what an exciting world of explorations of thought and feeling he seemed to reveal. His great honesty of mind and remorseless poking fun at any sham forced others to be honest too and showed a world in which one need no longer be afraid of saying what one thought, surely the first step to anything that would be of interest and value.'[6]

It is at this point that the term 'Bloomsbury' takes on meaning. The inner group of friends had now coalesced, become more intimate, more particular, peculiar and isolated. Lacking any manifesto, Bloomsbury, as Leonard Woolf has said, was 'primarily and fundamentally a group of friends'.[7] Now that Adrian and Virginia were also holding regular 'at homes' in Fitzroy Square, it met regularly in that area of London from which it took its name, not to achieve any programmed aim, but simply to talk. The chief philosophical influence on their thought was G.E. Moore's *Principia Ethica*, particularly its tenet that 'personal affections and aesthetic enjoyments include *all* the greatest, and *by far* the greatest, goods we can imagine'.[8] Discussion of 'the good' was an important aspect of their talk which, in an age badly in need of self-criticism, was deliberately investigative, depreciative, ironic, but also often chatty and frivolous. Among those who excelled at conversation was the critic Desmond Mac-Carthy who, like Lytton, Saxon and Leonard, had been educated at Cambridge and was an Apostle. Like the Stracheys and the Stephens, MacCarthy came from a highly educated sector of the upper-middle class which occasionally mixed with the aristocracy. An intricate network of intermarriage and social relationships knit these families together. Leonard Woolf, a Jew born into a family that had only just risen into the professional middle class from the lower stratum of shopkeepers, was made acutely aware of the privileges they enjoyed: 'Socially they assumed things unconsciously which I could never assume either unconsciously or consciously. They lived in a peculiar atmosphere of influence, manners, respectability.'[9] This was the background from which Bloomsbury drew its strength and against which it rebelled, enjoying, like many an avant-garde, a symbiotic relationship with the establishment. Thus Raymond Williams has written of Bloomsbury's 'significant and sustained combination of dissenting influence and influential connection',[10] in his assessment of the Group's contribution to a specific moment in the development of liberal thought. They wanted to replace hypocrisy and cant with a free, rational, civilized (all epithets that are crucial to an understanding of the Bloomsbury 'attitude') society, dedicated to the pursuit of truth and beauty. Though all were reacting against the Victorian intellectual and moral pressures that had, to a greater or lesser extent, weighed on their youth, Vanessa and Virginia did so from a different standpoint; unlike Lytton, Saxon, Leonard, Adrian, Keynes and MacCarthy, they had not gone to the best schools and attended university; they could not now enter the more powerful professions, nor could they vote. How, then, could they express discontent and effect change? As Vanessa realized, for the moment language was their most vital means: beneath her frivolous bawdiness lay a deeply serious intent.

A relaxed, elegant background for their talk was provided by 46 Gordon Square, for Clive and Vanessa, now that they and their four servants had the house to themselves, were comfortably situated. A new note of luxury had been created by the wedding presents they had received, by the chairs and beds they had bought in Paris, by the silver and unbleached linen acquired in London, and by the Augustus John painting *The Childhood of Pyramus* (now in Johannesburg Art Gallery) that had appeared on their walls. The era of Sargent and Furse, Virginia observed, was over. Yet despite the additional artefacts the house looked bare and informal by contemporary standards. For a time the drawing-room contained no carpets or wallpaper, an early Victorian mahogany table, a pianola, a Louis XIV bed and two basket chairs. Puritanism and good taste mixed. Clive, observing that the blue and yellow matchboxes clashed with the prevailing colour scheme, hid them from sight.

Virginia noticed with envy the ease with which her sister now entertained. Vanessa was not, however, turning into a society hostess, for marriage had in no way weakened her desire to paint. Clive, too, engaged in regular periods of work. He contemplated writing a book entitled *The New Renaissance* which would assess the foundations for a new age of enlightenment and in 1906 he began writing book reviews for the *Athenaeum*. His chief gift, however, lay not in his own creativity but in his ability to appreciate the work of others. He was unusually receptive, both to painting and writing, but had no driving need to turn his sensitivity to words into a vocation. Vanessa had a tendency to align herself with the aesthetic point of view of the person closest to her; she had earlier accepted Thoby's estimate of Tintoretto, now she approved Clive's praise of Augustus John. But during these first few months of marriage his dilettante attitude to the arts would have thrown into contrast her dedication: when she retired to the studio she crossed into a realm that he respected but could not enter.

Even when visiting Clive's parents in Wiltshire, during the summer of 1908, Vanessa managed to spend a significant part of her day painting.

After breakfast she and Clive retreated to his dressing-room which they had made their studio-study. After lunch they generally walked alone together while the rest of the family took more strenuous forms of exercise. In this way Vanessa managed to see relatively little of her in-laws. She could not, however, ignore the oppressive hideousness of her surroundings.

Cleeve House is a Victorian pile masquerading as a Jacobean baronial mansion. It aspires to grandeur but only succeeds in appearing small. It had been built in 1857 in a semi-Palladian style, but in 1897 Clive's father had surrounded the original building with pseudo-Gothic and Jacobean accretions, following a wilful eclecticism that determines the decoration throughout. He made lavish use of expensive materials. The house is built entirely in stone and a Gothic porch leads directly into a large wood-panelled hall, boasting a minstrels' gallery round two sides, an alcove in one corner (with raised floor to provide a stage for recitals) and a tall, vaulted ceiling. Certain of the doors leading out of this hall are made out of solid yew and are ornamented with huge metal fingerplates that clumsily imitate Morris's medievalism. Upstairs some of the bedroom door-handles are made out of claw-like iron rosettes, uncomfortable to hold and, like much of the house, aggressive and ostentatious. In Mr Bell's day polished wood and brass gleamed in every room and trophies of the chase hung on the walls. At his request, bells had been carved into the stone over every doorway or mullioned window and on the scutcheon mounted over the front door. Here and on the central arch in the main hall he had his and his wife's initials carved in large capitals, a final statement of his pride in the house that he had built to look like an Oxford college in pleasant country-side far removed from the Welsh pits and slag heaps where, as colliery owner and mining engineer, he had made his wealth.

'Squire' Bell, as Clive's father was called by the villagers, enacted the part of benevolent autocrat in imitation of the aristocracy to which he aspired. He employed a good many people in the village, gave land for the Women's Institute Hall and during the First World War provided the village with a potato sprayer. He became a Justice of the Peace, sat on the local Parish Council and was for some years Chairman of the Melksham Rural District Council. Young village girls would drop him a curtsy as he strode over the footpath from Seend to Melksham with his two dogs, to attend the Petty Sessions. At Cleeve House he encouraged his family to lead a 'county' life-style which involved a regular round of hunts, tennis parties, local events and nondescript conversation. The Bells played an important part in the village life; they belonged to various clubs and assisted with charities. When a branch of the Women's Institute was founded in Seend in 1919, Clive's sister Dorothy became its first President.

Dorothy was the nicer of the two sisters; Lorna, the elder, was sharp, aggressive and tended to bark. Both, however, had been well educated, but Vanessa dismissed their competence and composure as 'awful rich fox-hunting complacency'. The only member of the family with whom she made friends was Clive's brother, Cory, who was intelligent and could have succeeded in a number of professions, but he chose the life of an artilleryman as it suited his unashamedly hedonistic temperament. He endeared himself to Vanessa by once muttering 'nearly dropped the fucking thing' as he clutched at the heavy family Bible and read aloud at morning prayers.

The combination of wealth and the lack of intellectual dedication made Cleeve House unsympathetic to Vanessa. She observed that the conversation was mostly confined to the weather, the army, sport and local gossip. She found the cheery exchange of received opinion and common sense enervating, as she told Virginia:

> I often feel singularly boorish and crude. But here I feel subtle and clever and almost a genius. Unluckily the feeling is not so pleasant a one as you might suppose. It is only contrast with Lorna and Dorothy that makes me feel so, and it would be truer to say that I feel like a dolphin stranded high and dry, lashing about to find some water. When one first comes here, one thinks, well they really aren't so bad – there are virtues in vegetables and one has plenty to say oneself. But gradually with no nourishment from without, one's own stream of talk runs dry and one lapses into silence – and then the too awful torrent of commonplaces on tennis and the weather – oh Lord, how much can be said on the weather . . . one can do nothing but subside into gloom.[11]

At Seend, Vanessa found herself once again living among two generations and was reminded of how iniquitous family life could be. Having recently discovered that she was pregnant, she asked Virginia: 'What shall I do with *my* family of 4 when they grow up? I'm beginning to think 2 will be enough. Do you think we shall gradually fall into all the old abuses and that I shan't have any idea what my children are like or what they want to do?'[12] She was alternately delighted and terrified at the thought of having children, but all the while certain that she would be unreasonably fond. Meanwhile Clive taught her an artful method of dealing with Mrs Bell's and Lorna's requests: if asked to do something against his wish, he simply went his own way without argument or fuss, proffering a jocular refusal that baffled them.

On Sundays the self-congratulatory atmosphere at Cleeve House noticeably thickened. In the mornings Clive and Vanessa were left alone in the house while the entire family went to church where they occupied the front pew. Mr Bell was himself an atheist but he thought the Church a stabilizing social force and once the service had begun he would turn round to make sure that all his tenants were present. The family returned home to a large Sunday lunch and in the afternoon received visitors who obliged Vanessa by asking stilted questions about painting. When Mrs Raven-Hill called, Vanessa found her the exception. 'I like her', she told Virginia, 'and it is a relief occasionally to see people who do understand what you say and have some feeling for other things beside the crops.'[13] One can only guess at the curiosity tinged with jealousy with which Mrs Raven-Hill regarded Vanessa, for she had been momentarily put out when Clive terminated their relationship after his marriage. Vanessa, as yet unaware of Mrs Raven-Hill's former role, took additional pleasure in Virginia's letters, especially when two arrived on the same day. 'I found more relief than you can [k]now in escaping from the Bell breakfast conversation into Sweet William's [Virginia's] lively wit and hairy embrasures.'[14] She had also decided that their life in London had become too cumbrous and expensive and was in need of change; the degree of freedom she had so far won still did not fully satisfy her needs. But for the moment she was hampered by her pregnant state. 'I have made no autumn plans this year as yet,' she admitted to Virginia, 'for I suppose that the arrival of the infant will be my chief winter event, and my plan for disposing of servants can't come into force till next summer. It would involve of course leaving Gordon Square – but it's all too nebulous yet.'[15]

On 4 February 1908 she gave birth to a son whom they named Julian Heward Bell. Twenty-nine years later, in some fragmented pencil notes, Vanessa tried to recollect this and other events in his life. On first holding him she forgot instantly the pain of childbirth and felt overwhelmed by feelings that at the time she did not understand.[16] As her strength returned she observed with pleasure the infant that had invaded her life. 'We are both flourishing,' she told Madge Vaughan, 'and Julian came into the world shouting healthily and has continued to do so ever since.'[17] He had dark brown silky hair, was naturally greedy and after the first week gained weight without any trouble. Vanessa followed the then customary precaution of remaining in bed for a month after the birth. To entertain her, Clive invited his friends upstairs for an hour or two after dinner. One who now began to make a regular appearance at Gordon Square was the brilliant young economist Maynard Keynes who had recently left Cambridge and was employed at the India Office.

By Easter Vanessa was well enough to travel down to Seend where Julian was received with honour. Though he had revolutionized Vanessa's life, bringing out strong instincts which until then had lain dormant within her, she was not so submerged in maternal feelings as to despise intelligent company. When Virginia sent her an essay she had written, a mock life of Violet Dickinson, Vanessa told her, 'It brings back to me the atmosphere of rarefied culture and free talk which is so congenial to me and is a solace from talk of Julian or the winter of '81.'[18] At Seend she suffered from the exchange of banalities which composed lengthy discussions on the present heat, the exceptionally hot summer of 1882 or the harshness of past winters. At the same time she received from Virginia one of the most important essays she had so far written, a lengthy evocation of their past, focusing particularly on herself, Julia and Stella.[19] Vanessa was overwhelmed by it. 'My word, what a scene of gloom it becomes after the tragedies! I felt plunged into the midst of all that awful underworld of emotional scenes and irritations and difficulties again as I read. How did we ever get out of it? It seems to me almost too ghastly and unnatural now ever to have existed.'[20] She was also confronted with prose of exceptional limpidity and beauty, autobiographical writing so subtly nuanced and observed as to compare with the best of this genre. As Vanessa read, her past took on the shape of a work of art. Perhaps wary of giving too much praise, she offered small criticisms and described the whole thing as 'remarkably well constructed'. But while it remained in her mind, life at Seend dwindled to insignificance: 'I think in future you will have to keep me supplied with works of yours whenever I am here, for contact with your wits lifts me out of their dead level of commonplaces and I sniff the air like an old war horse and snort with delight.'[21]

During Holy Week the Bells went to church every day. As the drama of Christ's death and resurrection approached, Clive and Vanessa began to look forward to a thoroughly pagan evening, to be spent dining with the Raven-Hills and another *Punch* illustrator, George Denhelm Armour and his wife. On their way down to Seend, in the train to Devizes, Clive and Vanessa had been obliged to listen as a clergyman from Bristol described to all those in his carriage his wife's long and fatal illness, accused the Liberal Party of enslaving the people of England and concluded that the country's only hope lay in 'wiping out the blacks'. By contrast, conversation with the Raven-Hills would at least be civilized, Vanessa thought. Far from being bigoted, it ran freely over a number of subjects, including one that no one had apparently discussed with Vanessa before. 'Talk of freedom in talk – she stops at nothing,' Virginia was informed of Mrs Raven-Hill. 'Different methods of stopping children and the joys of married life were freely discussed and notes compared by her, Mrs Armour and myself and I quite enjoyed myself as you will believe. Also I see that I can get some useful tips from Mrs Raven-Hill as to the best methods of checking one's family, and I mean to make use of the dance at Devizes for the purpose, though as she is very deaf I shall probably cause a scandal.'[22] After the mincing insinuations exchanged by the Bell daughters with other Seend spinsters, Mrs Raven-Hill's unblushing animal delight in the flesh came as a relief. With her illegitimate five-year-old daughter, she sat like an unexploded mine of scandal in Wiltshire society, for in spite of her seductive appearance (even Clive's father had once pinched her leg) her chief concern was to maintain her respectability. Clive, watching his beautiful wife talk bawdy with this pretty, well-preserved Wiltshire lady, with her faint but perceptible hint of vulgarity, was aware of the conflict between abandon and reserve at work in both their natures. To Virginia he wrote:

> Mrs Raven-Hill, Mrs Armour, Mrs Clive Bell; three young or youngish women: mothers, how beautiful do they sit, each in her own day nursery smiling down Madonna-like on a smiling child. Last night they dined with three men; Mr Raven-Hill, Mr Armour, Mr Clive Bell; artists, young members of the youngest Bohemian clubs, stained by drink and lust and too warm contact with a sin-be-sodden world ... but Vanessa like some beautiful black velvet foil takes the measure of her peeresses and can judge their colour to a shade. Her appreciation is so sure that she is rarely descried, and yet she continues to get confidences. Explain me that.[23]

Vanessa, however, saw comparatively little of Mrs Raven-Hill and a great deal of her mother-in-law, Mrs Bell, a small, kind lady whose slightly bulging eyes gave her the appearance of a frightened rabbit. She lived entirely in the shadow of her stiff, stout, white-haired husband who was occasionally prone to outbursts of violent temper. Once when Clive's brother Cory accidentally broke a decanter, Mr Bell turned on him in fury in front of the entire company though Cory was by then in his forties. When Mr Bell was absent from the house Vanessa found the atmosphere noticeably less oppressive. Her spring visit ended with her making plans for a holiday in Cornwall. She sent Virginia, who had gone on ahead, instructions concerning rooms, carriages and luggage. The prospect of rejoining her sister delighted her. 'I shall look for your handsome red tie and soft nose at St Ives – Oh God what a joyful sight.'[24]

In her anticipation of pleasure, Vanessa overlooked the effect that her small son would have on the rest of the party. Virginia and Clive had been delighted and relieved by his safe birth but once this was over had not been unduly enthusiastic about his presence. Clive, fearful of mess and alarmed by fragility, had at first declined to hold the child. At Seend he had been infuriated by Julian's loud screams and had begun sleeping in a different room from Vanessa. To Virginia the infant, with its devouring need for attention, must have threatened her own habitual presumption on Vanessa's maternal affection. As it was she had never overcome her resentment of Clive who, in her opinion, did not equal the Stephens either in intellect or looks. If Clive was irritated and frustrated, Virginia was experiencing a more agonizing sense of real loss. In Cornwall both were infuriated by Vanessa's habit of interrupting the conversation in order to discern whether it was Julian or the landlady's two-year-old who was crying. The caterwauling increased their discomfort and both sought some form of escape.

They began to take regular walks along the sea's edge. Alone together they talked easily and at length because for some time Clive had acted as Virginia's mentor. He was also a delightful companion, well-read, witty, responsive to others' feelings, entertaining and even-tempered. But never before had he spent so much time alone in her company and he was therefore able to establish their friendship on a new footing. What happened next has been attributed to Clive's tendency, which grew marked in later years, to indulge in flirtatious teasing when in the company of the opposite sex. What was surprising, and fatal, was Virginia's willingness to respond. Quentin Bell has argued that Virginia, out of possessive love for Vanessa, 'had to injure her, to enter and in entering to break that charmed circle within which Vanessa and Clive were so happy and by which she was so cruelly excluded'.[25] By obtaining Clive's love she was, by proxy, sharing in the love which he got from Vanessa; in the same way that as a child she had broken into the intimacy that existed between Thoby and Vanessa, so now she sought to establish a triangular relationship in the mistaken belief that it would bring her again closer to her beloved sister. Therefore if this flirtation was stimulated partly by Virginia's malevolence, it was also fuelled by her need for affection.

For Vanessa it was a double betrayal. On the one hand it exposed the limitations of Clive's love and therefore of their marriage; on the other it was, she remembered, a curious experience feeling so jealous of Virginia at a time when she thought her the most fascinating woman she knew. This was her dominant memory of this incident: therefore it would seem that it was Virginia's behaviour which hurt her most. Up to this moment the relationship between the sisters had been unusually close; when apart they wrote to each other daily, exchanging teasing compliments and much affection, their love also finding physical expression in what Vanessa called 'petting'. Moreover Virginia was able to contribute to Vanessa's creative life in a way that Clive could not, and at this period one receives the impression that Vanessa needed Virginia almost as much as Virginia needed her. Now this reflexive intimacy was to be exposed to a corrosive jealousy, for though Vanessa realized that Virginia's flirtation with Clive was more a game of wits than a matter of passion, this did not lessen the outrage.

When exactly Vanessa became aware of what was happening is difficult to ascertain. Clive, as his letters to Virginia reveal, had fallen in love and probably chose to hide from his wife the extent of his feelings. Immediately after Virginia left Cornwall, Vanessa wrote:

> I wonder what you have said about us. 'Of course Nessa was quite taken up with the baby. Yes, I'm afraid she's losing all her individuality and becoming the usual domestic mother and Clive – of course I like him very much but his mind is of a peculiarly prosaic and literal type – And they're always making moral judgement about me. However they seem perfectly happy and I expect it's a good thing I didn't stay longer. I was evidently beginning to bore them.' Now Billy, on your honour haven't you uttered one of these sentiments?[26]

This vignette, informed by the watchfulness that protected their relationship, suggests that as yet Vanessa was unaware of any treachery.

In physical terms Clive and Virginia's transgression was of small account. 'I was certainly of opinion,' Virginia wrote to Clive, recalling one moment during their Cornish holiday, 'though we did not kiss – (I was willing and offered once – but let that be) – I think we "achieved the heights" as you put it.'[27] To which Clive replied, 'I wished for nothing in the world but to kiss you. I wished so much that I grew shy and could not see what you were feeling; that is what happens always, and one of the worst things in human nature.'[28] But as none of them cast a sentimental eye on chastity, the extent of their dallying was not the issue: they had violated not so much the state of marriage as Vanessa's trust, offending against the sanctity accorded by Bloomsbury to personal relationships. 'My affair with Clive and Nessa', Virginia significantly termed this episode, when she looked back on it seventeen years later. '... For some reason that turned more of a knife in me than anything else has ever done.'[29]

Vanessa, when she became aware of this affair (if such it can be called), found herself in a difficult position. If she gave vent to the anger and jealousy it aroused in her she was in danger of alienating one if not two of the people she loved most. It was therefore necessary for her to contain her emotions. She created no fracas, made no 'scene': she simply withdrew into herself. She had an instinct to preserve things, people, relationships, and therefore did not allow her suffering to become destructive. In so doing she found that she could bear it so long as it was kept within herself. Admittedly she was motivated in part by selfishness but also by a formidable capacity to contain and thus control pain. 'You know', Virginia once observed, 'only very rich soft natures like Nessa's absorb their experiences.'[30] This explains why she remains a central figure within Bloomsbury, her presence embracing others, like Piero della Francesca's Misericordia Madonna extending the protection of her cloak to those around her, a figure offering large repose, wise tolerance and an extraordinarily rich, mellow understanding.

Clive, meanwhile, was unsettled. He, Vanessa and Julian went down to Seend that summer. There he sat in the garden, emotionally drained and undirected, wondering whether either the Greek scholar Walter Lamb or Lytton had proposed to Virginia. He was made disconsolate by the noise of hammering which mingled with Julian's cries, as a huge marquee was being put up in preparation for a garden party. By the evening he had recovered enough to write to Virginia: 'When the world is asleep all sorts of nice things happen at Seend; hares and small rabbits come up into the garden and nibble the heads of carnations, owls hoot from fir-tree to fir-tree, and the flowers make violent love.'[31] At other moments the less attractive aspects of life at Cleeve House made him irritable and slightly depressed:

> Life here is very like a bad novel: Dorothy's nurses coming and going, Lorna's tennis parties, family news and neighbours' delinquencies. Discussion without thought, joviality without wit, dissertation without intellect or knowledge. Quantities of feeling without subtlety and endless activity without result. The simplest causes continue to produce the most inevitable effects, and the effects to provoke the most unfeigned astonishment! *Tout va bien, le pain manque!*[32]

More revealing is his analysis of himself, for his excitement over Virginia caused him to reflect in another letter to her on the limitations of his character.

> I feel like an emotional convalescent as I lie in the shade and gradually recover the power of dreaming. No longer always about the future either, I have a little scrap of a past to dream about too. By midday Lytton and Walter [Lamb] have become remote, my family has ceased to exist, I am as detached as a French novel and as unreal. Everything gets form – not its real form, the form which I believe you see or come at somehow by sheer force of imagination – but a form which it borrows from me and which I borrow from the National Gallery or the British Museum. Still I don't think you ought to despise it, though I admit that almost anyone with five hundred a year and no encumbrances and a Trinity exhibition can learn to fill his pockets with it and give some away when the summer makes him pensive. I sometimes ... could almost cry for the beauty of the world; that is because I am not great, I can't lay hold on it; I just go fingering the smooth outside, for ever pushing it out of my grasp ... I am

condemned all my life, I think, to enjoy through an interpreter; but then as the interpreter is art one must not complain too much.[33]

When the garden party took place Clive and Vanessa acted the perfect young couple and opened the dancing while all Seend, dressed in their Sunday best, stood round and watched. Few would have guessed that this demure wife had in her baggage some of Lytton's indecent poems which she had brought with her to read. Meanwhile the rest of the Bells seemed as somnambulant as ever.

> Oh God [she exclaimed to Virginia] this life amazes me more and more. Mr Bell is now sleeping over his one bit of literature during the day – the *Cornhill* with your article in it – (he has not told me what he thinks of it). Mrs Bell is reading I don't know what, a thick black book, probably a novel from the library. Lorna has just gone to bed with many yawns. How can people waste their lives like this? It goes on all the year, all the time that we in London are wondering whether we are growing old or railing at Saxon's dullness ... I don't know that it much matters that people spend their lives like this, but it's monstrous and criminal, isn't it, that *we* should have to spend any portion of ours in this swamp and fog.[34]

She wrote daily to Virginia and received many letters in return, not only from Virginia but also from Saxon Sydney-Turner who sent lengthy descriptions of scenery and weather and on one occasion resorted to giving her an inventory of the smoking-room in which he was writing. His letters left no impression at all on her mind but the images that Virginia tossed at her through the post led her to speculate, half-jokingly, 'how envied I shall be of the world some day when it learns on what terms I was with that great genius'.[35] But Virginia's isolation also roused her pity; she waited anxiously to hear if Lytton had proposed, and when Virginia took herself off alone to Wells to work on 'Melymbrosia' (*The Voyage Out*), she arranged that they should meet for a day in Bath. Their relationship still seemed as close as ever; their shared past enabled them to assume certain knowledge and understanding: when Clive and Lytton discovered the then unfashionable George Eliot, Vanessa reminded Virginia that they had known of her since the nursery.

Vanessa was still in a rebellious mood when in September she made the mistake of accompanying Clive on a shooting holiday in Ross-shire. The mountains and heather so attractive to tourists were to her hideous reminders of Landseer and Christmas cards. Then, too, the all-male company was of the dullest kind; at lunch they discoursed on various kinds of beer and spent most of dinner comparing wines. 'They go on for hours,' Vanessa told Lytton, knowing he would appreciate how excruciating it was, 'always at the same level and each new sentence imparting an exactly equally uninteresting piece of information or anecdote. No woman would do it for two minutes.'[36] Like invisible ink made visible by heat, her contemptuousness brought her French aristocratic ancestry to the fore, or so Clive thought, for among this company she appeared strikingly intelligent, beautiful, and very conscious of her femininity. She wrote to Virginia:

> There is an atmosphere of undiluted male here. How you'd hate it! If only you were here we should now light a fire and sit over it talking the whole morning, with our skirts up to our trousers. You would say 'Now what shall we talk about?' and I if I were tactful would say 'Our past', and then we should begin to discuss all our marvellous past and George's delinquencies, etc., and so come to our present and then to your future and whether and whom you would marry and then at last to the one great subject 'Now what do you really think of your brains Billy?' I shall say with such genuine interest that you'd have to tell me and we should probably reach the most exalted spheres. Why aren't you here?[37]

Virginia did join them in September when Clive and Vanessa, leaving Julian in care at Seend, took a holiday in Italy, staying at Siena and Perugia and making a day visit to Assisi. It was on this trip that Vanessa, through a combination of vagueness and ruthlessness, displayed how unsociable she could be. When some acquaintances were sighted – people whom they had met often at social occasions in London but had no wish to see – Vanessa turned her back quickly and stared intently into a shop window. Her attempt to avoid encounter was made painfully apparent by the fact that the window into which she stared with such unbroken interest belonged to a tallow–chandler and had nothing in it. When accidentally the two parties met again, the friends of the Booths responded to the Bells' greetings with a cold, frigid bow. From then on Virginia, Clive and Vanessa seemed to arrive at every church and gallery for ever on the tail of the other party who fled instantly. It was a relief to return home and to stop at Paris on the way. 'I really think we shall have to spend a winter in Paris some day,' Vanessa told Margery Snowden. 'All the painters one meets there talk constantly of pictures as they do nowhere else – and I enjoy it enormously.'[38]

Her own painting now began to reflect an increase of confidence. She concentrated chiefly on still lifes and portraits, most of which have been either lost or destroyed. One that remains from this period is the small oil sketch of Saxon Sydney-Turner playing the piano.[5] It is primarily a study in tone, the whites in his collar, the keyboard and sheet music being offset by the surrounding browns, greys and blacks, but it also conveys a moment of rapt concentration. At one time this portrait hung in his parents' home at Hove where Virginia thought it stood out curiously in its impoverished middle-class surroundings. It marks an advance upon that Vanessa painted of Lady Robert Cecil, for every touch now contributes to the mood of the whole. The light falls from behind, striking the back of the sitter's head and highlighting the lobe of his ear, leaving his face in shadow as he stares fixedly at the music. The handling is authoritative, the design calculated but not cold, the fall of light indirectly expressing Vanessa's affection for the sitter at the same time as it stills the casual scene.

'I see nothing of Nessa,' Clive complained to Virginia in December 1908, 'I do not even sleep with her; the baby takes up all her time.'[39] Even Vanessa had been surprised how completely a child had revolutionized her life. Though he gave her great joy he took up a good deal of her time – half her mornings and often her evenings too, as well as one afternoon a week when her nurse had a day off. And no amount of paid help could modify the anxiety he sometimes caused her. She never forgot her terror when he thrust a sharp crayon holder into his face, narrowly missing his eye but making a gash deep enough to require stitches. She watched him closely, marvelling at the iridescent sheen on his eyelashes, catching his likeness in paintings and drawings. Her earliest oils of Julian show him lying in the cradle. Later, when he began to stagger about, she resorted to quick sketches. He absorbed her interest more intensely than anything other than her painting.

Almost certainly Julian drove a wedge between her and Clive who, like most upper-middle-class fathers at this time, left the work involved entirely to mother and nurse. Moreover his flirtation with Virginia had caused Vanessa to deflect more of her affection and attention on to her son, deepening still further her emotional ties with her first-born. But these were not the only reasons why Vanessa and Clive began now to draw apart. Her letters to him are still fond (she nicknamed him 'Peak' and always signed herself 'Dolphin') but it is noticeable that she often resorts to a fey, teasing manner, subtly flattering him by underlining her lack of intelligence and literary ability in comparison with his own, all of which suggests an inequality in their relationship. At some point Vanessa saw through Clive's glamour and realized that the qualities in him that had attracted her at the time of Thoby's death no longer satisfied all her needs. If gradually their love for each other evaporated, it distilled into a lasting affection. Around 1909, while still writing flirtatious letters to Virginia, Clive again took up his affair with Mrs Raven-Hill, which he pursued until the outbreak of war. For the rest of his life, while never ceasing to admire his wife, he was rarely without a mistress. If Vanessa was aware, at this time, that his sexual interests lay elsewhere, she no more mentioned this matter to others than she had done his flirtation with Virginia. Her honesty, perhaps, prevented it. But it is interesting that this member of Bloomsbury now felt the need for reserve.

If the emotional tenor of her marriage had diminished, there was never any rift between her and Clive. She continued to depend on his ebullience to transform any social occasion, particularly those 'at homes' at Gordon and Fitzroy Squares which could still be disastrous if non-Bloomsbury friends were present. Vanessa, in 1909, was seeing a great deal of Lytton, the Cambridge mathematician H.T.J. Norton, and Maynard Keynes who sometimes brought Duncan Grant in his wake. She was also painting a friend called Irene Noel who hoped that Tudor Castle, who worked at the Admiralty, would propose. In Clive's absence these friends were incapable of making an 'at home' a success, as Vanessa describes:

> At Fitzroy Sq. were Pernel [Strachey], Keynes, Duncan, Castle and Irene. The evening was awkward in the extreme I thought. Irene was almost tearful and very much agitated. She and Castle talked the whole time to each other. The Goat [Virginia] was silent with occasional attempts at an affectionate whispered conversation with me which had to be curbed. Your presence would have been a great help. ... The evening was also blotted by the fact that Hans [the dog] was violently and most obviously sick in the middle of the rug. The Goat and Adrian rushed heroically to the rescue but – one could only turn one's head away or I felt I should do likewise.[40]

Yet despite the gaucheness that still affected their social evenings, the inner core of friends was now firmly established. Their bawdiness if anything increased when in the summer of 1908 sexual inversion flourished like German measles. H.T.J. Norton fell momentarily in despair over James Strachey who was besotted with Rupert Brooke; Lytton was distraught because Duncan had fallen in love with Keynes, who had now returned to King's College, Cambridge, as a don. At a time when homosexuality was still illegal, Bloomsbury's interest in the affairs of buggers, though it took the form of gossip and jokes, instanced their radicalism. Sexual humour often strikes us as comic because it names with ease those aspects of life that are mostly hidden from sight; the greater the taboo, the more comic and explosive will be the exposure. Maynard Keynes, at this time, indulged most frequently in this subversive humour and was startled to discover that Vanessa could share it. After she and Clive visited Cambridge this year, Keynes wrote to Duncan Grant:

> In the afternoon Norton and I and Vanessa and Clive happened to meet and walk. ... In the morning I breakfasted with [G.L.] Dickinson and later with

[Gerald] Shove where Clive and Vanessa again appeared. . . . At half past four Clive, Vanessa, Rupert [Brooke], James and [J.T.] Sheppard came to tea with me. That lasted till half past seven, and got, towards the end, rather amusing. Vanessa explained how interesting it was for her to come up and have a look at us, Lytton having explained every one of our secrets. She was perfectly lovely – I've never seen her more beautiful – and very conversational. Is she always so now? She seemed to hold the floor.[41]

The daughter of Sir Leslie Stephen was clearly at home among intellectuals, but it is significant that they were all – at least at this date – homosexuals. When certain of her female friends discussed women's suffrage, Vanessa was occasionally irritated by their disconnected ideas; she once upset Marjorie Strachey who, like her sister Pippa, was dedicated to the cause, by declaring women more hysterical than men. Though the suffragette movement in recent years had been increasing in strength, Vanessa took no part in it. Yet she was by nature a feminist, determined to fight for her own freedom and, if only by her example, for that of others. Paradoxically it was not the suffragists who increased her confidence in herself as a woman, but her conversations with these Cambridge homosexuals. While she had lived at Hyde Park Gate, power, action and creativity had seemed a male prerogative; but in the company of these intellectuals a less obviously masculine approach to life seemed to encourage sensitivity, imagination and wit. Vanessa need no longer perceive herself as 'that terrible low creature, a female painter' because femininity was no longer a thing to be despised. Rather, it was the deadening male conventionality, upheld by the Duckworths among others, that these friends ridiculed, collapsing into giggles when a newspaper misprint described a politician as a 'newly erected member'. Nor did the persistent harping on buggery irritate Vanessa, as it sometimes did Virginia, because she could view it with amusement from her vantage point as wife and mother. Lytton observed that when in the company of these Cambridge friends Vanessa appeared the most complete human being of them all.

It was to Lytton that Vanessa sent amusing descriptions of their Italian holiday in May 1909. She tempted him with a description of a row of naked boys saluting their train as it passed, and detailed the cumbrous English family with whom they had shared their carriage. The holiday was not, however, a success. Virginia came out to Florence to join them, and as she and Clive still tended to flirt with one another, the situation was uncomfortable and a quarrel broke out in the Bargello. After a fortnight Virginia cut short her holiday and returned home alone. Vanessa felt melancholy after her departure and, in order to distract her mind, attended mass at Santa Maria Novella, watching the ceremony as if it were a piece of theatre.

During this holiday they took tea with the brusque, imperious author Mrs Janet Ross in her castle Poggio Gherardo, and called on the Berensons in the nearby Villa I Tatti where they met the architect Geoffrey Scott. Vanessa, in her spare moments, read Choderlos de Laclos's *Liaisons dangereuses*, and suffered horribly one night from bugs, soaking her pillow in turpentine to prevent their return. She was painting a portrait of Rezia Corsini at their palace on the Lungarno Corsini. It proved a difficult task not only because Rezia's family often descended on them and, with animated chatter, unintentionally blocked Vanessa's view, but Rezia herself after a couple of sessions suddenly cancelled an appointment without making any arrangements for another.[42] Earlier, she had confessed to a youthful infatuation for George Duckworth and had been distressed to learn of the rift between the Stephens and their half-brothers. Though Rezia (who lived to be ninety-two) all her life cherished her memory of Sir Leslie Stephen and his family, this visit more or less ended her friendship with Vanessa who now realized that their previous familiarity had only been superficial.

Vanessa was not drawn easily into intimate relations with women. When Lady Ottoline Morrell made friendly overtures Vanessa treated them cautiously. 'Is Ottoline becoming my rival in your affections?' she wrote to Virginia from Florence. 'You will have a desperate liaison with her I believe, for I rather think she shares your sapphist tendencies and only wants a little encouragement. She once told me she much preferred women to men and would take any trouble to get to know a woman she liked, but would never do the same for a man. If I had not brutally said that I generally preferred men, what might not have happened?'[43] Already established as a leading hostess, Lady Ottoline seemed anxious to annex Bloomsbury to her court, where her favourite of the moment was Augustus John, with whom she was having an affair. She had first met the Bells in John's studio in the summer of 1908; Clive had showered admiration on John's painting, while Vanessa had stood silent at his side, her head bent, approving. By 1909 they were dining fairly frequently with the Morrells, who in turn accompanied the Bells and the Stephens to an artists' fancy dress ball that summer. Ottoline had envisaged a Mozartian scene, something light, elegant and aristocratic, and had dressed herself in a full black taffeta dress with a black lace mantilla for the occasion. She was a little disappointed at the dinner beforehand at Gordon Square to find Virginia unsuitably attired as Cleopatra and Vanessa looking decidedly improper in a white satin petticoat tricked out with ribbons and with roses rakishly stuck into her hair. But still more jarring was the jumble of bare

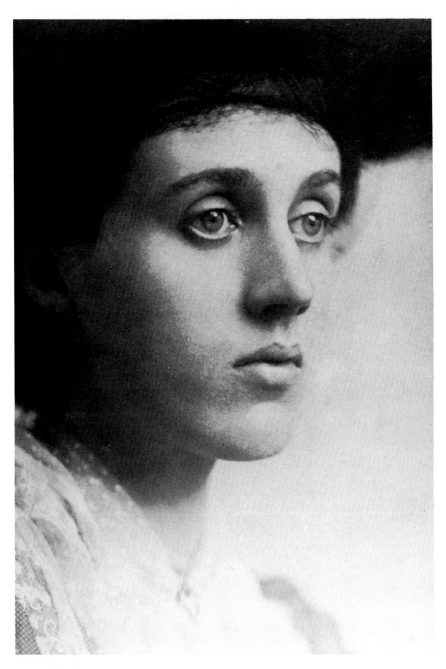

Vanessa Stephen, 1903

Sir Leslie Stephen

Julia Stephen

Vanessa, Stella and Virginia Stephen, c. 1896

Lady Robert Cecil, 1905

Saxon Sydney Turner, c. 1908

Vanessa Bell by Roger Fry, 1911

Roger Fry, 1933

The Bathers, 1911

Studland Beach, 1912

Landscape with Haystack, Asheham, 1912

Bathers in a Landscape, screen painted by Vanessa Bell for the Omega Workshops, 1913

Table, pottery and cloth sold by the Omega Workshops. The cloth, entitled 'Cracow',
was designed by Vanessa Bell.

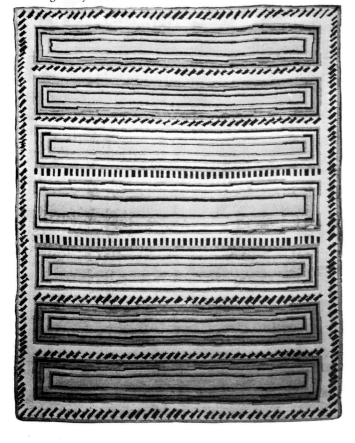

Omega Workshops carpet
designed by Duncan Grant

The entrance hall at Durbins, Guildford; wall
decorations by Roger Fry, Vanessa Bell and
Duncan Grant, 1914

Vanessa Bell at Asheham

The main hall at Durbins, showing Vanessa Bell's *Woman and Baby* in the
top right corner

limbs and ill-fitting costumes found at the party itself, where the mood was anything but Mozartian.

Nevertheless, undeterred in her pursuit of Bloomsbury, Lady Ottoline sailed like the Bucintoro across Gower Street, intent on wedding herself in friendship to the daughters of Sir Leslie Stephen. At first her high-key moods seemed expansive and generous, and beneath the prominent façade of dress, red hair, pearls and teeth Vanessa detected a sense of judgement. She told Clive that Ottoline thought Lytton was 'wrapping himself up in a narrow and Voltairian world and shutting out all common experiences. I thought she was really rather acute, but it may have been second-hand.'[44] It was not her extravagance that eventually lost Vanessa's respect, but her need to parade it. There was something frantic and omnivorous about her desire to give, introduce and entertain. 'Life lived on the same plane as poetry and music is my instinctive desire and standard,' she declared.[45]

Always suspicious of insincerity, Vanessa still turned more to her old friend Margery Snowden than the resplendent Lady Ottoline. With Margery she could discuss in detail the progress of her work: 'I have taken your advice about my still life and got the vase in drawing – at least I think I have. I can find nothing wrong, measure it as I will à la Nicol [J. Watson Nicol, tutor at Cope's]. But I don't believe I shall ever have the courage to send it or anything else to the New English.'[46] The New English Art Club, originally set up as an alternative to the Royal Academy, had by now become a prestigious exhibiting society. Vanessa, no longer content with the Friday Club, not only attempted the NEAC but had the year previously sent to the Allied Artists Exhibition at the Albert Hall which accepted five pictures for exhibition on payment of a guinea. Already she disregarded the Academy and when her friend Sylvia Milman had a work accepted for the annual exhibition Vanessa felt little enthusiasm or envy. Despite her own lack of outward success she was gaining steadily in confidence. When Henry Lamb, on Virginia's request, made some drawings of Vanessa, she enjoyed talking with him about painting and observed the Augustus John influence on his drawing style. His obvious talent did not depress her as she had just completed a still life with which she felt satisfied. She sent it, together with a portrait of Marjorie Strachey, to the New English Art Club in the spring of 1909. The portrait no longer exists but Vanessa described it in a letter to Margery Snowden. From this, and the few paintings that remain from this period, it is clear that one guiding interest was light and its compositional role. She also, at this time, contemplated renting a studio in Fitzroy Street, which she hoped Margery Snowden would share so that together they could hire models and paint from the figure.

Her portrait of Marjorie Strachey was rejected by the New English; her still life entitled *Iceland Poppies*, however, was accepted and when exhibited drew praise from Sickert and from Duncan Grant in one of his rare pieces of criticism, written for the *Spectator*. It may only be a coincidence that at this time when a triangular relationship was troubling her life, Vanessa produced a still life based on triplicates: there are in *Iceland Poppies* three still-life objects, three bands running across the background, three flowers, two of which are white and slightly separated from the third which is red. In her choice of subject she may have been influenced by Duncan Grant's liking for simple, Chardinesque still lifes. The few sparse objects enable her to concentrate on interval, highlight and shadow, and from these limited means she extracts an introspective, bitter-sweet mood, for the composition is sustained like a strain of music that lingers on dissonance before resolution. With its cool silvery tonality and concentrated mood, it remains one of her finest paintings.[5]

This picture also conveys a feeling of life suspended (the poppies and medicine bottle may contain a deliberate reference to sleep) and is therefore expressive of Vanessa's position at this time. While her sister wrote regular reviews for which she was often praised, her own development was at a standstill. Maternal obligations curtailed her career and for some reason or other the Fitzroy Street studio had not been taken, the model never employed. She still painted regularly, however, and on a visit to Cambridge executed a portrait of her cousin Katherine Stephen, then a Vice-Principal at Newnham College and subsequently Principal; but the portrait, which may have been commissioned, is now lost and the official likeness of Katherine Stephen that today hangs in the College is by Glyn Philpot. At home Vanessa often found it difficult to devote herself to her painting because Julian provided considerable distraction despite the assistance of his nurse.

In London that winter their life seemed vague and directionless. Stirred by a feeling of dissatisfaction, Clive and Vanessa proposed moving permanently to Paris and attempted to convince Virginia and Lytton of the sense behind this proposition. Had they carried out their intent it is unlikely that the change would have repaired their marital relationship. In a telling letter to Virginia, written on Christmas Day 1909, Clive confessed:

At heart, I'm on the side of the vulgar and efficient. Vanessa, I believe, gets further and further away from the daily; that's because she's refined. ... I met Mrs Raven-Hill at Paddington on Thursday and thought her delicious and flashy in a fur coat; and then I dreamt about Sapphism all night, and read the prolifics in *The Times* next morning. The truth is, I fancy, that I look at life in a good many ways, and that I don't necessarily dislike what I know to be second or third rate.[47]

Though his mood was buoyant, he too felt they had come to an *entr'acte*. Nothing seemed to happen: London struck him as depressingly ugly; its romanticism in certain lights and atmospheres was, he thought, a fluke. 'London has no beauty of design,' he complained to Lytton, 'there is no aesthetic intention. Sun and shade and nature play pretty tricks, but there is no splendour of harmonious composition such as ravishes my soul in Paris. There is a much deeper reason [for the proposed move], I have no friends in London. Saxon is but half alive, I see him once a fortnight perhaps – and then', he concluded, searching around in vague discontent, 'what is there left for us to think and feel?'[48]

FIVE

Petticoats over Windmills

1910–1912

Early one morning in January 1910 on Cambridge railway station Vanessa encountered the person who was to alter the course of her life. Their meeting was the result of chance but it could not have been better timed.

For one moment she hesitated to approach for she was uncertain if Roger Fry would remember her; they had met only twice, some four or five years before. Around 1905–6 she had attended a dinner given by the MacCarthys and had sat next to this erudite man whose reputation as a scholar of Italian art had earned him the position of art critic to the highbrow periodical, the *Athenaeum*. Vanessa had known of him since Hyde Park Gate days, when he had delivered a series of lectures in nearby rooms affiliated with the Albert Hall. Disliking lectures, she had never heard him talk, but had been intrigued when, seated in King's College Fellows' garden at Cambridge, Walter Headlam had pointed to a tall couple in the distance and announced that they were Mr and Mrs Roger Fry. At the MacCarthys' Vanessa had sat by this critic prepared to be silenced by his eminence; she expected that, like Tonks and Charles Furse, he would make her uncomfortably aware of her inferiority. Instead she found someone who listened to her remarks, understood and encouraged her to continue. To her surprise she talked easily and hotly defended the merits of John Singer Sargent's art, for she had been stung by Roger Fry's dismissive comment that the man could not draw. Looking back on this evening, Vanessa recalled: 'It was and seemed for long almost unbelievable that one could really talk, chatter, express oneself to one of these dreaded members of the upper world, one who already had grey hair but such kind, brilliant interested dark eyes and coal black eyebrows.'

At the end of the evening Roger Fry invited Vanessa to visit him and his wife at their house in Hampstead. Helen Fry had for some years been suffering intermittently from bouts of mental illness, and when Vanessa arrived at their Hampstead home she was made instantly aware of this woman's unhappy condition for she looked tired, ill-at-ease and forlorn. She responded to Vanessa and openly confessed her depression at not having enough time to paint. While they talked, two small children came in and Vanessa observed that the son, Julian, had Roger's dark eyes. He, meanwhile, tried to cheer his wife and talked with Vanessa about a painting he had seen that morning at a London dealer's. She left slightly in awe of him, aware also of the tragedy of his domestic life. 'I cannot remember what we talked of – ', her recollection of him continues, 'only the general impression remains of a strange alive household, not altogether happy but with a tremendous force and interest of some kind at work in it. I never went there again. My own life was completely upset and when I saw them again I was married myself.'[1]

Nothing further had come of this visit to Hampstead partly because in 1906 Roger Fry had been enticed across the Atlantic by New York's Metropolitan Museum of Art where he had acted first as Curator of Paintings, then as European Adviser. In this latter capacity he had travelled Europe, acquiring Old Masters for the Museum, taking part in an international network of scholars, collectors, connoisseurs, critics and dealers. At the Museum he had initially enjoyed the confidence and support of the trustees but this had quickly deteriorated, largely because Fry spent most of his time in England and Europe and very little time in New York. Finally a dispute with the Museum's autocratic chairman, the millionaire J. Pierpont Morgan, had terminated his appointment in February 1910. All through this period Fry had kept up his association with the scholarly *Burlington Magazine* which he had helped to found in 1903, and in 1909 he accepted a part-time position as joint editor. It did not interfere with his work for the Metropolitan but his wife's illness was a constant distraction: it had now become so severe that for long periods she had to be taken into care. In 1910 she was finally certified and committed to an asylum where she remained for the rest of her life. 'You have certainly fought hard to help your wife, and shown a devotion I have never seen equalled,' wrote Fry's doctor, Henry Head. 'Unfortunately the disease has beaten us.'[2]

Therefore when Vanessa unexpectedly caught sight of Roger Fry on Cambridge station and resumed their acquaintance, she met a man who had been jolted out of a highly successful career. Now aged forty-four, he failed to get the Slade Professorship at Oxford when it fell vacant that year, and was out of the running for the more prestigious jobs (though when offered the Directorship of the Tate Gallery he refused it). He was leading a patched-together domestic life, having just moved into the house he had designed and built at Guildford. As he was often away from home, his children, in Helen's absence, were looked after by his sister Joan. He had lost any former ambition and had turned his back on the knighthood that at one time seemed likely to come his way. When his wife had written him letter after letter in a pathetic, incoherent, child-like scrawl constantly begging him to take her home, he had formed, as he admitted, a callus to enable him to get through the inane tragedy of life. Unshackled by suffering from worldly concerns, he cared chiefly at this moment for art and had already decided to bring the Post-Impressionists to London. When he sat down in the same railway compartment as the Bells that morning, he brought out materials with which to write an article, but abandoned it when he discovered Clive's interest in and knowledge of modern French art. The two men kept up an unbroken conversation until they reached London. Vanessa was largely silent, studying the older man's face. He had penetrating but friendly eyes, made larger by his thin-rimmed spectacles; his mouth curled back over his slightly projecting teeth in an engaging smile; his deep, sonorous voice was unusually musical and expressive. 'As he sate [sic] opposite me in the corner', Vanessa wrote in October 1934, 'I looked at his face bent a little down towards his MS but not reading, considering, listening, waiting to reply, intensely alive but quiet. "What astonishing beauty" I thought looking at the austere modelling in the flat bright side lights from the train windows. I do not think I talked much but he was becoming a real person to me, and it was suggested that we should go and see him at Guildford.'[3]

At Vanessa's invitation, Roger Fry spoke at a Friday Club meeting the following month. In turn, Clive agreed to sit on the committee that Roger formed to carry out his idea for an exhibition of modern French art. Then in the spring the Bells made their first visit to his house, Durbins, at Guildford. His children had been sent to stay with their grandparents near Bristol as one last attempt was being made to reintegrate Helen into home life. During lunch she was so obviously cut off from communication that Roger made no attempt to involve her in the conversation. She sat in silence, occasionally murmuring to herself and later that day suffered the delusion that she heard her children calling, which aroused in Vanessa inexpressible pity.

After this visit the Bells did not see much of Roger Fry until the autumn. Vanessa was again pregnant, the child expected towards the end of July and already named Clarissa as its mother was certain it would be a girl. The arrival of her second child was to modify Vanessa's absorption in Julian into a more normal relationship. Her love for her children, however, had not ousted her need to paint, which was as strong as ever. When she heard at second hand that Alice, the wife of the diplomat Sydney Waterlow, had criticized a Mrs Meredith for an apparent lack of maternal feeling, Vanessa astutely remarked: 'I suppose the truth is that Mrs Meredith is a woman of some intelligence who apparently can be interested in her work as well as the twins.'[4] On the other hand, she did not underrate the suffering that children could cause when writing to Madge Vaughan, one of whose daughters had died a few months before: 'It seems to me as if there could be nothing quite so hard to bear as the death of one's child. . . . It is too terrible and too useless to dwell on the pain, though I know it is difficult not to do so.'[5]

Another melancholy event this year was the return of Virginia's mental illness. She suffered from headaches and acute nervous tension. In March Clive and Vanessa, in an attempt to effect a cure, took her and Julian down to Studland where they had gone the previous summer. They lodged, as before, with a Mr Joseph Gibbons. The weather was good, they rode donkeys, played patience, ate semolina pudding and slept on lumpy beds. And when they returned to London three weeks later Virginia seemed restored to health.

The short holiday had not, however, effected a cure and before long the old symptoms returned. In early June Vanessa and Clive were again obliged to take Virginia away from London, this time to the Moat House at Blean, near Canterbury. After two weeks had passed, Vanessa, aware that her sister's health was still not improving and anxious to find someone to look after her before she herself went into labour, consulted Sir George Savage. He advised a private nursing home at Twickenham run by a Miss Jean Thomas and there Virginia went on 30 June. Cut off from her family, friends and from her work, Virginia resented the treatment and at one point threatened to throw herself out of the window. Vanessa, in letter after letter, had to reason with her and convince her of the need for rest.

If Virginia's illness cast a blight over the summer, Vanessa was content enough in herself and in her fecund state. She also experienced a sudden access of affection for Clive and when he left her in London while he made a visit to Seend she wrote:

> I don't believe you have ever been away so long before. I am quite cheerful but I do feel curiously lop-sided without you, and things crop up that I want to say to you every minute. I have been meditating on marriage! How odd it is – it seems to give me something that those other people and I before I married had no conception of. It is you who give it to me I suppose not marriage. Your nature gives it to me. It is like being always thirsty and always having some

delicious clear water to drink. You do make me astonishingly and continuously happy.[6]

With Virginia at Twickenham and her son Julian with his nurse at Seend, Vanessa suddenly found herself free of responsibilities, able to relax, gossip and read. She strolled through volumes, including *War and Peace*, and felt pleasantly removed from the routine of ordinary life.

Into this spacious, unhurried world stepped Lady Ottoline. She kissed her hand to Vanessa one night across the theatre pit, a gesture which Vanessa had neither the grace nor the self-confidence to return. When they met in the interval, Vanessa thought Ottoline, who had long wisps of hair trailing over her eyes, looked exhausted. Earlier this year she had accompanied her husband on a political tour of Lancashire. The true cause of her exhaustion, however, was her agitation over the artist Henry Lamb, an affair that left her in a condition of near collapse. Vanessa, intrigued by the rumours that swarmed round Ottoline, extracted from her this summer the admission that she had had nine affairs. As her husband Philip was present the conversation could go no further, so Vanessa invited Ottoline to tea with deliberate intent. Ottoline was equally inquisitive about Vanessa and the two women circled round each other with vague generalizations about male and female jealousy. Finally Vanessa, tenacious but discreet, got from Ottoline the admission that she had never been in love with Philip but had married him on the rebound from an earlier love; she found him a pleasant, soothing companion, but had little physical response to him and their marriage was now celibate. On Henry Lamb (who had admitted intimate knowledge of Ottoline's physical charms) she would not be drawn though she repeatedly referred to him in conversation. The relationship between the two women was still close and when Ottoline left England at the end of July for a long and much needed holiday in Europe, Vanessa was thankful that their farewells were said at a crowded party which prevented too emotional an exchange.

Ottoline's affair with Henry Lamb was not the only subject of gossip that summer. 'I am inclined to be somewhat sceptical about the great passion,'[7] Vanessa wrote to Virginia about the relationship that had begun between her brother Adrian and Duncan Grant. Adrian had suddenly talked to her at length about 'inversion', describing an imaginary affair that clearly mirrored his own, for Duncan was now in and out of their houses at Fitzroy and Gordon Squares. The only thing about their emotional involvement that struck Vanessa as odd was Adrian's apparent want of real affection for Duncan, though after her brother's death she looked back on this relationship as one of his happiest.

Duncan was, as Maynard Keynes remarked in November 1910, 'rapidly becoming celebrated'.[8] At the Friday Club exhibition in June 1910, his *Lemon Gatherers* (Tate Gallery) caused Vanessa to write to Clive: 'I was very much impressed by it and really think that he may be going to be a great painter. There seems to me to be something remarkably fine in his work, and in the grand manner. He is certainly much the most interesting of the young painters.'[9] The only other artist whose work Vanessa praised was the seventeen-year-old Mark Gertler. The next day she wrote again to Clive explaining that she had bought *Lemon Gatherers*. She excused herself by reminding him that their forthcoming baby would bring in a gift of a thousand pounds from his family.

Clarissa was expected towards the end of July. As Vanessa's confinement approached, she restricted her entertainment to the receiving of visitors. Marjorie Strachey arrived and announced that she had at last fallen in love with a man. Clive's friend from Paris, J. W. Morrice, suddenly called but was not, Vanessa thought, drunk enough to be at his best. H. T. J. Norton was a frequent visitor, for his Cambridge background, wide reading and love of indecent humour made him at home in Bloomsbury. He was not the most handsome of men, having an unusually high forehead, three double chins and an unhealthy appearance. Depression and ill health were, in fact, to destroy his career as a mathematician, and after a breakdown he cut himself off from his former friends. In 1910, however, while Vanessa was nine months pregnant, he discussed with her promiscuous love, declared his warm feelings towards her and asked her to call him Harry.

Unable now to make the journey to Twickenham, Vanessa wrote to Virginia, 'Harry said he supposed I was very lonely without you. What an idea! Clive seems to think the same. I can only suppose that you have told them so so often that they have begun to believe it.' Yet Virginia's absence was not the only reason why these months, full of visitors and much gossip, were strangely void, and she added: 'Everyone agrees this summer has been a mournful one, whether on account of your disease or the King's death does not seem to be certain. Of course Clarissa also has not added gaiety to the scene, but I feel that I really chose the best possible time for her, that is the time when she has least interfered with anything else. I hope she won't have a mournful character in consequence.'[10]

On 19 August, three weeks later than expected, Clarissa arrived. A boy was contrary to all Vanessa's expectations, and he was hurriedly renamed Gratian. 'Gracious', joked Aunt Anny, as she breezed in to admire the new baby who, she declared confusingly, looked exactly like Clive *and* the first Sir James Stephen. Gerald Duckworth exploded when he heard Vanessa's choice of name: 'Oh my dear – just think of the poor chap at school.' Vanesssa calmly replied that she was considering not educating her children

in the normal way. Nobody seemed to like the name and so when Clive
went off to Seend, to see Julian and his family, she began to think of
alternatives. 'I hope you'll see your whore soon and get some amusing
gossip out of her', she wrote to Clive, referring to Mrs Raven-Hill (about
whom, clearly, she was now informed). In his absence Margery Snowden
arrived, in order to help nurse Vanessa, and made many bright quips about
the baby's name. Saxon Sydney-Turner meanwhile sat silently in one
corner, methodically going through Latin dictionaries and the index to
Gibbon, occasionally murmuring aloud Viggo Bell, Pausanias Bell or
suggesting with a small hysterical laugh, as a complete alternative,
'Crippen'.

Vanessa again took a month to convalesce and enjoyed receiving callers.
'I had a very nice visit from Duncan yesterday,' she told Clive. 'Snow
[Margery Snowden] was there all the time of course and we talked mostly
about painting as we could not discuss any really improper subjects freely
in her presence. However I like talking to him about painting more than
about most things.'[11] Clive's letters also brought her pleasure. They had
a peculiar mixture of suavity and force that convinced her he would one
day write a book. In mid-September she returned to everyday life, feeling
strange without a child inside her and glad to have recovered her figure.
But, as if not wanting this period of confinement to end, she began reading
War and Peace again.

Virginia had meanwhile gone on a walking tour in Cornwall with Miss
Jean Thomas who ran the nursing home at Twickenham. She returned
home very much better and anxious to start work again. First, however,
she took a holiday with her sister and brother-in-law at Studland where
Vanessa was reunited with Julian. He struck her as now curiously like
Thoby: he played with a greater degree of concentration than he had done
before and told her to shut up when she called him a pig for eating paper.
It was a hot Indian summer and Vanessa decided to stay on, with her nurse
and baby, after Clive, Virginia and Julian returned to London. While
Clive travelled to Paris, she made a visit to Corfe Castle, which reminded
her of Steer and where she expected to see industrious Slade students
perched on the hills. Then overnight the heat haze that had hovered over
the beach dissolved and drizzle set in. Left alone in the company of the
nurse, the lodging-house keeper and his wife, Vanessa grew irritated. 'My
brains are becoming as soft as – yours?' she wrote to Virginia, admitting
her restricted sympathies, ' – by constant contact with the lower classes.'[12]
By post, she heard that Desmond MacCarthy and Roger had gone to
Paris, to join Clive and look for paintings for their forthcoming exhibition.
While they were there Lady Ottoline arrived, on her way home from her

holiday, wearing, Desmond said, a hat 'like a crimson tea-cosy trimmed with hedgehogs'.[13] Vanessa's letters to Clive, meanwhile, were hungry not for news of Ottoline, but of painters and painting. She had been isolated too long and was now anxious to return to London.

A few weeks after her reappearance at Gordon Square the paintings of Van Gogh, Gauguin and Cézanne were shown in London, for the first time in any considerable number. 'Manet and the Post-Impressionists', as the show was called, opened at the Grafton Gallery on 8 November, having unleashed three days earlier, when a press view was held, a storm of controversy. Roger Fry's inspired idea (the actual organization of the show was fairly haphazard, the selection largely determined by what was available) had struck home. Aware of the etiolated traditions and insularity currently feeding British art, he had deliberately intended to rock accepted artistic standards. But because art is a carrier of ideology, Fry, by challenging received opinion concerning taste, had also thrown into question the social values implicit within it. To an Edwardian audience the paintings by these French Post-Impressionists seemed crude, aggressive, vulgar in colour, perspectively incorrect and in drawing unskilled. Some argued that they were merely the work of lunatics and bunglers, but their angry scorn merely confirmed the real challenge that these paintings presented. What differentiates the Post-Impressionists from their predecessors was that they were no longer content to record the shifting pattern of appearance but instead wanted to make the image more durable, either by emphasizing an underlying structure, as in the work of Cézanne, or by emphasizing an expressive response to the scene and therefore selecting and to some extent rearranging visual facts to create the desired effect. Compared with the tired mimetic skills that most English artists brought to their subject pictures, which depended upon easily recognizable sentiment, the Post-Impressionists had confronted experience afresh, ignored conventions and spurned the comfort provided by habitual ways of seeing. In the Post-Impressionists, Fry perceived a new expressiveness of design, a new search for structure, scale, interval and proportion. These paintings were vivid not because their sentiment was familiar but because of the freshness and directness of the means used. Nothing now was allowed to come between the artist's sensibility and his mode of expression; liberties could therefore be taken which before had only been allowable in a sketch. At a time when formality in dress and behaviour sustained a man's or woman's position in life, the informality of these paintings looked shockingly subversive, their lack of finish impolite. In their expressive vigour, they hit an English audience like a rude unwelcome shock.

To Vanessa, these pictures seemed to unleash feeling, to chart expression previously excluded from art:

It is impossible I think that any other single exhibition can ever have had so much effect as did that on the rising generation ... here was a sudden pointing to a possible path, a sudden liberation and encouragement to feel for oneself which were absolutely overwhelming. Perhaps no one but a painter can understand it and perhaps no one but a painter of a certain age. But it was as if one might say things one had always felt instead of trying to say things that other people told one to feel. Freedom was given one to be oneself and that to the young is the most exciting thing that can happen. Even the elderly caught the spirit. Sometimes one or two old painters who had plodded patiently all their lives painting as they understood they should paint, threw their petticoats, should one say, over the windmill and became comparatively honest and sensitive. Of course many did foolish things ... but that does not matter. The important thing, how important one cannot know, is that one or two perhaps who might, like the old brigade, have said their say by the age of 35, may, owing to that influx of new life and all that followed, find as did Rembrandt, Titian and Cézanne new things to say, fresh feelings to express as long as they lived. Such surely should be the fate of the artist. But in England at least he needed rescue in the early years of this century.[14]

It was not the first time that Vanessa saw the Post-Impressionists. At the New Gallery in London, which occasionally showed French art, she had been struck by a Cézanne of bare trees and houses with a pool in front. She had also seen there paintings by Degas and a small Van Gogh of flowers in a jug. But it was not until Roger Fry brought together a mass of these paintings that she perceived their honesty and freedom of expression, qualities, of course, highly valued by Bloomsbury. These French paintings confirmed her low opinion of contemporary British art. 'London knew little of Paris,' she recalled, 'incredibly little it seems now and English painters were on the whole still under the Victorian cloud, either conscientiously painting effects of light, or trying to be poets or neo-pre-Raphaelites.' Even Sickert's followers, the Camden Town Group, looked timid and tasteful in comparison with the robust vermilions in Matisse's *Girl with Green Eyes* or the fuchsia harmonies in Gauguin's Tahitian scenes. Most of the paintings on show were for sale and Clive considered buying a Cézanne of Monte Sainte-Victoire but found £400 beyond his means. He settled instead for Vlaminck's *Poissy-le-Pont*.

The effects of this exhibition reverberated throughout London society. 'That autumn of 1910', Vanessa recalled, 'is to me a time when everything seemed springing to new life – a time when all was a sizzle of excitement, new relationships, new ideas, different and intense emotions all seemed crowding into one's life. Perhaps I did not realize then how much Roger was at the centre of it all.'[15]

It was at first difficult to see much of him alone. So great were the crowds of people who pressed into the gallery, eager to see the paintings being denounced and mocked in the press, that he was constantly being called upon to explain and defend the French artists. But on a couple of occasions Vanessa and Roger went round the rooms together at a snail's speed, uncovering relations of form and meaning in each picture. She was at first a little distrustful of his theory that likeness to nature was irrelevant in art unless it contributed to the idea or emotion expressed. His attitude cut across much of the teaching she had so far received and made J. Watson Nicol's concern with exact measurement seem silly. Though Roger could be persuasively eloquent in front of paintings, he did not overwhelm her with his views but looked, waited, listened and was in no hurry to impose his own interpretation. When he did deliver an opinion it was always in such a way as allowed room for further comment. He showed her many things in art that she had not previously perceived. 'I think I can truthfully say', she reminisced, 'that I have learnt to see them, not only to know that they were there.'[16]

The man who stood at her side was tall, gaunt, his hair often dishevelled, his clothes a little awry. 'He wore good clothes badly,' Clive asserted.[17] Though he had little interest in dress, he bought the best as he thought it economical and pioneered a taste for blue shirts which he sometimes wore with a yellow pullover (on informal occasions) and his favourite Irish tweed suit. Ruffled by energy, he lacked Clive's self-conscious veneer of urbanity and made other Cambridge intellectuals look, by comparison, sedate. His difference from them at first made Vanessa a little nervous of him. When during the winter of 1910–11 he slept one night at 46 Gordon Square, he admitted in the morning that though he had slept perfectly on the *base* of the bed, the mattress had proved so intractable he had had to remove it. Vanessa still did not know him well enough to ride this complaint without embarrassment.

All the while, behind the excitement caused by the French paintings, Vanessa was experiencing acute anxiety because her new baby refused to gain weight. Each week she was tormented by the evidence of the scales. Because none of her friends had small children and Clive was terrified by the mere suggestion of illness, she had no one to turn to. Then one evening Roger came to dinner and for a few moments she was alone in his company while Clive fetched wine from the cellar. In reply to a question about the baby, she told him of her problem and he instantly understood her state of mind and offered a sympathy more intimate than any she had previously experienced. It left her aware that not only had the world of painting suddenly opened up but the possibility of human understanding seemed wider and more profound.

Despite this *éclaircissement* Roger remained throughout this winter a mystery to Vanessa:

> I had discovered something of his power of sympathy. I could see that his interest in human beings was as intense and quick as in works of art. I knew that his wife's insanity must have meant an appalling tragedy for him. But I was puzzled about his own feelings for and relationships with other human beings. Then sometimes I thought that underneath his possibly [?] ascetic exterior there were hidden immense depths of passion and emotion – sometimes I thought he had been through too much and had become almost aloof and detached from that side of life. I was not sure whether he took any interest in women as such and my own relationship with him at that time seemed to depend almost entirely upon common interests. Perhaps it was because these were so strong that they seemed to account for any amount of pleasure in our growing intimacy and companionship.[18]

By the spring of 1911 Claudian, as Vanessa's baby was now called, had recovered from his illness. Free of anxiety, she felt able to accompany Clive, Roger and Harry Norton on a trip to Turkey in April but suffered a fainting fit which delayed her and Clive's departure. When finally they arrived at Dover there was such a strong gale blowing it seemed likely their crossing would be delayed and they would miss the Orient Express. Clive urged Vanessa to return home but she refused. Once on board, the announcement of a half-hour delay in starting bred in Clive fresh despair. He implored Vanessa to admit defeat but again she ignored his pleas. When the boat eventually started he sank down on his seat with a groan and expected the worst. However the rough sea soon calmed, the boat picked up speed and they arrived at Ostend in good time, Vanessa feeling vindicated and triumphant.

Roger Fry and Harry Norton had gone on ahead and were waiting for their companions at Brussels. They had visited Ghent and in between sightseeing had played lengthy games of billiards and chess. In his spare moments Roger had also been penning anxious notes to Lady Ottoline as he had not yet got over his surprise at having taken this lady to bed immediately before his departure. He was not too unsettled, however, to take charge of all practical matters. It was he who haggled with waiters in French and German, with porters and petty officials. Clive, meanwhile, fussed over Vanessa's precarious health. She meekly followed his precautions, but inwardly exulted at finding herself abroad. 'Nothing gives one the same sense of complete irresponsibility and freedom,' she wrote happily to Virginia.[19]

She had only vague recollections of Constantinople and was delighted afresh by its beauty, likening it to a dish of soap bubbles. When they explored the streets, either on foot or in a horse and trap, she was surprised by Roger's ability to communicate directly with the natives, to uncover local customs and places of interest that more orthodox tourists never visited. His coming had been made known to certain officials but he managed to evade their invitations and only dined once at the British Embassy. Clive cut the dinner and instead wrote a long letter to Virginia. Mellowed by wine, smoking a cigar and looking across the ridge of Pera and the Bosporus, he admitted to feeling superbly Byronic:

> Today was Roger's day. Precisely what he originally intended to do I am not sure. Ultimately, we got afloat in a little skiff, with two rowers, about noon and pulled up the Sea of Marmara in a cutting cold wind, with nothing better to warm us than some slices of bread and meat and an orange. After an hour or so on the water we scrambled ashore over slimy boards and a beach of orange-peel and egg-shells. And V and R sat down on the nearest railway bank to sketch to the admiration of some twenty children and half as many adult Turks and Pharasites. Norton and I explored the walls; and then I took the train to Stamboul, went to Cooks and bought tickets for Broussa [Brusa]. . . . Now they have all returned – Roger carrying a brace of pictures as though they were partridges.[20]

On board the Greek steamer the next day they watched a swarm of boys selling newspapers, gingerbread, blankets, oil stoves, Turkish delight, shortbread and canary seed to the passengers. Once the journey began Vanessa and Roger dashed off sketches of the passengers, quickly becoming the centre of attraction; Norton sulked in his greatcoat; Clive shivered in his. A small German train took them the last part of their journey up from the sea through olive and mulberry groves, while they cheerfully lunched on oranges and bread, for only Roger could eat the canary seed. Brusa, the original Ottoman capital, is situated at the foot of Mysian Olympus and famous for its ancient monuments. The four friends put up in the Hôtel d'Anatolie and at first their holiday proceeded much as before; Vanessa and Roger sat painting together in the hills, while Clive and Harry felt rather superfluous. On one occasion the two painters were offered coffee by a Turk who also invited them into his house. There Roger painted his portrait while Vanessa executed an oil sketch of his wife, her black robes starkly outlined against a bare whitewashed wall. They could not communicate with the Turks, but Roger charmed them with his valiant efforts. The visit, however, ended disastrously, as Vanessa describes:

> We were taken to the garden to wash our hands in the well, which was quite small but deep and clear. I took off my rings, put them in my lap as I sate [sic] on the ground and when I got up one of them, a very pretty old French ring given me by Clive when we became engaged, fell into the well. It was impossible to see it or reach the bottom. The Turk brought a pane of glass and held it in the water, so making it possible to see clearly to the bottom but it could not be found. Then the wife was terribly distressed, burst into torrents of speech and finally into tears. Did she think we suspected her of anything? Of what could we suspect her? But I had to do my best to console her and the only way was by embracing her, which I am afraid wasn't very effective. However we went back to the hotel. Again I was more distressed than I could quite understand. It seemed to me as if something obscure but terrible had happened.[21]

Her sense of alarm may have been engendered by her precarious state of health. Exhausted by the travelling, sightseeing and painting, a couple of days later she fainted after lunch. Things went from bad to worse for she then suffered a miscarriage (probably the result of having conceived another child too soon after her last) which brought on a complete physical breakdown. In addition she suffered bouts of mental instability. These terrified her as she feared she was losing control of her mind.

Scant medical help was available and the Greek doctor eventually brought in was able to give little advice. It was Roger who took charge of the situation and, having nursed his wife through much more serious illness, insisted that Vanessa was in no real danger. Clive, meanwhile, was almost frantic with anxiety, and Norton was incapacitated by his obvious jealousy of Roger and dependence in his understanding of Vanessa's illness on a knowledge of animal rather than human biology. For several days Vanessa was utterly prostrate. Roger watched over her at night. When her senses revived, Vanessa often experienced panic and terror but was soothed by Roger's presence and his confident assurance that she would get better. As her health gradually returned, she grew increasingly familiar with his character, which alternately charmed, amused and irritated her. When he was able to leave her for short intervals, he returned to fill her room with clutter, with the bargains he had obtained in the bazaar, spreading out rugs and silks for her to admire as well as quick oil sketches that he had painted. He was tired by the nursing and she suffered from guilt at having ruined the holiday; but her complete dependence on him deepened their intimacy and she read in his face a new happiness.

Clive's prescient anxiety regarding this trip proved justified. 'While we are apart', he had written to Virginia, 'a good deal may happen; and I have an irrational foreboding that something will.'[22] But his foreboding had concerned Virginia with whom he was still in love. 'In your black velvet coat and hat and red-pink carnations', he had written in January of that year, 'you looked so lovely that I utterly lost my nerve and head for a time, and could only stumble through the end of a conversation and tumble silent into a taxi-cab',[23] which, for Clive, was unusual.

Virginia travelled out to Brusa to help bring Vanessa home. She was put on board the Orient Express and had recovered enough strength to enjoy the journey, most of which she spent talking with Roger. When Harry Norton got off the train at Vienna he took a sad farewell of Vanessa. On her return to London her physician Dr Wood threw doubt on whether or not she had suffered a miscarriage. He had clearly been wrong to let her make the journey and, on Roger's advice, she now changed her doctor. The new man – a Dr Lankaster – took an aggressively hearty view, told her to do as she liked and not indulge in the vapours. She decided therefore to visit Roger at Guildford.

The visit was not an entire success. At first Vanessa painted, enjoyed the peace of the countryside and won the confidence of Roger's nine-year-old daughter Pamela. She and her brother were looked after by Roger's kind but strict Quaker sister, Joan, who had been denied the education that her brother had enjoyed. She had been forty-five when allowed, for more than a week, to leave home unaccompanied. Any Edwardian 'lady' would have been daunted by Vanessa's unconventionality; for Joan Fry, who had already adjusted to a great many new experiences, Vanessa was more of a bombshell than a blessing. She regarded Vanessa's arrival as an invasion and because she, like her guest, was a person of great power, friction was inevitable. Meeting this woman, later to organize Quaker relief in Germany after the 1914–18 war, as well as allotments for the unemployed during the slump, Vanessa saw only her limitations. 'I rather pity him, poor man,' Vanessa wrote of Roger, 'when I see what his life is here, for evidently Miss Fry, though she is very nice and very fond of him and the children, is also quite stupid and sometimes rather difficult. Considering how much he enjoys the freedom of *our* society I think it's rather hard on him to have to live with people who make such freedom impossible.'[24] Meanwhile Vanessa tried to throw herself into life, as her doctor had suggested, but was troubled by the sensation that she was 'on the verge of some obscure abyss'.[25] Then suddenly she collapsed. Pamela eyed her sick state with the blank incomprehension of a child; Joan Fry did not disguise the fact that an invalid was a burden. As soon as was possible Vanessa returned to London where she saw the nerve specialist Maurice Craig, on Roger's suggestion.

She was told it might take six months before her health fully returned: in effect it took two years. During the next few months she painted hardly at all but sat or slept in deck-chairs, leading an invalid's life. In late July she took lodgings at Millmead Cottage, Guildford,* in order to be near Roger but not dependent on Joan Fry's hospitality. It seems she wanted to consolidate her position in his life. Almost certainly it was she who caused Roger, on their return from Turkey, to manufacture a row with Lady Ottoline which ended their brief affair. That summer he went to Paris, as had earlier been arranged, to meet Edith Burroughs, the wife of a former colleague of his at the Metropolitan Museum; with her he had enjoyed a mild flirtation. Again something must have been said, as when Edith came to London later that summer she met Vanessa and renounced all claim to Roger's affections. But if he was now emotionally uncommited, Roger was still legally married. Discretion necessarily surrounded his affair with Vanessa which at first was kept from Clive. Nor was Virginia told though she very quickly guessed. There were several reasons for this discretion; one was Vanessa's need for familiar affection. If Clive had failed her as a husband, he had never failed her as a friend; she had not the slightest desire to cast him off, or to put him in a position where he would be obliged to take any action that would affect their lives.

That summer England enjoyed exceptional heat, which encouraged a mood of moral laxity. 'Are you changing with the rest of the world?' Vanessa mused in a letter to Lytton.[26] She had earlier been in London at the time of the coronation, and though too weak to join the crowds watching the procession, had sent Roger a lively report:

Duncan ... thought it very beautiful, with the grey sky and charming China-men lolling back in their carriages smoking cigarettes. But perhaps he was a little prejudiced in favour of it all by his intense admiration for the Duchess of Devonshire's footman who was the most exquisite creature he had ever seen. Also the Prince of Wales stirred him a little! He doesn't seem to be changing his tastes very quickly does he? He and I have decided to emulate [Eric] Gill and paint really indecent subjects. I suggest a series of copulations in strange attitudes and have offered to pose. Will you join? I mean in the painting. We think there ought to be more indecent pictures painted. . . . I want to talk to you for several

*One painting that remains from this summer is an oil sketch of Millmead Cottage (now called The Weir House) which has previously been incorrectly titled *Adrian and Virginia Stephen on the Lawn at The Steps, Playden*. (See 'Vanessa Bell' catalogue to an exhibition at the Anthony d'Offay Gallery, London, 1973, no. 1, and 'Vanessa Bell', catalogue to an exhibition at the Davis and Long Gallery, New York, 1980, no. 2.)

weeks on end about painting and I want to enlarge upon my theories of composition in front of your paintings. They were very vague and confused when I did talk to you. Will you give me your lectures to read? I think it might be good for me and would also perhaps save me from telling you things you know already. . . . When I think about you and I begin to try to draw you, but luckily only in the air, I know the shape of all of you pretty well now – even your hands, I think I know almost as well as you know mine. I don't talk about them as much but perhaps I have felt them even more intimately.[27]

Though her marriage had been a success, it was Roger who fully unleashed Vanessa's sexual passion. In her letters to him there are none of the submissive endearments that she had earlier given Clive, but instead a teasing, provocative humour in which, if anything, she has the upper hand. She played upon the voluptuous streak in his nature. 'It is tantalizing to hear your voice at the other end of the telephone and not be able to see you,' she once wrote. 'I wanted to see you try to look disturbed when I insinuated such disturbing things as I did yesterday. It always makes a peculiar look come into your eyes which I enjoy. Have I ever told you of it? You look very much on the alert and rather wicked and your mouth takes on a very nice shape, drawn back over your teeth a little.'[28] No longer was her sexually liberated attitude mere theory. Moreover she seems suddenly to have become more aware of her sensuality and of its power. Roger accused her of flirting with Harry Norton and causing him unnecessary suffering. Vanessa affected meekness and promised in future to be kinder to men. This led to a long and revealing conversation with Sickert, as she told Roger. It was, she teased him, far easier, she had now discovered, to get on intimate terms with a man than a woman. 'Duncan is coming tonight', she confided, 'and has something private and important to say to me! He has wanted to talk to me for some time but finds it difficult to see me alone! No, you needn't wriggle and sharpen your eyes. I know what it is and it's nothing to do with me.'[29]

Roger did not fear losing her at that moment, however, for she seemed to want and need him in every way. She had surrendered to his ideas, sharing his enthusiasm for the Post-Impressionists and trying herself to paint in a new style. Mentally he was more sympathetic to her than Clive, less orientated towards literature and more actively involved in art, for he had initially trained as an artist and had painted for many years. If Clive contrived to give pleasure, Roger demanded more of every occasion. He was driven by a vision of how things should be, saw what was important and pursued it. His Quaker background had left him independent of mass opinion, given him a passion for justice and a hatred of cruelty. Because he never expected anyone to be anything but completely truthful he was inclined to be credulous. He had inordinate energy and a questing mind, also a streak of simplicity in his nature. Clive observed that he had 'the air of one who is perpetually surprised by life';[30] 'a kind of genial, yet astonished, serenity born of wisdom', wrote Osbert Sitwell.[31] He taught Vanessa to look for the genuinely felt, to spurn pretence, and encouraged her to think and feel for herself:

> Being with you [she told him] is like being on a river and being with most people is like driving a jibbing horse along a bumpy road. ... You know you have given me something quite new and very large and beautiful – both you and your character and your whole view of life – and I, who don't pretend to be so silly as not to like it, feel that it has made and will make the most tremendous difference to me to be allowed to come so near it and feel it and know it. It will make everything better for me and spoil nothing.[32]

At Seend in August she found she could now look with a painter's eye at the thick stone mullions that barred her window and imaginatively transform them into a Constantinople pattern, and the hideous fir trees in front of the house into a purple, green and yellow post-impressionist painting. But she felt more alone than usual at Cleeve House for Clive's kinship with his family instantly reasserted itself. She watched bemused as they relentlessly played lawn tennis in the hottest of weather. Wandering round the house, finding matches, ink and paper-knives laid out in every room, Bradshaw's Railway Guide, Whitaker's Almanack and the Army List in their appointed place in the hall, she was as always staggered by the prosperous efficiency with which the house was run. Roger, meanwhile, was overseeing the decoration of the dining-hall at the Borough Polytechnic, London, with large-scale post-impressionist murals by Duncan Grant and other artists. Marooned in Wiltshire, Vanessa, on impulse, showed a photograph of Roger to Mr and Mrs Bell who remarked that he looked odd and extraordinary.

After her three-week confinement at Seend, Studland in September offered many simple delights. She, Clive and the children drove round in donkey carts, received several visitors and sat on the beach. Vanessa began a large painting, *The Bathers*, in a style indebted to Maurice Denis, whose *Grandes Baigneuses*, lent by Vollard to Roger's 1910 exhibition, may have inspired her choice of subject. Three months earlier Roger had largely devoted his review of the French Salons in the *Nation* to this artist.[33] Like Denis, Vanessa composes her figures into rhythmic groups, the emphasis on silhouette showing a concern for the decorative unity of the picture surface. The figure lying down and wearing a straw boater is said to be Virginia, who visited Studland during the last week of September. The standing female on the right may represent Vanessa herself. 'I've been trying this morning on the beach to paint your subject', she told Roger, ' – the one with my colossal figure in the foreground, but it is a failure.'[34]

At Studland she regularly turned for advice on her painting to Roger, who visited as often as he could, staying with his children in nearby lodgings. Vanessa was still surprised that such an influential critic should take pleasure in her company for she often had little energy and felt troubled by egotistic broodings. In October she was left alone in London while Roger, Clive and Duncan went on a touring holiday in France. Despite her affair with Roger, she had not yet become physically estranged from Clive; in one of her letters to him she was able to unburden her mistaken fear that she might again be pregnant.

While they were away, Vanessa received a visit from Leonard Woolf, now back from Ceylon with tantalizing descriptions of its exotic colours and more natural existence. The next day Vanessa helped Virginia inspect some Adam rooms in Fitzroy Square. 'I believe elegance is becoming rather tiresome,' she announced,[35] as she took herself off in protest to Debenham's to buy green and red stockings. Colour obsessed her more and more. 'Tell Roger I am haunted by his objection to yellow green,' she informed Clive,[36] shortly before joining him in Paris where they bought a small still life by Picasso which Vanessa praised, in a letter to Virginia, for its colour.

That autumn she and Virginia decided to share the rent on a house in Sussex where they could enjoy greater freedom than life in London allowed. Clive disliked the plan and it contributed to the spell of glumness that hit him in November. He complained to Vanessa that Roger was now ever present at 46 Gordon Square; he disliked seeing so much of one visitor and observed rather bitterly that he now rarely saw her alone. Not wanting to reduce the amount of time she spent in Roger's company, Vanessa for a moment considered telling Virginia of their affair so that they could meet at Brunswick Square where her sister was now living with Adrian, Maynard and Duncan. Ironically, Roger's attentions to Vanessa had diverted Clive's away from Virginia and back to his wife, a fact that pleased Vanessa but made her situation difficult. She decided against approaching Virginia, feeling that such an act would be disloyal to Clive. Instead she agreed to keep the house emptier of visitors and thus ensure that they had more time together. In this way she diplomatically juggled her allegiances and kept her complicated loyalties intact.

It is significant that all her life Vanessa's favourite author remained Jane Austen, the novelist who specialized not just in character and action but above all in personal conduct, bringing to it a cool, controlled observation and an uncompromising morality. Vanessa herself shared the Bloomsbury attitude to morals which rested on paradox: while dismissing conventional values and behaviour, they yet remained severely judicial, employing scrupulous honesty in their evaluation of their own and others' behaviour. If their moral energy was no less rigorous than that of their parents against whom they were in reaction, they directed it, as Michael Holroyd has said,[37] not into public life like their Victorian forebears, but into their private lives, bringing an almost missionary fervour to their examination of personal relationships. Their standard was not any code of behaviour based on religion or humanist philosophy but simply a belief in the need for personal honesty. This left them suspicious of the emotionally ill-bred for there was little chance of a genuine relationship forming if a person's feelings were either false, exaggerated or uncontrolled. When Roger Fry was visited by a woman whose marriage was in ruins, he listened at length to her tale of misery and then pointed out that the logical course of action was for her and her husband to separate; when she replied that on no account would she consider breaking her marriage vows, he despaired of her ever finding happiness. Under Roger's influence, Vanessa became more firmly convinced that she should follow where her feelings led regardless of convention, that personal morality should be directed by need. Roger might have been warned of the dangers inherent in such a hedonistic attitude when he learnt that winter that Vanessa had taken a bath in Duncan's presence: 'You see he wanted to shave and I wanted to have my bath (he stayed to dinner) and he didn't see why he should move and I didn't see why I should remain dirty, and Clive was there and didn't object – and so! But I'm afraid he remained quite unmoved and I was really very decent. I felt no embarrassment and I think perhaps it was a useful precedent!'[38]

Emboldened not only in her attitude to life but also in her opinions on art, she visited the New English Art Club exhibition that winter and damned most of what she saw: Augustus John's drawings were sentimental; Steer was quite done for; Henry Lamb's paintings, deadly, academic, niggled and polished, very skilful and utterly commonplace. Now she saw how insubstantial and insidious early success could be, and wrote consolingly to Roger:

> You know it's utter nonsense for you to talk of having done everything at the wrong time of life. Really intelligent people with something in them like you and me, always are old and sedate when they're young. . . . You know painters especially often don't do anything very good till they're nearly 50. Isn't that true?[39]

In January 1912 she took a short holiday alone at Niton on the Isle of Wight, having found, on the postmaster's advice, accommodation with a Mrs Sheath at Springvale. Roger paid a three-day visit, and though he arrived feeling ill, he started painting and recovered instantly. 'I did a sketch of Roger yesterday', Vanessa told Clive, 'in Duncan's leopard manner with odd results but very like and today R is doing one of me. I've persuaded him to try the leopard technique too and he isn't at all happy in it but is spotting away industriously in the hopes of getting at something in the end.'[40] When they walked along the cliff-tops Roger dived down every bypath in his insatiable desire for interesting discoveries. He also had with him materials with which to write an article, and a book to review, Charles Holmes's *Notes on the Art of Rembrandt*, which Vanessa also read. Before the three days had ended he was on his third portrait of Vanessa, who was content to pose and not paint as she was having trouble with her eyes and now realized her need for glasses. (Two years earlier at the Moat House, Blean, her short-sightedness had caused her to mistake a group portrait of gospel preachers through the ages for the landlord's family.) She also listened to Roger's account of his one-man show at the Alpine Club Gallery, which had already sold £277 worth of his post-impressionist-inspired paintings. While he was present the Isle of Wight seemed horribly mid-Victorian and 'gardenified', Vanessa told Clive, adding, reflectively, 'Do you really want me I wonder? I am beginning to think how glad I shall be to get back to you again and to ordinary life.'[41] Already, perhaps, she found Roger's life-style a little exhausting, though her letters to him give no indication that she was tiring of his person. 'Roger, it was delicious having you all to myself for 3 whole days,' she wrote two days after he had left, 'but you're a taste that grows you know. How well we should be married to be sure.'[42] It was a safely impossible suggestion, fired perhaps by talk of Leonard Woolf's proposal to Virginia who arrived at Niton just as Roger left. The week before, Vanessa had advised Virginia by letter not to marry unless she was in love and to disregard Woolf's jewishness. 'Leonard is the only person I have ever seen whom I can imagine as the right husband for you.'[43] She expressed the same confident assertion in a letter to Leonard, trusting entirely to instinct as she knew him hardly at all. In order to get to know him better, she invited him to a house-warming party at Asheham, the Sussex house she and Virginia jointly rented that winter.

Asheham, a small early-nineteenth-century house, sits beneath Itford Hill looking across the Ouse valley to Rodmell. Though still isolated, its position is now obscured and greatly spoilt by the mounds of spoil from the chalk pits dumped at the back of the house and by the trees that now block its view across the valley. It is set back from the main Lewes to Newhaven road and reached by a farm track lined with beech trees. Though Virginia is said to have found the house in Leonard's company, Vanessa may have heard of it through the sculptor Eric Gill who lived near by at Ditchling, for in 1910 he and Epstein had proposed building a modern Stonehenge in the six acres of land that then belonged to the house, but nothing had come of this project. The house itself has a fragile, unreal appearance; its small, compact central block and two single-storey wings are pierced by tall, thin French windows with arched lights which give it more the appearance of a hunting pavilion than a farmhouse. David Garnett found it 'a little set apart, not quite of the real world, like the houses in Walter de la Mare's novels', and that under the influence of Virginia it came to suggest a 'timeless, underwater world'.[44] On it she based her short story *The Haunted House* and the belief that it is haunted still persists today. Despite the grace of the exterior, the house proved to be functional enough to accommodate a large and persistent stream of visitors once the summer had begun.

If Asheham was very much preferable to lodging-house accommodation at Studland or the Isle of Wight, it did not replace holidays abroad and in the spring of 1912 Vanessa, Clive and Roger visited Italy, stopping *en route* in Paris where they hung a small exhibition of avant-garde English art at the Galerie Barbazanges. Vanessa was pleased with the result though she thought the Camden Town artists looked weak. The gallery belonged to Percy Moore Turner who introduced them to the poet and art dealer Charles Vildrac and to the artist Henri Doucet, both of whom praised Duncan's work. That evening they all dined *chez* Vildrac. The following day they left for Milan where, to Vanessa's annoyance, she began to feel ill. They moved on to Bologna where a doctor diagnosed that Vanessa had measles and she was sent to bed. Roger again acted as nurse while Clive despaired, convinced that his wife had typhoid. The illness had one positive result: while Vanessa was bedridden, Roger brought her some coloured papers which she cut into small squares and stuck on to board, making paper mosaics. She was delighted by the brilliancy of colour this achieved and became convinced that mosaic was a medium they ought to develop. After a fortnight at Bologna, where Roger, in between his nursing duties, produced fourteen oil sketches, they moved on to Florence, abandoning their intended visit to Ravenna and Venice. Vanessa had been advised to travel as little as possible. She could not therefore accompany Clive on his day visit to Arezzo and was stung with envy on hearing his account of Piero della Francesca's frescos based on the story of the True Cross. She greatly admired this artist and catches an echo of his statuesque simplicity and contemplative mood in certain of her post-impressionist pictures.

That summer she made a breakthrough with her painting. Immediately after the close of the 1910 Post-Impressionist Exhibition she had begun to rely heavily on what Fry termed her 'slithery handwriting', freely outlining her forms in black, a technique often found in the work of Gauguin and the Nabis. What is distinctive in Vanessa's use of the dark outline is its relaxed unselfconsciousness; instead of merely encasing a shape and making it more emphatic, the line frequently breaks off and gives the impression that she was discovering the forms and shapes as she drew. This gives her early post-impressionist paintings a remarkable openness and sensitivity. As her control of this new style developed, she began to strike a balance between design and description, marrying evanescent effects of light with a concern for decorative unity. This 'impressionistic' Post-Impressionism is best seen in her paintings of Asheham; but it was a passing phase *en route* to a more solid, architectonic and abstract style. She toyed briefly with Duncan's semi-pointillist manner, but soon realized that she preferred to work in larger patches of colour, which first began to appear in *The Spanish Model* (Leicester Museums and Art Gallery) on which she was at work in June 1912. The heavily made-up model in Spanish costume had been hired by Duncan and they both painted her in his studio. Robert Ross and Charles Aitken, on a visit to Duncan's studio, saw Vanessa's painting and bought it for the Contemporary Art Society for five guineas; it was the first painting she sold.

Contemporaneously with this portrait she executed *Nursery Tea*[§], her largest painting so far and one which marks a new stage in her development. 'I have been painting my nursery scene,' she wrote to Roger, 'which is rather comic, but I am just in an exciting stage as I flatter myself that I am painting in an entirely new way (for me) ... I am trying to paint as if I were mosaicing, not by painting in spots, but by considering the picture as patches.'[45] Compared with *The Bathers* of 1911, a greater degree of abstraction now controls her design. It is held together by the compositional tensions set up between the figures and still-life objects and by the warm and cool colours placed around the central expanse of the white table-cloth. Compared with Sargent's paintings, which only a few years earlier Vanessa had greatly admired, this is a lean, conceptual painting, almost academic in its dispassionate formal organization and its deliberate eschewing of bravura or skill. The human situation presented is almost totally subordinated to abstract considerations and conveys little of her affection for her children, though it does record her delight in her younger child's colour. 'Quentin [as he was now called] is the one spot of satisfactory colour with his orange hair in a bright pink dress,' she declared. 'Someone at Studland thought he must be Winston Churchill's son, he was so like him! I hope he won't turn out to be a politician.'[46]

Since her relationship with Roger had begun, her letters to Virginia had become noticeably less intimate and informative. That summer a certain phase in their relationship was brought to a close by Virginia's marriage to Leonard Woolf. The ceremony took place in St Pancras Register Office, in a room overlooking a cemetery. Reminded by the bleak formality of the occasion that she had registered Quentin's name as Claudian and ought to have it changed, Vanessa interrrupted the proceedings to enquire how this should be done. Afterwards the handful of guests present returned to 46 Gordon Square for the wedding luncheon. When everyone had left, except for Roger and Saxon, Clive sat down and wrote a short, painful letter to Virginia, declaring his love for both her and her husband. Near by, in the same room, Roger sat painting Vanessa while Saxon looked on.

SIX

Asheham
1912–1914

While Leonard and Virginia remained on honeymoon, Vanessa took herself off to Asheham. She arrived at Lewes station on 16 August 1912 with a perambulator, bath, mail-cart, linen hamper, nine other pieces of assorted baggage, and Roger in tow. As she intended staying until winter, she immediately altered the arrangement of the house to suit her convenience; Roger, in between reading Ibsen and painting, pushed furniture around at her request. She then abandoned her London clothes in favour of loose skirts and a brightly-coloured handkerchief wound round her head. Her bohemia, however, had a respectable base; Sophie Farrell, who had left Vanessa's service to work for Virginia, provided excellent meals and with the help of a maid kept the house in good order. When Vanessa asked how long it was since she had ordered dinners from Sophie, she received the reply, 'Exactly 3 years on August 25th Miss Nessa'.[1]

Shortly before her arrival at Asheham there had been a fairly unsuccessful trip to Cologne. Desmond MacCarthy had recently returned from this city, having seen and praised the Sonderbund exhibition. As a result Clive, Vanessa and Roger set out for Germany on the evening after Virginia's wedding.

> We had the most hellish time in Cologne [Vanessa wrote to Virginia] at least all but the pictures was hellish. Why does any sane person go to Germany? . . . The pictures were good but on the whole the show was disappointing. Except for some Cézannes which Roger will probably secure for the Grafton there was nothing but what one could see elsewhere. Our hotel was comfortable and the food very good, the trains luxurious and all one's needs catered for. But the horrors are unspeakable. The country is completely coloured in mustard and pepper. The women are without exception ugly and ill-dressed. But the worst

of all is the art, which is everywhere, no house, no train is left alone. All are covered with refined German art. It got so irritating that one longed for England.[2]

The children had meanwhile been sent with their nurse Flossie to Seend. They were returned to Vanessa three days after she had arrived at Asheham and she went up to London to meet them at Paddington. Julian was overcome with delight on seeing his mother, while the two-year-old Quentin strode solemnly down the platform, making even his nurse look small. In the train to Lewes their high spirits could barely be contained and at Asheham they rolled boisterously on the mattresses that Vanessa had laid on the floor of the day nursery.

With two rumbustious boys in her care, life at Asheham, despite the external prettiness of the house, could never be elegant. More and more Vanessa found herself disliking the self-consciously artistic and earlier that year had been amazed and slightly appalled by the excessive good taste displayed by the painters Ethel Sands and Nan Hudson at Newington House in Oxfordshire. The two women entertained regularly, including among their friends Henry James, Sickert and Roger Fry. Invited with Clive for a weekend, Vanessa quickly perceived what immense care had gone into the choice of colours both in the house and garden: the grey walls offset the white lawn curtains, the rich hues in the spotless chintzes and silks, the green and purple quill pens. Even the deep plum-coloured clothes worn by the two women, and decorated with orange, grey or yellow buttons, seemed to have been chosen to match their surroundings. The pictures that hung on the walls – John drawings, eighteenth-century prints and Japanese panels – merged with the discreet, expensive restraint that governed the whole, while outside pale grey and green tubs held flowers specially selected for the colour of their blooms. Vanessa wondered what would happen if a small child were let loose in the house for, though she preferred it to the philistinism at Seend, she felt that the perfectionism of the two friends lacked a creative freedom; they muffled or drove out feeling in pursuit of the refined. 'It isn't what we want even for the minor arts is it,' she complained to Roger when he proposed involving Ethel and Nan in his scheme, that had already begun to form, for the Omega Workshops, '... I do think we shall have to be careful, especially in England where it seems one can never get away from this fatal prettiness. Can't we paint stuffs etc which won't be gay and pretty?'[3]

At Asheham her first concern was to make it habitable for her family and friends. After Roger departed she spent the first week alone with the children and servants, making red curtains with mauve lining and borders for one room and at intervals attempting, unsuccessfully, to teach Julian to read. Roger returned the following weekend and with his help she got to work on the garden. He cut down a holly-bush and fir-tree to improve the view and make room for badminton which Vanessa now instituted. She planted flowers which her new sheep-dog – a replacement for Gurth – promptly dug up. Her only neighbours were an old shepherd and his wife, Mr and Mrs Funnell, whom she employed to pump water for the house and to empty the earth closets. Each day she wrote to Clive, who was on a shooting holiday in Scotland, detailing the small activities that occupied her time. She also discussed with him whether or not to sell their Augustus John which Robert Ross thought the art gallery at Johannesburg would (and did) buy for the considerable sum of £600. She was inclined to accept their offer, preferring to use the money to buy a modern French picture. 'I wish we could get a Cézanne. It would be a great thing to have one in England.'[4] Meanwhile the heavy rains, which had earlier that month ruined the crops in the area, ceased and the warm weather returned. Vanessa began to paint, now and then basked in the sun or walked with Julian to the top of the Downs for a view of the sea.

Her first visitors, apart from Roger, were Frederick Etchells and his sister Jessie. Frederick had become friendly with Duncan the previous summer when he had contributed to the decoration of the Borough Polytechnic. His friendship with Duncan and Roger, together with his interest in modern French painting (he frequently travelled to Paris in the company of Wyndham Lewis) should have made him sympathetic to Vanessa, but his visit was not a success. She found him slow-witted and uncouth; he irritated her by bringing a book to meals and interrupting the talk by reading aloud passages; in conversation he was long-winded, in behaviour ungallant; only after she herself had seized the size and whiting was he shamed into assisting with the layout of the badminton court. In an atmosphere that must have been thick with antagonism as well as the smell of oils, Vanessa painted them painting, Jessie seated on the floor, Frederick standing at an easel outlined against an open French window (Tate Gallery). To reinforce form, she omitted all detail, including facial features. The view of the garden seen through the window is reduced to flat bands of colour that seem to negate the suggestion of space, so that the distant white wall appears to be on the same plane as Frederick's dark figure. Cool greens counterbalance hot orange and yellow ochre, while one of Vanessa's red and mauve curtains creates an emphatic vertical and picks up the red of Jessie's stockinged leg.

During their visit Mr Funnell suddenly announced that not only would he no longer pump the water but that the pump itself was broken. Clive, who had arrived from Scotland, immediately despaired and announced that the children should straightway return to London. Roger and Frederick, meanwhile, went to investigate and within ten minutes had the pump working again, and more effectively than before. Clive was so cheered by this that he promptly employed a farmhand to pump water each morning.

Apart from the Etchellses, most visitors fitted in well with the arrangements at Asheham and Vanessa found she got to know several of her friends on more intimate terms. Duncan came for a weekend and stayed for almost two weeks; Maynard Keynes appeared and Vanessa enjoyed his company more than she had ever done before. Another guest, and one who was to remain a life-long friend of Vanessa's, was Molly MacCarthy. She had been born Mary Warre-Cornish, the daughter of the Vice-Provost of Eton and was, like Vanessa, the niece through marriage of 'Aunt Anny', Lady Ritchie. In 1906 she had married the conversationalist and literary critic, Desmond MacCarthy, and for the first few years of their married life they had lived in a Suffolk farmhouse. In 1910, however, they moved into a house in Wellington Square, Chelsea, and from then on Molly became a part of Bloomsbury's inner core. But whereas Maynard had been drawn to Asheham by Duncan's presence, Molly came primarily to see Clive who employed all his verbal skill to turn cartwheels in her presence. He was stimulated by her paradoxical character, by her combination of oblique humour and reserve, by a certain primness that was at odds with her original mind and gifts as a novelist. Molly, it seems, was undecided this summer how far their flirtation should go. It did not trouble Vanessa who remarked to Virginia: 'Molly's visit was quite successful, though she and Clive did not have all the tête-à-têtes they had hoped for. She is very nice and amusing, the worst of her being an unexpected moral sense which crops up suddenly and is rather tiresome.'[5] Molly remained a central figure within Bloomsbury but this association did not ease the conflict within her character, as a conversation that she had with Vanessa the following year in Gordon Square suggests. 'She and I sat and talked rather aimlessly about marriage, etc,' Vanessa recounted to Clive, 'as she generally does now, but it is always more or less in the abstract unluckily. I think she is rather worried about the subject and said how she thought I managed so well and she didn't know how to – and how one couldn't deceive those one loved, etc.'[6] At Asheham, in the summer of 1912, even Duncan found Molly's restraint an invisible barrier to free speech: 'She is we all thought very nice, but it was rather a strain on our tongues which had wagged rather free before.'[7]

Other visitors included Saxon, Sydney Waterlow, a Cambridge intellectual and friend of Clive, Oliver Strachey (brother of Lytton), Harry Norton, Adrian Stephen, and Violet Dickinson. The last, for once, got on well with Clive and amused him by asking Vanessa dozens of questions without waiting for any replies. Most visitors seemed unable to leave, for under Vanessa's influence life at Asheham was relaxed and full of ease. Even Clive stopped complaining of its dankness and agreed that they should keep on the rent. Apart from badminton there was little entertainment provided and Vanessa left her guests entirely to themselves; on a hot September day Oliver Strachey and Norton were left unmolested to discuss aesthetics indoors with all the windows closed. Vanessa's capacity to create an almost tangible atmosphere of freedom aroused Roger's wonder:

> I imagine all your gestures [he wrote] and how you'll be saying things and how all around you people will dare to be themselves and talk of anything and everything and no idea of shame or fear will come to them because you're there and they know you'll understand. And then I think of how beautifully you'll be walking about the rooms and how you'll take Quentin on to your knee and how patient you are and yet how you are just being yourself all the time and not making any huge effort just living very intensely and naturally and how perfectly reasonable you are (except when one muddles with your pictures) and yet how your being so reasonable is never dull or monotonous or too much expected and is in fact much more exciting to me than if you were all whims and caprices like the professionally seductive.[8]

Her ability to put others at their ease reflects her own inner content. At Asheham she appears to have rid life entirely of all those remaining impediments that prevented complete freedom of existence. From the photographs of this period, showing the children running naked in the garden and Vanessa made even more statuesque by the simple line of her plain clothes, one catches a glimpse of a gloriously casual existence, made possible by the accord with which all her faculties – maternal, mental, sexual and artistic – flowed together. Now in her early thirties, she was at the height of her beauty; moreover the sensuality that she radiated was combined with an unusual strength of character. Remembering her at this age, Leonard Woolf declared:

> Vanessa was, I think, usually more beautiful than Virginia. The form of her features was more perfect, her eyes bigger and better, her complexion more glowing. If Rupert [Brooke] was a goddess's Adonis, Vanessa in her thirties had something of the physical splendour which Adonis must have seen when the goddess suddenly stood before him. To many people she appeared frightening and formidable, for she was blended of three goddesses with slightly more of Athene and Artemis in her and her face than of Aphrodite. I myself never

found her formidable partly because she had the most beautiful speaking voice that I have ever heard, and partly because of her tranquillity and quietude. (The tranquillity was to some extent superficial; it did not extend deep down in her mind, for there in the depths there was also an extreme sensitivity, a nervous tension which had some resemblance to the mental instability of Virginia.) There was something monumental, monolithic, granitic in most of the Stephens. . . . There was a magnificent and monumental simplicity in Thoby which earned him his nickname The Goth. Vanessa had the same quality expressed in feminine terms. . . . It was the strange combination of great beauty and feminine charm with a kind of lapidification of character and her caustic humour which made her such a fascinating person.[9]

She had also inherited the Stephens' dedication to work and at Asheham, despite its relaxed ambience, never lapsed into inactivity. Clive, after scything nettles, mowing the badminton lawn, entertaining his children and finally settling down to contemplate what was to be his most famous book *Art*, thought the combination of physical and intellectual work made for a 'blameless, humdrum existence'. Asheham encouraged work and thought and much of their discussion that summer concerned the forth-coming Second Post-Impressionist Exhibition which Roger was preparing for the Grafton Galleries to open in November. This time an English selection was to be included, selected by Clive, also a Russian contingent chosen by Boris Anrep. Vanessa and Duncan were both to exhibit and certain of the paintings done at Asheham that summer would have been executed with this forthcoming show in mind.

Working beside Duncan at Asheham, Vanessa began more and more to see her painting in relation to his; after three days spent working on the same still life, she perceived how dull hers was by comparison. Yet she was not uncritical of his art and was constantly on the look-out for any suggestion that he was failing to fulfil his initial promise. 'It's too awful if everyone turns out a failure,' she once declared, 'and if even Duncan at his age is already going for less fine things than he did.'[10] At one point she thought he had never done anything as good as *Lemon Gatherers* (Tate Gallery) which she had bought; she also considered his *Queen of Sheba* (Tate Gallery), which he sent to the Second Post-Impressionist Exhibition, rather sweet in conception and limited. 'I thought that the usual English sweetness was coming in and spoiling all.'[11] All this summer she resisted falling a prey to his skill and charm and in September claimed positive independence in a letter to Roger: 'I find that I am not now much impeded by working with Duncan although of course I always think why didn't I see it like that. But as I have come to the conclusion that I didn't see it like that I no longer try to think I did.'[12]

One painting which stylistically can be dated to the autumn of 1912 is *Landscape with Haystack, Asheham*[S]. It boldly exhibits her point of view, having a monumentality that is hers and not Duncan's. If Monet had made the haystack an object of study, Vanessa uses it to underline the difference between Impressionism and Post-Impressionism, for here the effect is entirely dependent on form and design, the colours being restricted, as in *Iceland Poppies*, to a subdued range of greens and greys, warmed only by a touch of orange. One characteristic peculiar to her vision at this time is the use of flattened but full, boldly encompassing forms.

It was she who suggested that the advertisement for the Second Post-Impressionist Exhibition should show a fashionable lady looking with horror at the announcement of the forthcoming event. Duncan took up the idea and designed the poster in a semi-cubist style. As the opening date approached, tension mounted. 'Roger is in the thick of it all and the troubles are beginning,' Vanessa informed Leonard who had agreed to act as exhibition secretary on his return from honeymoon.

> Pictures and hangings won't arrive but that's all inevitable. Duncan has done the poster which is rather fine. We expect a lively autumn with visits from Matisse and Vildrac and other distinguished foreigners. I am also proposing to give 3 evening parties to introduce young women to the house. Once introduced it is hoped that Clive will find no difficulty in doing the rest.[13]

Five days later she journeyed to London with certain of her and Duncan's paintings to help Roger hang the show. Duncan, meanwhile, admitted nervously to Maynard: 'I have been working like hell to get something finished for the Grafton show which opens next week. I do nothing but ruin what I have already done which drives me to distraction. A great many of the French painters have already come and are very interesting. The Matisses are radiantly beautiful.'[14]

Matisse dominated the Second Post-Impressionist Exhibition for he was better represented than any other artist and his first version of *The Dance* (Museum of Modern Art, New York) fitted one wall in the end gallery. It was Matisse's vibrant colour and bold reductionism of form that had most influence on Vanessa and she, Duncan and Roger must have had his *The Dance* in mind when in April 1914 they decorated the hall of Roger's Guildford house with three life-size nudes[S]. This second exhibition was much more up to date than the first; Picasso was now represented by certain of his analytical cubist paintings, Derain, Marchand, Vlaminck and others by recent work. The Russian section was a mixed success, containing work by several painters associated with the semi-mystical World of Art Group whose symbolist productions Roger found too literary and romantic for his taste. The English section was also uneven and was made to look derivative by comparison with the dazzling assurance of the French. But even the French section contained work of unequal importance. The four paintings bought from this show by Hilton Young (later Lord Kennet) and which still remain with his family – a Marchand, two Chabauds and a Lhôte – reflect the kind of lesser work interspersed between the Picassos and Matisses, while Villette's *Bois Colombes* (private collection), then in Roger Fry's possession and which he must have admired for its naïve vigour, clumsily imitates Van Gogh. It was not, however, these artists whom the critics attacked.

Paul Nash argues in his autobiography *Outline* that it was the deformation of the human figure which made this show painful and incomprehensible. Matisse and Picasso were the worst offenders, and the more philistine element in the British press reviled them at length. The *Morning Advertiser* found in Matisse's *Conversation* a 'wholesale abnegation of technique' and said of Picasso's *Le Bouillon Kub*, 'If a satire upon the cubist formula it is inimitable; if anything else it is unintelligible.' Post-Impressionism, it declared, was a suicidal development and one that could not last.[15] The newness of this art also partly explains the adverse critical reaction: only four years previously Bernard Berenson had come to Matisse's defence in the American *Nation*; England was now not very far behind in critical appreciation. Nevertheless even the cultivated A. J. Finberg, the authority on Turner and English watercolour painting, turned a scornful eye on this show, arguing that most of the paintings were 'vapid, empty, stupid and above everything dull', and that those by Picasso consisted 'merely of lines and angles with a few touches of dirty grey and brown tones'.[16] Among the English artists, Duncan received the most praise for his *Pamela* and *Queen of Sheba*, the latter satisfying the English love of literary appeal. His *The Countess*, however, was compared by the *Observer* critic, P. G. Konody, to 'Matisse at his silliest'. 'Mrs Bell's *Asheham*', he continued, 'belongs to the inlaid linoleum type of Post-Impressionist landscape; whilst in her *Nosegay* she is so bent upon searching for non-existing angles that the flowers look as if they had been badly cut out of paper.'[17]

Roger Fry saw in Post-Impressionism two important developments: expression released from the tyranny of representation and, in the work of Picasso for example, a search for 'the intellectual abstract of form'.[18] This emphasis on the constructive aspect of Post-Impressionism explains why in this show Cézanne, with his 'pure structural design',[19] had been chosen to represent the older generation of painters. What unified both tendencies was the desire to create not an illusion of but an equivalent to life. Despite the evident distortions in a picture like Matisse's *The Dance*, his art, Fry argued, convinces us of its reality by 'the continuity and flow of his rhythmic line, by the logic of his space relations, and, above all, by an entirely new use of colour'.[20] Though Roger Fry always stressed in his lectures the social and economic background to artistic production, he came more and more to believe that great art, like that of Matisse, belonged to the timeless realm of the imagination. Post-Impressionism was for him an appeal to the imagination, not through the imitation of nature, but through the rhythm of line and harmony of colour.

In lectures, articles and catalogue introductions Roger energetically argued the case for Post-Impressionism. As the excitement and furore increased during the course of this second exhibition, it began to seem necessary to find some unifying aesthetic that would give the new art theoretical respectability. The publishers Chatto and Windus had earlier asked Fry to consider writing a book on Post-Impressionism but as he was now more interested in preparing his scheme for the Omega Workshops, he suggested that Clive should undertake it. The result was *Art*, published in 1914, in which Clive drew upon many of Roger's ideas. It was the first book published in England to propound a cogent, easily understandable formalist theory of art. It became something of a manifesto for the English post-impressionist movement and, as its author later admitted, a whiff of propaganda emanates from many of its pages. Vanessa was not only present on the many occasions when Roger and Clive discussed aesthetics, but she also read *Art* in both manuscript and proof forms, herself correcting some of its errors. Its basic tenets provided the theoretical standpoint which she clung to all her life.

Clive's aim, in writing this book, had been to look for that essential quality in all works of art that distinguishes them from other objects. By page 8 he had discovered it to be 'significant form' – 'lines and colours combined in a particular way, certain forms and relations of forms, [which] stir our aesthetic emotions'. At the time this oversimplification seemed a refreshing and urgently needed antidote to the sentimental miasma that clung to the confectionery English art of the day. Clive rightly perceived that paintings with sentimental subjects used form 'not as an object of emotion, but as a means of suggesting emotions', and that this emotion was often false because 'it suggests . . . not pity and admiration but a sense of complacency in our own pitifulness and generosity'. With, surprisingly, an almost Ruskinian fusion of ethics and aesthetics, Clive insisted that the moral value of art was related to its aesthetic excellence: trivial story-telling in paint not only offended the eye, it was also nugatory. That which he admired in great primitive cultures was 'absence of representation, absence of technical swagger, sublimely impressive form'. His theory justified and encouraged Vanessa's crude blocking out of form in her pictures, for suddenly much that had formerly been put into art could now be left out. Once when she and Roger were obliged to make love in inhospitable surroundings, she pointed out that, as in a Matisse painting, they were forced to consider only the things that mattered.

In January 1913 the Second Post-Impressionist Exhibition ran for an extended period in slightly altered form (a large display of Cézanne's water-colours were sent from Paris by Bernheim-Jeune). Vanessa, meanwhile, returning to her own work, sometimes fell into despair. She told Roger:

> I have been doing designs with Duncan all day, and his are much better than mine and I'm rather depressed. His are so gay and lively – mine rather dull and stupid. I want you to tell me if they have any good in them after all ... and then Duncan's colour – oh, it's long since I've been so depressed by working with him. Do you know I am still overcome by thinking of that Giotto. It has been before me all day. My God, how divine. I see it does the whole thing. ... It also makes me feel how little one can analyse one's feelings before really great art. One is simply lifted into a different life and carried off in it. ... And why doesn't *that* depress one? It doesn't. In fact I feel if one can have these things to see it doesn't the least matter what one does oneself. It's enough that they should be in the world and one's lucky to see it.[21]

If Giotto consoled, Duncan continued to unsettle her. His style was more eclectic than hers, absorbing inspiration from many sources: from visits to Ravenna in 1910 and Tunis and Sicily in 1911, from literature and the theatre, from pointillist and cubist paintings and from the African influence in the art of Picasso. His natural talent as painter and designer had recently overflowed into murals, in the Borough Polytechnic, in the house he shared with others at Brunswick Square and in Maynard's rooms in King's College, Cambridge. He employed a richer palette than Vanessa and his line was animated by a more complex and varied sense of rhythm, often creating vibrant surface decoration. While she hewed out blocks in her compositions, he seemed to dance with mocking lightness over the canvas, touching in patches of shimmering colour.

A similar gaiety guided his character; he had an almost childlike delight in the absurd, the fantastic or unexpected. With his agile mind he never became a victim of habit but seemed to improvise according to the situation. Angelica Garnett has recalled how 'objects in his hands seemed constantly alive, never simply things; just as repeated actions never bored him but became a source of reiterated pleasure'.[22] He also had very good manners and exquisite pronunciation, and with just a few words could win over the most difficult of matrons. Few remained impervious to his insouciance and his ability to discover in everything either an amusing element or a source of wonder and surprise. The delightful originality of his mind made him particularly attractive to the highly educated; both Lytton Strachey and Maynard Keynes had been bewitched by Duncan, and not just by his grey-blue eyes, dark hair and sensuous good looks. His passionate interest in painting left his character free of constraint; he seemed devoid of petty egotism, entirely without an axe to grind, untroubled by practicalities. He could on occasion be melancholy and downcast but was never dissatisfied, never expecting from circumstances more than they had to give. Keenly perceptive, he had given Lytton the impression that he was a genius. Though he was frank about his homosexuality among Bloomsbury, he once complained to Maynard that, being 'sodomitical', he had to hide his philosophy of life from most people. Despite this training in reserve, his emotions were often dangerously close to the surface and once when Adrian Stephen abused the Stracheys in his presence he burst into tears. He was proud but never arrogant. Though he had taken part in the 1910 'Dreadnought Hoax', and like Adrian, Virginia and others had dressed up as an Abyssinian and boarded the largest and most modern battleship in the Royal Navy, when certain officers came to take their revenge and whisked him off to Hampstead Heath, intending to cane him, his lack of resistance unmanned them, turned their fury to embarrassment and resulted in his only receiving two ceremonial taps. His marked unworldliness, his casual and often shabby dress, as well as his habit of blinking when he spoke, meant that, like Prince Myshkin, he could sometimes be mistaken for an idiot. To entertain others he did sometimes play the fool but underneath was wily and knowing. To some extent his gentle manner and uninsistent courtesy were deceptive, for they veiled subtle and audacious reasoning. With beguiling simplicity and no apparent display of effort, Duncan usually got what he desired.

An only child, he had been brought up in India and Burma where his father, Major Bartle Grant, was posted. He was exceptionally close to his mother whose good looks he had inherited, and all her life he wrote to her and visited her regularly. At the age of nine he had been sent to England to be educated, first at Hillbrow preparatory school, then at St Paul's in London, and had lived first with his grandmother at Chiswick, later with Lytton's parents, his aunt and uncle, Sir Richard and Lady Strachey. As a child he had first begun to draw because he wanted to record all the trappings that accompanied army weddings. At school he seemed impervious to organized education, and Lady Strachey, perceiving that his real love was painting, allowed him to leave St Paul's early and attend Westminster School of Art. Simultaneously Simon Bussy, the French artist who had married his cousin Dorothy Strachey, advised him to copy the Old Masters, to acquire the habit of working daily and to develop an imaginative understanding of form.

From the start of his career Duncan gained more sustenance from Italian and French art than from native traditions. He had copied in the Branacci Chapel and the Uffizi in Florence, and in the Louvre while studying under Charles Cottet, Lucien Simon and Jacques-Emile Blanche at the last's studio, 'La Palette'. From early maturity Duncan exhibited a self-protective ability to close his mind to things and people he either disliked or did not need. In Paris he felt an instinctive aversion towards Wyndham Lewis despite his intriguing ideas. He also temporarily chose to ignore Matisse whose *Bonheur de vivre* caused an outcry at the Salon des Indépendants in 1906. After one of his friends had drawn a sketch of this picture, Duncan saw that it had nothing in common with the Chardin he was copying and therefore did not go to see it. When a little later he saw the Matisses in Gertrude and Leo Stein's collection he felt them to be 'so beyond anything I was used to'[23] that he did not permit them to affect his own work. The most modern French painting that he admired at this time was Degas's *Interior* (Coll: Henry P. McIlhenny, Philadelphia) which he saw among a collection of Impressionist paintings at Durand-Ruel's. In this the tension set up in the shadowy room between the dressed figure of the man and the half-dressed figure of the woman caused several writers who had known Degas personally to aver that the title of this painting should be *The Rape*. Duncan's own interest in psychological drama emerged in 1909 in his painting *Le Crime et le Châtiment* (Tate Gallery) in which Marjorie Strachey sits with her head in her hands having just completed Dostoevsky's novel of the same title. Partly due to the Stracheys' influence, Duncan was himself unexpectedly well read. While in Paris he devoured, among other things, *Tristram Shandy*, Shakespeare, Molière and Conrad.

Despite his obstinate refusal to look at modern French art in 1906-7, his response to the Post-Impressionists in October 1910 was dramatic. Earlier that year he had completed a suave portrait of his cousin James Strachey (Tate Gallery) in a naturalistic style, bringing careful control of drawing and tone to his likeness of this elegant young man. Before two years had passed, however, he was exhibiting in the Second Post-Impressionist Exhibition *The Tub* (Tate Gallery), in which all the skills found in the former painting are noticeably absent. Instead of modelling form, he employs flat areas of colour, simple outline drawing and crude hatching to delineate the figure and the furnishings, the whole having an expressive vigour and decorative strength which the earlier painting lacks. Vanessa had watched this startling, revolutionary development and on several occasions had sat painting at his side. As we have seen, she tended to partner herself aesthetically with others and now found that as her interest in Duncan's painting grew, she was increasingly engaged by his personality and natural charm.

At Christmas of 1912 she fell ill with exhaustion and was unable to accompany Clive and the children to Seend. She remained in London and spent Christmas Day in the company of Duncan and Adrian, reading passages aloud from her father's *Mausoleum Book*. The next day Duncan reappeared, lay on the floor, discussed what they had read the evening before and advised her to decorate her studio like a tropical forest, with red figures, birds of paradise and blue ceiling, and to hang up curtains of different colours as a protest against the darkness and gloom of London in winter. But it was Roger, and not Duncan, who then stepped in while Clive was away and helped nurse Vanessa back to health.

The difference in age between Duncan and Roger amounted to almost twenty years. Vanessa, though six years older than Duncan, felt herself his contemporary and more often compared her paintings with his than with Roger's. The praise others bestowed on Duncan only served to sharpen the focus of her attention. 'Duncan's art is supposed to be improving', she told Virginia in February 1913, ' – and I think his latest works are very good. There is hope after all that he may be the long looked for British genius.'[24] There were also certain similarities in their natures: Duncan was deeply sensuous, his passions chiefly physical and uncomplicated, and, like Vanessa, he was without shame. Never to be ashamed was one of Duncan's favourite maxims, as Angelica Garnett has recounted;[25] Vanessa, when once asked in conversation what was the meanest action she had ever committed, was obliged to admit, 'I couldn't think of any, not because I'm a saint, but because I never think of them again once they're committed.'[26] Duncan's morality was still more self-centred. In the above-quoted essay, Angelica Garnett declared, 'Duncan was a consummate egotist, with a clarity of vision that is rare, doing neither more nor less than he wanted.' Like Proust, he believed that an artist is under an obligation to live for himself. Many years later Duncan confessed in a letter to Helen Anrep that he had once shocked Lady Ottoline by declaring selfishness the one great human virtue.

At Asheham Vanessa had established a life-style that suited her nature: unhurried, untrammelled, purposeful, sensual and free. There Roger, with his faster pace, blinding enthusiasms and sudden spells of irrational pessimism, occasionally jarred on her nerves. Duncan, less emphatic and more adaptable, slipped easily into her ambience, making no plans but staying as long as the weather and present company permitted.

In May 1913, when Duncan accompanied by Vanessa, Clive and Roger on a holiday to Italy, it soon became obvious that it was he and not Roger with whom she felt most accord. On this occasion they managed to see the mosaics at Ravenna and visit Venice, and stopped also at Padua, Urbino, Spoleto, Nemi, Arezzo and Rome. Vanessa was disappointed by Venice and disliked Urbino, but on the whole the holiday was a success and the two wooden figures that Duncan bought from an exquisitely beautiful Italian called Dante Paradiso still hang in Charleston studio. The flavour of the trip is caught in a letter Vanessa wrote to Virginia from wet and cold Urbino, with its dour and hostile people and dirty hotel:

> You can imagine the activities and otherwise of the party. Roger is up with the lark, does many sketches, sees all the sights and he and Clive are indefatigable in their attributions and historical discoveries. I can't say I listen to much and after Padua I stuck at sightseeing and now refuse to see more than about one thing a day. I find that Duncan sympathizes with me and if he and I had the conduct of the party in our hands, we should settle down somewhere for a month and spend most of our time loafing. Perhaps it's as well we can't. We have seen today one of the best pictures in the world, a very beautiful Piero della Francesca [*The Flagellation*] and so it has been worth staying here in spite of all the horrors of the place. One of my principal amusements is reading Roger's family letters which throw an amazing light on their lives and characters.[27]

This Italian holiday probably made apparent to Roger what Vanessa had already half-jokingly insinuated; when in February he had visited the academic, Melian Stawell, who was very obviously in love with him, Vanessa had teasingly written, 'But you may be in Melian's arms when you get this and I, alas, am not in Duncan's, but all alone in the depths of Sussex.'[28] But at first she did not fully comprehend the nature of her feelings for Duncan and never presumed that any could be returned. Duncan was in love with her brother Adrian, strongly attracted to the schoolteacher and mountaineer George Mallory and, in passing, to a number of other men. Vanessa was surrounded, as she was all too aware, by homosexuals; when Maynard Keynes, a former lover of Duncan's, took the rent of Asheham temporarily in the spring of 1914, she wrote:

> Did you have a pleasant afternoon buggering one or more of the young men we left for you? It must have been delicious out on the downs in the afternoon sun – a thing I have often wanted to do but one never gets the opportunity and the desire at the right moment. I imagine you, however, with your bare limbs entwined with his and all the ecstatic preliminaries of sucking sodomy – it sounds like the name of a station. . . . How divine it must have been. I hope you didn't make your throat worse as you lay in that delicious drowsy state afterwards on the turf. Perhaps this is all imaginary however and it really took

place in a bedroom. I wonder whose? Not Gerald's at any rate for one really couldn't have the heart to disarrange his exquisitely tight trousers. I hope they got brushed before he returned. Well it was a very nice interlude and I felt singularly happy and free tongued.[29]

Her freedom with words did not parallel her behaviour. Though she did shake free the upper part of her clothing and danced naked to the waist at one of the frenzied pre-war parties, it is unlikely that she copulated with Maynard Keynes in public on the sofa at Brunswick Square as it was improbably rumoured. On the whole their high spirits were more chaste than their talk led people to suppose. A great deal of dressing-up went on, inspired partly by the recent success of the colourful and exotic Russian Ballet, and at one fancy-dress ball Roger arrived as a Brahmin, Duncan as a whore great with child. Duncan gave frequent midday champagne parties in Brunswick Square, depleting Maynard's store of champagne as the latter discovered one evening when he invited the politicians Austen Chamberlain and Reginald McKenna to dinner.

At certain moments Vanessa came close to shedding civilization entirely. In August 1913 a camp was organized at Brandon in Norfolk by the four daughters of the Fabian socialist and civil servant, Sir Sydney Olivier, all of whom delighted in the outdoor life and in the poetry of their friend Rupert Brooke. Vanessa had collectively nicknamed them the 'neo-Pagans'. Vanessa, Clive, Molly MacCarthy, Maynard and Roger agreed to take part and at the last moment before they set out, Duncan also arrived at Gordon Square, wearing paint-stained clothes and a spotless white hat, clutching various packages, a collapsing easel and stool, and a bottle of champagne. For some the conditions of the camp were scarcely bearable; Clive never forgot the discomfort he endured; Molly appeared like a fish out of water and soon returned home with a cold. Vanessa, on the other hand, though she slept in a nearby farmhouse and not in a tent, found the simple life very much to her liking and sat guard over Roger's excellent chicken stew flavoured with apple and mint like a rustic peasant, full of ancient earthy wisdom. 'They were all very friendly and easy', she told Virginia,

and I found it possible to adopt a pleasant grandmotherly attitude towards them. In fact I got the reputation of 'running on' without ceasing all day and every day, and I don't think I ever have talked so much before in my life. I lectured them on life and morals and I only hope it did them good but the young are very crude aren't they? It will take years before they really reach our point of mature wisdom, and of course they haven't had any of the experiences we had had at their age.[30]

On her return to London she engaged in a spell of hard work for the Omega Workshops. Founded earlier that year with Roger, Vanessa and Duncan as co-directors, the venture had officially opened in July with a display at 33 Fitzroy Square which housed both workshops and show-room. Roger's aim was to provide young artists with the opportunity to earn some money and to allow the influence of Post-Impressionism to invigorate decoration. The Omega agreed to almost any commission, be it for murals, mosaics, stained-glass windows or garden pots. It sold painted furniture and any item capable of some form of surface decoration, as well as fabrics, rugs and carpets made to artists' designs, pottery and stuffs brought back from Turkey and Italy, and some brightly-patterned cloth made by Foxtons in Manchester for the African market. Roger admired the freshness and spontaneity found in primitive and peasant work and encouraged the 'family' of artists which he attracted to the Omega to follow an impulse towards free expression. As such the venture was a demonstration of his generosity; it gave a number of young artists such as Frederick Etchells, Gaudier-Brzeska, Edward Wadsworth and others the chance to experiment boldly, even, as in the case of Wyndham Lewis, to contradict him and discover their own preferences.

Surprisingly, the results had a remarkable homogeneity, mainly through the use of pure colour. The Omega scorned the Edwardian taste for pastel shades and matching tones; it flung reds, greens, blues and purples across table tops and on to screens. Duncan painted one screen with blue sheep against an orange ground; Vanessa decorated another with a semi-cubist memory of Brandon camp, with green figures resting outside tents[§]. In both, design and colour had a violence that even today looks inharmonious amid the restrained asceticism often equated with good taste. Anti-taste, anti-refinement, anti-expense, Omega products were a shocking intrusion upon the English love of prettiness. Rarely have the applied arts in England displayed such unabashed creativity. Moreover at their best the designs and decorations had a crispness and dynamic elegance that was in advance of its day. The fabrics, in particular, had a refreshing openness and sim-plicity, Vanessa herself designing two, entitled 'Maud' and 'White'.

It seems probable that Vanessa played an important psychological role in the Omega. Her newly-won independence and willingness to experi-ment boldly may have helped stimulate the exchange of ideas among the other artists. Her tall figure cut a commanding presence and her deep voice and slow speech, together with her unhurried calm, made a striking impression on the young assistant Winifred Gill. (Will Arnold-Foster, who had studied painting at the Slade, once declared that Vanessa had only to enter a room to change it completely, to make things – as Virginia put it

– 'real, and large, and infinitely composed and profound'.[31]) As she had earlier decorated the nursery at Gordon Square with stalking lions, zebras and jaguars pouncing on deer, it was almost certainly due to her suggestion or example that the Omega, during the winter of 1913–14, displayed a prototype nursery, its walls decorated with a tropical landscape and an elephant made out of cut paper, in a style that anticipated Matisse's paper cut-outs. The design even spread on to the ceiling because, as one reporter was told, small infants spend a lot of time on their backs.

Throughout the second half of 1913 Vanessa was fairly constantly involved with the Omega. In the summer she painted one of the three panels to decorate the Ideal Home Exhibition room that autumn; they were based on the Russian Ballet, largely inspired by Matisse's first version of *The Dance* (which had been included in the Second Post-Impressionist Exhibition) and were said by Marjorie Strachey to be hideous enough to attract the attention of the police. In Roger's company Vanessa went down to Mitcham and learnt to throw pots, though she proved less good at making than at decorating them. In Roger's absence that autumn she took over the management of the Workshops; after a row with Wyndham Lewis concerning the decoration of a room for the Ideal Home Exhibition in the autumn of 1913, it was Vanessa who acquired a letter from the *Daily Mail* that effectively cleared Roger's name. It was she, too, who tried to persuade Etchells, who had left with Lewis, that the disagreement had resulted from a mistake. By December 1913 she had poured so much of her energy into the Omega that she felt it was having an adverse effect on her painting; for a period she withdrew and only decorated items that could be done at home. In the spring of 1914, however, she became involved in designs for Lady Ian Hamilton's house, No 1 Hyde Park Gardens, and executed a mosaic pavement for the hallway, using the design she had originally submitted for the stained-glass window. Vanessa also played her part in attracting patrons. Clive's father had promised financial support on first hearing of the venture, but renegued after a visit to the Second Post-Impressionist Exhibition. Lady Ottoline promised to order a set of dining-room chairs. Shortly afterwards Vanessa was invited to dine and found to her surprise antique chairs installed. When she exclaimed at this Ottoline excused herself by saying that the Omega chairs had been too expensive. Vanessa, not easily rebuffed, asked Ottoline to name the price of the Omega chairs. When Ottoline produced a sum double that which the chairs actually cost, Vanessa relentlessly pressed her to say who had given her this information, at which Ottoline, desperate in the face of Vanessa's uncompromising veracity, weakly replied, 'Oh, the *usual* young lady.'

Experience of working for the Omega broadened Vanessa's attitude towards painting. No longer need it be confined within a frame on the wall, to the realm of rarefied aesthetic discourse. Shape, line and colour now tumbled over the most ordinary object, weaving pattern and decoration into everyday life, releasing creative exuberance. Her experience as a painter gave confidence to her designs, while the habitual need to design liberated the compositions in her paintings, making them simpler and bolder. One lasting effect of the Omega was that, in general, it made Bloomsbury painting more immediate, more decorative, concerned rather to gratify the senses than to reason with the mind.

During this period prior to the First World War, Vanessa's paintings grew increasingly architectonic. Her *Studland Beach* of 1912-13[§] marks a radical advance upon her treatment of the same subject in *The Bathers* of 1911. Everything is now flattened and reduced to its simplest components. The diagonal shoreline, slicing right across the picture surface, pulls in the opposite direction to the compositional tension set up between the two groups of figures. The image of the figure in the tent with the children clustered at her feet may contain a reminiscence of Piero della Francesca's *Madonna della Misericordia*. The block-like standing figure with the hair hanging down the back has a surprising resemblance to Matisse's *Nu de Dos III* of 1916-17 which it may have influenced, as it is possible that Roger Fry included *Studland Bay* among the photographs of recent English work that he showed Matisse on a visit to Paris in June 1916.

In *Studland Beach* and other paintings of this period, Vanessa's use of abstraction makes each shape static and separate. This reduction of form to elemental shapes expresses a feeling which is often austere and remote, but also, I think, related to her maternal experience. All her life Vanessa revered her mother and the powerful influence she had had over others. In her paintings and designs of this period she often turns to maternal subjects. Apart from the Piero-like vignette in *Studland Beach*, she put a stylized image of the madonna and child on to an Omega tray (Coll: Kenneth Rowntree) and into a small clay statuette, also made at the Omega (Charleston Trust). In October 1912 her desire to express maternity in monumental terms led her to begin work on a six-foot-square canvas of the Nativity. She admitted that it was difficult to balance the necessary amount of description that the scene demanded with her desire for abstract design: 'What a fool I was to embark on such a thing. ... How is one to get form into heads and figures without saying more than one wants to about them.'[32] When complete the painting hung in the main hall of Roger's house at Guildford. By 1914 Vanessa had taken such a dislike to it that she painted another six-foot-square canvas, entitled *Woman and Baby*, to replace it. The *Nativity* was almost certainly destroyed; the *Woman and Baby* is known nowadays only from a photograph.⁵ In the latter a woman and her new-born baby lie on the bed while three figures look on. The spare design in which the figures are reduced almost to flat silhouettes, combined with the emotive subject, suggests that this may have been one of her most important post-impressionist paintings. All detail is omitted, the faces hardly delineated because, in a series of recent portraits of Virginia, Vanessa had discovered that character and feeling could be conveyed simply by the tilt of the head.

The logical outcome of this paring down of her vocabulary was the move into pure abstraction. Around 1914-15 she produced a handful of abstract collages and paintings. 'With hindsight', Simon Watney has written of her small abstract oil, now in the Tate Gallery, 'her entire career bears down relentlessly on this point of technical and conceptual sophistication.'³³ In this and her only other extant abstract painted on canvas, Vanessa comes close in style to the Czech artist Frantisek Kupka's *Amphora: Fugue in Two Colours* which, exhibited at the Salon d'Automne in 1912, was one of the earliest non-representational paintings in European art. Vanessa's use of flat, abutting and overlapping planes, may, however, owe more to the insistent vertical emphasis often employed by Sickert whose work she admired. But discussion of Kupka's abstracts and those by Kandinsky shown at the Allied Artists Salon in London in 1913 and at the exhibition of the Grafton Group – an exhibiting society recently founded by Fry – in March that year, may have encouraged her experiments. However, Bloomsbury abstraction never matured into a confident style because, unlike that of Mondrian or Kandinsky, it lacked a philosophical base. G. E. Moore's insistence on the precise definition of meaning may have indirectly encouraged Vanessa's use of elemental shapes and the extreme openness and honesty of her abstract style; but a more immediate influence upon Bloomsbury abstraction was the desire for liberation from nineteenth-century representationalism and its often mawkish sentimentality.

Bloomsbury's abstract period, like that of Wyndham Lewis and the Vorticists, was short-lived. It was destroyed partly by the loss of confidence caused by war and partly by the English intellectual climate which was unsympathetic to such work. It is probable, however, that in Vanessa's case interest waned because she needed to bring to her art more of her experience of life than the conceptual purity of abstract art allowed.

Post-Impressionism had encouraged not only a more informal treatment but also a broader range of subjects. It had brought Vanessa, as she said, 'a sudden liberation to feel for oneself', and now she had no hesitation in putting her own life into her paintings: she portrays her friends chatting around a fire, reading or sewing, in relaxed, unselfconscious poses; instead of conventional landscapes or carefully arranged still lifes, she turned to the casual and everyday: at Studland she had painted the arbitrary configurations of figures on the beach; at Gordon Square she had made the daily routine of 'nursery tea', as the Edwardians called it, her subject. Moreover her choice of forms may reflect on her maternal experience for there is an emphatic fullness in the sweep of certain lines, in the curve of the tablecloth in *Nursery Tea* or the arc of the sea in *Studland Beach*.

It was partly her delight in the world around her that led her to share Clive's distrust of narrative painting. In print he had declared the representative element in art to be always irrelevant: Vanessa was to adopt a more modified stance. 'A work of art', wrote Matisse in 1908, in his famous *Notes d'un peintre*, 'must carry in itself its complete significance and impose it upon the beholder even before he can identify the subject-matter.' It is precisely this point that Vanessa makes in a letter to Leonard Woolf, written in 1913, which remains one of her rare statements on aesthetics:

> It can't be the object of a great artist to tell you facts at the cost of telling you what he feels about them . . . I often look at a picture – for instance I did at the Picasso trees by the side of a lake – without seeing in the least what the things are. I saw trees, but never dreamt of a lake or lakes although I saw certain colours and planes behind the trees. I got quite a strong emotion from the forms and colours, but it wasn't changed when weeks afterwards it was pointed out to me by chance that the blue was a lake. . . . The picture does convey the idea of form . . . but not the idea of form associated with anything in life, but simply form separated from life. As a matter of fact we do first feel the emotion and then look at the picture . . . at least I do. The reason I think that artists paint life and not patterns is that certain qualities of life, what I call movement, mass, weight have aesthetic value. But where I should quarrel with Clive . . . is when he says one gets the same emotion from flat patterns that one does from pictures. I say one doesn't, because of the reason I have just given – that movement etc. give me important aesthetic emotions.[34]

Her divergence from Clive's opinion explains why pure abstraction never wholly absorbed her. Abstract art, for her, lacked this sensuous relationship with the everyday world. Though she asserts that she looks at form separated from life, it is separated not from visual and tactile experience, but from concepts of use, value, from sentimental associations and other non-visual content.

Even at a time when she was experimenting with abstraction and enjoying close links with the Parisian avant-garde, she never completely turned her back on subject-matter. In January 1914, on a visit to Paris with Roger, Clive and Molly MacCarthy, she was taken by Gertrude Stein to meet Picasso in his studio. It was bristling with cubist constructions made out of bits of wood and coloured paper as well as certain portraits from his Blue period. Vanessa was astounded by his creativity. She also met Matisse in his studio and saw more of his work in the collection of Michael Stein. It was on this visit that Clive bought a still life of eggs by Juan Gris and Vlaminck's *Village in Provence*. Later that month Vanessa's paintings hung alongside those by Marchand, Lhôte and Friesz in the second of Roger's Grafton Group shows; photographs of Picasso's recent constructions were also included. Then in May she sent four works to the Whitechapel Art Gallery's important survey of twentieth-century art. One of these was her six-foot-square *Woman and Baby* which had caught the attention of the press when exhibited with the Grafton Group in January. The *Daily Telegraph* called it 'powerful and expressive'; the *Pall Mall Gazette* gushingly discerned a sentiment not so very far removed from that of the Victorians:

> Her large subject 'Woman and Baby' is one of the most poignant designs that one remembers in modern painting. The broad sculpturesque composition may be derived from Puvis de Chavannes, but it has an intensely human interest, clothed in a primitive passion, that seems to sweep aside all conventional barriers. . . . None but a woman, none but a great artist, could have so perfectly expressed, with a new sympathy, all the pathos and bewilderment of this time-worn theme.[35]

Vanessa's maternal feelings now played a dominant role in her life. Roger Fry must have perceived this when around 1913 he carved in wood a mother protectively clutching to her side two children; the same motif is found in the Christmas card that he made in 1913. Something of Vanessa's absorption in her two sons is conveyed in many photographs that she took of them at Asheham where they ran about the garden naked. Her love for them had increased as her marriage daily lessened in importance: confirmed in her role as mother, she was now dismissive of her role as wife. Even in her youth she had instinctively reacted against the male-dominated conventions that her Duckworth half-brothers and others upheld. She liked men as friends, but her new-won independence may have left her disinclined to re-enter a relationship where she would be the submissive partner. This perhaps troubled her affair with Roger who could be demanding, his intellect, energy and enthusiasm challenging the very independence that he had helped her to achieve. Duncan presented no such threat. Like many homosexuals, he was extremely close to his mother and had preserved a streak of juvenile irresponsibility. This, combined with their six-year difference in age, perhaps enabled Vanessa to look on him as a younger brother or even son. Roger demanded of her a more complete role, wanting her to be in all but name a wife. He suffered greatly as she gradually transferred her affection to Duncan. She suffered too, more intensely, perhaps, than she expected, but not in a way that ever threatened her position as mother.

Duncan was not easily caught. Even his age was elusive: in January 1914 he told Maynard, 'My mother tells me I am only 28 which is a great surprise. I thought I was 29. So I have a whole year to spare.'[36] In order to draw Duncan closer to her Vanessa began to underline their difference as painters from the others in their circle. While he was away during the early part of 1914, first at Menton and then in North Africa, she wrote to him from Asheham. 'Norton says I have become a slut and have quite changed all my habits since he has known me. A good deal is put down to your example. One painter alone is simply mobbed I find. Nothing escapes notice, holes in one's stockings, green paint on one's face, shoes down at heel, slowness of mind – all is put down to being a painter.'[37] Meanwhile Duncan sent her branches of oranges and lemons from Africa (which she painted) and she in turn sent him reports of the Grafton Group show where Duncan's *Adam and Eve* was causing offence. 'I believe distortion is like Sodomy,' she wrote. 'People are simply blindly prejudiced against it because they think it abnormal.'[38] But if she was compatible, he was not in love: in February 1914 she jokingly suggested in one letter that they should elope and potter harmoniously together; in August, however, when Clive considered visiting Asheham, she had to admit: 'You will be very welcome and will interrupt no lovemaking. Only Duncan is here and he as you know is impervious to my charms.'[39]

Many years later Duncan recalled that he first became aware of the nature of Vanessa's love when he caught sight of her in a mirror watching him shave.[40] To another, he said that awareness of her love struck him after a party given at Lady Ottoline's.[41] This must have been after April 1913 as it was not until then that Ottoline reopened her friendship with Vanessa and Duncan after her quarrel with Roger in May 1911. 'I went to tea with Ott.,' Vanessa told Roger. 'We had a most touching scene! She kissed me warmly and said how nice it was to be friends again. That the whole thing had been so dreadful, but we agreed there was no need to go into that again! Then she kissed me passionately on the lips! And so we made friends and sat and had a long talk about other things. ... Isn't it odd.'[42] After this she and Duncan (but not Roger) often attended Ottoline's parties at which the guests were invited to dress up in her store of Persian and Turkish clothes and where Duncan performed wild improvisations to one of Brahms's *Hungarian Dances*, pedalled out on the pianola by Philip Morrell. At one of these parties the violinist Jelly d'Aranyi embraced Duncan on the stairs as he was about to leave. Vanessa, who was waiting for him in the hall below, spun round and without a word promptly left the house. From now on, Duncan realized, Vanessa's feelings would have to be taken into account.

This shift in her affections had begun during their trip to Italy in the spring of 1913. She had decided then to assert her independence and had refused to do some of the things Roger suggested. Many years later he recalled in a letter to Helen Anrep: 'I knew so well when Vanessa was falling out of love with me and on her way to falling in love with Duncan ... one of the symptoms was an almost eager seizing on things where she could disagree with me and be in the opposite camp.'[43] On their return to England they had both worked intensively towards the opening of the Omega, and though Vanessa saw Roger daily, she was less able to set aside time for their affair. At the same time she was attempting to re-establish normal relations with Clive as she wanted to have another child.

When in the spring of 1914 she went on a short bicycling holiday in France with Roger, it would seem that her complicated affections were equally divided between him, Clive and Duncan. Each day their talk far outpaced the mere ten miles travelled and in the evenings she wrote to Clive. 'Roger is depressed about his life and his art. He finds me "rébarbative" and says I look like the heroine of a story in the Strand magazine, I am so neat and prim. I do my best to cheer him up about life and art without being too kind – but of course you and Duncan are absurd really – our relations are much too fixed and old-established to be altered now. I find no new excitements in that line and shall be glad of some contemporary company.'[44]

If her affair with Roger was changing, so too was her relationship with Virginia. Even before her marriage to Leonard, Virginia had begun to feel that her sister was drawing apart, into a world of her own making: 'As a painter, you are much less conscious of the drone of daily life than I am, as a writer. You *are* a painter. I think a good deal about you, for purposes of my own, and this seems to me clear. This explains your simplicity. What have you to do with all this turmoil? What you want is a studio where you can see things.'[45] Virginia did indeed begin to make use of her sister for her own purposes and gave certain of Vanessa's characteristics to Mrs Ambrose in *The Voyage Out*. Throughout her life Virginia seems to have had a need in her writing to draw on her knowledge and understanding of Vanessa. She also found that by underlining and exaggerating certain aspects of Vanessa's character she retained her hold on her. She seized on Vanessa's 'generous talent for losing umbrellas and forgetting messages'[46] and on her hilariously muddled use of proverbs. As early as 1910 Vanessa had warned Clive: 'Virginia since early youth has made it her business to create a character for me according to her own wishes and has now so succeeded in imposing it upon the world that those preposterous stories are supposed to be certainly true because so characteristic.'[47] Nevertheless Vanessa herself was to develop a line of self-mockery, underlining habits that touched on the absurd – her reliance on safety-pins, for instance, or her wildly inaccurate dressmaking – so that, like Gertrude Stein's steady transformation into the likeness that Picasso had earlier painted, she came more and more to resemble Virginia's invention.

But during this period, while interest in the Post-Impressionists raged, the intimacy between the sisters noticeably cooled. On honeymoon, Virginia learnt that Vanessa had broken confidence and told Leonard how in 1911 Virginia had received a proposal from Walter Lamb. On her return to London Virginia had for a period kept her distance from 46 Gordon Square but had been dissuaded from quarrelling with Vanessa by Leonard. Both sisters now felt that the other had been disloyal, for Virginia had earlier been indiscreet about Roger's brief fling with Lady Ottoline, a fact that had determined Vanessa to tell her sister nothing about her own affair. Both sisters therefore temporarily withdrew from their former intimacy, and the breach was never wholly repaired. When Virginia tried to re-establish close relations she sometimes received the impression that Vanessa was deliberately repressing affection. Yet Vanessa's maternal care for her sister had not suddenly ceased, for Leonard, following Virginia's custom, turned to Vanessa for advice on whether or not Virginia should have children. Vanessa told them to obtain all the advice they could and then make up their minds themselves. In a letter to Virginia, she pointed out that all women ran some risks in having a baby, but that Virginia should be warned against it if it meant running an appreciable risk of another breakdown or a permanent state of nerves which would prevent her from enjoying the child when it arrived. On the whole Vanessa felt that if Virginia waited a while and took adequate care of herself there would be little danger to her health, and she repeated Jean Thomas's view that a baby would do Virginia good. The case against her having children was, at least in January 1913, less clear-cut than Leonard Woolf in his autobiography *Beginning Again* suggests. However, what must have decided him against procreation (for it was he who finally took the decision) was the two subsequent nervous attacks which Virginia endured in July and September of that year. During the second of these she attempted suicide by taking an overdose of veronal. Vanessa was immediately called for. After the doctors had given Virginia a stomach pump, Vanessa sat up with her all night while the exhausted Leonard slept. She was the first to tell him in the morning that Virginia had pulled through.

Looking back on this period immediately preceding the outbreak of war, Vanessa felt some explanation was needed for Bloomsbury's lack of prescience:

> It must now be almost incredible how unaware we were of the disaster so soon to come. I do not know how much the politicians then foresaw, but I think that we in Bloomsbury had only the haziest ideas as to what was going on in the rest of Europe. How could we be interested in such matters when first getting to know well the great artists of the immediate past and those following them, when beauty was springing up under one's feet so vividly that violent abuse was hurled at it and genius generally considered to be insanity, when the writers were pricking up their ears and raising their voices lest too much attention should be given to painting: when music joined in the general chorus with sounds which excited ecstasy rage and disdain: a great new freedom seemed about to come and perhaps would have come, if it had not been for motives and ambitions of which we knew nothing. But surely such unawareness can never come again and it is difficult to explain it to those who cannot hope to feel it.[48]

Clive and Vanessa were visiting Seend when the outbreak of war was declared. Clive was made speechless with gloom, but the rest of his family adopted a hearty jingoism, rejoicing in the government's action despite the fact that their son Cory would now be in danger. Already the increased demand for coal was making them large profits. Depressed by their lack of foresight, Vanessa longed to return to London, and once back was disappointed to learn that Roger's plans for a third show at the Grafton Galleries, to be divided into two sections, one devoted to contemporary art, the other to the Parisian dealer Ambroise Vollard's Cézannes and Impressionist paintings, had been terminated by war.

The final act of this period in her life was played out at Asheham. She went down to Sussex with her children towards the end of August, Quentin waving excitedly at the soldiers that they saw on every station, and most of Bloomsbury presently followed. First to arrive was Duncan with whom, Vanessa told Roger, she was on 'friendly but quite cool terms'.[49] They talked mostly about painting, maintaining a state of ignorance about current affairs which the arrival of Clive and Maynard destroyed. Then came Desmond and Molly MacCarthy, the Cambridge economist Gerald Shove, Harry Norton, Lytton and a young creature from the Slade with hair like a thatched cottage, Dora Carrington, all settling on Ashcham like a flock of birds preparing to migrate. Finally Virginia arrived, looking physically so much altered by her last bout of illness that Vanessa felt strange talking to her. Meanwhile she did a great deal of painting while Duncan busied himself with an abstract scroll which he intended should be viewed through an aperture as it wound past to musical accompaniment (Tate Gallery). When Adrian appeared, bringing with him Mary Berenson's daughter by her first marriage, Karin Costelloe, Vanessa observed that they behaved much like an engaged couple. This depressed Duncan, who was still sharing a house with Adrian, for he felt Karin not good enough for his friend. Something was clearly said, as Adrian left Asheham in tears. But this tension was localized and did not blight the general mood. Most evenings those present gathered in one room to write indecent poems and sing Scottish songs, making the small house at the foot of the Downs ring with laughter.

The following weeks were filled with anxiety and indecision. Adrian announced his intention of enlisting; Clive, ineligible for active service because of an unhealed rupture that he had had since his teens, considered seeking employment as an interpreter in the Army Service or Medical Corps. Still more unsettling was the despair that Roger, now disabused of the belief that Vanessa still loved him, unleashed in his letters. 'You can't help being the one woman I know who fits me perfectly in every turn of your mind and soul and body,' he implored.[50] In order to rebuff his demands and complaints, she became self-absorbed, even a little callous. He refused to visit Asheham while Duncan was present. 'No letter today,' he wrote acidly. '. . . Duncan's never written to say when he was going so I suppose that you've told him you've told me not to come and persuaded him to stay on. Perfectly reasonable of course but it makes me feel with a fresh bitterness how utterly I am out of it.'[51] When they did meet conversation was painful and strained; for a period neither could talk freely to the other, and only when Vanessa picked up a copy of the *Nation* and read in it an article by Roger did she again feel in contact with his mind.

Roger was too passionate to agree to a still intimate but secondary role in Vanessa's life, as Clive had done. It was therefore difficult for her to remain on an easy footing with him as he demanded more than she could give. But when in a calmer mood, he could shrewdly remark, 'Decidedly and in the long view I doubt if ever you can afford to get rid of me as completely as your immediate inclination is to.'[52] With which Vanessa, after a period of considerable agony and reconsideration, could only concur: 'When I came back I wondered how I could ever have thought I was less dependent on you! . . . for really I *do* want you dreadfully in all the things I most care about, and I see quite clearly that I always shall.'[53]

SEVEN

Granite and Rainbow
1914–1916

Without any perceptible change in their outward relationship, Duncan had steadily grown in importance for Vanessa. It was one thing to admire his work and accept the current opinion that he was one of the most talented artists of his generation; it was quite another to discover in herself an involuntary passion for this homosexual who for the last few years had been living with her brother. For a long period it would seem that Vanessa was unable to admit to herself the true nature of her feelings. Then suddenly she broke down and, it is said, in Virginia's presence wept at the hopelessness of her position.

While living with Adrian, Duncan had been attracted to George Mallory, a graduate of Magdalene College, Cambridge, who, according to Geoffrey Keynes, was 'fond of argumentative discussion and had an interesting mind though he was not outstandingly clever'. He also had 'good looks in the Botticelli style' and 'the build of an ideal athlete unspoilt by overdevelopment in any part'.[1] He posed naked for Duncan who did not disguise in these paintings his response to Mallory's physical appeal. When the young man took up an appointment at Charterhouse School in Godalming, Duncan visited him there. Then in July 1914 Mallory married. A month or two later Duncan was distressed by the attention Adrian paid Karin Costelloe and shortly after the outbreak of war they too married. It was at this point that Duncan drew closer to Vanessa and told her that to some extent he returned her love.

Those nearest to Vanessa in 1914 must have thought it highly unlikely that an intimate relationship between her and Duncan would last. Though Duncan enjoyed the company of women and was attractive to them (the violinist Jelly d'Aranyi was thought to be in love with him), his homo-

sexual passions had excluded other sexual pursuits, save for a single experimental visit to a Parisian brothel. (Even this had not been at his own
instigation but that of a friend whose uncle had kindly sent money for this
very purpose.) Moreover the speed with which he had already tumbled
into and out of several affairs suggests that he was disinclined to commit
himself wholeheartedly to a single relationship. Lytton observed, when his
love for Duncan was at its height, that he seemed 'afraid of me, of my
affection – as if he didn't dare to face something he couldn't reciprocate'.[2]
Confronted with Vanessa's feelings Duncan ought to have shied away in
terror: that he did not tells us much about Vanessa.

One characteristic response that Vanessa aroused was a sense of reverence. It was not just her tall, statuesque beauty that gave her an unusual
emotive power over others but, as Leonard Woolf observed, the combination of this beauty with feminine charm, strength of character and ironic
humour. Marjorie Strachey noted that she emanated 'a sense of repose and
understanding',[3] for she had a profundity of feeling which was directly
linked to her innate honesty. After visiting her in the country on one
occasion, Virginia found London 'glittering and unreal'.[4] Her monumentality aroused a devotion which did not lessen but increased with intimacy.
Her largeness of mind enabled her to joke about 'sucking sodomy' with
Maynard and allowed homosexuals to gossip freely in her presence.
According to Quentin Bell, she at one moment proposed the creation of
a libertarian society with sexual freedom for all.[5] Tolerance, understanding, love and a capacity to create freedom now drew Duncan gradually
into an intimate relationship that lasted for the rest of Vanessa's life. And
as she had for some time courted unorthodoxy it need not surprise us that
the game of love involved not two players but three.

Duncan first became familiar with David Garnett while visiting Lytton
at The Lacket, Lockeridge, near Marlborough, over the Christmas of 1914.
Bunny (as Garnett was familiarly known) was a botanist by training,
currently engaged in research under an eminent zoologist at Imperial
College. He came from an extremely distinguished literary family: his
grandfather had been Keeper of Books at the British Museum, his father,
Edward, was a doyen among publishers' readers, and his mother, Con-
stance, famous for her translations of the Russian classics. Bunny had inherited their interest, enjoyed the company of authors and in 1912 had met
and walked in the Tyrol with D.H. Lawrence. He himself was to publish
his first serious book in 1923 and to make a career as a literary editor and
prolific novelist. In 1914 he was still only twenty-two, somewhat diffident,
gauche and shy. He had occasionally attended Adrian Stephen's poker
parties during the previous year and there gained the impression that

Duncan, seven years his elder, disliked him.

Bunny had gone down to Lockeridge in the company of Francis Birrell and was meeting Lytton for the first time. He listened intently as his host read aloud 'Ermyntrude and Esmeralda', a witty, risqué sexual satire designed to entertain his friends. Bunny, already dedicated to a life of promiscuous heterosexuality, recalled in his memoirs that Lytton's reading confirmed him as a libertine and enabled him thereafter to lead a sexual life free of all conventional constraints.

While walking on the Marlborough Downs that Christmas, Duncan and Bunny enjoyed a conversation that began their intimacy. The subsequent development of their relationship can be traced in David Garnett's unpublished diary for 1914-15. On 6 January 1915 the two men met again when Maynard, with cunning percipience, placed Bunny between Vanessa and Duncan at a dinner that he gave at the Café Royal which preceded a party at 46 Gordon Square. Later that night Duncan told Bunny that he loved him and soon after this they began sleeping together. On Duncan's side the initial attraction was almost certainly physical. Bunny had exceptional good looks and a muscular figure; he was tall, fair-haired, had startlingly blue eyes and a slightly protuberant mouth. Due to a muscular deficiency caused at birth, he rarely looked sideways but always turned his entire head, a gesture which seemed to confirm the sincerity of his unaffected manner. Though he had previously flirted with Maynard and Lytton and enjoyed a sentimental attachment with Francis Birrell, he had so far always refused to pursue a male friendship into bed; that he did so now with Duncan greatly upset Birrell. Garnett later claimed that he only complied with the physical side of their relationship to avoid hurting Duncan's feelings. Certainly he continued to carry on with various women friends, taking a delight in the other sex that he could not get from 'dull sodomitical twaddle'. He was also from the start slightly appalled by Duncan's 'black emotional collapses' and his capacity to talk all afternoon with tears in his eyes without ever getting off an emotional plane.[6] Yet he found himself entranced by Duncan for the next four years. Soon after their relationship began Bunny sat to Duncan for the first of several portraits which, like those of Mallory, expose the sexual attraction that the sitter had for the artist. 'It was partly my good looks,' Bunny years later conceded, 'but chiefly I think because of my simplicity and absence of ulterior motives.'[7]

It would seem that Vanessa was aware of what was happening from the start. Bunny, who had previously admired the thirty-five-year-old Vanessa from a distance, on finding himself seated next to her at the Café Royal dinner, invited her to tea. A week later she arrived at his dingy flat in Pond Place, off the Fulham Road, and found sticky chocolate éclairs and China

tea bought in her honour. Impressed more by his character than by his
intelligence (an opinion she was later to reverse), she made a point of
embracing him warmly on leaving. After this Bunny became a regular
visitor at 46 Gordon Square, dropping in like other of their friends at any
hour of the day and gossiping with Vanessa about Lady Ottoline with
whom he was already familiar. When he cancelled a supper arrangement
with Duncan in order to attend one of Ottoline's parties, Vanessa, anxious
that Duncan should not be upset, reprimanded him. It was as if she were
aware that she could only build a Heaven in Hell's despite if Duncan's
emotional and sexual needs were fully satisfied.

Almost overnight Bunny, on whom Duncan's love was now focused,
became an intimate friend of Vanessa's despite their thirteen-year difference in age, for if Bunny were on hand, Duncan would also be close. In a
memoir of Vanessa written in the late 1970s shortly before his death, David
Garnett recalled: 'When Vanessa realized that Duncan loved her and would
give her what he could in return, she was wildly happy and so was he.'
Bunny himself was also half in love with her. 'Vanessa is a darling', he
wrote on more than one occasion in his diary. In his later memoir, which
is not always reliable, he claimed that Vanessa verbally agreed to spend a
weekend with him when Clive went away. He also provides an evocative
description of her appearance at this date:

> What was she like? A tall woman who stooped and swayed while she walked
> and moved erratically, swiftly for a few steps and then slower. These undulating
> movements had won her the nickname Dolphin with Virginia ... I thought
> Vanessa more beautiful than Virginia. Her face had a grave beauty in repose:
> the perfect oval of a sculptured Madonna. Her straight dark brown hair, parted
> in the middle, was swept in wings over her ears to be fastened in a loose knob
> on the back of the angled pedestal of her neck. Her mouth was lovely, not small
> or too large, rather turned down at the corners, often impudent and full of
> humour. The eyes, under deeply hooded lids, were like those of her brother
> Adrian and her son Quentin: blue-grey and deceptively innocent. No one who
> looked out of such eyes, one felt, could have an *arrière-pensée*. And then they
> would sparkle and the Madonna's face reveal that one was being teased. Her
> hands were large but fine with long fingers: aristocratic hands which she had I
> believe inherited, together with her special beauty, from her French ancestors
> – the Chevalier Antoine de l'Etang and his wife Mlle Thérèse Blin de Grincourt.[8]

Duncan's attractions were likewise many and complex. At thirty, he
was still exceptionally handsome, in manner idiosyncratic, unaccountable
and utterly charming; always and invariably himself. His single-minded
devotion to painting continued to free him from the ambitions and desires
constraining more conventional lives. Recollecting him at a later date but

nevertheless pinpointing a lifelong characteristic, Angelica Garnett has written: 'He possessed the instinctive wisdom of an animal, never undertaking responsibilities that belonged to others, never promising more than he could perform. He bobbed on the surface, gently irrepressible, impervious as a duck to water, elusive as a leaf on a pond.'[9] His disinterestedness had a potent appeal to Vanessa who no doubt perceived the connection between his inner freedom and his creativity. She was also to discover that beneath his airy manner lay strong feelings and tenacious loyalty. He regularly visited his parents, whose marital happiness depended on discreet extra-marital affairs, his mother's allegiance being given to a certain Colonel Young. Like his parents, Duncan believed that matters of the heart were essentially private, and though with certain of his male lovers he indulged in masochistic emotionalism, he was otherwise exceptionally circumspect; even his closest friends sometimes had difficulty in assessing the depth of his feelings. His dislike of any public form of emotional disturbance gave a classical bias to his appreciation of art; he once told Bunny that he thought the finest poetry 'an expression of all apparent aloofness from the human feelings involved in a person who has suffered all feeling'.[10]

'Have you finished Virginia's novel?' Vanessa asked Roger in the spring of 1915, shortly after the appearance of *The Voyage Out*. She too demanded a sense of detachment in art and her chief criticism of this book was that Virginia had not sufficiently distanced herself from her material.

> It seems to me extraordinarily brilliant almost too much so at times. It makes it too restless I think. However it is of course very good in its descriptions of people and conversations and all the detail. The obvious criticism I suppose is that it isn't a whole but I haven't quite finished it yet so I oughtn't to make a final criticism. ... Novel writing does seem a queer business at least this kind. If it's art it seems to me art of quite a different sort from making a picture but I don't think all novel writing is. The quotation from Jane Austen even though it's only a sentence seemed to me at once to put one into a different world, one that's the same really that one is in when one looks at a Cézanne. Did you feel it? I suppose it's because one knows the rest of the book and one could feel it from only one sentence. Reading Virginia's book is much more like being with an extraordinarily witty and acute person in life and watching all these things and people with her.[11]

The book appeared amid a season of unparalleled social gaiety. As if in defiance of the war, Lady Ottoline Morrell was holding parties every Thursday at which, Vanessa told Hilton Young, 'you might see Bertie Russell dancing a hornpipe with Titi (Hawtrey's young woman), Lytton and Oliver and Marjorie Strachey cutting capers to each other, Duncan dancing in much the same way that he paints, [Augustus] John and Arnold Bennett and all the celebrities of the day looking as beautiful as they could in clothes seized from Ottoline's drawers – and Ottoline herself at the head of a troup of short-haired young ladies from the Slade prancing about . . . one can't describe the queer effect all these people had on each other'.[12] In addition there were occasional concerts at the Omega given by Belgian refugees, and one evening a week Bloomsbury met for a play-reading. On the night that Bunny sat between Vanessa and Duncan at the Café Royal, all the guests had retired to 46 Gordon Square to hear Racine's *Bérénice* performed by Duncan, Lytton and Marjorie Strachey with the aid of three eight-foot puppets made by Duncan out of cardboard. These monstrous effigies still leant against the end wall of the sitting-room when two months later Ottoline paid a farewell visit immediately prior to Vanessa's departure for West Wittering on the Sussex coast.

Her destination was Eleanor House, a small cottage surrounded by farm buildings situated down a rough track about half a mile outside the village. The rent of this house had been taken the previous year by Clive's friends Jack and Mary Hutchinson on the advice of Professor Henry Tonks who himself moved into the nearby disused boatshed which made a good studio. Its double doors, which rolled back, faced directly on to the estuary and at low tide overlooked a view of exposed mudflats, broken by inlets and small pools, the iridescence of the scene throwing into contrast the dark, barn-like interior of the shed. On the landward side the shed had a small bedroom and kitchen.

Duncan went down to Wittering ahead of Vanessa and put up in the shed, Mary Hutchinson having given him the key and the warning that Tonks's possessions were not to be disturbed. At weekends he received visits first from Adrian, then from Bunny. While Duncan painted, Bunny began the novel which they intended writing together. The sun shone and sandpipers wheeled overhead. 'After lunch', Bunny's diary records, 'we suddenly raided Tonks' wine and drank it in the sunlight and fought drunkenly and lustfully. And then we shook the dust out of our clothes and went growling at each other down to the point. The open sea came tumbling in.'

Vanessa arrived towards the end of March and put up at Eleanor House.

I have been having a very nice time here alone with Duncan [she told Virginia]. Now we have a house party for the weekend. Maynard and Margery Olivier are here, Ka [Cox] is coming and possibly Marjorie Strachey. . . . This is a small house done up rather in the New English Art Club style of decoration with spots and stripes and bright colours everywhere, very pretty for the most part with some lapses. Tonks has a large studio just by, all as neat as a new pin with his own pots and pans hanging up in shining layers and a few incredibly bad niggled sketches. Those people – I mean the New English artists – are even worse than one thought when one sees them unframed – at close quarters.[13]

To her relief, their visitors never stayed long. Marjorie Strachey, however, came twice, pursuing her eccentricities with unflagging energy. She taught Duncan and Bunny Dalcroze's eurhythmics and introduced games guaranteed to cause discomfort, such as the writing of each other's obituaries. She insisted on reading her friends' characters from the lines on the palms of their hands and discovered in Vanessa sadism and inconstancy. She also excelled at the recitation of nursery rhymes which she delivered with such unexpected and exaggerated emphasis that the most innocent tale became blood-curdling or full of sexual innuendo. In conversation she would tackle any subject, bringing the Strachey intellect to her analysis of childbirth, military strategy, boxing or the attractions of the sexes, each remark being hurled at her listener like a sarcastic insult.

It had been bitterly cold when Vanessa first arrived at Wittering, too cold to paint in the boatshed and instead she and Duncan made use of the dining-room at Eleanor House. Vanessa sat for her portrait, leaning back in an armchair and occasionally falling asleep. 'I have done no painting myself yet', she told Clive, 'and seem in fact to do little but eat and sleep – alone. No little Grant has yet had a chance to come into existence.'[14] If Clive had given his approval to Vanessa's new love for Duncan, she in turn teasingly encouraged his affair with Mary Hutchinson which was temporarily held in check that spring while Mary gave birth to a son. It was not Clive, however, whom Vanessa feared offending but Bunny; she was therefore pleased when he expressed unfeigned pleasure at the idea of her having a child by Duncan. By announcing her intention she put an end (perhaps conveniently) to Bunny's hopes of sleeping with her. But she still needed him as a link between her and Duncan and in her letters to the younger man underlined her and Duncan's love for him. 'He [Duncan] seems to think of you a great deal and we often talk of you. Yesterday we talked of your looks and decided that we liked looking at you and after all what more can one say of anyone?'[15]

While Vanessa plaited their three lives into a single, binding cord of affection, wartime hysteria continued to rage. It was rumoured that a German invasion was imminent, that the country was rife with German spies. Innocent people were victimized. Women distributed white feathers among farm labourers and other men who had not enlisted. Toyshops sold patriotic games, and Union Jacks and photographs of the King and Queen appeared in many shop windows. In the *Daily Mirror*, the paper at which Vanessa most often glanced, the war industry and the effects of gas in the trenches were brought home daily by a double-page spread of photographs; even its serialized love story was coloured by war, its hero being awarded a VC. With their lives set against this oppressive background, Vanessa and Duncan grew increasingly ebullient and irreverent. They referred to Clive and Lytton, when they arrived at Wittering, as 'the old gentlemen', and Duncan, uttering terrifying growls and butting Lytton with his head, pushed him into the sea. When Vanessa attempted to leap a broad dyke and fell up to her waist in black mud, Duncan was left helpless with laughter.

All this time Julian and Quentin had remained with their nurse Mabel Selwood in London where they were now attending a small primary school. On many occasions Vanessa left her children in the care of others, sometimes for weeks on end; her fondness for them never excluded other interests and her need to paint remained dominant. When Brynhild Olivier, one of the neo-pagans, a younger generation of friends heartier, insistently commonsensical and orientated more towards Socialism than Bloomsbury, had a child, Vanessa was horrified to learn that she was going to manage without a nurse. This 'sounded to me too awful', she told Virginia, 'for she'll never be able to go away or hardly to leave the house I should think. When I think of what Julian used to be even with a nurse I pity anyone without one. But these young neo-pagan mothers evidently mean to do the thing thoroughly.'[16] When her own children joined them at Wittering at Easter, however, she delighted in their presence and they contributed still more to the holiday mood.

At Eleanor House she relished in particular the absence of bells, for at Gordon Square the telephone or doorbell rang constantly. She relapsed into a life of ease and the few newspapers that reached them were now often left unread. After the children returned to London in May she moved into the boatshed with Duncan and found that its cavernous gloom suited her unconventional mood. If their love was by now firmly established, so too was the pattern of compromise and generous tolerance necessary to sustain it. It was an odd but not unmanageable relationship. Vanessa cannot have wished for any intrusion on their intimacy, yet she wrote to Bunny asking him to join them at Whitsuntide. He came. Six months later she remarked: 'I feel as if I had spent years in that shed with you and Duncan. ... The life there was quite unlike anything else.'[17]

Vanessa's letters to Bunny are deceptive; she affects an easy familiarity but in fact her teasing flattery and racy humour disguise a nervous desire to please. Aware of Bunny's relative immaturity, she knew that her fascination for him lay in the discovery that a woman of her class, age and beauty could talk so freely about licentious subjects. She once enchanted him at a dinner by picking up her rolled-up napkin and pushing it to and fro in its ring, alluding to a bawdy joke which they had encountered in a play-reading. When alone with Duncan and Bunny in the boatshed, she abdicated in favour of the younger man, as a letter to Clive makes clear: 'I am now alone with the two young men so you see we're three and I suppose I ought to feel *de trop*. But I can't say I bother about it much. After all if you have your nights together it seems to me your days can be spent *à trois*. Don't you think so?'[18] Roger drew from her a more painful account: 'I think perhaps it was a rather difficult situation,' she admitted, 'but on the whole I am happier about Duncan and Bunny because I see that Bunny really does care a good deal for him. I had been afraid he didn't and that it would mean unhappiness for Duncan ... I can't pretend I was always happy for it's impossible not to mind some things some times. ... But it is an odd disease we all suffer from and I see one can't expect always to be rational.'[19] Her position left Duncan at times overcome with guilt. While on a visit to his mother in May, he wrote to Bunny: 'I am so fond of Nessa I am ashamed she should be so fond of me and you are fonder of me than I deserve and I must just abjectly love both of you and hope not to be too much noticed for it.'[20]

If in her private life Vanessa was walking a tightrope, albeit with a certain audacity, her painting had never before blazed with such assurance. At Eleanor House she translated a view of the farmyard into a mosaic of light pinks, ultramarine, purple and yellow. Bunny sat bare-chested for the artists, and while Duncan gave him the beauty of a god, Vanessa portrayed a rather inert, red-nosed young man, colouring his lumbering body a luminescent pink. Before making a picture she drew only a rough outline sketch and then, as an unfinished portrait of Duncan reveals, began to create form directly with touches of pure colour. Shadow was now automatically rendered not by changes of tone but of hue. In her portrait of the young actress and poet, Iris Tree[§], also painted this year, the shadows under her eyebrows and neck are painted chrome yellow. The face is scarcely modelled at all and merely punctuated by two blue dots and a red mouth. Iris's plump figure is clothed in a plain black dress and seated on a small sofa covered with a boldly-patterned red and white cloth in which Vanessa has introduced a note of yellow to balance that used elsewhere. Behind is a red screen. Though the portrait conveys little of the sitter's character, its colours clamour for attention.

Both painters were probably still experimenting with non-representational art as in June Duncan sent two abstracts to the Vorticist exhibition organized by Wyndham Lewis. They were also doing occasional decorative work for the Omega, Duncan that summer designing a signboard and making a mosaic out of glass and seashells found on the beach; Vanessa tried her hand at dress design. Her ideas were far in advance of accepted taste. On her visits to Paris Rose Vildrac had taken her to the Galeries Lafayette where few women of Vanessa's social distinction would have bought their outfits, since it was still many years before *prêt-à-porter* clothes became widely acceptable. But Lafayette's demonstrated to Vanessa that gay and fashionable clothes need not be expensive. Evidently, as few sold, her own dresses were a little too *outré* for Omega clients. Even Virginia was shocked by her influence: 'My God! What clothes you are responsible for! Karin's clothes wrenched my eyes from the sockets – a skirt barred with reds and yellows of the violent kind, a pea-green blouse on top, with a gaudy handkerchief on her head, supposed to be the very boldest taste. I shall retire into dove colour and old lavender, with a lace collar and lawn wristlets.'[21]

Though saddened by the news of the deaths of Rupert Brooke, Henri Doucet, the French painter who for a time worked at the Omega, and the sculptor Gaudier-Brzeska, from the evidence of her work Vanessa seemed as yet unaffected by war. Her sympathy for others outside her circle of friends was restricted. She was sometimes just too 'damned sensible', Roger felt, for he was still made utterly miserable by his hopeless love for her. 'Nessa dear I hope you'll never really know what I suffer. I mean I hope you'll never know it by experience. If you could know it a little more by imaginative sympathy you could be more tender to me you could help me to begin life again more – you could not hurt me so terribly.'[22] Like an animal caught in a trap, he thrashed out in all directions, occupying his mind with excitements and ceaseless activity, but finding no escape from pain. It was a haphazard life he led, he felt, in which everything seemed strange and dull. He felt his deprivation more keenly, knowing that Vanessa and Duncan were painting in each other's company, their happiness making a mockery of his solitary efforts. 'Will it ever stop this pain, this sense of exile from all that makes life worthwhile for me,' he despaired in one letter to her, '... the beauty and loveliness of you, the atmosphere you make of joy in life simply fill my mind incessantly with a passion of regret.'[23] To distract his mind, he left England in April for an extended visit to France.

Soon after he left, Virginia suffered another breakdown, having been ill with nervous depression since March. During this and her previous breakdown, Vanessa, though greatly concerned, remained uninvolved. She herself was seriously ill at Gordon Square during the first week of June.

The precise nature of her illness is unclear and it may just have been a severe form of fatigue as within a few days she had recovered. She gave temporary lodging that summer to the economist Gerald Shove whose probable engagement to her cousin Fredegond, the daughter of Florence Fisher and F.W. Maitland, Sir Leslie Stephen's biographer, was hotly discussed. With the arrival of Fredegond came also her intellectual friend Alix Sargent-Florence to whom Bunny felt himself attracted. Ka Cox, who had studied at Newnham College, Cambridge, where she had become emotionally involved with Rupert Brooke, brought further distraction for her description of Brooke's mother who had just suffered the loss of a second son stuck in Vanessa's mind. 'Ka said she thought the death of one's children when one was getting old was the worst of all and I expect she's right.'[24] Then too she was concerned for Duncan because at the end of June Bunny left for France, having decided, as his research had come to an end and he had no prospect of a job, to join the Friends' War Victims' Relief Fund.

But as yet the horror of war reached her only intermittently. For entertainment, she encouraged Duncan to gossip about his visit to Garsington Manor which Lady Ottoline and her husband Philip had recently taken and decorated in bizarre fashion. 'There is a lake in which they all bathed,' she recounted, at second hand, to Clive, 'Ott with a red greek headdress and hair all on end and high heeled pink satin shoes, groaning in the water that she was only decent out of the water and all naked below. But Duncan of course didn't play up and dive.'[25] Sceptical but curious, she herself accepted an invitation to visit Garsington in July. The beauty of the Elizabethan house impressed her and she got much pleasure from the patched, gilded and slightly fantastic element in its decoration and from the sight of Ottoline swathed in Turkish cloaks and hung with ropes of pearls. She sat in the garden writing to Bunny who was now at work building sheds to help rehouse war victims in the district of the Meuse. She told him that Duncan was gloomy but that if Bunny were suddenly to appear from behind an ilex, 'How everything would change and what a nice excited furry little bear would be rolling about on the lawn instead of the rather pathetic quiet caged creature sighing beside me.'[26]

Her next letter to Bunny was dictated to Duncan while she crocheted. 'Duncan', she insisted, 'has been thinking of you all day (!!!!) (Starting in bed before breakfast when he had a vision of you so he told me) even when this afternoon he had to keep an assignation with a soldier at a music-hall.'[27] In his replies Bunny returned her affection, his warm words smothering any tension that existed between them. His heterosexuality, however, weakened their threesome, as Vanessa was aware. When he left for France she gave him a writing-case, with a note punning on the euphemism for contraceptive sheaths – French letters. 'F Ls always gratefully received by the giver of this. Honi soit qui mal y pense – Vanessa' (under which she drew a bell). She wrote teasingly to him in France, 'Do you make love to all the young women in the way I've so often had to blow you up for?'[28] Often his emotional involvement with the women to whom he made love, such as the drug-addicted model Betty May or the young Slade student Barbara Hiles, was slight, but before his departure for France he had told Lytton that he was out of his senses about Alix Sargent-Florence. His compulsive need for women slowly aroused Duncan's jealousy and placed on their triumvirate a strain which Vanessa's refusal to sleep with Bunny may have increased.

Shortly after Bunny left for France, Vanessa sent Roger an account of how things stood:

> I don't know how to describe the whole arrangement between the 3 of us. It is odd, I suppose, but as far as the relations between me and Bunny go it is in a way simple. We should not see very much of each other I expect if it were not for Duncan. As it is we like each other very much. He is not in the least in love with me nor I with him. Duncan provides a curious meeting ground for us as we are both so intimate with him. I think B is now not exactly in love with D but depends on him a great deal, and is very fond of him. At the same time I think he is really more attracted by women and generally has several flirtations on hand. . . . He is certainly very generous which I like and has strong affections. Sometimes of course it has been difficult for I couldn't help minding some things and feeling out of it and in the way but that was less so lately and we seemed to have settled down to a possible relationship . . . I don't think I can write about my relations with him [Duncan] . . . it's too difficult . . . and I don't think there's any great change in either of our feelings. We have seen more of each other and I have been happier.[29]

What she could not tell Roger was her conviction that her love for Duncan was absolute and final: beside this, the restrictions on their relationship counted for little.

In August she, Clive and the children returned to the Sussex coast, renting a house called The Grange at Bosham, which placed them in easy reach of the Hutchinsons at Eleanor House. Although in June Mary had stayed at Gordon Square, her husband Jack was as yet ignorant of her affair. 'I am alone here,' Vanessa wrote to Maynard, soon after arriving, 'Clive having gone off with Mary to visit Ott and then Lytton. Jack has had to put up I think rather against his will with again not being asked. Poor man, it is getting a little marked I think, and what my servants think I can't imagine. They're very kind to me. Mabel and Flossie talk to me a

Iceland Poppies, 1909

Lytton Strachey, 1911

A Conversation, 1913–16

Abstract, c. 1914

Interior with a Table, San Tropez, 1921

Poppies and Hollyhocks, c. 1940

Interior with Housemaid, 1939

Self-portrait, 1958

great deal.'[30] Though she had initially encouraged Clive in his pursuit of Mary, now that she had become a part of their circle Vanessa felt uneasy.

Mary Hutchinson (née Barnes) was a cousin of the Stracheys and like Duncan had spent her childhood in India. Her mother had died young and she had been brought up by her grandparents in England and sent to Effington School. This background had been inhibiting and not until she met, and in 1910 married, the genial, broadminded barrister Jack Hutchinson had her personality begun to develop. He encouraged her interest in art, and in general began her education in a way that Clive was to continue. She quickly outgrew her husband, however, who had, Vanessa thought, 'that peculiar type of open-minded tolerance which is more deadly than anything',[31] and whose love of telling bawdy tales exhausted even her own taste for this genre. Mary's love of irony amused Clive and he perceived that she had many unrealized talents. She had a sprightly sense of humour and with her two children would go through the medicine cabinet inventing different personages for each bottle. But she was presented to Vanessa in an unfortunate manner; in front of Mary, Clive held forth on her talents as a writer, praising her brilliant conversation and her caustic analysis of the *faux bon*. 'Mary sat silent as though unaware that she was the subject of these eulogies,' David Garnett recalled. 'Sometimes Duncan would make an effort and ask some question. But Clive would not be directed from the subject of Mary's perfections while the two women sat looking on in silence. There was sometimes a gleam of humour in Vanessa's eye.'[32]

Clive's praise was not unjustified. Mary was intelligent, well-read, a devotee of Proust and a close friend of Eliot and Aldous Huxley. She was to publish a volume of short stories with the Hogarth Press and wrote occasional reviews for *Vogue*. She could be biased and opinionated in her views but this did not antagonize Vanessa so much as her taste and appearance. Whereas Vanessa rarely did anything to enhance her looks, Mary personified the fashionable and chic. She bought her clothes from Poiret, later from Charlie James, and inclined towards the bizarre. Tall, pretty, but not beautiful, her mouth being too pronounced for her small face, she appeared pale, fastidious and slight beside her large, strawberry-red, ebullient husband. She always sat upright, never leaning back in a chair, and would never have fallen asleep while posing for Duncan as Vanessa did. The artist Adrian Daintrey observed: 'Mary gave the impression that, should you come upon her suddenly, she would always present just such a front as she would wish you to see.'[33] This disconcerted Vanessa who objected: 'Mary I think is made for salons. Her exquisiteness is not lost upon us but it ought really to be seen by the polite world.'[34] Bloomsbury, particularly Virginia, imposed upon Mary a more fashionable image than was in fact true, for though she went frequently to parties, she refused invitations from the leading hostesses, Sybil Colefax and Lady Cunard. Her morals, too, were less disciplined than her appearance, and her tendency to flirt roused in Clive furious jealousy.

Vanessa could not disguise her feelings towards Mary when she came to paint her portrait.[§] Here the personalities of the two women meet and clash, Vanessa's broad handling being at odds with Mary's tight composure; Mary's likeness and outward coldness are accurately caught in a painting that also triumphantly reveals Vanessa's attitude towards her sitter. She satirizes Mary's sly expression by painting the whites of the eyes blue and the sideways-glancing irises blue-black. Across one cheek slithers a green diagonal, indicating shadow; it directs the eye towards the mouth with its exaggerated lower lip, the whole painting culminating in a rubescent pout.

While at Bosham, Vanessa attempted to improve her lodging-house surroundings by placing her and Duncan's paintings over the dreary prints that hung on the grey walls. She also swam daily, like the rest, for the weather was hot. The children spent most of their time outdoors. Julian's hair, bleached by the sun, hung in pale streaks over a darker ashen gold; Quentin regularly played the buffoon. When the wind dropped the estuary stretched before them like a sheet of glass while herons stood sentinel on the mud and gulls and curlews wheeled overhead.

One evening Duncan and Vanessa sailed up the estuary to attend a party given by the Hutchinsons at Eleanor House for the novelist Gilbert Cannan and his wife Mary and two subalterns. Vanessa and Duncan, with masks, performed a piece called *Euphrosine ou les mystères du sexe* in which Vanessa changed into boy's clothing half-way through. Charades followed, on the words 'sodomy' and 'passion'. The last scene, acted by Duncan and Mary Hutchinson, again parodied life, as it ended with Jack, playing the deceived husband, discovering them in bed together, Duncan escaping through the back window in nothing but his shirt, to the surprise of the fisherman who was laying his nets outside.

When Duncan left Bosham to visit his parents, Roger arrived. Vanessa, normally content to paint what was on her doorstep, now found herself carrying her easel for miles in search of motifs. She came down to breakfast to find that Roger had already bathed, visited the village church and done countless small tasks. On his last day he announced his desire to sail up the estuary with her and Clive. Eager to set out, he fumed while they procrastinated, the situation reminding Vanessa of their travels in Italy. By the time they reached the shore all the boats had been taken, but as the day was hot, Clive and Vanessa sank down contentedly on to the sand, prepared to wait their turn. Roger, who knew little about sailing, meanwhile haggled with each boatman in turn until eventually they found him a boat, larger than the usual kind and boasting enormous sails. In this they shot down the estuary with ease. When they had almost reached the open sea Roger turned back, only to discover that the wind had dropped and the tide was now against them; despite persistent tacking they made no advance. Clive despaired and declared they could do nothing but drop anchor and wait till midnight when the tide would turn again; Roger, tacking remorselessly, ignored him. Eventually a breeze sprang up and carried them home. Vanessa, while silently resolving never to let her children sail in Roger's company, thought the expedition typical of his determination to conquer – men, wind and tide.

The war continued to set an oppressive background to their holiday mood. Maynard, on his visits, brought inside news from the Treasury and terrifying descriptions of Zeppelins. Earlier that summer Clive had courageously written a pamphlet entitled 'Peace at Once' as a challenge to the shallow optimism of the militarists. It must have lost him the regard of a good many of his friends and acquaintances outside Bloomsbury; it caused his father temporarily to cut off his allowance, G.K. Chesterton to attack him violently in the *Nation*; and the Lord Mayor of London ordered the pamphlet to be burnt. At the same time Vanessa received letters from Margery Snowden detailing which members of her family had enlisted and how her time was occupied with garden parties for war charities. From this Vanessa concluded, 'I see more and more that we are completely isolated from our kind.'[35]

Towards the end of September Vanessa began to make plans for Bunny's return. At Bosham her portrait of him with a red nose had hung over the mantelpiece, reminding her that while she enjoyed freedom and happiness he was labouring in harsh conditions in France. She wrote to him with easy affection:

In spite of wars and conscription and all horrors and disappointments, I must tell you ... that I have been extraordinarily selfishly happy lately. One of the advantages of being old is that one isn't happy without knowing it – I have known it often lately ... it has been hot and sunny and I sit out or in and paint with the animal and he takes me for walks in the evening and he's there when I wake up and when I go to bed and sometimes in between too (which in between can be read either way) and he's so extraordinarily charming and odd in his ways and so amazingly nice to me that I have been as childishly happy as one can be. ... The only drawback sometimes is that one can't tell him so or say anything but some platitude about 'what a nice creature you are'. ... Of course I've suffered too from some of the bad tricks you have taught him. I've often been bitten to the quick and there's an awful new habit he's got of tickling – in the road or anywhere and he carries it to such a point that sometimes the only escape has been to throw myself in the road regardless of cuts and bruises.[36]

Having no prospect of any job in London, Bunny felt unable to return home for he had no wish to live off his friends. Vanessa, realizing his straits, sent him £5 and promised to do all she could to find him employment. In October he took a fortnight's leave and returned to London, learning *en route* that there was a possibility of employment at the Institut Pasteur in Paris. At the same time Duncan received an invitation from Jacques Copeau to execute scenery and costume designs for a performance of *Pelléas et Mélisande* at the Théâtre du Vieux-Colombier in Paris. He received official approval from the Foreign Office to undertake this work and when Bunny's leave ended the two friends crossed the Channel together. At Dieppe they were wrenched apart by government officials who declared Duncan a 'pacifist anarchist' and offered him the choice of imprisonment in a concentration camp or immediate deportation. He returned to England the next day, suffering taunts and insults from both passengers and officials, and arrived back at 46 Gordon Square to find a play-reading in progress. 'It all seemed familiar but far off, especially when Clive started to make an academic harangue on the liberties we were supposed to be fighting for',[37] he told Bunny, who, after a brief, unhappy period in Paris, returned to the Mission Anglaise at Sommeilles.

Duncan, separated again from Bunny, ran to Vanessa with his depression. She plotted and schemed, approaching Maynard and Dora Sanger, the wife of a Chancery barrister, in the hope of finding employment for Bunny. She dreamed of setting up a colony in Cornwall where all could exist freely, enjoying a large studio and a communal dining-room and where they would never take a newspaper. She sent Bunny money for his return journey and invited him to join them at Asheham in the New Year. Duncan's restlessness made her now pathetically eager for Bunny's re-appearance. She spent Christmas at Garsington, amused by the disparity between Ottoline's extravagance and Philip's parsimony, and afterwards joined Virginia and Leonard at Asheham.

The new year began with the government's introduction of conscription. Vanessa was alone with the Woolfs when the news first came through, and she was thankful when Clive, Duncan and Bunny, who had now returned from France, joined them. Maynard, Lytton and Harry Norton also arrived and the talk constantly returned to the implications of the forthcoming bill. All agreed it would be better to go to prison than become a soldier, as they were opposed to the diminished responsibility for one's own acts that military service entailed. They may also have been aware that Asquith's Military Service Act was politically expedient rather than necessary, satisfying not the needs of the army but a demand made by popular feeling.

Nevertheless conscription shattered Vanessa's carapace of ignorance. Once, at the Morrells, she distinguished herself by asking the man next to her at dinner if he was interested in politics: Mr Asquith, whose face at that time appeared regularly on the hoardings exhorting the country to save for victory, if not amused, must have been very surprised. Until now she had merely glanced at newspapers, taking the *Daily Mirror* because its many illustrations gave her ideas for paintings. But the new act, which called up all single men resident in England who were without dependants and between the ages of eighteen and forty-one, affected the lives of those closest to her. Like other of her friends, she now undertook simple office work on a voluntary basis for the National Council for Civil Liberties, while Clive, at the request of Lloyd George, sat on a committee to look into what provisions could be made for conscientious objectors. Tribunals were set up all over England, empowered to grant absolute or conditional exemption. If conditional exemption was awarded some form of non-combatant service had to be found. Duncan and Bunny knew that their own cases would receive a better hearing if they were already engaged in useful labour. It was therefore their good fortune to discover that a farmhouse, formerly belonging to one of Duncan's aunts, Miss Florence Ewebank, who had recently died, was vacant and the six acres attached to it in need of cultivation.

Miss Ewebank had lived at Wissett Grange in a small Suffolk village of the same name and had rented out the nearby Wissett Lodge. Duncan's father, Major Bartle Grant, had been left in charge of her estate and with the two young men went down to inspect the Lodge, its land and the orchards, half a mile off, that belonged to the Grange. They found the apple trees badly in need of pruning and the blackcurrant bushes infected with disease. Though the major could barely veil his disapproval of his son's pacifism, and in Garnett's presence spoke of him to Duncan as 'your friend Garbage', he agreed to their moving in.

Aware of the grim alternatives awaiting conscientious objectors, Duncan and Bunny immediately set to work. Neither had any knowledge of farming and their unprofessional methods roused suspicion and distrust among the local inhabitants. When Bunny's friend Barbara Hiles visited she was first coerced into weeding an asparagus bed and then, with Bunny, made to act the part of a horse while Duncan tried to plough a field. They suspected that some of their white leghorns were being stolen and so died their tails blue, giving the birds a patriotic look for their colours were now blue, white and red. This unorthodox practice caused further resentment and was felt by the locals to make a mockery of poultry farming.

Once they were settled at Wissett, Vanessa joined them, bringing with her the children, her cook Blanche and the nursemaid Flossie. Virginia was upset at the thought of her moving permanently to the country, but Vanessa ignored her pleas. Duncan returned to London to assist her with the move. The day of their journey was warm and sunny, only marred by Duncan, who was suffering from a hangover, vomiting on the cab floor while they drove to Liverpool Street. They caught a train to Halesworth and probably made the last part of their journey in a horse and cart belonging to a local gypsy whose services they occasionally employed. The Lodge is situated about a mile outside the small village of Wissett; its large, half-timbered façade overlooks the road but in those days was partly hidden from it by an enormous evergreen oak.

The next day Vanessa sat in the sun without her jacket and wrote a letter to Clive. Everything, almost, met with her approval: the nineteen white leghorns had so far produced ten eggs and more were expected in the course of the day; the children were running wild in the garden; the house was ample, peaceful and even more isolated than Asheham. 'It is amazingly remote from the war and all horrors, though Bunny saw a Zeppelin on Friday night and heard some explosions. We hear rumours that one came down in the mouth of the Thames, but we get no papers – is it true? How absurd it seems that people shouldn't be allowed to live this kind of life in peace. One could be perfectly happy like this I believe. Only the time goes too fast.'[38]

Under her influence the house was quickly put in order. Paintings were hung, and Clive, who had proposed a visit with Mary Hutchinson, received instructions to bring some collapsible rhorkee chairs. The chimney was swept and missing bricks replaced. To counter the darkness of certain rooms – for in 1916 the house had squeezed into its steep roof an additional attic storey which has since been removed – they applied a brilliant lime-blue distemper to the walls. Next she banished from sight the remains of the previous tenant, including the numerous ornaments and small tables. 'I find that there are things one *does* object to, to live with,' she told Roger. 'Especially the imitation Morris and early Victorian chintzes, and things which merely create dirt and stuffiness, and things which are peculiarly thin and *mesquin*.'[39] She dyed the chair-covers with coloured inks and before long the rooms became vibrant and alive. Once this had been done she began to look around for a studio, discovered a working space in the top of a nearby barn that was partly filled with old beehives, and arranged for the shutter over the window to be replaced with glass.

With purposeful organization she again created a situation in which those around her could live and work happily. Blanche took charge of the cooking; Flossie flirted with soldiers from Halesworth; Duncan and Bunny worked on the land all day; the children, who had developed a passion for war games, spent most of their time outdoors and needed little attention. A new addition to the household was the sheep-dog with one blue eye, given to Duncan by a neighbouring farmer, and named Henry after Ottoline's brother, Lord Henry Cavendish Bentinck, who had recently bought some of Duncan's paintings.

When Mary and Clive arrived on a visit, the *bon viveur* found the Lodge sadly lacking in comfort; he complained of the cold, the cooking, the puppy and the fleas. At Easter Maynard arrived and while he was there Vanessa saw her first Zeppelin which passed over the house making a noise like a threshing machine. Lytton and Harry Norton came next, for a week in June, and were bemused by the rampant growth and absence of civilization. Lytton wondered whether the inhabitants of the house had arrived at the secret of life. Or was it, rather, incurable oblivion? Vanessa had earlier warned him: 'I feel that all our ways are changing. We are so much overcome by the country as compared with London that I doubt if I shall ever return to Gordon Square. The delight of having no telephone, no crowd to tea and all the rest is so great. Then the positive delights also of flowers and trees and innumerable unexpected sights and sounds keep one perpetually happy.'[40] Lytton, however, suspected a danger in its somnolence: 'Everything and everybody seems to be more or less overgrown with vegetation, thistles four feet high fill the flower garden, Duncan is covered with Virginia (or should it be Vanessa?) creeper, and Norton and I go about pulling up the weeds and peeping under the foliage.'[41]

Lytton, and Mary before him, brought news of Garsington where Philip Morrell was now employing conscientious objectors as farm labourers. This, in itself, invited a parallel with their life at Wissett and though Vanessa had neither Ottoline's wealth nor her authority, her intense interest in Garsington suggests that she regarded it as a rival outpost. When Roger visited it at Easter, Vanessa wrote to him for more news, but he, having spent his time virtuously crocheting hats to sell at the Omega, had little to give her. Garsington's exotic décor and eccentric way of life preyed on Vanessa's mind; but she doubted if Ottoline was creative and quizzed Lytton on the matter. 'Norton and Duncan and I', she announced to Roger, 'took the line that she has a terrifically energetic and vigorous character with a definite rather bad taste . . . but that it was different from having any creative power – but Lytton thinks Garsington a creation. . . . To me it seems simply a collection of objects she likes put together with enormous energy but not made into anything.'[42] She was perhaps comparing it with Wissett Lodge where one bedroom now had Fra Angelico copies, painted in watercolour, on the bare whitewashed walls. She herself had executed a Visitation but had not stuck rigidly to the original design. In between these decorations they hung columns of marbled paper.

In May Duncan's and Bunny's case came up before the Blything Tribunal; their appeal for exemption was rejected despite representation on their behalf by Philip Morrell, Maynard and Adrian. The Suffolk farmers who sat on the jury suspected the two young men of having moved to the area in an attempt to evade call-up; they were irritated by Adrian's legalistic arguments, and when Maynard, speaking for Bunny, mentioned that his mother had visited Tolstoy, they replied that it made no difference to Garnett's case where his mother had been. After this their only chance of avoiding prison lay with the Appeal Tribunal which met at Ipswich on 19 May. This time Maynard adopted an aggressive approach. He began the proceedings by placing his bag stamped with the Royal Cipher where all could see it and announced that he hoped for an expeditious hearing because important work awaited him at the Treasury. Afterwards he telegraphed Vanessa with the news that both men had been granted exemption from combative service with leave to appeal to the Central Tribunal regarding alternative employment. Prison had therefore been averted but to avoid uncongenial labour Duncan and Bunny had to prove that they were engaged in work of 'national importance'.

Vanessa now wrote to Virginia asking if Lady Robert Cecil (Nelly) would speak on Duncan's behalf to her brother-in-law James Cecil, fourth Marquis of Salisbury and Chairman of the Central Tribunal. This Lady Robert did, though nothing was allowed to sway Lord Salisbury's careful impartiality. While waiting for further news, Vanessa distracted herself by making artificial flowers for the Omega, some of which reappeared in her paintings and decorated the room at the Omega when in February of this year she put on a small show of her work, which ran for two weeks. She also began reading the two-volume life of Sir Edward Burne-Jones written by his wife.

> How perfectly awful and how provincial those Victorians were, except Rossetti and Morris and I'm not sure Ruskin wasn't better in many ways than most. B J himself simply deteriorated into a machine I think. He went on with his incredibly sentimental owl in an ivy bush view of himself and his holy mission completely ignorant of the whole of French art of this time, impressionists and

all. My God his evidence about Whistler [at the Whistler *v*. Ruskin trial] was too awful and gave him away pretty well. I see the only hope for the English is to get outside their island pretty often.[43]

Still uncertain about the future, they received a visit from the Woolfs. 'I've seldom enjoyed myself more than I did with you,' Virginia afterwards wrote, 'and I cant make out exactly how you manage. One seems to get into such a contented state of mind. I heard from Lytton who feels the same, and says he would like to live with you forever.'[44] Vanessa's gift for creating mental freedom and domestic comfort remained unchanged. Disliking fuss, enjoying relaxation, she brought to any situation a combination of maternal warmth and critical intelligence, as well as an element of creative risk. Once when Ottoline compared Dorelia John, now established with Augustus at Alderney Manor amid harmonious disorder, with Vanessa, Lytton, in his shrill Strachey voice, replied: 'Yes, but she hasn't got that sharp cutting intellect of Vanessa's.'[45] Virginia discerned that a certain conflict in Vanessa's nature enabled her to combine vulnerability with granitic strength. While visiting Wissett, she arrived at the initial idea for her novel *Night and Day* in which Katherine Hilbery is based on Vanessa. 'But try thinking of Katherine as Vanessa, not me,' Virginia later told her former Greek teacher Janet Case; 'and suppose her concealing a passion for painting and forced to go into society by George [Duckworth] – that was the beginning of her.'[46]

At Wissett Vanessa painted for several hours each day. The barn had proved too cold for comfort and she did most of her work in a bedroom. She painted a view out of the window of the pond in front of the house, placing an Omega jug and box in the foreground on the sill. The view through the window was to become a popular motif during the twenties as it satisfied the modernist concern with the flatness of the picture plane, the window frame forcing up the external scene into a firmer relationship with the picture surface. Vanessa's recurrent use of this motif, however, suggests that it had for her more personal significance. It may reflect on her need for domestic security and on the protected position from which, because of her sex and class, she viewed the world. It is interesting that the photograph of her mother which she kept for many years on her desk shows Julia leaning against a closed window, her face turned to the light.

A window also plays an important role in her picture *The Conversation*§ (sometimes called *Three Women*), begun in 1913 and partially repainted at Wissett. From the surface movement visible beneath the top layer of paint, it would appear that she reworked the women's dresses, probably darkening their tone in order to bring out their contrast with the brightly coloured flowers seen outside. These become the visual equivalent to the animated chatter of the three women, absorbed in their talk as the curved lines of their figures suggest. In both choice of pose and subject Vanessa may have been influenced by Duncan's *The Queen of Sheba* (Tate Gallery), though Vanessa's humour is more biting, less sweet. On seeing this picture, Virginia declared: 'I think you are a most remarkable painter. But I maintain you are into the bargain, a satirist, a conveyor of impressions about human life: a short story writer of great wit and able to bring off a situation in a way that rouses my envy. I wonder if I could write the *Three Women* in prose.'[47]

Because Duncan was largely occupied with farmwork, Vanessa painted mostly on her own at Wissett. She therefore welcomed external stimulation and when Roger visited Paris in June she begged him for news of Picasso's and Matisse's recent work. In search of new ideas, she imitated Roger and painted a joke portrait of Queen Victoria based on a photograph, telling him, 'She's just the sort of middle-class woman I am always wanting to paint, entirely dressed in furniture ornaments'.[48] When he sent her a black and white reproduction of a Giotto to copy, together with a precise description of its colours, she interpreted it freely and felt as elated by the venture as if the subject were her own. She turned easily from the sacred to the profane, executing designs for a bed for Mary Hutchinson. 'One side is a woman asleep, rather like "Flaming June" by Lord Leighton with poppies and waves (I think) all very symbolical. On the other is the remains of the dessert she has been eating and down below flowers tied in a true lover's knot of white satin ribbon.'[49] Only a sketch of the sleeping woman remains (Swindon Art Gallery), its rhythmic use of distortion indebted to the example of Matisse.

The arrival of Lady Ottoline disrupted their routine existence. Vanessa had dreaded her visit, foreseeing that her extravagant presence would quickly become claustrophobic in the small cramped rooms. There was also the danger that Quentin, an advanced six-year-old, might pinch her bottom and accompany this gesture with winks and giggles. However Harry Norton was present when she arrived and helped alleviate the burden of conversation. Even so, Vanessa blazed with rage after her visitor left. 'We're recovering from Ott. whose visit nearly destroyed us. ... I've decided that woman isn't for me. I can't stand it and hope I shall never spend more than a few hours at a time in her presence again – or at the most one weekend a year. This is final. Not that I dislike her but the strain is too great.'[50] Ottoline herself cannot have enjoyed the visit; on more than one occasion Norton gave her Bengal Lights disguised as matches with which to light her cigarettes and they ignited with a blinding flash leaving her shaking and furious.

Soon after this the Central Tribunal announced that Duncan and Bunny could not be their own employers and they would have to seek farm work elsewhere. Vanessa now moved quickly. In May she had received from Virginia a lengthy description of a farmhouse called Charleston which was only four miles from Asheham. Further mention of the house had again been made in August when Adrian and Karin thought of taking it, but a week later Virginia reported that they had changed their minds. Vanessa now went down to Asheham to seek out the farmer Mr Gunn and to enquire about work for Duncan and Bunny. He promised to introduce her to a certain Mr Hecks (who farmed the nearby New House Farm) at Lewes market the next day. Sleeping that night alone at Asheham, Vanessa reflected how different Sussex was from Suffolk for it felt far less remote. Bicyling out from Lewes station she had been overtaken by motor vehicles transporting horses for use in the war. 'But once past the Eastbourne road', she wrote to Duncan, 'it was quite quiet and one is overcome by the extraordinary peace and beauty of the place. The colour is too amazing now, all very warm, most lovely browns and warm greys and reds with the chalk everywhere giving that odd kind of softness.'[51] The next day she met Mr Hecks who agreed to employ her two young men. Before finally departing she bicycled out to Charleston for a quick look at the house, received an unfavourable impression and returned by train to London.

Something, however, must have caught at her mind for a day or two later she travelled down to Sussex again and this time was met at Glynde station by the tenant of Charleston, a Mr Stacey, who was prepared to sublet. He took her all over the house, showing her the many larders, the cupboards, the cellar and the outbuildings. The rooms had recently been papered and when Vanessa said she would prefer to whitewash over them or paint them a single colour, he did not object. This time the house seemed to her quite different and she wrote excitedly to Duncan, describing its 'large lake', its orchard and overgrown tennis lawn that looked like a field. After seeing the house and agreeing to take it, she lunched with the Staceys in their house at Firle, keeping her feelings disguised while Mrs Stacey voiced her thoughts on the war. She then returned to Wissett and did not see Charleston again until she arrived to take up residence.

The move out of Wissett caused turmoil and dispute. The earth closets had to be emptied, dead chickens buried, twenty-five parcels of luggage packed. 'Here all is confusion and horror,' wrote Bunny to Lytton. 'Duncan's parents insist that every particle of paint shall be scraped and washed off. Vanessa, the children, servants and Barbara [Hiles], who has been staying here, leave today with ten bales of canvases, easels, rorky [sic] chairs and pet rabbits.'[52] Added to this list were ducks, packing-cases, a sack of globe artichokes, two bicycles and the sheep-dog Henry. To make matters worse, Quentin, who had recently cut his knee, had to travel on a stretcher. Though five packages disappeared *en route* (afterwards turning up at Gordon Square), the inspector at Liverpool Street Station declared they had more luggage than was allowed, and charged them an excess fee of nineteen shillings. This was more than all the money they had between them and Duncan's offer to leave his watch as security offended the chief clerk who refused to let them take any of the luggage and everything had to be left at the station until the next day.

Duncan then returned to Wissett to dispose of the livestock and the apple crop and Vanessa remained in London for a short while. It was Bunny who first went down to Sussex, in the company of two ex-Slade students Barbara Hiles and Dora Carrington. All three went to look at Charleston, Bunny afterwards telling Vanessa that he thought it open, easy and roomy. Carrington sent her a still more enthusiastic note, perceiving that there were many things in the house and garden that would make subjects to paint. She and Barbara left Bunny at the Ram Inn at Firle, where he initially put up while he began work for Mr Hecks.

Soon after Vanessa herself arrived at Charleston her fears that she had misjudged the house vanished. To Roger she wrote:

> Anyhow it's most lovely, very solid and simple, with flat walls in that lovely mixture of brick and flint that they use about here and perfectly flat windows in the walls and wonderfully tiled roofs. The pond is most beautiful with a willow at one side and a stone or flint wall edging it all round the garden part, and a little lawn sloping down to it with formal bushes in it. Then there's a small orchard and walled garden and another lawn and bit of field railed in beyond. There's a wall of trees – one single line of elms all round two sides, which shelters us from west winds. We are just below Firle Beacon which is the highest point on the downs. . . . Inside the house the rooms are very large and a great many. . . . One [bedroom] I shall make into a studio. It is very light and large with an east window, but the sun doesn't come in much after quite early morning, and it has a small room out of it with another window, so one might get interesting interiors I think. The house is really much too big at present of course, but it's nice to have space and no doubt it will get filled in time. There's hardly any furniture in it yet. . . . The Omega dinner service looks most lovely on the dresser.

She decided that the bedrooms should be kept relatively empty. For the rest of the house she bought furniture in Lewes and, on Barbara Hiles's suggestion, visited the Caledonian Road but found to her dismay that it was Thursday and all the shops were closed. Nevertheless odd and ugly pieces of furniture kept appearing unexpectedly in corners of the house and were to contribute to its unique character. Neither the initial bareness nor the lack of comfort mattered. At nine o'clock in the morning, with Duncan and Bunny having set off for work at seven-thirty and the children still in care in London, she had time to consider her new surroundings and the promise they presented. 'It will be an odd life', she concluded her letter to Roger, '... but it seems to me it ought to be a good one for painting.'[53]

EIGHT

One Among Three
1916-1918

Like Asheham, Charleston is remote, situated at the end of a farm track leading off the main Lewes to Eastbourne road. In 1916 it was even more cut off than it is today and visitors arriving by train either had to walk, taking a short cut through the fields, from Glynde, or travel on to Berwick in the hope of finding a taxi. The surrounding countryside was then less intensely cultivated, the roads mere dusty lanes bordered by uncut hedges and alive with wild flowers and small animals. Charleston is situated almost at the foot of Firle Beacon, the highest in a line of downs that stretch from Newhaven to Cuckmere. These dominate the landscape, rising so abruptly out of the flat fields that their presence is felt even from a distance. On the days that a sea-mist rolls in they are obliterated from sight until the impenetrable fog frays at the edges like wisps of cotton wool.

Though mainly eighteenth-century, the house in part dates back to the seventeenth and, in the course of recent repairs, structural features have been revealed that go back still earlier.[1] A substantial, three-storey farmhouse, its unornamented front elevation is broken only by six wide sash windows. Around the turn of the century it had been used as a guest-house and porcelain number-plates are still nailed to the bedroom doors. A photograph of Charleston at this date shows the garden in immaculate order and guests in Edwardian costume punting on the pond, its edges kept neat and trim. Since then the Gage family, who owned the surrounding estate and nearby Firle village, had leased the house to the farmer Mr Stacey who had sublet. When Vanessa took over the rent, the garden was overgrown, the tennis lawn knee-high with long grass and studded with wasp-hollowed apples and pears that lay unharvested on the ground.

The house faces east and overlooks the pond (Vanessa's 'large lake') on which Duncan at one point considered breeding flamingos. In 1916 the front door was surmounted with a gabled porch (later removed in favour of a brick surround). The interior of the house was also slightly more rambling than it is today for in 1939 Vanessa introduced fairly extensive alterations. But even in 1916 the rooms, though low-ceilinged, were generously proportioned and they convey comfort and seclusion but not claustrophobia. One room (which became known as the garden room) had French windows that opened on to the large walled garden situated on the north side of the house. Beyond it lay a paddock and an orchard, and a line of elms that protected house and garden from northerly winds. Even here, amid the peace and isolation that Charleston offered, war could not be forgotten, for when the winds blew in the opposite direction the noise of gunfire sometimes carried across the Channel.

Charleston became Vanessa's permanent home for the next three years. After 1919 it was only used in the holiday periods and not until 1939 did she again reside there permanently. With its ample size and rural surround-ings, it suited family life and from the start her children were at the centre of its existence. It also encouraged the unfolding of her and Duncan's decorative talent and, though at first many rooms remained bare and empty, over the years to come pattern and colour were to appear around fireplaces, on overmantels, doors, walls and furniture, echoing and har-monizing with the paintings, textiles and embroidered cushion covers, giving the house its unique character.

The secret of Charleston's colourfulness lies in its use of grey. Soon after moving in Vanessa, having obtained Mr Stacey's permission to do so, obliterated all the existing wallpapers with a wash of distemper. She and Duncan mixed Indian red and cobalt blue into the white paint to achieve a warm grey. This mid tone, unlike white, allows other colours to retain their strength without making them look brash. It is also sympathetic to light which it both absorbs and mutedly reflects, enabling it to spread into the dim corners of the low-ceilinged rooms.

This grey provides the basis for Vanessa's decorations in one upstairs bedroom. The long wall, opposite the window, contains a fireplace and two doors, one leading into a small dressing-room. In February 1918 she filled the upper panels of the doors each with a vase of flowers, and the lower with marbled circles, a motif she repeated in the three discs orna-menting the fireplace. The slightly austere geometrical decorations hold in check the exuberance of the flowers. These are freely handled and do not follow closely the underlying, quickly-sketched pencil design. In places Vanessa incorporated the pale colour of the ground into the design, so that it becomes the white of the Michaelmas daisies or the glass of the vase, and this interlocking of positive and negative shapes may reflect her contemporaneous interest in woodcut. Finally, in order to turn doors and fireplace into a decorative whole, she painted the surrounding architraves and skirting-board Indian red. These decorations, together with those in the downstairs room to the right of the front door, where again circles ornament the fireplace and flowers the wood panels beneath the window, were the first to be executed. To this day they remain gay and fresh.

These exuberant decorations belie the harsh conditions in which they were produced. They had neither piped water nor electricity; water had to be pumped, earth closets emptied, wood chopped before fires could be lit. Food was rationed and in short supply. Vanessa therefore kept chickens and ducks and later rabbits, while Bunny kept bees. The house was difficult to heat and often freezing; in winter it was sometimes necessary to break the ice on a basin of water before washing. Vanessa did however employ three servants – a cook, a maid and a tweeny, as labour was still cheap. (Just how cheap can be assessed from the fact that in 1913, when Clive and Vanessa discovered they had overspent their income that year by £600, and therefore abandoned a proposed trip to Spain, they were paying their nurse who lived in at the standard rate of £25 per annum.) And though she was obliged this year to sell a Thackeray manuscript that had remained in the family in order to pay for the move and furnish the house, her financial security was never threatened. She still received an allowance from Clive (temporarily domiciled at Garsington), despite the fact that they now led more or less separate lives; and he had enough invested capital to live comfortably off his unearned income, even after 1929 when the Wall Street crash drastically devalued his Canadian and American securities. Vanessa herself had a small amount of capital which she invested on Maynard's advice. In 1918 he estimated that this stood at £3,600, bringing her in an income of around £200 a year. In 1917 her total income must have been more than £533 as this was her expenditure for that year which, Bunny noted in his diary, was within her means. Nevertheless, with Duncan and Bunny labouring often in harsh conditions in the fields, life at Charleston was not luxurious and at first only rarely pleasurable. Vanessa therefore tended to mock Leonard's fear that their decadent way of life and close proximity to Asheham would pollute the atmosphere and put a strain on Virginia's health. Vanessa herself was anxious to guard her privacy and when Lytton proposed himself as a lodger, she refused him, arguing that her household was already too oddly composed to allow for another permanent addition.

One friend who did become a regular visitor and who made substantial financial contributions to the running of the house was Maynard Keynes.

At both Asheham and Wissett his intelligence, wit and brilliant conversation had always made him a welcome guest. He could turn a commonplace into a paradox, find a truism in the unexpected, believing that 'words ought to be a little wild, for they are the assaults of thought upon the unthinking'.[2] He had a quick mind, was exceptionally well informed and had unusual powers of concentration; as a schoolboy at Eton he had kept a record of the number of hours he worked, regarding three or four a poor effort, seven or nine more satisfactory. His Fellowship dissertation, 'A Treatise on Probability', written between 1906 and 1908, had restored him to King's College in 1909 as an economics lecturer, but since January 1915 he had been in the employment of the Treasury, involved with the financing of war. This had placed him in a difficult position with his pacifist friends in Bloomsbury, for to them it seemed that 'his job must have involved calculating the cheapest way to kill Germans'.[3] In February 1916 Lytton had tackled him on this matter during dinner at 46 Gordon Square, with Vanessa, Duncan and Bunny sitting round in approving silence. Despite this, friendly relations had been maintained and Maynard had been of valuable help to Duncan and Bunny at their tribunals.

Maynard's Cambridge background, conversational skill and shattering wit were not the only factors that endeared him to Bloomsbury: he was also adept at indecent jokes and himself highly sexed. At one time he had rivalled Lytton for the affections of Arthur Hobhouse, a handsome but conventional Cambridge graduate who momentarily capitulated to Duncan. Keynes himself had fallen heavily in love with Duncan during the summer of 1908 and had suffered greatly when Adrian Stephen superseded him in Grant's life. Since then the arbitrariness of Maynard's sexual encounters with both sexes had given rise to the rumour that he had copulated with Vanessa on a sofa in Gordon Square. Only his devotion to her makes this improbable. He had an inordinately high regard for artists and writers and his affection for both Vanessa and Duncan was mixed with reverence. And though his high office and friendship with the Asquiths made him a regular guest at political house parties, he readily exchanged this more worldly ambience for Charleston and over the next three years made it his spiritual home.

It was Maynard who had taken over the lease of 46 Gordon Square when in August 1916 Vanessa realized that she would be tied to the country as long as war lasted. 'The theory is, I understand,' he had written to her, 'that in the break-up of no. 46, Duncan takes you, Mary takes Clive, and I take the children.'[4] In practice things were less simple. Vanessa took the children with her to Charleston and Clive, meanwhile, insisted on retaining his right to reside at Gordon Square whenever he wished. In addition it was to remain as a town house for all those living at Charleston and therefore Maynard was understandably worried that when he, Norton and, John Sheppard, a Fellow at King's College, Cambridge, moved in, the house might on occasion be too full for comfort. However, the changeover went ahead and though Clive did find cause for complaint, the new arrangement worked well. From London Maynard assisted Vanessa with the furnishing of Charleston; he ordered mattresses from the furniture shop Maples, sent down a Chinese carpet and offered Vanessa the furniture left at his disposal by his previous tenants in Gower Street. In turn Maynard, when driven to the end of his tether by excessive work, would go down to Sussex for a rest.

Once the house was furnished Vanessa confronted the problem of her children's education. She disliked the idea of sending them away, suspecting that public schools, with their asphyxiating pressures to conform, treated children mechanically and did not take enough care of their health. As an alternative she decided to set up a small school at Charleston and, as a preliminary experiment, in January 1917 she borrowed from the young socialist and erstwhile mistress of H.G. Wells, Amber Blanco-White, her two daughters, Anna-Jane and Justine. Vanessa's maid, Mabel Selwood, was elevated to the position of governess and made chiefly responsible for the children, though Vanessa herself taught them French and elementary music. In order to feed her extended family, Mabel's sister Trissie was lured away from the Hutchinsons, a fact that did little to improve Vanessa's relations with Mary. With two small girls living in the house, Julian and Quentin immediately became more self-conscious and at first things went well. Quentin played happily with Justine but Julian grew increasingly irritated with Anna-Jane. His civility broke down when the children were on a walk with Mabel, and seizing handfuls of gravel he pelted the elder girl and hit out at the younger with a stick. He was returned home in disgrace and Vanessa told of his misdeed. Though she rarely scolded or punished her children, when that afternoon she walked into the kitchen, where the children had their tea, the tone of her voice as she said 'Julian' was such that all four children promptly burst into tears.

Even under adverse wartime conditions Vanessa continued to impress others with her shaping control over the circumstances of her life. Roger, not wanting to know in detail the domestic circumstances that she enjoyed with Duncan, put off visiting Charleston until January 1917. He was then surprised by how much she had already achieved and slightly pained by her evident absorption in her surroundings. In March he succeeded in extracting her from Charleston by inviting her to visit Durbins. There both painted a madonna lily placed in front of a beaded African arrow case, a savage black stripe running down its centre. Both painted the same flower, but Vanessa chose only to include a select number of blooms which form a burst of pale colour at the top of the straight bare stem. The naturalistic colours and representational style reveal that Vanessa was sharing in a general move, affecting artists in England and France, away from abstraction. Three years earlier, in *The Mantelpiece* (Tate Gallery), the forms and colours which she arrived at had only a tenuous relationship with the actual still life. In *Madonna Lily* it is the actual look of the flower that engaged her attention and which, with the artist's powers of selection and compression, she strove to reproduce. When many years later her son Quentin asked her why she had turned away from abstraction she replied that she had come to the conclusion that nature was much richer and more interesting than anything one could invent.

Her reaction, however, coincided with a widespread move away from experimentation in the arts and was therefore influenced as much by impersonal forces as personal considerations. If war and its effects on social and economic life were the dominant catalysts, a more local influence was the retrospective mood encouraged by the exhibition of copies and trans-lations from the Old Masters shown at the Omega in the spring of 1917. Roger had intended this to bring out the unity within ancient and modern art and he encouraged all the artists associated with the Workshops to copy or freely translate from great art of the past. Vanessa sent, among other things, a copy of a Bronzino, an artist then very out of fashion, and with this won praise from Sickert.

Roger was nettled that the exhibition attracted few visitors and no reviews. The Omega continued to fill him with enthusiasm and leave him often irritable and out of pocket. In June he discovered to his fury that Vanessa and Duncan had agreed to decorate two rooms for Mary Hutch-inson in her River House, Hammersmith, for £12, thus undercutting the Omega by £8. Vanessa protested that Duncan had done a great deal of low-paid work for the Omega in the past; and as he had been unable to do much decorative work recently, he now did not wish to sacrifice his potential earnings from this one-off commission by going through the Omega. As it was, the increased assurance and calm disposition of form in Vanessa's recent decorative work left her out of sympathy with the in-choate patterns and muddy colours that Roger's less talented assistants at the Omega sometimes employed. When he took her to see the flat which the Workshops had recently decorated for the wife of a Belgian diplomat, Mme Lalla Vandervelde, Vanessa's immediate reaction was one of horror: the small rooms were crammed with painted objects in which the colours did not tell but cancelled one another out. They also appeared thin and shiny in quality. Unable to disguise her lack of enthusiasm for the venture as a whole, Vanessa hurriedly singled out individual items for muted praise.

Life at Charleston, meanwhile, throve on its isolation. A mile or two distant even from any nearby village, it encouraged an existence entirely free of the usual social pressures. 'Nessa is 4 miles on the other side of the downs, living like an old hen wife among ducks, chickens and children,' Virginia announced to Nelly Cecil in April 1917. 'She never wants to put on proper clothes again – even a bath seems to distress her. Her children are for ever asking her questions and she invents all sorts of answers, never having known very accurately about facts.'[5] She repeated this view to Violet Dickinson:

> Nessa and Duncan came over yesterday, having previously washed themselves; and then went back in a storm late at night to help ducklings out of their eggs, for they were heard quacking inside, and couldn't break through. Nessa seems to have slipped civilization off her back, and splashes about entirely nude, without shame, and enormous spirit. Indeed, Clive now takes up the line that she has ceased to be a presentable lady – I think it all works admirably.[6]

The children were not so sure. They had begun to realize, on visits to their friends' houses, that their own home life was totally improper: the front door of 46 Gordon Square had glared crimson in contrast with the discreet greens and blacks elsewhere; the unframed paintings that decorated the walls at Gordon Square, Wissett or Charleston were of a different colour from those that hung in gold frames in other peoples' houses. Then, too, nobody at Charleston seemed to take much interest in the war, while everywhere else it dominated conversation and invited religious dedication to its cause. The seven-year-old Quentin was quite certain that the adults he lived with were mad, but it did not really seem to matter. Though technically the children were living in a broken home, Clive, who made regular visits, was not missed. Duncan, Quentin has recollected, was 'a delight, a kind of absurd elder brother and Bunny a very stable sensible comforting figure'.[7] Life at Charleston that spring and summer was secure, serene and happy.

Only occasionally did the strain of balancing all her responsibilities against her involuntary determination to paint cause Vanessa to despair. 'Roger, why do you admire me now?' she flung out, in a moment of self-doubt. 'No, I'm not fishing, but it really seems to me very odd. I often seem to myself to make such a mess of things. You don't know how desperate I sometimes get about everything, painting, bringing up the children properly, etc.'[8] To which came the reassuring reply:

Oh why do I admire you – my dear it would take ages to tell you all I do admire you for but you see I think you go straight for the things that are worthwhile – you have done such an extraordinarily difficult thing without any fuss, but thro' all the conventions kept friends with a pernickety creature like Clive, got quit of me and yet kept me your devoted friend, got all the things you need for your own development and yet managed to be a splendid mother. . . . You give one a sense of security of something solid and real in a shifting world. Then to [sic] your marvellous practical power wh. has of course really a quality of great imagination in it, because your efficiency comes without effort or worry or fuss. No I don't think you need ever doubt yourself. You have genius in your life as well as in your art and both are rare things.[9]

Of considerable importance for Vanessa was the founding of the Hogarth Press. In the summer of 1917 Leonard and Virginia sent out its first publication, *Two Stories*, with woodcut illustrations by Dora Carrington. Vanessa's interest was immediately aroused and she suggested that the Press should publish a book of artists' woodcuts. The Woolfs approved the idea and Vanessa had already invited Roger to collaborate in its compilation when the project foundered because she could not agree to Leonard's having control over the book's appearance. Two years later the Omega Workshops took up Vanessa's idea and published a book of woodcuts, including two of her own, *Dahlias* and *The Tub*.

In spite of her disagreement with Leonard, Vanessa continued to take an interest in the Press. The illustration work that she produced for it provides visual proof of the way in which Virginia's writing stirred and enriched her imagination. 'Why don't you write more short things,' she asked, soon after the appearance of *Two Stories*, '. . . there is a kind of completeness about a thing like this that is very satisfactory and that you can hardly get in a novel.'[10] Virginia then wrote *Kew Gardens* and as soon as she read it Vanessa volunteered an illustration. 'It might not have very much to do with the text,' she admitted, 'but that wouldn't matter. But I might feel inclined to do the two people holding the sugar conversation.'[11] Roger Fry once claimed that Vanessa never illustrated anything, but her *Kew Gardens* frontispiece proves him wrong. One of the elderly women holding the 'sugar' conversation is observed staring at a flower like a sleeper who wakes from a heavy sleep and sees a candlestick reflect the light in an unfamiliar way. Vanessa, taking up the concept of indeterminacy, brings an impressionistic handling to her woodcut so that the two women merge with the flowers in the background. She also executed a small tailpiece of a caterpillar and a butterfly. When the pamphlet was printed in May 1919 (running into a second edition the next month), she was infuriated by the uneven printing of the woodcuts. Virginia, the recipient of certain harsh remarks, felt lacerated by her criticisms. Nevertheless Vanessa continued to make an important contribution to the Hogarth Press. Never again did Dora Carrington or any other artist except Vanessa design illustrations or dust-jackets for Virginia's books. When in 1921 the Press published a collection of Virginia's short stories under the title *Monday or Tuesday* Vanessa designed the cover and made four woodcut illustrations. This time the prints were, if anything, too heavily impressed on paper of inadequate quality.

Inevitably this collaborative work encouraged consideration of the relationship between literature and art. Formerly Virginia had on occasion been slightly repelled by the Bloomsbury painters' insistence on purely visual qualities. Now suddenly her interest in painting grew stronger; she visited the National Gallery and tried to describe to Vanessa her response in front of certain pictures; she borrowed certain of Vanessa's paintings to hang on her walls; she found her sister's subtle colours showed up the inadequacy of those in an Omega chair cover in the same room. In turn Vanessa began to take a more critical interest in books. In the evenings at Charleston, while they sat round the fire in the garden room, she occasionally read aloud to the others from Dickens. She turned automatically to the classics, admitting a taste for the 'simple and domestic', but also took great delight in those memoirs and autobiographies that reflected all the middle-class virtues that had helped strangle her youth. 'Do you know anything about Harriet Martineau and her works?' she enquired of Virginia. 'I'm rather fascinated by her autobiography. She was evidently so right minded and so unpleasant. You see what works one's reduced to reading in the winter evenings in the country. I find autobiographies absorbing. I wish you'd write yours.'[12] The memoirs which she fell upon with glee, so much so that she and Duncan learnt passages by heart, were those written by an old family friend, Mrs Humphry Ward. 'What is the peculiar mixture of commonplace banality, snobbishness, arrivism and boastfulness which makes her hit the bull's eye of British middle-class taste with such amazing skill each time?' she asked Virginia. 'It's really fascinating, taken in small doses. I hope you're going to expose her somewhere.'[13] She recognized in Mrs Ward a character worthy of Lytton and, after the appearance of his *Eminent Victorians*, suggested her as a future subject. Lytton had earlier read his life of General Gordon aloud at Charleston and Vanessa had been critical: 'It seems to me the Strachey mind is purely dramatic and that the result in writing biographies is to give a superficial and unreal effect.'[14] But, she added, she could not at the time judge it with any degree of fairness because throughout the greater part of the reading both she and Duncan had been asleep.

Lytton was not the only person to make demands upon her attention. The cook, Trissie Selwood, frequently interrupted Vanessa while she was painting with queries and a desire to talk. Julian also absorbed more of her time for he was now able to see that Mabel was intellectually his inferior. In a fit of irritation with her and the maid Flossie, he suddenly attacked them both, pulling the latter's hair. 'Julian is a difficult character,' Vanessa admitted to Roger, explaining that her son's needs made it difficult for her to visit London: 'he's fearfully sensitive and really needs a lot of patience. He gets upset and then everything irritates him, but he will always tell me about things in the end.'[15] In addition the house that summer was often full of visitors, among them Clive and Mary, Molly MacCarthy, Gerald and Fredegond Shove, Lytton and Dora Carrington and Harry Norton. Finally Barbara Hiles arrived, uninvited, with her tent, and for the next few weeks camped outside Vanessa's front door.

Barbara was small, pretty, vivacious and unconventional. She had dark blue eyes, red cheeks, an elfin face and short, curly hair. Like Carrington and Dorothy Brett, with whom she had been at the Slade (where Tonks had advised her to take up sewing), she had first been observed by Bloomsbury at Lady Ottoline's parties. There, like many others, she had danced with abandon, once giving Bunny a black eye when she spun unexpectedly into the air. She had dallied briefly with Maynard and Bunny and was often seen in the company of a friend's brother, Nicholas Bagenal, who followed her down to Charleston. She also had an admirer in Saxon Sydney-Turner who arrived at one of her parties in her Hampstead studio with a neatly wrapped present of some soap and fell silently but decisively in love with her. After her first party at 46 Gordon Square she had flung her arms around Clive and Vanessa on leaving and on her visit to Wissett in 1916 had charmed Duncan with her carefree behaviour. Like Carrington, Brett and Iris Tree, whom Virginia termed 'the cropheads', she had been one of the first to bob her hair; she also wore trousers and during the war rode a motorcycle. She was willing to undertake any task, helping pull the plough at Wissett and painting walls and staining floors at Tidmarsh where Lytton and Carrington were now living. At Charleston that summer she helped Duncan and Vanessa dye material and make up costumes for a performance of *Pelléas et Mélisande* in Paris. In this and many other ways over the years to come Barbara earned Vanessa's gratitude but never won her affection. Vanessa and Virginia were both aware that though Barbara gambolled like a puppy in their midst, her character was brittle and egocentric. 'She still frisks into the room,' Virginia observed in

1919, 'but she is fundamentally sedate.'[16]

Vanessa's suspicion that Barbara's rapturous behaviour hid a fatuous mind was confirmed when the young woman announced that she was keeping Saxon as a lover but marrying Nick Bagenal who had been called up. 'I myself think that Barbara has behaved idiotically', Vanessa declared, 'and will live to regret it, but there's no way of saying so. But how anyone with the imagination of an owl can conceive of life as she conceives of it passes me – half the year with one, half with the other, a child by each, etc, and no-one to have any jealousy or cause for complaint, and she like a looking glass in the middle reflecting each in turn.'[17] Aware of the tensions inherent in her own situation, Vanessa did in fact send Barbara a letter, which is said to have arrived the morning of the wedding, advising against marriage. Behind her ruthless act lay genuine concern. Later when she heard that Barbara intended having an abortion, not wanting a child until Nick was safely returned from the Front, Vanessa dissuaded her. She herself was by then pregnant by Duncan and she told Barbara that if anything happened to Nick their two children could be brought up together.

Towards the end of the summer she revived the idea of a school at Charleston. Mabel had now left to get married and in October a new governess arrived, a Miss Eva Edwards, chosen because her face reminded Vanessa of a Sassoferrato madonna and would therefore be a good subject to paint. Miss Edwards, who had been educated in a French convent, very quickly saw that life at Charleston was irregular and let her dissatisfaction appear permanently on her face. On her very first evening she drove Vanessa nearly demented with her conversation. The children liked her even less and once, when out on a walk, expressed their feelings by pushing the unfortunate woman into a ditch. Not anxious to stay, she was desperate at the thought of leaving without alternative employment, which made it awkward for Vanessa to dismiss her. After six weeks she left and soon after sent Maynard a letter offering to become his mistress if he could find her a job in London.

She was replaced by a Mrs Brereton, a friend of Roger's who had earlier nursed his wife Helen. She was separated from her clergyman husband and had two children, one of whom, her daughter Anne, she brought with her. Vanessa was now ready to employ anyone who was independent and tolerably nice and Mrs Brereton's severe ugly face and frizzy grey hair, though unpaintable, were overlooked. She was quiet, sensible and congenial. Vanessa took the first opportunity that arose to discover her attitude to religion. Mrs Brereton admitted to being agnostic but wished her daughter Anne to attend church. Vanessa agreed that all the children might occasionally attend a service on Sunday, adding, to Virginia, 'to which I don't object as long as they aren't taught it's all gospel truth'.[18] When she outlined her proposal for a small school at Charleston, Mrs Brereton agreed to the idea and offered to find a young tutor.

Mrs Brereton's arrival in January 1918 seemed to augur well for the new year. That winter had been particularly severe. The dung on the farm track froze into ridges and each time the farm wagons drove down it the great wheels caused the vehicle to shudder and groan as they laboured over every rut. Duncan, unused to heavy labour, had lost weight and exhibited symptoms of nervous exhaustion which were aggravated by the lack of fat and shortage of meat in their diet. When Vanessa applied to the Pelham Committee for permission to employ Duncan as her gardener, and thus ease his situation, her request was refused. Moreover a medical report had to be obtained from Dr Maurice Craig before the Committee of Work of National Importance agreed in February that Duncan need work only half of the day for the next two months.

In January all the inhabitants of Charleston fell ill with colds. In Vanessa's case this developed into influenza after she had struggled into Lewes one day in order to send Adrian, on trial experiment, the sheep-dog Henry who had been frightening the servants with his bark and bite. Her illness left her prone to migraines and utterly run down; Duncan told Maynard that she could do not the slightest thing without becoming completely exhausted. Maynard sent 'essences' to help build up her strength and by mid February she had more or less recovered for she wrote to Virginia: 'It's awful being cut off from one's principal occupation, isn't it? I'm thankful to be able to paint again. One gets that tetchy without it and off one's balance.'[19]

For a period nervous strain troubled the triangular relationship between her, Duncan and Bunny which, now in its third year, had grown unbearably tense. One evening that spring, while Duncan was absent, Bunny broke out in exasperation and told Vanessa that he had for a long time wanted to sleep with her and that if she did she would find he got less on her nerves. He recollected – and his recollections were sometimes modified by time – 'Vanessa looked at me with those childlike blue eyes and agreed that it might be so, and said gently that it was impossible. We could not conceal what we had done from Duncan and it would upset him dreadfully.'[20] Bunny's 1918 diary reveals that relations between them were less cordial than this suggests. There was no outward change in their relationship (and the children did not notice that anything was wrong) but Bunny sensed in Vanessa unconscious malice towards himself and others. He also found her ungenerous to those for whom she felt no affection, and he was aware that she now rarely listened to anything he said. He had also been hurt by Norton's recent observation that both Lytton and Vanessa had chosen to live with their inferiors.

Still worse was the passionate antagonism binding Duncan and Bunny. Small inconsiderate requests led to stormy disagreements: when Bunny took to his bed with a cold and asked for a fire to be lit in his room, Duncan was outraged by his selfishness for they were suffering from a shortage of coal. The main cause of their misery, however, was Alix Sargent-Florence, whom Bunny wrote to regularly and slept with on his visits to London. Duncan was uncontrollably jealous and on one occasion was found by Bunny in the barn banging his head against a beam and threatening suicide. They fought regularly, Duncan lashing out blindly at Bunny until both were half dead with exhaustion. 'Duncan now thinks I do everything out of kindness to him,' Bunny's diary records. 'Really he is an owl. After living with me for three years he hasn't yet discovered that I am a very affectionate slowcoach with no grand passions and am perfectly happy with him, if I am sometimes allowed to have the distraction of an affair with someone else.'[21]

If these emotional scenes represent one aspect of life at Charleston at this date, another is caught in Duncan's large canvas of Charleston dining-room (Ulster Museum, Belfast). Painted during the period when his jealousy was at its height, it shows Vanessa at work on a still life by the window and Bunny seated at the table writing. The mood of quiet concentration suggested by the two figures is conveyed throughout the picture by the balancing of tone and directional movements. The colour, though sober and realistic, is richly varied and sustained. It celebrates the peaceful working existence that their domestic surroundings encouraged.

Very different in character is *The Tub*§ begun by Vanessa in 1917 and completed in the spring of 1918. She originally intended it as a decoration for the garden room and this may explain why stylistically it is relatively unaffected by the greater degree of realism now found in both her and Duncan's work. Mary Hutchinson had posed for this picture wearing a chemise. As the painting progressed, Vanessa decided that the figure would look more decent if wholly naked. She took out the chemise as well as the pitcher to the right of the tub and other objects in the left-hand corner. As Simon Watney has remarked, the act of undressing is 'a curiously apt metaphor for this further paring down of her pictorial vocabulary'.[22] We are left with the stark, uncompromising relationship between the standing figure and the tub. This juxtaposition may contain a reminiscence of Matisse's *Le Luxe I* (shown at the Second Post-Impressionist Exhibition) in which the curved form of the crouching nude, like Vanessa's tub, is set against the nearby upright figure. As the pentimenti in *The Tub* reveal, the pose of Vanessa's standing figure was originally almost identical with that in the Matisse. Moreover her handling of paint is, like Matisse's, deliberately anti-illusionistic; its insistent texture helps to create space and conveys her sensuous involvement in her medium. But whereas Matisse's line, with its fluent, persuasive rhythm, leads the eye from one figure to the next, she insists on the separateness of each element. By contrast her painting is static; its equilibrium is tense, discomforting.

The disquiet expressed through the formal relationships arises chiefly from the separation between the figure and tub. As there were no baths in Charleston at this date, a tub of the kind shown here was in common use. In the picture it is so severely tilted up towards the picture plane that it creates an almost perfect circle. The circle was a motif frequently employed by Vanessa in her decorative work which, in its combination of fullness and stability, she must have found peculiarly satisfying. It is therefore possible that the strained relationship between the tub and the standing figure in this large painting is an unconscious expression of her own sense of incompleteness. She herself, with her distaste for narrative or literary content, would have firmly denied any conscious symbolism. Nevertheless, her position at this time was one of relative isolation: she was cut off from Duncan by his love for Bunny; she spent most of the day alone because while the men worked in the fields her children were looked after by servants. Living in a remote part of the country with no telephone, she was, when no visitors were present, cut off from social life and from her friends. Her severe illness in January 1918 suggests that her health was poor and it is perhaps not surprising that very few paintings remain from this period. All this lends an importance to *The Tub* that cannot be denied. It may be only coincidental that, as in *Iceland Poppies*, painted when Vanessa was suffering intense jealousy over Virginia's flirtation with Clive, three flowers again appear in *The Tub*, in the vase on the window that overlooks the pond. As before, one is separated by its colour from the rest, for two are red, the third yellow.

If Vanessa was again undergoing a personal crisis, she told no one. Despite her belief in honesty there were certain matters on which she maintained a guarded reticence, an impenetrable privacy. Her letters reveal a great many details concerning her daily life, but when it comes to what she was feeling or suffering as a result of those dear to her it is as if she disappears into another room and firmly closes the door. Yet the extent of her emotional deprivation can be gauged from the diary that Duncan kept during the first part of 1918.

Duncan shared a bedroom with Bunny and if this diary was written for anyone but himself it was in the hope that Bunny would read it. Nothing that Bunny did was at this time free from suspicion; when he wrote a thriller entitled *Dope Darling* under the pen-name Leda Burke in order to earn some money, Duncan suspected that the characters in it were based on himself, Alix and James Strachey. He was further distressed when he discovered that Bunny was still taking advantage of his earlier affair with Barbara, and in a letter to Alix had said that he needed to think of himself as married to her. Alix, meanwhile, had fallen in love with Lytton's brother James Strachey who was temporarily infatuated with one of the Olivier daughters, Noel. In this merry-go-round there was little satisfaction for anyone and Duncan frequently gave way to moods of black despair. His angry scenes with Bunny often ended in tears which were mercifully followed by periods of quiet affection.

Vanessa had little part in this drama. Duncan went to her for sympathy and advice, and to relieve frustration. Bunny was absent from Charleston for five days in February and Duncan recorded in his diary: 'I copulated on Saturday with her [Vanessa] with great satisfaction to myself physically. It is a convenient way the females of letting off one's spunk and comfortable. Also the pleasure it gives is reassuring. You don't get this dumb misunderstanding body of a person who isn't a bugger. That's one for you Bunny!'[23] From this it would seem that for him Vanessa's physical attractions counted for little; it was her character he loved and admired, as another entry in the same diary makes clear:

Last night Bunny and Nessa had a terrific conversation over my body after supper, about my jealousy and the treatment of it. Some things that were said in fact the fact that the whole conversation was so exciting to me made me feel rather upset. But at the end I felt only increased affection and respect for Nessa. The scene about Barbara was gone into and Nessa gave me her views of how a person in my state should be treated. She spoke about me so much as I should have myself had I dared to defend myself, that I left everything in her hands. It was quite conclusively proved that B had never in his life had a pang of real physical jealousy when in love. . . . Nessa said she thought one soon got over unreasonable jealousy but we both agreed we would both entirely give up a love affair rather than suffer reasonable jealousy as its result.

We all discussed later whether our high opinion of a rival made us more or less jealous. Nessa thought the higher the opinion the greater the jealousy with which I later agreed. She produced Virginia of whom she had been more jealous than anyone at a time when she admired her more than any woman she knew. . . . Nessa said she pitied neither B or me and thought I had less cause to [be] jealous than anyone in the world . . . but I was hurt slightly by her saying she got no more from me than a brotherly affection. I was paralysed by this as I always am. I am so uncertain of my real feeling to V that I am utterly unable to feign more than I feel when called upon to feel much, with the consequence that I seem to feel less than I do. I suppose the only thing lacking in my feelings to her is passion. What of that there might be seems crushed out of me, by a bewildering suffering expectation of it (hardly conscious) by her. I think I feel that if I showed any, it would be met by such an avalanche that I should be crushed. All I feel I can do in this case is to build slowly for her a completely strong affection on which she can lean her weary self.

Shortly after this exchange, Roger and Clive arrived on a visit. Bunny was in London and in his absence a conversation began about homosexual love and whether it differed emotionally from heterosexual love. Clive was certain that it did because for him the root cause of love was the complementary appeal of the different sex; Roger, on the other hand, had no difficulty in understanding homosexual love; for him the most important aspect in any relationship was the realization of a separate personality. He described from his own experience the sudden development of a 'great illusion' about a person whom one had previously regarded coldly. Clive argued that 'illusion' gave the wrong idea of the importance that the loved one's character suddenly took on for the lover. Vanessa agreed with Clive that there should be a sense of some absolute value in the beloved but thought that only when one was conscious of this *and* of the 'illusion', of which Roger had spoken, was the relationship at its best.

Next the question arose as to whether a person should go to bed with someone who did not return his or her love. Clive came out decisively against the idea, saying that the favour offered would be too humiliating. The conversation was now well under way and it was impossible for Duncan to attempt to divert it. He glanced at Vanessa and saw that she appeared lost in her own thoughts; she said very little more that evening, even when the talk moved on to absent friends. Afterwards, Duncan visited her in her bedroom before he retired and discovered, as he had expected, that Clive's remark had made her bitterly aware of what she had lost in loving Duncan. He did his best to comfort her, but all the time his mind was agitated with the thought of Bunny who had not returned that evening as he had promised.

Vanessa, now the lover and not the loved, learnt to draw upon reserves of self-denial and restraint. Under the present circumstances she understood Roger's predicament all too clearly, and she advised him not to expect more from her than she could give:

I can say ... from my own experience on the other side too, that there's no good in trying to force oneself to feel more than one feels or even to show more than one feels inclined at the moment to show. But one *can* force oneself not to expect or even want much more than is freely given, and I think any good relationship depends in the end upon the one person being able to do that. At least I have found that this is what I have to do.[24]

If during the first three months of 1918 the emotional situation at Charleston had come near breaking-point, by April the worst was past. Duncan's jealousy suddenly abated; he became indifferent to Bunny's affairs, was deeply absorbed in his painting and greatly refreshed by the sight of Blake's illustrations to Dante which he saw at Christie's on a visit to London. He had also been caught up in the excitement over the sale of the Degas collection. On seeing a catalogue of the sale in Roger's studio, Duncan had persuaded Maynard to obtain money from the Treasury with which to buy works for the National Gallery. The outcome was successful and Maynard thanked Duncan for his part in this by giving him a Delacroix drawing bought at the sale. Maynard himself acquired a small painting of apples by Cézanne which became the object of intense study among Bloomsbury painters. Then in April Vanessa conceived a child by Duncan and later that year when she repeated the motif of the tub for the Omega book of woodcuts, she compressed the design so that the figure, in easier relationship with the tub, now overlaps it. Simultaneously she reduced the number of flowers in the vase behind from three to two.[§]

Life at Charleston continued to be harsh and rigorous; coal was hard to come by and in order to supplement their meagre food rations Vanessa began to breed rabbits. Their spartan existence was broken when the sound of a taxi at the gate announced the arrival of Maynard or Clive and Mary, bringing iced cakes from Buzzard's, chocolate, dates, fish and copies of the *Tatler*, their presence filling the house with infectious laughter and gossip of the *haut monde*. Another source of civilization was Roger who sent copies of the *Burlington Magazine*; after reading his review of Vollard's *Cézanne*, Vanessa was eager to borrow the book. Virginia, still impressed by her sister's adamantine exterior and inner vulnerability, was also a regular visitor. 'I've been writing about you all the morning,' she told Vanessa, for she was now recomposing her sister as Katherine Hilbery; '... you've got to be immensely mysterious and romantic, which of course you are; yes, but it's the combination that's so enthralling; to crack through the paving stone and be enveloped in the mist. You must admit that puts the matter in a nutshell.'[25]

As the spring and summer of 1917 progressed minor domestic crises seemed to accumulate. In March Vanessa took Julian and Quentin to Durbins to be operated on respectively for tonsils and adenoids while Roger's daughter Pamela also had her adenoids treated. At Charleston

Mrs Brereton still took most of the responsibility for the children though her authority was increasingly resented. One day Vanessa looked out of the window and saw Julian rain blows on the governess's face in a fit of rage at her attempts to discipline him. The formidable Mrs Brereton withstood his attack and dragged him into the house where, on catching sight of Vanessa, he stopped struggling. For a few moments he and Vanessa sat in miserable silence in the garden room while Mrs Brereton, her face visibly swelling, recovered in the dining-room. She then ordered Julian to go to his bedroom and told Vanessa not to visit him until six in the evening. When eventually she went upstairs, Vanessa found him still tearful and argumentative, but he responded to her reasonableness and agreed in future to obey Mrs Brereton.

With the arrival of Mr Henry Moss, whose shyness, silence, stammer and physical weakness did not bode well for his role as tutor, Vanessa was now able to carry out her plans for a school. In April she advertised for pupils in the *Nation* and asked an annual fee of £100. She hoped to take in eight small children but by June had only acquired two day boys and one boarder, the last being Mrs Brereton's nephew. The school effectively ran only for one term.

Meanwhile 'the servant problem', as Vanessa called it, began. Trissie's announcement that she would shortly be leaving to marry the son of the farmer Mr Stacey obliged Vanessa to look for a new cook. Virginia offered her own cook and maid, Nelly Boxall and Lottie Hope, as temporary help. Then, because Leonard wanted to economize, it was suggested that if the two servants enjoyed being with Vanessa they could stay put at Charleston. Nelly and Lottie were understandably wary of being moved permanently to the depths of the country; one minute they agreed to the scheme but the next changed their minds. Meanwhile the high wages being offered to women in factories and munition works made it very difficult to obtain servants prepared to live in. After considerable difficulty Vanessa employed a dark-haired sloe-eyed Scottish girl called Emily as house parlourmaid and, one after the other, two temporary cooks. Then in October she borrowed Nelly from Virginia until Emily's sister, Jenny, arrived to take up position as cook. Once both sisters were firmly installed they proved to be unreliable; they went off to Lewes, promising to return by five but did not reappear until ten in the evening. When reprimanded Emily promptly gave notice but, as Vanessa's baby was almost due, agreed to stay on until after the birth.

When Vanessa first knew she was pregnant, she allowed three months to pass before telling anyone. 'Clive took Nessa's news in the greatest good part', Duncan told Maynard, 'and is already hoping the parent Bells may stump up some money.'[26] But the question of money was a side issue for it would have exposed Vanessa to much adverse comment from an intolerant society had this deception not been practised. Clive's generous willingness to pretend responsibility for Duncan's child contrasted with Roger's gloomy view of the situation. In June he stayed at Bo Peep Farm, only a mile away from Charleston, and Vanessa, feeling sick and hot, walked along the old carriageway at the foot of the downs to visit him. He complained that her pregnancy had further reduced her interest in himself or his life. She grew irritated with his tendency to denigrate everything English and felt unable to cope with his depression. They argued bitterly and that summer their relationship nearly came to an end.

In September Vanessa lost the heel of her shoe as she was going down stairs and fell heavily on her side. A week later, while visiting Roger at Guildford, she had a haemorrhage and feared a miscarriage. The doctor who examined her thought the cause might have been a slight movement of the placenta and he advised her to take extreme caution during the next two months. When that same month she visited London, Maynard hired a brougham which made it possible for her to attend a performance of the Russian Ballet at the Coliseum and a party given by the Sitwells. Duncan was also anxious that she should listen to good music for he was convinced that embryos could hear. But for most of the time, while she was in London, Vanessa lay on the sofa watching Duncan decorate Maynard's rooms.

She was at Charleston when news of the Armistice came through. Bunny dashed off to join the celebrations in London, Duncan went into Brighton to observe the festivities there. (Roger, painting away in London, was said to be unaware of any change.) When Bunny returned he began eagerly to discuss his plans for the future; Duncan had suggested that he should become a picture dealer and he rambled over this idea incessantly, constantly asking Vanessa's advice. In order to help with the running of the house – the chopping of wood and pumping of water – he agreed to stay on at Charleston until after the baby was born, and with Vanessa read a book that told them what to do if the child arrived when no doctor was present. She was determined to have the baby at Charleston because in her opinion sympathetic colours in her surroundings far outweighed the sanitary advantages of a meanly-decorated nursing home. After hearing that Barbara Bagenal had given birth to a daughter, she made plans for her own *accouchement*: Julian and Quentin were to be sent to the Woolfs and Virginia warned in advance of their needs. As Christmas approached a letter arrived from Roger, gloomily predicting that the baby would absorb all her strongest feelings and cause their friendship to fade. 'One cares for one's children in themselves,' she tersely replied, 'not as connected with anyone else. ... But of course a baby absorbs one for a time. After that I expect I shall be only too glad to feel well and free and be able to paint again. You can't think how much I already long to.'[27]

She went into labour sooner than was expected and at two o'clock in the morning on Christmas Day gave birth to a daughter. Julian and Quentin, who were still in the house, scuttled about like mice, until distracted by stockings and presents; Duncan and Bunny sat up all night talking with the doctor. Bunny was surprised that the perfectly formed baby already exhibited signs of intelligence and independent will. When placed in a shoe-box on the kitchen scales she was found to weigh $7\frac{1}{2}$ lb. 'Its beauty is the remarkable thing about it,' he wrote to Lytton on Christmas Day, adding the afterthought: 'I think of marrying it; when she is twenty I shall be 46 – will it be scandalous?'[28]

Later that day Vanessa woke to hear the farm labourers singing carols as they went about their work. She experienced a moment of peace; but in the days that followed anxieties quickly crowded in.

First, Julian and Quentin proved too much for Virginia and the onset of one of her malignant headaches dispatched the children to 46 Gordon Square where they were looked after by the cook Blanche and the maid Jessie. At Charleston, meanwhile, Emily and Jenny began to take advantage of Vanessa's confinement; they produced barely edible food, were slovenly, unpunctual, careless and rude. A nurse, employed to live in, left the day she arrived, horrified by the conditions that prevailed under Emily's and Jenny's interregnum. Vanessa was now obliged to dismiss Emily. Before the maid departed, Vanessa asked her to open her luggage as she suspected her of stealing Duncan's pants, and as a result had flung at her three cakes of soap and some blankets which, to her relief, Emily had indeed stolen. With Emily gone, Nelly Boxall arrived again, on temporary loan from Virginia until a new parlourmaid was employed. Meanwhile Mrs Brereton discovered that Jenny had stayed out all night with a young man who reappeared the next day prepared to spend all afternoon in the kitchen. Upbraided by Mrs Brereton, Jenny now gave notice but in conversation with Vanessa admitted she had no real wish to leave. Vanessa kept her on but put Mrs Brereton in charge of housekeeping.

Next the new maid, Phoebe Crane, arrived. She had, according to one of her referees, refused in her past employment to go to church. She had bulging eyes, a missing front tooth and a hacking cough; she was a little deaf and very slow, in conversation full of past grandeurs and hatred of the church. Intent on doing good, she achieved disasters, on one occasion upsetting the baby's bath water all over Vanessa's bedroom floor. The mere sight of this woman turned Mrs Brereton purple with rage and several times a morning she appeared in Vanessa's room with tales of the Crane's incompetence. The only positive improvement in the house at this time was the installation of a boiler which made hot baths easier.

The 'servant problem' paled into insignificance beside the anxiety caused by the baby. Vanessa's pleasure in her daughter's dark blue eyes, well-shaped head and delicate features quickly turned to pain when she observed that the child suffered indigestion and refused to put on weight. The local doctor prescribed orange juice and dilute carbolic which left the baby critically ill. In growing panic Vanessa sent letters to her London doctor, Craig, while Duncan visited another in Brighton and Bunny wired to his medical friend, Noel Olivier, for help. She sent Dr Marie Moralt to Charleston who promptly changed the baby's diet and within a few days the crisis was over, the baby gaining nine ounces in two days. To placate the local doctor who had a strong prejudice against women doctors, Vanessa pretended she had known Moralt for years. The two women did in fact become friends and Moralt returned to Charleston a few months later as a welcome guest. The only remaining problem was the baby's name. Bunny drew up a list of suggestions which ranged from Canada to Minerva and the child was at first named Susannah Paula, then Claudia (which Virginia thought pompous), was registered Helen Vanessa but finally called Angelica (which amply pleased Virginia). Duncan was the first to draw her. The tiny, scrawny creature he portrayed was such a painful reminder of this agonizing time that in later years Vanessa could hardly bear to look at these drawings.

Bunny stayed on at Charleston until mid January when he left for a brief visit to his parents. While away he began another affair with a young woman employed as a professional gardener to the Duchess of Marlborough. On his return to Charleston he brought her with him for she had agreed to help out in the garden, but he was disappointed, on seeing her in Duncan's company, to realize how much less amusing and civilized she was than his friend. Duncan exhibited slight jealousy of the young woman, but seemed at the same time to be tiring of Bunny, though the two friends still shared the same room at night. Shortly after this Bunny moved back into his father's flat in Pond Place, in order to begin his career, not as a picture dealer, but in bookselling, finding a job in Museum Street and later setting up a shop of his own with Francis Birrell in Taviton Street.

Towards the end of May he visited Charleston unexpectedly, arriving late and finding the young South African painter Edward Wolfe sleeping in his bed. Duncan was annoyed that Bunny had given no warning of his coming; Wolfe was obviously distressed at Bunny's sense of having been ousted. Angry words were exchanged which brought Vanessa to their room. 'I discovered suddenly', Bunny wrote in his diary, 'that only the thinnest veneer had ever existed in Nessa's attitude to me. . . . But for the time being I felt furiously jealous of Wolfe, told Duncan so and burst into tears that were not comforted. I told D that I never wanted to see him or to come to Charleston again and quite lost all my control. At this . . . he consoled me with the best grace he could. I slept in the paddock and the next day all was well.'[29] Ironically Bunny, who had caused Duncan so much jealousy, was now feeling a possessiveness towards Duncan that he could neither rationalize nor control. He also sadly reflected that Duncan was probably his only true friend within Bloomsbury.

Bloomsbury had never tolerated bores and Vanessa had become critical of Bunny partly because he bored her. She also felt he was 'muddle-headed'. She herself always upheld the controlling power of reason. Her baby was a 'reasonable creature' because she cried only when in need. When confronted with any problem Vanessa avoided emotional turmoil and calmly sought the simplest solution. She could side-step issues with skill: Mrs Brereton did not take pepper and always forgot to pass it and so instead of asking for it repeatedly, Vanessa simply bought an extra pepper-pot: it was, Duncan and Maynard agreed, a Nessian solution. By avoiding confrontation, mitigating disturbance and by silently absorbing her suffering into herself, she had emerged from these difficult, early years at Charleston with the elusive Duncan still at her side. Where Lytton, Maynard, Adrian and Bunny had failed, Vanessa had created a loving relationship that, however delicately balanced, had survived.

At Home and Abroad

1919–1926

Living in the country in wartime conditions, Vanessa had necessarily led a rather private existence. When she emerged from her seclusion in 1919 and started again to attend London parties, she found that 'Bloomsbury' had changed. Like the Pre-Raphaelites, Bloomsbury really began to exist in the public imagination at the moment when the original group had dispersed. By 1919 Vanessa was convinced that the term 'Bloomsbury' no longer had any meaning, yet it was now constantly employed in the press to label a loose conglomeration of artists and writers that might include T.S. Eliot, the Sitwells, Aldous Huxley, Raymond Mortimer and many others who had never attended a Thursday evening or engaged in those discussions that had been made possible by the intimacy of their group. As Vanessa observed, 'the sense of feeling of any small society depends not only on the presence of its members but on the absence of others, who inevitably prevent the ease and freedom necessary for saying anything which comes into one's head. It is that which matters not the subject of conversation which must change according to the topics of the day.'[1]

It was perhaps in order to maintain a semblance of unity that the Memoir Club was founded. This was a revision of the Novel Club, formed in an unsuccessful attempt to draw from Desmond MacCarthy his long-awaited masterpiece. Molly MacCarthy, with habitual vagueness, took charge, inviting 'probable members' to hear papers read in February 1920 though the first meeting did not take place until March of that year. 'Old Bloomsbury', as Leonard Woolf termed these friends, quickly decided on a single strict rule concerning membership: no new person could be invited to join without the approval of every other member. They looked for an attentiveness to those habits of feeling that the group prized. 'I know, being civilized as we are,' Virginia once told Saxon Sydney-Turner, 'we can't help watching our feelings, and being incredulous of them. But that I believe to be the proper way to feel, and later when things are less new, one loses this self-consciousness, and enjoys the fact that our feelings have been so watched, and are therefore so good.'[2] The Club tapped a rich vein of autobiographical writing, providing invaluable material for the historian. Six of Vanessa's own contributions remain as well as a fragment of her tale concerning a mad servant,* which revealed 'a remarkable talent in a fantastic narrative of a labyrinthine domestic crisis', as Leonard Woolf has remarked.[3] The Club, which at first convened frequently, continued to meet irregularly until Clive's death in 1964, after which it was brought to a close.

Vanessa's return to a more sociable existence in this post-war period forced her to realize just how unorthodox her way of life had become. When two of her Stephen aunts expressed disapproval of her oddly-composed household, Virginia rushed to her defence. In the spring of 1920 Vanessa exchanged letters with Madge Vaughan who was considering renting Charleston for three weeks in April. Then suddenly Madge decided that Vanessa's immoral way of life made it impossible for her, a head-master's wife, and her children to take the house. Vanessa was infuriated by her absurd and offensive behaviour.

> Why on earth should my moral character have anything to do with the question of your taking Charleston or not? I suppose you don't always enquire into your landlord's character. ... As for the gossip about me – as to which of course I have not been left in ignorance – I must admit that it seems to me almost incredibly impertinent of you to ask me to satisfy your curiosity about it. I cannot conceive why you think it any business of yours. I am absolutely indifferent to anything the world may say about me, my husband or my children. The only people whose opinion can affect one, the working classes, luckily have the sense for the most part to realize that they can know nothing of one's private life and do not allow their speculations about what one does to interfere with their judgement as to what one is. The middle and upper classes are not so sensible. It does not matter as they have no power over one's life. But it seems to me tragic that you should be of their mind.[4]

Her furious contempt reveals both the strength of her character and the insecurity of her position. She had previously kept up a desultory corres-pondence with Madge. By now they had little in common and Vanessa probably had little inclination to repair their friendship, but she did make one attempt at reconciliation.

* See page 188.

Dearest Madge, I daresay it was very stupid of me to get so angry with you. The fact that we differ on some important questions shouldn't make me angry. But I think if you tried to put yourself in my place and realize what you would feel if I asked you to tell me about some thing that was a most intimate concern of yours and Will's – asked you to do so not because you seemed particularly in need of sympathy or help but in order to satisfy practical considerations of my own – you would understand.

You say you tell Will everything although your married life has been full of restraints. What reason is there to think that I do not tell Clive everything? It is perhaps because we neither of us think much of the world's will or opinion, or that a 'conventional home' is necessarily a happy or good one, that my married life has not been full of restraints but on the contrary full of ease, freedom and complete confidence. Perhaps the peace and strength you talk of can come in other ways than by yielding to the will of the world.[5]

Five years later Madge died and Vanessa attended her funeral. Virginia wrote to Madge's daughter Janet, 'She was such a part of our childhood – I can't describe to you what she was like when she used to stay with us at St Ives, and how we worshipped her.'[6] Some years later still Janet Vaughan returned Vanessa her letters to Madge, with a note blaming her father Will Vaughan for destroying this and other of his wife's friendships. Sadly, the rift with Madge in 1920 had never been repaired.

The return of peace did not solve Vanessa's domestic problems at Charleston. The First World War had radically changed the opportunities open to women and Vanessa now found it difficult to obtain resident staff. She employed a nurse called Nellie Brittain who was liked by everyone and seemed to fit in; though it was discovered that in one of her letters she had described Charleston as a 'washout'. Vanessa often found it difficult to establish easy relations with servants. She instinctively disliked the old-fashioned authoritative stance which insisted on 'us' and 'them'. Sophie Farrell had been a product of this system and Vanessa's inability to maintain it had been the chief reason why Sophie had left and was now happily employed in the paternalistic establishment run by George and Margaret Duckworth. Embarrassed by servility, Vanessa nevertheless found the alternative of greater equality between employer and employee equally hard. With class distinctions then very much more deeply entrenched, the business of living in the same house with young women who came from very different backgrounds from her own often proved intolerably difficult. She was glad therefore to find in a Mrs Pitcher and her husband a part-time cook and gardener who simply got on with their jobs and required very little attention. Meanwhile Mrs Brereton, who still acted as governess, was discovered to be writing a novel in which several of the conversations that occurred at Charleston reappeared verbatim. Though she remained at Charleston until the summer of 1919, in the spring Vanessa bluntly told her that her presence in the house was extremely disagreeable to them all. It was Vanessa's maternal instinct, Virginia thought, that made her 'splendid, devouring, unscrupulous'.[7] Maynard, at this time, took to calling her Ludendorff Bell, after the Quartermaster-General who had largely controlled military and political power in Germany during 1916–18 by the simple expedient of threatening resignation if chancellors advocated policies of which he disapproved. With such powers of command as were hers, Vanessa bowled through domesticities and in May 1919 wrote happily to Virginia: 'I am painting again quite steadily. It's wonderful. I am really freer than I have ever been here as after 9.30 in the morning I have done with my household for the day.'[8]

She maintained her routine even when visitors arrived. One of the most regular was Maynard who continued to be a figure of considerable importance in Vanessa's life, almost rivalling Roger for her affections. He regularly bought and sold shares, employing her capital to bring in small profits, and took much interest in her family. 'Your nurselessness sounds intolerable,' he had written in March 1919, but, mindful of how easily she had attracted Trissie Selwood away from the Hutchinsons, he added: 'I suggest that you select the nurse from amongst those employed by your friends whom you most favour and then offer her double her present wages to come to Charleston. Mrs Ludendorff Bell ought to be at least good for that.' This letter was written from Paris where Maynard, as the chief representative of the British Treasury, was attending the British delegation concerned with German indemnities. 'I wish I could tell you every evening the twists and turns of the day for you'd really be amused by the amazing complication of psychology and personality and intrigue which make such magnificent sport of the impending catastrophe of Europe.'[9] Three months later he wrote again: 'I shall be back very soon indeed and in great need of Charleston. I shall want desperately to spend a good part of the summer with you, if I can, to recover my health and sanity.'[10]

During August and September he wrote *The Economic Consequences of the Peace* at Charleston in the first-floor bedroom facing the top of the stairs. This bitter, brilliant account of the Paris Peace Conference, of the deceit and hypocrisy which had undermined any hope of achieving a fair peace treaty, outlawed Keynes from British official circles for some time. Describing the Council of Four, he created portraits that revealed his eye for detail and grasp of the most furtive characteristic. The book, a product of bold independent thought and cutting analysis, increased Bloomsbury's respect for Maynard, though in later years they sometimes suspected that he was prepared to sacrifice his principles to his ambition. Even in 1919 this thirty-six-year-old genius, who sat listening to the talk at Charleston with his hands tucked up his sleeves, smiling gently but rarely laughing aloud, for the most part a kind benevolent presence, could invite censure. His table manners sometimes reflected his greed, and in argument the speed of his mind, his analytical prowess and ability to summarize, occasionally left him impatient and irritable with the conclusions of others. However, one endearing characteristic that manifested itself at Charleston was his love of weeding; taking out a penknife, he would inch his way along a path methodically removing even the tiniest seedling.

Maynard gave several parties at Gordon Square to celebrate the return to London of the Russian Ballet, which was currently exciting widespread interest. In May 1919 Vanessa accompanied Roger to a performance of *The Firebird* and was greatly impressed by Stravinsky's music. The previous autumn Lydia Lopokova had been the talk of the season when she danced Mariuccia in Massine's ballet *The Good Humoured Ladies*. Duncan and Bunny, on different occasions, had been taken backstage by Lady Ottoline to meet her and both had been charmed by her vivacious manner and appearance; her hair, fluffed up in front and gathered in to a bun behind, her small blue eyes and upturned nose combined to make her at once pretty and slightly absurd. In 1919 she starred again in *La Boutique fantasque*, the décor of which was by Derain. As both Derain and Picasso arrived in England this summer, in connection with Diaghilev ballets, Lydia's attractions, at least for the Bloomsbury painters, were temporarily eclipsed.

Vanessa lent Derain 36 Regent Square, a small flat she had leased from Alix Sargent-Florence (now living with James Strachey) – but which she did not make use of until the autumn. She first met the French painter when she took round some curtains and to her delight saw some of his drawings and the beginning of a painting. That summer he was well represented in the exhibition of contemporary French art organized by the Sitwell brothers in Heal's Mansard Gallery, which Roger reviewed at length and Vanessa certainly visited. After Derain left she moved herself, her children, her nurse and cook into this small flat, regretting that its distance from Fitzroy Street, where Duncan now had a studio, made it difficult for her to see him easily. He helped her decorate the flat and by September, Lytton, dining there with them, declared its style 'Charlestonian'.

Eager to engage once more in London life, Vanessa nevertheless discovered that it quickly palled. At one of the Sitwells' parties she found herself introduced to one person after another before any real conversation could develop; she also caught sight of Iris Tree who had arrived back from a visit to America married, thin, quiet and with enormous staring eyes (Vanessa preferred her fat and bold). At the same time her domestic life was difficult, for her temporary cook Budge Boxall (Nellie's sister) did not stay long. Vanessa herself had to cook and shop and sometimes take Julian to school when that September he started at Owen's in Islington. She collected him after his first day and found him white-faced but defiant, surrounded by bullies.

There was much to see in London that autumn – an exhibition of Matisse's paintings, Alvaro Guevara's much-talked-about portrait of Edith Sitwell and the London Group show, where Vanessa's portrait of Mary Hutchinson hung in a prominent position. She and Duncan meanwhile worked on decorations for the Hutchinsons' River House at Hammersmith. Apart from this commission, Vanessa did little painting that autumn and winter and in October wrote despairingly to Roger: 'I see no way of getting back to the old easy state of things and no prospect of my being free to do anything but paint and look after the children for years so that it does seem much more sensible to live in some place where one could paint easily – here I can't paint anything big and you know how difficult that is to me – and where at any rate physical life was pleasant and one could have light and warmth.'[11] London, often foggy, crowded and tiring, made her anxious to go abroad, as did the reports she now received from Clive and Roger of life in Paris where the art world was once again in full swing. Clive dined every evening with artists and writers and told Vanessa how one evening he read out her account of *Parade*, which she declared the best thing she had ever seen on stage, to Picasso, Cocteau and Satie, the three principal artists behind its creation. The only bright development in London that winter was the Bells' acquisition of the lease on 50 Gordon Square, which they shared with Adrian and Karin Stephen, Vanessa taking the top two floors which were self-contained. This brought her out of her cramped quarters at Regent Square back into Bloomsbury and nearer to Duncan.

In the spring of 1920 she agreed to take a holiday in Italy with Maynard and Duncan. It was arranged that in her absence Sophie Farrell should take charge of the running of 50 Gordon Square; a new housemaid called Mary was also employed. Freed of her everyday responsibilities, Vanessa was able to relax in Rome, in the old-fashioned Hôtel Russie which faced on to the Piazza del Popolo and had a large garden behind, its winding paths leading to the slopes of the Pincio, and in this ideal setting she read Henry James. Then, after a five-day tour of the surrounding countryside, she and

Duncan began painting. They hired a studio in the Via Margutta, an artists' quarter since the time of Claude Lorrain. Maynard also wrote there and all three might have continued to work in peace had not their landlady decided that a skilful arrangement of curtains would enable her to join them. She received a constant stream of visitors, including many cavalry officers. Finally Maynard erupted and the curtain arrangement ceased.

In Rome Vanessa noticed that Duncan's painting style was moving towards a greater solidity. This had less to do with their environment than with the general post-war trend which abandoned experiment and reverted to tradition. She too began to paint still lifes in a realistic style, with rich but sombre colour harmonies. Only in their decorative style was Roman influence felt, for on their visits to the many churches they noticed the varied fresco techniques employed, the patterning, *trompe-l'œil* and imitation marbling. Vanessa told Roger of their new enthusiasm and he wrote back, suggesting that she and Duncan should write an article on church decoration. They contemplated (but never wrote) one on the more general topic 'Taste in Rome' for they had admired also the colours in the peasants' clothes, the shape of the oil-carts, the beauty of Italian pottery, in fact everything that had escaped the middle-class tendency to vulgarize, prettify and deform.

Meanwhile Maynard had been speculating brilliantly on the fluctuating European exchanges: every day he announced that he, Duncan and Vanessa were richer than the day before. Vanessa and Duncan spent accordingly; they rummaged in antique shops and markets, buying old chairs, a settee, pots and antique frames. Vanessa acquired seventeen pairs of gloves and a great many stuffs in the Piazza dei Fiori. When Maynard went off to visit Bernard Berenson at his Villa I Tatti outside Florence, Vanessa and Duncan stayed behind a day or two before joining him there, in order to pack up and send off home by sea all they had purchased.

Despite their recent wealth they were unprepared for the luxury of I Tatti with its Louis xv furniture, its many bathrooms, private sitting-rooms and huge cars, all acquired through the money Berenson earned through connoisseurship. Vanessa could not help thinking, 'If only they had got in an ordinary Italian workman from the village to tell them what colours to use how different it would have been. Colour is simply non-existent as it is.'[12] She was still more troubled when Berenson discussed with her the pictures she had seen. Her friendship with Roger, with whom Berenson had earlier quarrelled, made him suspicious of her judgement; her admission that she admired the paintings of Raphael met with a reproving silence. She confided in Roger her feelings: 'If only he were honestly a stockbroker one could be quite at one's ease. . . . It seems so odd to come here and go to see pictures which of course excite one enormously and are most important to one, and to know that he's also grubbing away in private at the same kind of thing – and yet feel that it's a closed subject. He asks me what one has seen out of politeness, and sometimes out of curiosity to see what he'll say I ask him a question or two. But one knows one's on very thin ice. How absurd it all is. I'm sure he has no more notion of what it is that's important in a painting than a flea has. All this terrific business and income has been built up on the shakiest of foundations but I suppose he's really supported by the stupidity of the rich which after all is fairly safe ground.'[13]

During their stay a party was given for all those at I Tatti by the American collector Charles Loeser, who lived near by. Waiters in white gloves served ice-cold marsala and elaborate coloured cakes while Miss Loeser waylaid Maynard and showed him his host's collection of Cézannes about which he spoke with the utmost confidence. Returning to the salon he found Duncan calmly giving his opinion on the devaluation of the lira to the governor of the Bank of Italy. Realizing that there had been some confusion as to their identity, they did nothing to rectify it, but when a day or two later Berenson proposed throwing a return party, they incurred his anger by telling him of the mistake. Though Vanessa had played no part in the deception, she too was made to feel disgraced.

On their way home they stopped in Paris where Vanessa and Duncan sketched on the quais and attended a private view of a Picasso exhibition, afterwards visiting his studio where they saw a confusing mixture of recent abstracts and neo-classical nudes. They also dined with Derain and his wife, with the Braques, Satie and Dunoyer de Segonzac, and to the last, Vanessa lost her heart. 'He started a long account in the extraordinary way French men do of the joys of an artist's life, how foolish were the rich and how simple the pleasures which cost nothing and made an artist perfectly happy – the sort of thing one may agree with but could never say in English. However by way of variety I insisted upon the miseries, the horrors of letting oneself in for these awful problems and of never being able to do what one always had to go on trying to do. I really agreed with him but I was rather surprised as I shouldn't have thought from his painting that he had such an extraordinarily happy disposition.'[14] The respect and admiration were mutual; Segonzac ever afterwards referred to her as 'la grande Vanessa'.

Back in London Vanessa was confronted with two tragedies. Maynard's speculations on the fluctuating currency exchange had miscarried; the syndicate he had formed, and in which Vanessa and Duncan had placed all their capital, was suddenly bankrupt. Fortunately Sir Ernest Cassel was persuaded to refloat Maynard and, by a series of adroit moves and within a remarkably short space of time, he was soon able to repay Vanessa and Duncan all that he had lost.

The second tragedy concerned the housemaid Mary. While they had been away Blanche, the cook at 46 Gordon Square, had received several telephone calls from a district nurse in Bedfordshire announcing that a series of unmitigated disasters had hit Mary's family, killing off her parents and her boyfriend and leaving her brother dangerously ill. On receiving the news Mary had turned hysterical and for three weeks had raved wildly at night until Dr Moralt had placed her in an infirmary. The district nurse then wrote from Bedfordshire saying that Mary could be sent to her to recuperate and Vanessa agreed that she should go down with Blanche by train. Before they reached their destination Mary escaped Blanche's care and ran away. Vanessa herself now set out for Bedfordshire to explain what had happened but on arriving found that neither the district nurse nor Mary's family were known in the area. She then remembered that Mary had once mentioned a corn-merchant friend of her father's living in St Neots and went in search of him. He too knew nothing of Mary but found her father's name and address in his books. From there Vanessa went on to discover that Mary's parents were alive and well. The tale of disasters had been a concoction of Mary's; she herself had rung 46 Gordon Square from No. 50, forged the letter from the district nurse and was clearly mentally ill. Soon after she was seen wandering in the Bloomsbury area, was decoyed by Blanche into 46 Gordon Square, captured, certified and carried away in a plain van.

The most significant outcome of the saga concerning Mary is that it led directly to the employment of Grace. Grace Germany was only sixteen years old when she came to work for Vanessa; initially employed as a maid, she became Angelica's nurse after Nellie Brittain left, and later still Vanessa's cook; she remained in her employment until Vanessa's death and for some time afterwards continued to act as housekeeper for Duncan, earning for herself the well-deserved title, 'the angel of Charleston'. She came from Norfolk where her father had a smallholding and her mother acted as nurse to the American artist Sheldon Mills. As a young woman Grace was tall with unusually good looks. Her robust sense of humour and appetite for life made her able to adjust to almost any circumstances. When transported to France she learnt French because, as she once said, 'I'd learn Chinese if I had to, in order to talk.' Nor did she have any complaints about Charleston whither they all departed at the end of July, and where, according to Lytton, circumstances remained unchanged: 'The company in this house is its sempiternal self. Duncan and Vanessa painting all day in each other's arms. Pozzo [Maynard] writing on Probability, on the History of Currency, controlling the business of King's, and editing the Economic Journal, Clive pretending to read Stendhal. . . . The children screaming and falling into the pond.'[15]

In an old army hut which they had converted into a studio, Vanessa and Duncan were at work on a set of eight allegorical figures which were to decorate one side wall in Maynard's rooms over the archway of Webb's Court at King's College, Cambridge. The figures represent Science, Politics, Economy, Music, Classics, Mathematics, Philosophy and History, but the attributes given to the nude males and draped females do not, in every instance, make their role clear, the chief subject being apparently the beauty of the figures themselves. Beauty had once again become fashionable and Vanessa no longer felt the need to apologize for painting that which merely appealed to the eye. She began to paint the view of the garden through the French windows, or the children seated on the window-seat in the dining-room, catching effects of light and atmosphere which Post-Impressionism, at its most severe, had tended to ignore.

Compared with the beauty of Charleston, London in the autumn offered a rush of telephones and people, the steady grind of traffic, mist, damp and fog. In these less sympathetic surroundings Vanessa occasionally lost confidence in her work and was often in need of Roger's or Duncan's encouragement to boost her self-confidence. She spent a considerable part of 1921 working and reworking a family group, depicting her three children grouped round the paternal figure of Clive (Leicester Museum and Art Gallery). It required a complex organization of space, limbs, light and shade and after Roger had offered precise criticisms, she repainted certain parts. Dull greens dominate, denying her gift as a colourist and contributing to the tired, overworked look of the picture as a whole.

Vanessa cannot have been aware of the incongruity inherent in her choice of subject. As it is, Angelica remains a little separate, sliced off from the rest by the diagonal which begins with the gun Julian is holding and continues down through Clive's knee. If the formal arrangement of the picture encouraged an unconscious admission of difference, Vanessa, even with friends, kept up the pretence that Clive was Angelica's father. And so automatic did this pretence become that her birthright became, at least in Clive's mind, confused: some years later he fell into a discussion with Julian as to whether Angelica had more Stephen than Bell blood in her.

Clive himself continued to associate with Mary Hutchinson and, briefly, with the beautiful Juana Gandarillas. Vanessa observed the affairs of his heart with amusement, and reserved her anxiety for Duncan's boyfriends, one of whom, she realized, might one day cause him to change his feelings towards her. For the moment, however, they presented no serious threat. Duncan meanwhile had been upset by the news that Bunny was about to marry Ray Marshall. He tried forcible dissuasion: 'A legal marriage is at once a reality in the eyes of the world of the most odious sort (in my opinion) and it is impossible I sh. say to escape the pyramid that the world builds up every day round yr. personal relationship.'[16] He nevertheless forgave him and painted Ray's portrait as a wedding present; she sat, he told Bunny, a little unkindly, 'like cream cheese on a plate'. Bunny's place in his life had been taken by the Davidson brothers, Angus and Douglas, who, one after the other, became his intimate friends. While he was in Paris with Douglas in May 1921 Duncan sent Vanessa a letter saying that he had great confidence in her ability to make herself happy. She had little alternative.

Arriving at Charleston that August, Vanessa surveyed her surroundings with pleasurable surprise:

I am rather astonished [she told Duncan] on coming here again to find how much energy we spent on this place, how many tables and chairs and doors we painted and how many colour schemes we invented, considering what a struggle it was to exist here at all. I can't think how we had so much surplus energy. It is all still almost too full of associations for me, I suppose because one doesn't have much ordinary life here to obliterate them for I don't have at all the same feelings about Gordon Sq. though I might. But also a great deal was crammed into a very short time here. I feel as if I were drowning and rapidly review the different scenes.[17]

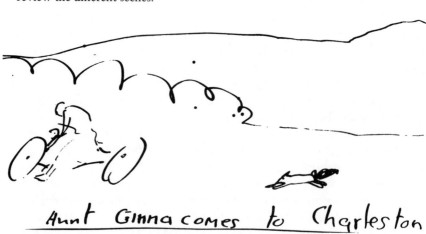

Aunt Ginna comes to Charleston

There was some uncertainty that summer whether they would be allowed to remain at Charleston as the farmer Mr Stacey considered taking it for his own purposes. As it was, they occasionally had to cede the use of the house to Mr Stacey over the winter months. Its total cost to them for 1921 came to £235, to which Maynard contributed £60 for his rent and keep, Duncan £42, while Clive and Vanessa paid the rest between them. Julian and Quentin had begun the habit of disappearing each evening in order to produce the Charleston Bulletin which, amply adorned with illustrations and peculiarities of spelling, chronicled the activities of the household. It recorded the comings and goings of visitors, Virginia arriving by bicycle, adventures in Lewes, the number of trippers sighted on the Downs. It drew upon a certain kind of journalistic bombast and inveigled Maynard, Roger and Virginia into making contributions. The editors declared it 'unique among daily papers in being controlled by no millionaire or political party. It is not perhaps unique in having no principles.'[18] It gave considerable space to the observation of nature, an interest stimulated by Bunny who had first directed Julian to the books of Richard Jefferies. And it took particular delight in domestic disasters, for life at Charleston could still be fraught with practical problems. These may have contributed to Vanessa's intermittent poor health. That summer Maynard gave her regular doses of milk and stout and made her take early nights, as she was planning to spend the autumn and part of the winter at St-Tropez where Roger was already established.

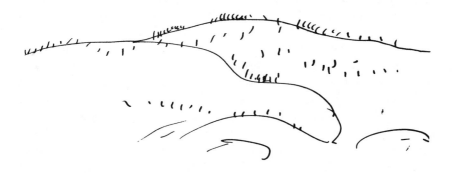

DISTANT VIEW OF THE TRIPPERS

Duncan went ahead of the rest in order to spend a few days in Paris. Vanessa followed with her children, Nellie Brittain and Grace Germany. On the journey out her chief pleasure lay in watching her sons' response to all that they saw. As the train approached Paris she stood in the corridor with Quentin awaiting the first sight of the city for, as he told her in his most ceremonious manner, he was most anxious to see it as he expected to live there one day. They disembarked at the Gare de Lyon to find Duncan waiting for them. During the next part of their journey they slept sprinkled with feathers as Quentin's pillow had burst. At Avignon in the early morning Vanessa, Duncan and the two boys dashed out for coffee and hot rolls, bringing back hot milk and rolls for the rest. The train continued its route and by the time it had reached St-Raphael where they were due to disembark everyone had again fallen asleep except for Vanessa, and she was incapacitated with Angelica on her lap. Not until the train was about to move off did they begin to unload the first of their numerous small packages and objects. The guard was furious, but just at this very moment, to Vanessa's relief, Roger appeared dressed in blue linen trousers and espadrilles, his face bronzed and beaming. With his help all their belongings were deposited on to the platform, Duncan finally leaping off the train as it moved away. Their journey was still not at an end: they took another small train to St-Tropez, then a tram and finally had to walk a mile up a dusty road before arriving at La Maison Blanche, tired, indescribably dirty but in the highest of spirits.

The villa belonged to Rose Vildrac and stood on a hill, a little way out of the town, overlooking the bay. Though small, the rooms were large and light; paintings by Derain, Vlaminck, Friesz and other artists associated with the Vildracs' gallery hung on the walls. As had been arranged, a French *bonne* called Louise came in each day to shop and cook. She threw occasional tempers and terrified Grace. 'Our French cook is very good,' Vanessa told Clive, 'does the marketing, cooks us delicious lunches and even does a good deal of the washing. She is very practical and I think looks upon Grace as a hopeless amateur – as indeed she is, trapesing about in exquisite transparent clothes, with a handkerchief tied round her head, very lovely and quite incompetent. However she picks up a few words of French occasionally and makes herself understood with the help of a dictionary. Duncan is very happy with excellent wine in unlimited quantities which costs us about 6/- a week.'[19]

The pattern of their days was quickly established. While the weather remained warm they ate breakfast on the terrace, after which Julian and Quentin went off for lessons with a round-faced ex-nun called Mlle Bouvet. In the afternoon the children bathed, sometimes with Vanessa and

Duncan who otherwise spent all the day painting, and in the evening they occasionally dined in the town, with Roger or other painters. Even when the cold weather set in and the wind rattled the ill-fitting windows, Vanessa found it still light enough to paint and in the evenings they lit a wood fire.

Life in the south encouraged a more sensual existence. Duncan warned Bunny that he had become completely 'animalisé' at St-Tropez. He had picked up in Paris the most recent volume of Proust, *Sodome et Gomorrhe*, and was transfixed by the opening description of M. de Charlus's meeting with Jupien. St-Tropez had a floating population of painters, many of whom were known to Roger, who had also attracted to his person a flotilla of admiring ladies. Among the artists whom Vanessa and Duncan met was Camoin who had known Cézanne and lived in a house near by. Painting was a natural ingredient in the life of St-Tropez and even Quentin now astonished Vanessa with his detailed, realistic pictures based on the theatre.

Vanessa was still worried that her painting was becoming too like that of Duncan. She had earlier determined that at La Maison Blanche they should paint in separate rooms and for a period not look at the other's work. Duncan's St-Tropez paintings are distinctive for their strength of design and earthy colours which nevertheless suggest light rather than solidity. Vanessa's palette, at this time, is quite different and less restricted in range. Her *Interior with a Table*[S] contrasts the orange roofs in the bright, sunlit valley, with the soft shades of grey-green, purple-brown and silver-blue inside the room. Vanessa's worry that her work was a pale imitation of Duncan's was unfounded; her *Interior with a Table* has a subtlety and density in its rich interchange of line, colour and form which make it one of her most satisfying paintings. Her temporary independence from Duncan seems to have increased her self-confidence. However, their shared profession was already the strongest link in their relationship; at St-Tropez sleeping arrangements were such that Vanessa shared her bed with Quentin.

They stayed at St-Tropez from October until early January when Rose Vildrac arrived to inspect the contents of the house prior to their departure. Her reputation had gone before her and all St-Tropez felt nervous on Vanessa's behalf. The house was spring-cleaned, scrubbed, scoured and polished. When they had almost finished and their energy was at its lowest ebb, the Vildracs arrived, Charles as charming and courteous as ever but completely silenced by his voluble wife. All final remnants of disorder were hastily bundled out of sight and they tried to keep Rose in the studio which was spick and span. The inventory was brought out and the number of breakages gone into. One cheap lampshade that Duncan had broken had been replaced with another of slightly different hue. Rose spotted it instantly and declared it vastly inferior to the original. It was, as Vanessa would have said, 'the last feather in the camel's cap', and they departed under a cloud.

By 1922 Julian, now fourteen, had received scant education of the more orthodox sort. Mr R.F. Cholmeley, the headmaster of Owen's School, had urged Vanessa not to take Julian with her to St-Tropez but she had ignored his advice as well as that of Miss Rose Paul whose small school in Gordon Square Quentin attended. Now, however, she admitted something had to be done about Julian's education and while in France she had arranged for him to start at the Quaker school, Leighton Park, in January. When the time came for him to leave home she could not disguise her distress. 'You will have the others,' said Julian, to which she replied, 'But they are not you.'[20]

On her return to London Vanessa had been severely depressed by the fact that none of her friends talked to her about her work; two of her recent paintings hanging in Maynard's room went unnoticed. With Julian at boarding-school, Quentin now attending Peterborough Lodge preparatory school and Angelica still in the care of a nurse, Vanessa decided to return to France for a period of uninterrupted painting at the first opportunity. To Virginia it seemed that French influence had not only affected Vanessa's dress but had deepened her calm tolerance of, among other things, Clive's continued philandering. She realized that her sister now sought an ambience outside Bloomsbury and this increased her awareness of their separateness. 'Nessa came again,' her diary records. 'How painful these meetings are! Let me try to analyse. Perhaps it is that we both feel that we can exist independently of the other. The door shuts between us, and life flows on again and completely removes the trace.'[21]

Within a month of her return Vanessa had disappeared to Paris where she put up at the Hôtel de Londres and painted in a small room in the rue de Verneuil, next to the larger room where Duncan both worked and slept. This was the first time she had ever done more than sketch in Paris and she revelled in the atmosphere which she had earlier tried to create in London with the Friday Club: where the issue of painting was alive and encouraging. She and Duncan visited Segonzac in his studio and thought his recent work fresher and more luminous in colour. He returned their visit, looked through all their sketches and greatly pleased Vanessa when he declared that, despite superficial likenesses, their work was fundamentally different. 'You see how terrified I am of the usual female fate,' she wrote in relief to Roger.[22] More willing to mingle socially in Paris than in London, she saw, among others, Roderick O'Conor, Marcel Gimond,

Zadkine, Kisling, Nina Hamnett and Teddy Wolfe. She visited the Salon des Indépendants, became quickly bored with the acres of efficient paintings that lacked any genuine feeling but admired the Derains. 'I hardly know myself with no family on my hands,' she told Maynard. 'How are they behaving? I have begun to paint again and feel more myself in consequence in spite of no family who are after all more of an after thought than one's painting.'[23]

The outcome of this two-month stay in Paris and her visit to St-Tropez was her first one-artist show, at Percy Moore Turner's Independent Gallery in April 1922. (An earlier show of her work at the Omega had been small and shortlived.) Now she exhibited twenty-seven paintings, many of which were French scenes, the rest still lifes and portraits, as well as a number of drawings. She was still relatively unknown to the general public and the show seems to have attracted no reviews. Her paintings, however, sold well.

In London she was immediately drawn back into the extreme vigilance which Bloomsbury brought to their own and others' behaviour. Under such conditions it was inevitable that disputes and misunderstandings should arise. Certain minor irritations, such as Mary Hutchinson's invitation of Duncan but not Vanessa to a party, could be overlooked, but the affair recently begun between Maynard and the ballerina Lydia Lopokova could not. While they had been in St-Tropez, Maynard had warned Vanessa of his feelings towards Lydia: 'Loppy came to lunch last Sunday, and I again fell very much in love with her. She seemed to me perfect in every way. One of her new charms is an [sic] most knowing and judicious use of English words.'[24] As her career was temporarily hit by misfortune and she could no longer afford her room at the Waldorf Hotel, it was agreed that while Vanessa was in Paris, Lydia should live in her rooms at 50 Gordon Square in exchange for a small rent. Clive, at this time, was considering moving away from the Square in order to set up home with Mary in Chelsea, an idea that Vanessa opposed as she liked the convenience of having Clive near at hand. The idea was eventually abandoned because, as Clive himself realized, the intellectual life offered by Bloomsbury was ultimately dearer to him than the delights of any female's charms. But while his departure remained a possibility, Maynard wrote to Vanessa asking if Lydia could stay on at 50 Gordon Square until rooms became vacant for her at No. 41. The situation would then be this: 'If L [Lydia] lived in 41, D [Duncan] and I in 46, you and family in 50, and we all had meals in 46 that might not be a bad arrangement. . . . A great deal depends on whether you can face Clive's leaving the square. We all want both to have and not to have husbands and wives.'[25]

Here lay the crux of the problem. Lydia, as Maynard's mistress, was a colourful, transient addition to Bloomsbury. It was impossible not to respond to her ingenuous gaiety and genuine astonishment with life. Unlike other ballerinas, she did not put on airs, but once outside the theatre would run or skip home like a child. She had an arbitrary control of the English language and her bizarre pronunciation added to her comic gift. To an intellectual like Maynard she was as rare as a hoopoe in a hop garden. At first Vanessa and Duncan were also captivated: when Lydia joined Massine's troupe at Covent Garden, Duncan painted her in a kilt dancing a divertissement; 'Vanessa gave me the drawing by Duncan of me,' Lydia recounted to Maynard, ' – I look like a Scotch whirlwind so much activity and not only in the legs, everywhere.'[26] She herself grew very fond of Vanessa and enjoyed gossiping with her. While Vanessa was in Paris, Lydia missed her sorely for Maynard spent most of his time in Cambridge where his companion was the elegant Sebastian Sprott. Once while Maynard was absent a letter was composed, begun by Vanessa, continued by Duncan and completed by Lydia: 'Dearest Maynard. We are all absolutely crazy drunk. We are slightly tipsy. Duncan invited Vanessa and me to a big jug of beer at Gaflis [?]. We all drank your health and we kiss you, and I too more than anybody. Lydia.'[27]

Such camaraderie did not last. It was dispelled by Maynard's announcement that he intended marrying Lydia after a divorce had been obtained from her former husband Randolfo Barocchi. Bloomsbury tried hard to dissuade him. Clive argued that Lydia could talk of nothing but the ballet, that her presence made conversation tedious and insipid; she could, as Quentin Bell has said, be 'an enemy to good sense'. While she remained at 50 Gordon Square Lydia once too often made the mistake of interrupting Vanessa at work. From St-Tropez Vanessa had advised Maynard: 'As for Loppi, *don't* marry her. . . . However charming she may be, she'd be a very expensive wife and would give up dancing and is altogether I'm sure much to be preferred as a mistress (dancing).'[28] On her return to London she remained firmly opposed to the idea of marriage: 'Clive says he thinks it impossible for any one of us, you, he, I or Duncan, to introduce a new wife or husband into the existing circle for more than a week at a time. We feel that *no one* can come into the sort of intimate society we have without altering it.'[29]

From this it is apparent that Vanessa was objecting not so much to Lydia herself as to the effect that her presence would have on Bloomsbury. Lydia's unconventionality would in fact have appealed to Vanessa's independent mind and made her far more acceptable than the chic, *mondaine* Mary Hutchinson whose visits to Charleston Vanessa had scarcely welcomed and who had never been allowed into the inner circle. If Maynard married Lydia she would immediately be drawn into the very heart of their lives; she would have considerable influence over her husband and possibly other of his friends: Vanessa's intimacy with, and dependence on, Maynard would be weakened if not destroyed. Moreover, their circle, which very obviously composed an élite, would only remain an élite if the intimacy which they cherished were not watered down by intruders. Lydia with her active life in the ballet would almost certainly introduce a motley crew of foreigners and dancers into their circle and the possibility of civilized conversation would decrease. Therefore if Vanessa's behaviour looks brutal and cliquish, it was nevertheless motivated by strong loyalty to that inner circle of friends and to the habits of feeling that they had achieved. She perhaps also suffered on Duncan's behalf. Though their affair had long since ended, Duncan's loyalty had kept his feelings towards Maynard intact. These, combined with his instinctive distrust of marriage, made the contemplation of Lydia as Maynard's wife agony to him.

Maynard's love for Lydia brought to an end his close association with Charleston. On one of his visits he had introduced an experiment with time (never a precise matter where Duncan and Vanessa were concerned), by putting the clocks back an hour, which threw the household totally awry. Lytton had arrived to find the house and its inhabitants resembling a Chekhovian drama, in which comedy just had the upper hand. 'Charleston is as usual,' Virginia observed this summer. 'One hears Clive shouting in the garden before one arrives. Nessa emerges from a great variegated quilt of asters and artichokes; not very cordial; a little absent minded. ... Then Duncan drifts in, also vague, absent minded, and incredibly wrapped round with yellow waistcoats, spotted ties, and old blue stained painting jackets. His trousers have to be hitched up constantly. ... Nessa, who concentrates upon one subject, and one only, with a kind of passive ferocity which I find alarming, took Leonard off primarily to discuss her attitude to Mary.'[30]

Virginia was pleased with the dust-jacket for *Jacob's Room* which Vanessa designed that summer, though the result was a collaborative effort: Leonard suggested alterations in the lettering and Virginia chose the colours used. It did little to help sell the book; as Leonard recalled, it was condemned by booksellers and laughed at by the public. It was perhaps too elliptical in style to achieve immediate popularity. She avoided the common mistake of attempting to do too much, and instead merely suggested table, flowers and curtains by a few simple shapes, taking care that the lines and shapes used should be both associative and achieve an unforced balance in their abstract design. She produced all the subsequent dust-jackets for

Virginia's books, and many others besides, as well as the colophon of a wolf's head. These all helped to create a certain house style and made a distinctive contribution to the Hogarth Press.

As a painter Vanessa's reputation was steadily growing. At the London Group exhibition in April 1923 John Alton's praise in the *New Statesman*, if vague, was affirmative: 'There is always a beautiful character pervading all the work of this, the best of our women painters. Her feeling for colour is personal and essentially feminine, using the word in its best sense.'[31] *The Times* critic admired her portrait of Lydia Lopokova (now lost) and an interior showing a nurse and child at tea for its 'pleasant openness and freedom'.[32] Such praise was badly needed for she frequently doubted her ability and had regretted sending pictures to this show. She shared her anxiety with Duncan: 'It is angelic of you to have retouched Lydia. I expect she wanted it badly. As for the compliments you send me, they're very welcome as I was really afraid my works were so bad that no one would dare to mention them to me. I saw [Frank] Dobson looking at Lydia for some time and as he said nothing I was sure it was utterly condemned.'[33]

The fact that her painting was now severely traditional made her acceptable. John Alton began his review with an attempt to explain why the whole show reflected so little experimentation when compared with the early London Group exhibitions. Like others, Vanessa had begun to measure her work less against that of her contemporaries than against the Old Masters'. She sought in her own paintings the resolution and complexity of formal relationships that she admired in Raphael's *St Catherine* (National Gallery) which she now copied. When in June 1923 she accompanied Duncan on a visit to Spain, where they met Roger and visited Madrid and Toledo, she sat in her studio on her return home utterly bewildered by the experience of the Prado: 'I feel rather crushed by all the pictures we saw,' she admitted to Duncan, '. . . I don't know what to think. It's very upsetting at my age to see important new masterpieces I find. In one's youth one's mind was always in such a dither it didn't seem to make much difference, but nowadays its a rare experience and I find rather an overwhelming one.'[34] Her way out of the impasse was to paint an 'unassuming' still life.

Vanessa often belittled her pictures in favour of Duncan's. When in June 1923 the Independent Gallery gave him a show, she was delighted to find in his work a 'solidity and richness', qualities that she sought but did not always find in her own. Her psychological need to uphold Duncan as the 'great' painter revealed the inequality in their relationship and her insecurity. 'I feel isolated in the world when I can't talk or even write to you', she once admitted to him.[35] Yet she also realized that the continuation of their relationship depended upon her ability to give him free rein. In April 1923 she had spent several days alone with Quentin and Julian at Monk's House, Rodmell, while Virginia and Leonard were abroad. She had known that Duncan, in her absence, was seeing the good-looking sculptor Stephen Tomlin and reveals in one of her letters that her fear of losing Duncan ran parallel with her fear of failure as a painter:

> You are at this moment no doubt sitting in the arms of Tommy, at least, feeling quite happy, I hope, also I hope not staying up too late, but no doubt relieved to think that you can stay up as late as you like and all night without my being a bit the wiser. But please my Bear write and tell me what you do for at this distance it won't matter and I feel very remote from you and want very much to know how the affairs of your heart progress. You seemed to me rather *distrait* and impenetrable. Are you keeping a great deal back from me? I cannot help wondering.
>
> I think with horror of my pictures at the L.G. [London Group]. Oh Lord this gave me quite a turn and I wished I hadn't sent them.[36]

Duncan replied that he had not had any hectic scenes with any of his young men, that Douglas Davidson was away and that he did not see much of Tommy. However uninformative he actually was, Vanessa need not have been seriously worried: Duncan, as he admitted in a note written immediately after Vanessa's death, had developed the habit of 'deferring' to her. He admired and respected Vanessa and needed the life-style that only she seemed able to make possible. He enjoyed her shrewd humour, her huge tolerance, and shared her voracious desire for the peaceful routine necessary for painting. Many years later he told Paul Roche that he loved Vanessa but had never been 'in love' with her. The love they shared, however, penetrated too far and too deeply into their lives to invite simple analysis or explanation, and an important factor in it was their shared love of Angelica. While Vanessa was away at Monk's House and Duncan and Angelica left in London, his daughter woke him one morning with the deafening cry, 'Mummy, are you awake?' hoping that Vanessa, in Sussex, would hear. On many occasions Angelica delighted him, not least when Lord Gage visited Charleston and risked a bawdy joke in her and Duncan's presence, only to find to his astonishment that the three-year-old child had dissolved into hysterical laughter. Fascinated by Angelica, Duncan nevertheless continued to conceal, even from the child, his parental role, and this inevitably made him uneasy towards her. He taught her much, was always an enchanting companion, but viewed objectively it is difficult not to conclude that he abdicated a certain responsibility and must have curtailed his emotional commitment.

More binding perhaps even than his daughter was the maternal and domestic comfort which Vanessa created at Charleston. Each year the house and garden grew lovelier, more adorned, more imbued with associations. It exerted a potent spell on all who visited it, spinning an invisible net of contentment over its occupants. Charleston gave to Duncan what he had lacked in childhood and youth – a permanent, family home. To have abandoned Vanessa and his life there would have required him to uproot and deny the better part of himself. Thus during the summer of 1923 things continued much as usual: the Charleston Bulletin purveyed an odd mixture of fact and fantasy; stoats were seen, moths and butterflies caught and fruit harvested; and canvases covered stroke by stroke with paint.

That Christmas Duncan went as usual to his parents while Vanessa remained at Charleston with Clive and the children. Surprised to find herself enjoying a traditional Christmas at home, with her husband and family like any other conventional, domestic couple, she thought of announcing their whereabouts in *The Times*. While there she painted a copy of a Raphael madonna, grew bored with the constant talk about the *Nation* (of which Leonard had recently been made literary editor), and was entertained by the illustrated 'Life of Mrs Bell', produced jointly by Virginia and Quentin. It recorded scenes from her life: her unexpected meeting with Mrs Humphry Ward by the Arc de Triomphe and prompt refusal of invitations to lunch, tea and dinner; her habit of arriving at the customs with three dozen trunks of pottery and everything else lost; her belief that jackdaws stole her spectacles when, according to the authors, six pairs could be found embedded in her hair.

Virginia, childless, continued to study every aspect of Vanessa's motherhood. In the spring of 1924 Angelica and her nurse were knocked down by a car. As it turned out neither was seriously hurt but on arriving at the Middlesex Hospital Vanessa and Duncan found Angelica laid out with her face to the wall and at first thought her dead. A young doctor arrived and did little to dispel Vanessa's acute anxiety as she sat down to wait for the surgeon's opinion. It was then Virginia saw on her face 'that extraordinary look of anguish, dumb, not complaining, which I saw in Greece, I think, when she was ill. ... What I felt was, not sorrow or pity for Angelica, but that now Nessa would be an old woman; and this would be an indelible mark; and that death and tragedy had once more put down his paw, after letting us run a few paces.'[37]

Yet it had been a false alarm. More serious was the illness Angelica suffered in April 1924. She had two teeth extracted and two days afterwards Vanessa took her and her new nurse Louie Dunnet down to Seend where she intended leaving them while she took Julian and Quentin to Paris. In the train to Devizes Vanessa noticed that Angelica's gums were still bleeding and her neck swollen. At Seend she was discovered to have a temperature and put to bed. A doctor was called who feared that an abscess was forming in her neck which would have to be lanced. This proved unnecessary but over the next few days Vanessa had to watch her small, thin child suffer pain; until the swelling went down she endured unmitigated anxiety. She stayed on at Seend while Clive took Quentin to Paris, as had been planned, where he spent a short period with a French family before following Julian to Leighton Park that autumn.

Once Angelica had recovered Vanessa herself paid a short visit to Paris with Clive in order to see that Quentin had settled in. They lunched with Derain and visited the latest ballet, for which he had designed sets, as well as another that had sets by Braque. They spent one evening in the company of Segonzac and his great friend Jean-Louis Boussingault. The previous year Vanessa had seen Segonzac in London when he came over in connection with his show at the Independent Gallery. Though she admired him primarily as a man, this 'virile Impressionist', as Arthur Jerome Eddy described him, may have influenced her painting, because for a period she seems to have imitated his earthy palette and his abrupt handling, using a palette knife to obtain a thick, overlaid texture.

Segonzac deepened further Vanessa's love of Mediterranean culture. At Charleston, in the evenings, conversation would quite often turn on the French or Italian way of thinking, feeling or living. A discussion might develop from something Clive read, for he would often be holding either a French or Italian book and had been indebted to Aldous Huxley for directing him to the plays of Alfieri. If Roger was present, his passionate love of France meant that the topic would be pursued still more energetically. The extent to which Vanessa and Duncan became imbued with Mediterranean culture is reflected in their decorative work. During the twenties they undertook several commissions, their style gradually becoming more baroque and more Italianate; they resorted to traditional motifs such as the nude, vases of flowers, fruit, musical instruments, swags, medallions and ornamental embellishments. Sadly, very little of this decoration survives. At first the commissions came from relatives and friends, from Adrian and Karin Stephen for their rooms at 40 Gordon Square, from Angus Davidson who lived at 3 Heathcote Street, off Mecklenburgh Square, and from Virginia when in 1924 she moved into 50 Tavistock Square. 'My rooms are all vast panels of moonrises and prima donna's bouquets,' she announced proudly in April.[38] A loggia decorated for Peter Harrison at his house Moon Hall at Gomshall in Surrey does not survive but was probably identical in design with the painting in the Victoria and Albert Museum which at one time covered an entire wall in Raymond Mortimer's house, 6 Gordon Place: Vanessa told Mortimer that they were charging him only £45 for this and other minor embellishments because they were using an idea they had already employed in a loggia. Mortimer proved to be an excellent patron; he was generous, encouraging, prompt in payment and threw a party to celebrate the room's completion. The wall decoration, however, is too like a painting and, in the central panel, for which Vanessa was responsible, the suggestion of illusionistic space conflicts with the need to create a flat, decorative pattern. More successful were those designs which had to be inserted into relatively restricted areas, such as in between and over the bookcases in Mary Hutchinson's library at 3 Albert Gate or on to the door panels and round the fireplace in Clive's rooms at Gordon Square.

Though these decorative commissions received much acclaim at the time and were often illustrated and discussed in magazines, their contribution to the history of interior decoration has, until very recently, been ignored. Instead of the concept 'fitness for purpose' upheld by the Design and Industries Association, these decorations, if they have any creed, are concerned with 'fitness for pleasure'. Their hedonism follows no theory and arouses distrust among historians. Unlike the leading designers and architects who created the International style, Duncan and Vanessa did not attempt to impose any rigid style or theory, but, in their eclectic pursuit of various styles and motifs, expressed an underlying belief in the individual's capacity to create his or her own environment.

Since the war the relationship between Vanessa and Roger had settled into one as comfortable and familiar as a well-worn glove. He confided in her with regard to all his various and often troubled affairs; she, in turn, assured him that her old one was all he had to reckon with. Then in the winter of 1924 she gave a party to which she invited Boris and Helen Anrep. Two years earlier Lydia had correctly summed up their marital situation: 'I visited B. Anrep and saw his wife, children, his sister. No harmony, that is why he searches for persons, to whom he can pour his lyric qualities.'[39] There was indeed very little harmony in the Anrep household where Boris insisted on keeping a *ménage-à-trois* and, as Vanessa had earlier suspected, Helen had already begun to fall in love with Roger Fry. Vanessa's party marked the start of their affair.

Boris received the news in Slavonic fashion: he raged, threatened murder, denied Helen the right to leave. The situation was made difficult by the existence of their two children, Anastasia and Igor, and by Roger's sister Margery who wished for no intruder in the domestic arrangement that she enjoyed with her brother. As usual, Roger turned to Vanessa for advice. Though she felt sorry for Boris, whom she liked, her advice was controlled by her feelings for Helen as a mother: it was essential for Helen to remain friends with Boris and achieve an amicable separation that would enable her to keep the children. She was impatient of the emotional harangue that went on for almost a year before Helen finally moved in with her new lover. On one occasion Vanessa dined with Roger, enjoying with him a flirtation that revolved round their discussion of Helen; the strong Italian wine added to his odd but delightful impression that the flavour of their former romance had outlived desire. Nevertheless it was sobering to be told by Vanessa that she had never been jealous of his affairs, only relieved when others gave him what she could not. Even he sometimes suspected that his goddess was made of stone. 'No you're not perfect,' he once wrote to Helen after she had expressed fear of comparison with Vanessa, '... I think Vanessa is an almost perfect being, but she buys perfection by very sharp and fixed limitations.'[40] He now realized that her capacity to compel life to suit her own ends left her imperfectly satisfied.

> Oh I daresay Vanessa is a more perfectly and harmoniously developed being but perhaps she's a demi-god and we are only human ... I doubt if V. has ever had the possibility of loving as we love because she hasn't found a demi-god. I daresay D. is the nearest she could get but then his response is imperfect whereas I do vibrate enough in unison with you to show all the splendour of your nature. V. will die without that having ever been seen.[41]

Vanessa's inability to love Roger had lost her much. What she had never forfeited was his ideas concerning form and content in art. Even when he began to modify his formalist viewpoint she held fast to his earlier ideas and throughout her life remained convinced that the foundation of aesthetic experience in art rested on the perception of forms, colours and spatial relationships. In January 1925 she was invited to give a talk on art at Leighton Park School; the simple, straightforward text that remains conveys the essence of her belief.

She began by underlining that she was there as an artist, not as a critic; she confessed her ignorance of dates and admitted that those who knew her well doubted whether she knew which came first – the Greeks or Romans. She then read passages from Virginia's famous essay 'Mr Bennett and Mrs Brown' and pointed out that in fact neither Wells, Bennett nor Virginia had 'seen' the old lady in the railway carriage; they had observed details that had human significance but very little of her appearance. Unlike the writer, she continues, the artist's principal occupation is with form and colour, and some of the greatest artists in the past had been those content to discover formal relations in pots and pans, fruit and vegetables. So absorbing is this study of shape and colour that the artist is in danger of forgetting all other aspects of the material world: 'One is almost incapable of being bored. Even a kitchen coal scuttle may become the most exciting continuation of curves and hollows, deep shadows and silver edges, instead of a tiresome thing to be filled with coal, or a half worn out thing that will soon need renewal.' She goes on to admit a dangerous heresy: her belief that skill is of no importance in art and that habits of hand only lead to mechanical productions.

> Suppose you are drawing a flower. If you are capable of seeing that flower with all its subtleties of form, the way its edges recede or are sharp against the space behind, you have to try to express your feeling about those things in line. It must be sensitive, everywhere – nowhere must it become mechanical . . . when art is on the downward grade, skill tends to get the upper hand.[42]

Though Vanessa did not pursue the philosophical implications behind her statements, this short essay rests on two unspoken beliefs: that the artist is she or he who can shape, contain or reproduce feeling and sensitivity in such a way that others can share it; that aesthetic expression, to attain universal meaning, must be disinterested. Neither here nor elsewhere did Vanessa choose to investigate the psychological motivation behind her work. Her praise of qualities like 'solidity' and 'richness' suggests that she was still looking for a monumentality, a generous containment related to her experience of motherhood. Her fascination with reflections and with the stroking, sensuous quality of light would suggest that she was searching in her art for that close, reflective relationship which the child enjoys with its mother. If, as Vanessa's close maternal relationship with Thoby and Virginia would suggest, this crucial, primary relationship with the mother had in Vanessa's case been unsatisfactory, then much of her painting may be about an attempt to resolve a psychological need. Julia Stephen, in her charitable desire to help others, may have denied Vanessa and Virginia adequate physical love, but in so doing she may also have given them the potential to become artists.

The earlier anxiety that they might be obliged to leave Charleston had now ended with a fourteen-year renewal of their lease; able to take a long-term view of their life there, Vanessa resolved to build a studio on to the house. Roger drew up a plan and a Mr Durrant, a builder from

Uckfield, estimated the cost to be £250. The only alteration made to Roger's original design, while work was in progress, was the addition of a dormer window over the north-facing lights below. Inside the walls were painted grey, the tall pitched ceiling white. In one wall is set a door which opens on to a brick courtyard while a small L-shaped extension to the far corner of the room has plain wooden doors which open on to the walled garden.

Compared with the more domestic proportions elsewhere in the house, this huge vaulted room offers both expanse and haven-like peace. On first painting in this studio that summer, Vanessa was struck by the cool still quality of the light. Immersed in this room, where the silence is broken only by natural sounds, she drew upon a contemplative calm that is found reflected in her paintings. With this addition life at Charleston had become the perfect existence.

Her freedom to paint continued to owe much to her organizational prowess. Earlier that year she had supervised the move out of 50 Gordon Square into the nearby No. 37, two floors of which she sublet to Dadie Rylands and Douglas Davidson. At Charleston she organized for Angelica and a few of her friends' children a 'summer school' which ran for two consecutive years during the summer term under Marjorie Strachey. The latter's dramatic, if somewhat biased, teaching of history rendered even the dullest events full of unsuspected interest. She bewitched the handful of children sent down to Charleston – among them Anastasia and Igor Anrep, Christopher and Nicholas Henderson and Judith Bagenal – and in her free moments would don a pair of breeches and stride off to the Downs where she declaimed Shakespeare in one of the chalk quarries. Vanessa taught the children to paint and draw. She was, Sir Nicholas Henderson has recalled, 'unassertive in manner and unimpetuous in movement'. However, during much of the 1925 summer school she and Duncan were absent; they visited Paris and saw the Pellerin collection of Cézannes on which Roger was writing an article. On their return they stayed in London where Vanessa painted, longed for Angelica and admitted feeling 'half-baked' without any family ties.

At Charleston Vanessa and Duncan enjoyed a routine working existence which both found satisfying and fulfilling. After visiting them one day Virginia remarked: 'I never saw two people humming with heat and happiness like sunflowers on a hot day more than those two'.[43] Charleston succoured Vanessa's inner reserve on which Virginia again commented when both dined, for the first time for many years, with Jack Hills in London. 'I'm more nervous of these encounters than she is,' Virginia opined. 'She has a sweet cordiality (odd term to use) which impressed me, recalling mother, as she led him on; and laughed; so sincere, so quiet, and then, when we went on to Roger's rather dismal gathering, gay and spirited, kissing Chrissie [Christabel McLaren, whose husband later succeeded to the title of Lord Aberconway] and flirting with Mrs Anrep, so careless and casual and white-haired – but enough of this.'[44]

At the start of 1926 the Charleston Bulletin was full of attack. 'We learn with the utmost horror and alarm that Angelica has succeeded in obtaining the right to paint in oils, with the promise of a complete outfit of her own. This deplorable weakness on the part of Nessa threatens to make life for the non painting inhabitants of Charleston intolerable.' In April it expressed further editorial disapproval:

Again as happened last Christmas, those irresponsible revolutionaries, the artists, have been improving Charleston out of all knowledge. On first entering the house one is struck by the overwhelming odour of paint, emanating from the new radiators. On first entering the bath one sticks to the bottom and turns white in patches owing to the imperfectly dried Chinese white congealed at the bottom. The old square hot water tank, so useful for drying clothes on, has been replaced by an obese cylender [sic] crowned with an abrupt cone on which no garment will remain.

Of the imitation Old English hearth [the inglenook recently discovered in the dining-room], of the eccentrically situated W.C., of the combined dustbin and crematorium at the foot of the stairs, there is no need to speak at length. Though time and use may accustom us to these innovations, yet the artists

THE BATH

would to [do] well to confine themselves in the future to their paints, and to refrain from experiments in other and more lasting mediums.

Vanessa was frequently the butt of her sons' facetious humour. 'Nessa knows nothing', they often declared, for they had begun to have interests that extended beyond her own. Quentin, when given a radio one Christmas declared he had spent one evening listening to Bolshevist propaganda broadcast from Leningrad; Julian, now in his final year at Leighton Park, demonstrated his growing interest in politics by entering a speech-day debating competition with the topic 'The Present Industrial System'. According to the *Reading Observer* he expressed himself vehemently, upheld socialism, declared money earned on the Stock Exchange to be stolen property and endured much heckling. When he announced that unless conditions changed soon England would have a violent and bloody revolution, the laughter was so great it was some time before he could continue.

Julian was speaking at the time of the 1926 General Strike. Vanessa was out of the country when this occurred and as yet politics remained on the very periphery of her life. In Venice, where she went that summer with Duncan and Angus Davidson, her chief role was to impress on the languid Angus that the Hogarth Press was making a loss and therefore he needed to work harder. They put up at the Hotel Manin before moving to rooms at 234 S. Gregorio. At first Vanessa indulged lazily in her surroundings, doing a little sightseeing, less painting and, as always when abroad, more reading than usual. Aside from French novels, she tackled Beatrice Webb's *My Apprenticeship*, finding this lady's persistent search for 'general principles' bearable in the Italian sunshine where few principles survived.

From Venice they visited Ravenna, to see again the mosaics; Ferrara, to see the Cosimo Tura frescos; and Padua for the Scrovegni Chapel, Vanessa finding Giotto more of a colourist than she had previously thought. Until now, she and Duncan had exercised restraint when they caught sight of pottery, but in Ravenna they were completely undone. In a shop filled with canaries of every shape and size – in the egg, in the nest and on the wing – the two of them fell with delight on jug, plate and bowl, making numerous acquisitions. In their enthusiasm they learnt from the shopkeeper that the pots were made by a family in a nearby village. The next day Duncan and Vanessa took a train out to this village, discovered the family and were made welcome by the women. They watched as the daughter freely decorated a pot and then the father appeared and began to throw pots with such economy of movement that it was obvious he could produce whatever shapes he desired. In the exchange that followed they asked if the potter would allow them to decorate certain pieces themselves and proposed a plan, which never matured, to return that autumn to commission an entire service. Laden with parcels they travelled back to Ravenna where Vanessa's bedroom had begun to resemble a pottery shop.

In Venice Vanessa paced the Giudecca deep in thought: Virginia had sent her criticisms of the first exhibition of the London Artists' Association. This Association realized an idea originally mooted in 1914 when, in order to bring in money for artists, a picture-lending society had been proposed (but never formed) which was to be called the Christian Dining Society to annoy Vanessa. The London Artists' Association, largely managed by Maynard and underwritten by three other wealthy sponsors, guaranteed a salary to a select number of artists which would be offset by sales of work at regularly-held exhibitions. Maynard's skill at business ensured its success and within the first three weeks of this show £1,600 worth of paintings had been sold and all the catalogues bought. Vanessa cared little for reviews, still less for H.S. Ede's article in the *Nation* which she thought 'imbecilic', but Virginia's comments on her work moved and provoked her, for they mixed high praise with perceptive criticism:

> What I think is this: there is a divinely lovely landscape of yours at Charleston: one of flashing brilliance, of sunlight crystallized, of diamond durability. This I consider your masterpiece. I do not think the big picture of Angelica etc, in the garden quite succeeds. I expect the problem of empty spaces, and how to model them, has rather baffled you. There are flat passages, so that the design is not completely comprehended. Of the smaller works, I think the blue boat by the bridge is my favourite. Indeed, I am amazed, a little alarmed (for as you have the children, the fame by rights belongs to me) by your combination of pure artistic vision and brilliance of imagination. A mistress of the brush – you are now undoubtably that; but still I think the problems of design on a large scale baffle you. .... It seems to me that when you muffle the singing quality of your tone, and reduce the variety and innumerability of colour (the pigeon breast radiance in which you are so supreme that, before hot pokers, or the asters (?) my mind shivers with joy) to bone, where the frame of the design is prominent, then, now and again, you falter, or somehow flatten.[45]

Colour continued to be Vanessa's forte and usually determined her choice of subject. In Venice it was not the traditional views or the lagoons that inspired her but the sight of a colour chord set up by a patch of wall, green shutters and a window-box. She painted directly on to the canvas with well-loaded brushes, making no attempt to disguise the brushmarks but often allowing them to create pattern or texture. Her colours were still resonant but now keyed in with her more naturalistic style. Around

Mary Hutchinson

Mrs Mary Hutchinson, 1914

ris Tree, 1915

Quentin Bell, 1919

Adam and Eve, 1913

The Tub, 1918

Woodcut frontispiece to *Kew Gardens*,
published by The Hogarth Press, 1919

The Tub, from *Woodcuts by Various Artists*,
published by the Omega Workshops, 1919

Kew Gardens

From the oval-shaped flower-bed there rose
perhaps a hundred stalks spreading into
heart-shaped or tongue-shaped leaves half
way up and unfurling at the tip red or blue or
yellow petals marked with spots of colour raised
upon the surface; and from the red, blue or yellow
gloom of the throat emerged a straight bar,
rough with gold dust and slightly clubbed
at the end.

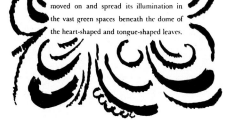

The petals were voluminous enough to be stirred
by the summer breeze, and when they moved, the
red, blue and yellow lights passed one over the
other, staining an inch of the brown earth beneath with a
spot of the most intricate colour. The light fell either
upon the smooth grey back of a pebble, or the shell
of a snail with its brown circular veins, or, falling into
a raindrop, it expanded with such intensity of red, blue
and yellow the thin walls of water that one expected
them to burst and disappear. Instead the drop was
left in a second silver grey once more, and the light now
settled upon the flesh of a leaf, revealing the branching thread of
fibre beneath the surface, and again it
moved on and spread its illumination in
the vast green spaces beneath the dome of
the heart-shaped and tongue-shaped leaves.

Two pages from the illustrated edition of *Kew Gardens* published by The Hogarth Press, 1927

Dunoyer de Segonzac

Vanessa and Angelica

Clive Bell

La Bergère

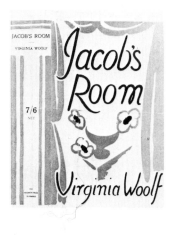

Nine of Vanessa Bell's dustjacket designs for The Hogarth Press

Judith Stephen, Mrs Uppington, Angelica,
and Grace Germany at Charleston

Duncan Grant as a Spanish dancer

Clive Bell and Duncan Grant

Quentin, Angelica and Julian Bell

Julian Bell (Photograph by Lettice Ramsey, c. 1931–2)

Vanessa Bell (Photograph by Lettice Ramsey, 1932)

Angelica at the easel

1926 she painted a half-length self-portrait in which she looks out through her horn-rimmed spectacles straight at the viewer. It is direct, forthright and in places rather summarily treated, a dispassionate examination of her appearance, entirely free of any posturing or the desire to impress or romanticize. In 1926 she also painted *The Open Door*[S], showing the double doors in Charleston studio open on to the sunlit patio. Compared with her earlier post-impressionist work, her pictures of this period sometimes lack intellectual astringency. Those done at Charleston, however, are richly evocative of the house, of its atmosphere, peace and sensuous beauty.

Each year Charleston underwent further change and by degrees became more civilized, though it was still a long way behind Tilton, the nearby farmhouse which Maynard and Lydia, who had married in 1925, now used as a country retreat and which boasted telephones and electric light. Clive, shivering in Charleston dining-room in April 1926, wrote to Virginia:

> If you could see me crouching in the ingle-nook recently discovered in the dining-room – with a candle insecurely balanced on a waste-paper basket and the waste-paper basket on a chair, and even so unable to see a stroke. ... The reason why I write in so wretched a position is that the new heating system leaves everything to be desired, at least on such a day as this when the sea-fog beats in at every chink. ... Tilton is gradually becoming what it should be, the neat retreat of a great financier. Charleston is frankly disappointing, and less commodious than a Sabine farm. But Nessa doesn't care a rap – not she.[46]

The 'Tiltonians' often accompanied the 'Charlestonians' on picnic outings and the like. They were also usually present at Quentin's birthday-party on August 19 when grouse was eaten and fireworks let off beside the pond. But Vanessa had never overcome the antagonism that she felt towards Lydia, and she would frequently groan or hide when she paid a visit. Even Roger found Lydia trying; when dining at Tilton during the summer of 1926 he wished 'she'd not make such an effort to entertain to be gay and dispense herself', as it prevented any general talk from developing and obliterated Maynard's natural wit and charm. Roger had been forced to spend the greater part of the evening talking to Julian and Quentin and he was impressed by the elder's intelligence. 'He's got much of Clive but is a more serious character with bigger ambitions and altogether more to him.' On the whole, his visit confirmed him in his admiration for Vanessa and all that she had achieved. 'It really is an almost ideal family based as it is on adultery and mutual forbearance with Clive the deceived husband and me the abandoned lover. It really is rather a triumph of reasonableness over the conventions.'[47]

Charleston
in France
1927–1930

During the late twenties and early thirties Duncan and Vanessa were at the height of their reputations. Within the exhibiting society, the London Group, they were key figures, though as yet they had little influence upon the committee. According to the artist Raymond Coxon, Vanessa 'never so far as I remember raised her voice in contradiction in meetings. Roger's booming voice boomed and all was agreed upon.'[1] Founded in the winter of 1913–14, the London Group had initially brought together the majority of progressive artists in England with the notable exception of those associated with Bloomsbury. They had joined late, Fry in 1917, Vanessa and Duncan in 1919, but since then their still lifes, landscapes and figure studies had dominated the twice-yearly exhibitions. In itself the London Group, whose membership had grown more amorphous over the years, could confer only limited celebrity. It was Maynard's London Artists' Association, with its select group of artists, which successfully steered Vanessa and Duncan into the limelight. Duncan, especially, now found himself fashionable and famous. Both, however, refused ever to court publicity for its own sake: Duncan, knowing that it would upset other artists in the group, complained when Maynard starred his name in an LAA advertisement; on another occasion he insisted that catalogues and advertisements should not make use of any personal details; even the artist's age was to be withheld. Most of the LAA exhibitions took place in the elegant Georgian rooms belonging to the Cooling Galleries at 92 Bond Street. Here Vanessa had her major triumph with the Association in February 1930. The show, devoted entirely to her work, was reviewed by the young artist John Piper who discovered the essence of her art to be 'its feminine quality'. 'The subtle delicacy of her painting is, perhaps, the most characteristic thing about it, but it bears scrutiny only because it is united to a hard-won but inevitable solidity of objects.'[2]

The LAA also encouraged Vanessa's and Duncan's decorative work which was now very much in demand: when in November 1930 Vanessa put on an independent exhibition at 46 Gordon Square of screens, lamp-shades, sofa-covers, cushions, tiles, trays, chairs, tables and artificial flowers, all either made or embellished by herself, Duncan, Roger, Keith Baynes and Frederick Porter, the crush was so great on the first day that an hour after the show had opened every item had sold and orders for replicas were being taken. Admittedly friends and relations still made up the clientele, but their decorative projects reached a wider public through illustrations in *Vogue*, the *Studio* and elsewhere, and public commissions were shortly to follow. In 1929 Dorothy Todd and Raymond Mortimer published *The New Interior Decoration*, illustrating work by Le Corbusier, Breuer, Oud and Mies van der Rohe, as well as that by Duncan and Vanessa; their fecund, exuberant, eclectic, sensuous style contrasting oddly with the streamlined asceticism and clinical anonymity of the International Style.

If their names were now linked in the public's mind, Vanessa occupied a secondary role to Duncan's greater reputation; in reviews of group exhibitions his paintings would be discussed at length, hers perhaps mentioned in passing along with the work of others. His pictures were often praised for precisely those qualities that her art lacked: an ability to create a melodious, rhythmic line, to draw directly with the brush and thus set up rhythmic repetitions that enliven the surface of the canvas; he was also a more inventive, imaginative artist than she, occasionally indulging his fantasy and love of conceit. There is an engaging persuasiveness in his art of this period, in his fluent handling of form and varied colour harmonies. He had moved away from the more sombre hues and dense, compacted brushwork found in his still lifes and portraits of the early twenties and had developed a more relaxed, pleasure-giving style. Yet the single, and crucial, advantage that, with hindsight, Vanessa's art has over Duncan's, is a greater commitment to the thing seen. Even her dullest still life can display more feeling and integrity than that discernible beneath the flourish and animation of Duncan's bravura. His fascination with the world of everyday appearances did not equal his abundant talent and, like Picasso, he seems to have had difficulty in discovering subjects of sufficient interest to absorb and contain all his skill. As early as 1923 his erstwhile teacher Simon Bussy, in a review of Duncan's 1923 one-artist exhibition, had observed 'too much facility, too much fluidity, a certain superficiality, a manner of using paint which makes the canvas look more like stuff that has been dipped in dye than like a painted picture. "La couleur", Gustave

Moreau used to say to his pupils, "doit être pensée".'[3]

Though she had at one time watched Duncan's development with a critical eye, Vanessa now never doubted that he was a better artist than herself. She had little interest in critical opinion and was probably glad that the attention paid to Duncan allowed her to get on with her work in peace. It was enough that their paintings were selling well and that they had several projects and commissions on hand. Celebrated, active, apparently contented with both her life and work, she was admired and envied by many at this time. She emanated an impression of solid personality and this made her, even when silent in company, the centre of the room. Her character was distinguished by a fullness, ripeness and serenity; one afternoon in April 1927 Faith Henderson, the wife of the editor of *Nation and Athenaeum*, and Virginia Woolf sat either side of a fireplace and discussed happiness, as Faith describes: 'Virginia said that practically everybody she knew was happy, or if they were not, they *ought* to be. I replied that nobody I knew was happy, except perhaps Vanessa who shone out as a star apart.'[4]

This outward serenity prevented even those close to her from seeing that she was not always happy and that beneath the calm, luminescent surface of her daily life lay fear. Vanessa was now approaching fifty. Her sexual relationship with Duncan had almost certainly ended; at one point, either quite soon after or before Angelica's birth, Duncan is said to have told her that he could no longer sleep with her, not because he disliked it, but because he found the psychological strain too great. In her thirties Vanessa had been highly sensual but never promiscuous; she had always been emotionally involved with her lovers and did not then or now seek sexual satisfaction for its own sake. In many ways she was extremely reserved and in order to let other interests dominate she had been able over the years to submerge her sexual appetite. Duncan remained predominantly homosexual by inclination. Therefore in order to retain his love, Vanessa had to continue the pattern of behaviour begun in 1915: she both tolerated his sexual adventures and defused the threat presented by his more permanent boy-friends by absorbing them into their social life, even agreeing to the presence of Angus Davidson on their 1926 trip to Venice. Because she made no fuss but just accepted homosexuality, several of Duncan's boy-friends became devoted to her and felt safe in her presence. Once their affair with Duncan ended, their bond with Vanessa often deepened for they shared her devotion to him and the unspoken, perhaps unconscious, sense of being cast-offs. If they were painters the exchange of sympathy was still easier. One such was the Viennese aristocrat, Franzi von Haas, whom Duncan met around 1924; another was the tall, rich, handsome dilettante artist Peter Morris. He had eyes the blue-green of winter grass, was shy, sensitive, diffident and cultured; he lived in Chelsea with his sister Dora, to whom he was devoted and whose beauty Vanessa caught in a portrait painted in 1937 (Leeds City Art Gallery). Later, in the 1930s, his asthma obliged him to leave London for the warmer climate of Mexico, but while he remained in London he claimed Duncan's attention. Vanessa had dreaded their first meeting. 'I have told him nothing about you and me,' Duncan wrote to her from Paris in January 1927. 'But of course I don't know what others have said. If I was there it would be perhaps easier but on the other hand you may really get to know him better yourself. ... If you cannot face it, I shall understand.'[5] Vanessa, of course, did face it and found Peter so entirely sympathetic that he became a lifelong friend.

Always Vanessa must have been aware of Duncan's imperfect love for her. Like Hester Vanhomrigh, Swift's 'Vanessa', after whom she had been cruelly named, she was destined to undergo what Leslie Stephen in his life of Swift described as 'a long agony of unrequited passion'.[6] She constantly feared separation from Duncan. To break with the person one loves is bearable when one is still young because the future is still unpredictable; to break with a loved one at the age of fifty is to sense that one will suffer a definitive loss for the rest of one's life. A hint of Vanessa's desperation is caught in her nervousness over her initial meeting with Peter Morris: she hoped she would be equal to the occasion, she told Duncan, 'for I know that getting to know him is the only hope as far as I'm concerned'.[7]

Early in 1927 Duncan had set out to join his mother at Cassis, stopping for a brief sojourn in Paris *en route*. There he enjoyed the company of the young painter Robert Medley and his friend the dancer Rupert Doone. He also spent some time with Julian who, since the previous autumn, had been living in Paris with a schoolteacher called Pinault and his family. Clive had hoped that, in this intermediary year between school and Cambridge, Julian would learn a little French history, more of the language, and broaden his experience of life; but the young man was less at home in Paris than his father had been. He attended classes at the Sorbonne, enjoyed lectures on Chinese history given by the poet George Luce and made friends with a Chinese student. Pinault shared Julian's interest in politics and left-wing ideas, encouraged the young man's fascination with the French Revolution and extended his knowledge of French literature. Yet despite these absorbing interests Julian spent much of his time wandering the streets, less aware of his environment than of his homesick longings for Charleston, Cuckmere Haven and the birds that could be seen there on a cold winter's day. It was in the city of Paris that he wrote his first nature poems.

Duncan travelled on to Cassis, where his mother and Aunt Daisy had rented Roland Penrose's Villa des Mimosas which had a studio in its garden. Soon after arriving he fell ill with bronchitis which developed into pneumonia. As had earlier been arranged, Angus Davidson arrived in Cassis shortly after Duncan and was appalled by his friend's condition. For once in his life Angus took the initiative and sent Vanessa a report of Duncan's illness. She repeated this over the telephone to Lytton's niece, Dr Elinor Rendel, who admitted that it was possible Duncan had typhoid. Just at that moment Virginia entered the room and was immediately struck by Vanessa's white face. As soon as was possible Vanessa left for Cassis and Virginia wrote in her diary: 'I think a left handed marriage makes these moments more devastating: a sense remains, I think of hiding one's anguish; of insecurity. Angus writes the most cautious alarming letters. Anyhow she went yesterday in a snowstorm, and we kissed on the pavement in the snow. We are very intimate – a great solace to me.'[8]

Vanessa, taking Grace and Angelica with her, stopped in Paris *en route* and there received a telegram telling her that Duncan was over the worst. No longer in a state of crisis, she chose to linger a couple of days in the city in order to see Julian at her leisure. In foreign surroundings he struck her as now fully grown up. She found to her delight that he saw through Mary Hutchinson's veneer of culture and was critical of her. 'I found it almost impossible to believe I was his mother,' Vanessa told Roger, 'it was so exactly like talking to a friend of one's own choosing only more intimate in many ways than most friends.'[9] Now that her formerly dependent son had become an independent equal, Vanessa felt her affection for him change and deepen.

At Cassis she found Duncan thin, bedraggled and bearded; still very weak and unable to walk far or do more than sit quietly in the sun. There was little Vanessa could do to aid his recovery as he was surrounded by adoring elderly females. In addition to his mother, who was quiet, distinguished and still remarkably beautiful, there was his bustling, energetic aunt, Daisy McNeil, and his mother's companion, Miss Elwes, who nursed a private passion for religion. Vanessa, realizing that she would have to time her visits to Les Mimosas when the others were absent, moved herself, Grace and Angelica out of the Hôtel Cendrillon on the waterfront and into a recently-built villa, owned by a Corsican doctor and named after his country.

Before a week had passed Vanessa had arranged for both Grace and Angelica to have French lessons each morning with a Mlle Chevalier and had herself begun stretching canvases. From the veranda of the Villa Corsica Vanessa had a view of the small town and its two harbours. She noticed that though it was only February, wild flowers, anemones and marigolds had begun to sprout in the red earth between the olives. Next the almond trees blossomed and wild narcissi and red tulips began to appear in the fields. That spring her love for the Midi became fixed.

> Painting is a different thing here from what it can be in the winter in England. It's never dark even when the sky is grey. The light in the Penrose studio is perfect and even now one could often work out of doors, if one wanted to. It makes so much difference to be sure one won't suddenly be held up in the middle of something by fog or darkness. Also the beauty is a constant delight. The people are very friendly and helpful and living is very cheap ... it seems more and more ridiculous for painters to spend half their lives in the dark.[10]

In conversation with Duncan, she had already begun to consider taking a house in the area. Meanwhile he convalesced at Les Mimosas and she spent most of her evenings alone or with Grace at the Villa Corsica.

Her thoughts turned often to Clive, for she had heard from Virginia that he had broken with Mary Hutchinson and intended coming out to Cassis to recuperate and work on his book *Civilization*. The precise reasons for the quarrel were unclear: Mary claimed, then denied, that she was in love with someone else; Clive declared untruthfully that he was tiring of the fashionable society in which Mary moved. A temporary reconciliation was achieved and then broken and Clive arrived at Cassis subdued and depressed. He put up at the Hôtel Cendrillon but went to the Villa Corsica for his meals. Vanessa did not pry into his affairs but allowed him to reveal as much as he wished in his own time. She did not regret the break as it seemed to her that Mary prevented Clive from working and had very little constructive influence on his intellectual life. Vanessa herself was too deeply ingrained with the Stephen heritage to take kindly to dissipation in any form. 'Still work is the only thing,' she once averred to Quentin. 'What a mercy you have that whatever happens. I often feel it.'[11]

She herself had the pleasure of knowing that, while she was in Cassis, her paintings were being exhibited in England by the London Artists' Association. The show was, she said, 'a humble affair, only a few sketches collected hurriedly at the last moment from last summer's sketches'.[12] Her doubts about it proved justified as the work did not sell well, but it earned her praise from Virginia: 'The point about you is that you are now mistress of the phrase. All your pictures are built up of flying phrases. This is to me a very exciting and congenial stage. They have an air of complete spontaneity. The downs seem to billow; yet the hay–cart is perfectly substantial. I daresay your problem will now be to buttress up this lyricism with solidity.'[13] Virginia was echoing a period concern: 'solidity' had become something of a catchword and in their search for it both Vanessa and Duncan could occasionally become heavily literal.

In order to paint, Vanessa was determined to lead an anti-social existence at Cassis. But at first she was slightly fascinated by the impoverished English gentlefolk who resided in the fishing village, forming a small, self-contained society much like that in a Jane Austen novel. Moreover her own forbidding reserve was often undone by her daughter's habit of calling out 'Bonjour' to any passing stranger who took her fancy. Vanessa also recognized in a certain Colonel Teed a fellow outlaw from polite society. He was a retired Bengal Lancer who had abandoned his wife for a small, dark-haired ex-nurse called Jean Campbell. He lived a little way out of Cassis in a small seventeenth-century château, Fontcreuse, and from its surrounding vineyards produced a wine then, as now, renowned in the area. Colonel Teed's role in Cassis was akin to that of an impoverished lord of the manor. He got on well with the local people and could be relied on for such information as the name and address of the local plumber. He had a distinctive appearance: his ugly face was seismically lined, his hands more often than not covered in car oil, his preferred outfit being a workman's boiler suit. While living at his ease in sin at Cassis, he yet remained colossally English. 'Damn picturesque place, Marseilles,' he would bark, 'when you get the hang of it.'

Through Colonel Teed Vanessa discovered La Bergère. This was a small farmworker's cottage situated in the middle of his fields, ramshackle, uninhabited and in need of repair. When she first asked if she and Duncan could take it over he refused, saying that he wanted to use it for chickens and other farmyard purposes. But before she left he had begun to reconsider her request and in the course of their subsequent correspondence an agreement was drawn up: in return for Vanessa's advance of £600 for repairs, she received a ten-year lease on the house. All repairs and additions to the house were then made in Vanessa's absence during the latter part of 1927.

While she remained at the Villa Corsica during the spring and summer of that year she managed to organize life very much to her satisfaction. At the end of February Duncan moved in with her as his elderly relations had now departed. A young woman called Elise Anghilanti came up every day from the town to help with the shopping and cooking. When the car did not start they found they could depend on the services of a nearby garage mechanic. In April Julian and Quentin arrived, accompanying the nurse Louie Dunnett who now took over responsibility for Angelica. Though the two brothers lodged in the town, they had their meals at the Villa Corsica where they had a noticeable effect on the conversation: Julian, large, uncouth and dressed in loose-fitting clothes temporarily objected to the artists' view of things and fought conversational battles with the rest; Quentin, by comparison slim and elegant, Vanessa now found completely sympathetic. Her absorption in her sons perhaps made her appear indifferent to Duncan, because when Virginia and Leonard paid them a visit the former, observing their settled relationship, let drop a reference to her sister's 'marmoreal chastity' which Vanessa could not afterwards forget. 'Anyhow you see how Duncan and I smart,' she confessed to Virginia after she had left. 'It is terrible to be thought chaste and dowdy when one would so much like to be neither.'[14]

Duncan's affairs were indeed temporarily chaste. He still wrote to Peter Morris, but 'as for love,' he told Bunny, 'in my case it hangs or lies suspended. Little by little I get used to or forget my little heart troubles and miseries. ... If I don't get what I want my *amour propre* comes into play a good deal which if it does not kill real love provides a corslet which deceives oneself, if not others.'[15] Both he and Vanessa were temporarily reviewing their affections, for she wrote to Roger: 'I believe one gets to think being "in love" less and less important, but loving people never gets less important and you are one of the people I love most, as you know well, and however much either you or I may happen to be in love with other people my real feeling for you doesn't change.'[16]

Early in May Roger arrived at Cassis, putting up at Les Mimosas. He persuaded Vanessa and Duncan to hire a boat in which they could explore the many calanques that cut into the coast west of Cassis. As they drew close to the shore where the white sand turned the sea the colour of aquamarine, the nine-year-old Angelica jumped in and swam until she could stay in the water no longer. She emerged for the picnic jabbering nonsense and intoxicated with happiness. Equally memorable was the evening at the Villa Corsica when a tapping was heard at the window. Roger declared it was only a bat or a bird, but on going to look they found an enormous female Emperor moth, with a six-inch wing-span. Intent on adding this specimen to Julian's collection, they caught it and dosed it first with ether, then chloroform, and after two days the moth eventually died.

Vanessa blamed the elaborate proceedings undertaken for her son's sake to ensure the death of the moth on her maternal instinct. Or so she told Virginia, when describing to her this incident which provided the initial inspiration for *The Waves*, originally entitled 'The Moths'. 'I wish you would write a book about the maternal instinct,' she ended her letter. 'In all my wide reading I haven't yet found it properly explored ... I could tell you a great deal! Of course it is one of the worst of the passions, animal and remorseless. But how can one avoid yielding to these instincts if one happens to have them?'[17]

The book of Virginia's that did arrive while she was at Cassis was *To the Lighthouse*. Virginia, relying on memories acquired during the first thirteen years of her life, had recreated their mother in the character Mrs Ramsay, in terms that Vanessa immediately recognized:

> Anyhow it seemed to me that in the first part of the book you have given a portrait of mother which is more like her to me than anything I would ever have conceived possible. It is almost painful to have her so raised from the dead. You have made one feel the extraordinary beauty of her character, which must be the most difficult thing in the world to do. It was like meeting her again with oneself grown up and on equal terms. ... You have given father too I think as clearly, but perhaps, I may be wrong, that isn't quite so difficult. ... it is so shattering to find oneself face to face with these two again that I can hardly consider anything else. In fact for the last two days I have hardly been able to attend to daily life. Duncan and I have talked about them, as each had a copy, whenever we could get alone together. ... Duncan who didn't know them says too that for the first time he understands mother. So your vision of her stands as a whole by itself and not only as reminding one of facts.

Whether or not *To the Lighthouse* presents a realistic portrait of Julia Stephen, this book with its emphasis on maternal love returned Vanessa to the mother she could both recognize and understand; to a character resolved into a unity by the healing power of art. To what must have formerly been a fragmented, incomplete and painful memory, she was now reconciled. In addition to this, she had the sensation that the book had been imagined and understood as a whole. She therefore ended her letter to Virginia on a note of high praise: 'I am excited and thrilled and taken into another world as one only is by a great work of art.'[18]

At the end of May Vanessa left Cassis, and on arrival in Paris bought clothes for Angelica at Lafayette's, or rather her daughter swiftly selected what she wanted and having done so proceeded to dance in the middle of the shop. Is it her de l'Etang blood, Vanessa wondered, as they extricated themselves with difficulty from the admiring crowd of women that had gathered round. Angelica then travelled back to England with Grace, while Vanessa stayed on for a short while in Paris with Duncan, eventually leaving before him and arriving home without misfortune, save that her bottle of Perrier water exploded in the luggage-rack.

While she had been abroad Clive's father had been seriously ill. On 21 June he died. He was given a dignified funeral at Seend, the procession winding its way through the village street, from Cleeve House to the church. He left £271,303 9s. 9d. and the shares that went to Clive brought him in an additional income of around £1,200 a year. Without any noticeable extravagance, several small comforts began to appear at Charleston.

That summer Julian and Quentin no longer disappeared each evening to write the Bulletin but shared in the after-dinner talk. Vanessa observed that Quentin was more a man-of-the-world than Julian but that Julian was intellectually ahead of his younger brother. Both had a good effect on Clive with whom they sparred verbally and with much humour. There was a willingness to discuss anything, a love of irreverent banter and ribaldry. But it was noticeable that Vanessa adopted a different attitude to her daughter's upbringing than she had done to her sons'. There was just a hint of sedate respectability in her manner as she murmured, 'Pas devant l'enfant' when Angelica was present, and the conversation would be steered in another direction.

She and Duncan were occupied that summer with designs for the loggia at the Château d'Auppegard, near Offranville, outside Dieppe. Ethel Sands and Nan Hudson had spared no effort in restoring this seventeenth-century château to its original condition. They had repaired the eighteenth-century wood panelling and stripped off the plaster on the south side to reveal the original timber and cow-pat façade, at the same time uncovering a loggia at the far end of the house. Vanessa and Duncan, on two visits made this summer in July and September, painted its walls an uneven green to suggest foliage, leaving in the centre oval spaces in which they drew pastoral and garden scenes. On the chimney-breast Duncan painted a lady leaning out of a window. All were done in a spirit of light-hearted pastiche, in a style sympathetic to the age of the château. The colours are soft and warm, orange and pale green predominating. The most striking thing about these decorations is the very obvious differences between the two artists' styles: in Duncan's work everything flows and billows, suggesting that movement was essential to his personal expression; in Vanessa's notice-ably more static pastoral scenes the vertical figures balance the horizontal lines in the landscape and sky, revealing her preference for stillness and detachment.

The château itself is only one room deep, one room opening into another on the ground floor and receiving light from both north and south. From the outside one can look right through the building and this spread of glass gives the château an air of delicacy and insubstantiality. Vanessa found, as at Newington, that the environment was a little too precious for her taste. She vented her feelings on Roger:

> Please send us a glimpse of ordinary rough and tumble, dirty every day existence. I am beginning to be in danger of collapse from rarefication here. The strain to keep clean is beginning to tell. Duncan shaves daily – I wash my

hands at least 5 times a day – but in spite of all I know I'm not up to the mark. The extraordinary thing is that it's not the house only but also the garden that's in such spotless order. It's almost impossible to find a place into which one can throw a cigarette end without it becoming a glaring eyesore. Ethel goes out at night and hunts snails till there are practically none left. Old men come in and polish the floors, women come and cut the grass, others come and wash, Nan makes muslin covers to receive the flies' excrement (I don't believe Nan and Ethel have any – they never go to the lav.). Everything has yards and yards of fresh muslin and lace and silk festooned on it and all seems to be washed and ironed in the night. No wonder they hardly ever paint.[19]

With the memory of Auppegard still fresh in her mind, Vanessa weeded furiously on her return to Charleston. She blamed the shocking state of the garden on the fact that she had three children and less income than Ethel, but eventually admitted to herself that the elegant precision at Auppegard and shabby disorder at Charleston were due to temperament rather than the advantages or want of riches and virginity.

She could not bring herself to leave Charleston that autumn. Duncan had gone with Bunny by car to Cassis in order to inspect the repairs at La Bergère, leaving Vanessa alone in Sussex with Angelica and her friend Judith Bagenal. Both girls were due back in London when the term began but they stayed on at Charleston while the Indian summer lasted. Vanessa gardened, made curtains and painted. She also began the designs for a new edition of Virginia's short story *Kew Gardens*. Each page was to be decorated with abstract and semi-abstract shapes alluding to the descriptions of light, movement and shape found in the text. It is the boldest and most effective of their collaborations. The decorations succeed because they are imprecise enough to echo but not to replace the sensations and images aroused by the text. Yet they have sufficient importance to make each page visually dramatic, text and image balancing each other as in Blake's illuminated books. The apparently artless spontaneity of her designs cost Vanessa much trial and error. Towards the end of the book she found she needed to try six or seven designs before she arrived at the one she wanted. The twenty-one pages vary considerably in style, the earliest having a bold openness of touch that the later ones lack. Towards the end of the book the line becomes thinner, the shapes and patterns more prettily clustered. 'I have always thought neatness was the quality to aim at in middle age,' Vanessa had opined to Virginia earlier this year, 'and here I am, as you say the worse for wear and untidy.'[20] It is interesting that, secure in the comfort and peace offered by Charleston, she could design with greater freedom and panache; in London her initial assurance evaporated, her style tightened and she wrote to Duncan telling him how badly she needed his advice. The 1927 edition of *Kew Gardens* demonstrates a dwindling of self-confidence; her style shifts from the slashing and bold to the carefully decorative. In both, however, she is able to express sensibility through the most economical of means. It was this simplicity that impressed Virginia; of Vanessa's dust-jacket for *To the Lighthouse* she wrote: 'I wish you'd signed your cover. Privately I thought it lovely. . . . Your style is unique; because so truthful; and therefore it upsets one completely.'[21]

While Duncan was absent in France Vanessa did not lack for company in London. She saw much of Angus Davidson and still acted as intermediary between him and his employers, the Woolfs. With him she went to hear the Léner quartet and afterwards went on to a supper party given for Clive by Edward Sackville-West. At unexpected moments London struck her as beautiful, but not its inhabitants: 'Never did I see so many middle aged sour looking females, all trying to be smart. They haven't the fascination for me of the females I see in waiting rooms at Lewes, whose choice of colour in dress and hats seems to be often equal to Velasquez – at any rate when helped by the astonishing backgrounds provided by the South Downs bus waiting rooms.'[22] But London offered parties, exhibitions, gossip, the glimpse of Ottoline in Wigmore Street, old, wizened, powdered and complaining sonorously about the vulgarity of modern life. It also brought new faces into their circle, such as that of the beautiful young actress Valerie Taylor who was flattered when Clive and Vita Sackville-West paid her compliments and invited her to parties. Both Clive and Duncan are said to have taken her to bed. She was also the only person ever to paint Vanessa's face blue, prior to a cocktail party at which everything had to be either blue or green. The young Angelica watched as her mother's face was made up and felt the situation to be unbearably tense.

If Vanessa was obliged to curtail her demands upon Duncan's affection, she drew considerable satisfaction from her family. This autumn Julian went up to King's College, Cambridge, to read history under the economic historian John Clapham. He lodged at 12 St Edward's Passage and Vanessa was anxious to hear how he had settled in. Though he wrote poems, beagled and spoke at the Union, his first motion being 'That England thinks too much of her athletes and their doings' (sport, he argued, was a kind of opiate used to keep democracy quiet), his first year at university was not a notable success. It wasn't until his second year that he established friendships with those who shared his literary or political interests: Anthony Blunt, Edward Playfair, Richard Llewelyn-Davies, Alasdair Watson, Harry Lintott and John Lehmann. In Cambridge, as in Paris, he found it difficult to put down roots, to establish with any degree of confidence a life cut off from that of his family. He found a valuable link with his past in Bunny who was now living with his wife Ray not far from Cambridge at Hilton Hall in the village of the same name. They provided Julian with hot baths and hospitality after he had been beagling in the surrounding countryside. Exhilarated with physical exhaustion, he would then sit by the fire happily exchanging stories about his family with Bunny.

During Julian's second term at Cambridge, Quentin went to Munich where he lodged with a Baroness von Massenbach on the recommendation of Duncan's friend Franzi von Haas. He hoped to learn the German language but as the very agreeable Baroness spoke excellent French the purpose of his visit was effectively negated.

With her family dispersed (Clive at this time was touring Germany with Raymond Mortimer), Vanessa fled London and, with Duncan, Angelica and Grace travelled to Cassis to take up residence in the newly restored La Bergère. They arrived, clutching rhorkee chairs, blankets, easels and a gramophone, to find the small house looking bright and new, with yellow walls and blue shutters, but still very much a part of the landscape. Everything was prepared for their arrival: Elise Anghilanti had lit wood fires, placed flowers in the rooms, prepared a meal and put wine on the table. They settled in with ease. A small bathroom had been installed and an extra room added on the far side of the house which could be entered only by an outside door. This became Vanessa's bedroom and studio for it enabled her to hide when unwanted visitors called. Duncan took over the large upstairs room, leaving two small downstairs rooms for Angelica and Grace. Situated at the bottom of a farm track, near the top of a valley, the house faces south, and from the terrace one looks down over the fields towards Cassis and the sea. Even today it is set apart from the other villas that spread out into the surrounding hills.

Their only neighbours were the Teeds who tactfully never imposed their presence. They sold them eggs, wine and jam, found a donkey for Angelica and offered her a small summer-house to play in. Aunt Daisy, whose Dutch barge was moored at Cassis, bought Angelica a piano. Elise Anghilanti came up from the town each day with the shopping, became a close friend of Grace and taught her much about cooking. The affectionate esteem that Vanessa felt for Elise was returned. When in 1934 a friend of Duncan's – the American journalist Jimmy Sheean – rented La Bergère, he quickly discovered that Jourdan, the local garage mechanic, Colonel Teed, Jean Campbell and Elise all adored Vanessa. She in turn was captivated by her new surroundings for La Bergère was, she observed, 'another Charleston in France'.

She quickly asserted her ownership: an oleander was planted beside the terrace; headed notepaper ordered from the Hogarth Press. She also sent Grace and Angelica off in the donkey-cart each morning to attend French lessons in Cassis, so that she and Duncan could paint. They bought a Renault car and began to explore the area. They made a visit to Aix and admired the Ingres paintings in the Musée Granet; they discovered the pottery at Aubagne which still used seventeenth- and eighteenth-century moulds and where Vanessa made several acquisitions. They frequently navigated the hairpin bends on the coast road to Marseilles with erratic skill. Once, however, Vanessa swerved to miss a bus, skidded and went straight into its side. No one was hurt but the car was badly damaged.

This year she was determined to evade Cassis society. She did, however, accept an invitation to dine with a Colonel Carruthers and his family. Apart from the inedible food, Vanessa was forcibly struck by what was in fact a standard form of grace: 'The grace was on completely new and original lines and ended up with some terrible snarl about "and ourselves to *Thy* service". Have you ever heard of such a thing? I couldn't hear the beginning and can't conceive what it can have been to lead coherently to such an ending unless the food was to be devoted to our service and so eventually to God's. Anyhow I nearly did for myself and hope that I did quite by the end of the evening, only I think they'll forgive everything.'[23] She herself was prepared to be 'at home' to no one except the Teeds and Duncan's Aunt Daisy. Nan Hudson's announcement that she was coming to Cassis for two weeks in March, to be near them, did not please her. When Barbara Bagenal arrived, bringing her daughter Judith who was to be left behind as a companion for Angelica, and stayed a few days before returning home, Vanessa dutifully took her to places of interest but before long had developed her father's habit of groaning aloud. At the same time she was writing to Virginia about Clive's social life: 'He wrote me a most extraordinary letter, simply that of a lady of fashion, telling me how he spent his day hurrying from the beauty specialist to the dancing master, lunch, dinner and supper parties. It sounded rather too hectic to be natural I thought. I agree with you he seems to be in an odd way sexually.'[24] Even Queen Victoria's social foibles now came under her review: while reading her letters to Disraeli, Vanessa detected what Lytton had overlooked, that the Queen was in fact a middle-class scold.

Despite Vanessa's horror of society, the small rooms at La Bergère were often surprisingly crowded, especially after the arrival of Julian and Clive in March. When Clive's friend Raymond Mortimer appeared in Cassis for a week, Vanessa found she enjoyed his company more than she expected. The Woolfs followed and, like Julian and Clive, stayed at Fontcreuse. While they were present a visit was made to Aix, Tarascon and St-

Rémy where they saw the asylum in which Van Gogh had stayed. Soon after Virginia and Leonard had left Roger arrived, having just delivered a lecture at Monte Carlo. While he was present the entire party dined one evening in Cassis with the young painter Tristram Hillier and his girl-friend Joan Ferminger. Clive flirted so outrageously with Joan that rational conversation was impossible; Vanessa again perceived that Clive's break with Mary had left him unbalanced. She was critical too of Lytton and Carrington when they lunched at La Bergère while touring near by. It seemed to Vanessa that Carrington had a funereal effect on Lytton, dampening his conversation and making him appear lifeless and depressed.

Duncan and Vanessa decided to travel home by car with Angus Davidson who was staying near by. To make this possible Vanessa sent Angelica and Grace home by train, arranging for Roger's friend Angela Lavelli to help them across Paris. On the day Vanessa and Duncan finally left, they at first drove off without realizing that Angus was not in the car, Duncan having also left behind his money and passport. Once these omissions had been rectified, the journey proceeded smoothly enough. They stopped at the small town of Brantôme (which Vanessa saw was paintable and afterwards recommended to Roger) and at Amboise before arriving in Paris in a shocking state – Duncan without a tie, buttons or socks; Vanessa equally informal in red espadrilles and a straw hat, but hoping to reclothe herself while there. On 16 June this daughter of Sir Leslie Stephen, so disreputably attired and obliged to co-habit with an unreformed homosexual while her husband gallivanted elsewhere, this shabby middle-aged female whose life, by normal standards, lacked glamour, respectability, security or appeal returned to England. And four days later Virginia wrote in her diary:

> Mercifully, Nessa is back. My earth is watered again. I go back to words of one syllable: feel come over me the feathery change: rather true that: as if my physical body put on some soft comfortable skin. She is a necessity to me – as I am not to her. I run to her as the wallaby runs to the old kangaroo. She is also very cheerful, solid, happy. The trifles that annoy other people, she passes off; as if her happiness were a million or two in the bank; ... never in a muddle, or desperate, or worried; never spending a pound or a thought needlessly; yet with it all free, careless, airy, indifferent: a very notable achievement.[25]

Though Duncan complained to Bunny that their life at La Bergère had lacked excitement, it had not been unproductive. Whether at Cassis, in London or at Charleston, Duncan and Vanessa continued to spend the greater part of the day painting. With 'a brush, the one dependable thing

in a world of strife, ruin, chaos',[26] they could return, whatever the stress
and discord of daily life, to that continuously absorbing interior world in
which the struggle to record observations of light, colour and form,
however agonizingly difficult and intractable, resolves into an enduring
happiness. Here, where the artist strives to shape, condense and order
thoughts and sensations until they take on a form that communicates, is
the promise of continuity as opposed to decay, of meaning as opposed to
senselessness, of value as opposed to waste. Vanessa painted, not in order
to forget anxiety and pain, but in order to transform them into the
permanence of art.

Such generalizations do not apply only to fine art. There was something
equally satisfying in the unfolding of an abstract pattern suitable for a
cushion cover; or in the decoration of a fan. When Helen Anrep's son
discovered on a market stall an old ivory fan decorated with an Italianate
scene and gave it to Vanessa to restore, he was slightly disappointed when
it returned totally transformed, with the relaxed curlicues, loose hatching,
dots and circles that defined her unmistakable style. At Charleston even
the log box was ornamented with angelic musicians and dancing figures
painted by Duncan. When Quentin broke the oval mirror over the
garden-room fireplace, by placing a lamp too close to its surface, Duncan
filled the space it had occupied with a decoration of ships at sea. Later this
was replaced with a basket of flowers which was illusionistically held in
position by two semi-naked females painted on the wall either side. In the
studio two equally robust figures had been squeezed on to the fireplace
surround. Before long one cupboard door in a bedroom was to be decorated by Angelica, in a figurative style noticeably lighter and more feminine
than Duncan's baroque nudes. 'At last I understand the real charm of the
female as opposed to the male and what vanity and amusement and colour
they give to life,' Vanessa now observed to Julian. '... Of course Angelica
isn't the only female who shows it to me – there are always Virginia and
one or two others, but as I'm really in love with Angelica for the time
being I think I can understand it as a man would.'[27]

If her affections were now almost exclusively given to Duncan, her
family and a few close friends, she did enjoy a mild flirtation with Segonzac
on a visit to Paris that autumn. She and Duncan dined with him at Foyot's
and afterwards danced at the Bœuf sur le Toit. In the cab on the drive
home the French artist, slightly tipsy but still very charming, held Vanessa's
hand. She and Duncan automatically gravitated towards the artistic quarter
and they now regularly stayed at the Hôtel de Londres in the rue Bonaparte
that led into the rue Jacob and was two minutes' walk from the rue de
Seine. Quentin was also staying at the Hôtel de Londres, having begun

work in an atelier that was visited by the artist Jean Marchand once a week. Though still a student of painting, he had already decorated his brother's rooms at King's College with a dado representing the storming of the Winter Palace.

Even Vanessa, though oblivious of their subject-matter, was appalled by these murals when she and Angelica accompanied the Woolfs on a visit to Cambridge in October. While Virginia dined and lectured at Newnham, Vanessa, having put Angelica to bed in the hotel, had supper alone with Julian. Now that he had rooms in college, an old car to drive, and had received the honour of being made an 'Apostle', he seemed happier and less gauche. The next day George ('Dadie') Rylands gave a small luncheon party at which Vanessa, the Woolfs, as well as Lytton and Maynard were present. They sat at a circular table in a room overlooking the lawn leading down to the Cam and ate the meal that was to reappear in *A Room of One's Own* where it makes a telling contrast with the one Virginia had had the night before at Newnham. But while Virginia savoured the gastronomic differences between men's and women's colleges, Vanessa was chiefly interested in Douglas Davidson's decorations around the doors and over the fireplace in Dadie's sitting-room. Being a 'sound critic', as Quentin has said, she disliked these tight, neat imitations of her and Duncan's style. She thought them 'old-maidish' and even less likeable than Quentin's execrable mural which sat so heavily on the wall.

If at Cambridge Vanessa had been impressed by Julian's increased sociability, the same young man sat silent, like his brother, at Cleeve House that Christmas under the eye of their grandmother. The death of Clive's father had made no appreciable difference to the life of the house; neither the conversation nor the fabric of existence, Vanessa thought, had altered since her first visit in 1906. At mealtimes old Mrs Bell sat at the head of the table, overseeing the conversation which therefore had to be reined in within very strict limits. Vanessa struggled to find some remark that was neither banal nor confined to the weather. Clive and Cory also struck out with indifferent topics, 'mostly confined to food, motorcars or other subjects sufficiently dull to be safe. The talk grew increasingly desultory until Mrs Bell disappeared to bed and then it instantly rallied, careering freely over a whole range of dissolute topics.

In January 1929, galvanized by descriptions of the art in German museums, Vanessa, Duncan and Quentin travelled to Berlin. The Woolfs also visited Berlin this month and Vanessa was struck by their awkwardness: they walked miles to avoid the difficulty of taking a cab; they ate in the hotel restaurant whereas Vanessa and Duncan automatically ate out, finding small places where they got better food for a third of hotel prices.

It was obvious, Vanessa thought, that most writers are miserable when removed from their studies and only painters know how to live abroad.

A good deal of their time was spent in the company of Harold Nicolson, currently employed in the embassy, and his wife Vita Sackville-West who was there on a visit. Her dislike of Berlin and the social duties that she was expected to perform made the situation tense: Leonard's refusal to attend a party where Harold had promised to introduce him to a certain politician made matters worse. The atmosphere was already uncomfortable when one evening the Nicolsons, their two sons, Vita's nephew Edward Sackville-West, the Woolfs, Vanessa and Duncan all set out for dinner. As no table had been booked and they numbered nine in all, they had to trudge the streets filled with deep slush in search of a restaurant that could accommodate them. After the meal they went to see the famous Russian film by Pudovkin entitled *Storm over Asia*, banned in England by the British Board of Film Censors. Vanessa enjoyed it in purely visual terms, for its display of landscape and old Mongolian types. But when they re-emerged she discovered that others in the party were incensed by the film's anti-British propaganda. Afterwards they stood in the street vaguely quarrelling with each other, Edward Sackville-West trying to distract Duncan's attention as he wanted to take him off on a tour of Berlin's night life without Harold being of the party. Vanessa, thankfully uninvolved, was amused by it all, despite her unspoken grudge that the Nicolsons were 'an unnecessary importation into our society'.[28]

Not many days had passed before her earlier dislike of Germany again overwhelmed her. It was not the people she disliked, for they struck her as kind and able to enjoy themselves unselfconsciously, but the tasteless food, the shapeless figures of the women and the general affront to the senses which no amount of sanitary conveniences and abundant hot water could disguise. Duncan shared her feelings; for him bad food constituted a serious threat to civilization. Both longed for France. Things however improved when they moved from Berlin to Dresden which Vanessa preferred and where she admired Raphael's *Sistine Madonna*. She began to copy in one museum but got into trouble for upsetting her water all over a chair and was told that watercolours were strictly 'verboten'. Meanwhile the presence of Quentin added to her pleasure. She saw that, like Virginia, he could enjoy Germany because he lived largely in a world of his own; that he could not sit in a train for five minutes without starting a flirtation; and that though he clearly thought her and Duncan half-witted, he was very kind. Thus they arrived at Vienna where they met Roger and had the pleasure of looking at paintings in his company, Vanessa still trusting more in his judgement than in her own.

On her return home, Vanessa declared the London climate soft and balmy compared with that of Berlin, though England, like the rest of Europe, was suffering intense cold. By mid February all the pipes in 37 Gordon Square were frozen solid; even the gas pipes had ice in them and only one fire would burn. The city was riddled with disease and influenza raged among their friends. Both Angelica and Grace fell ill but Vanessa still managed to work each day in Duncan's Fitzroy Street studio.

After this bleak winter Cassis in the spring was more enchanting than ever. The asperity in the landscape, with its line of rocks culminating in the Couronne de Charlemagne almost behind Fontcreuse, suited Vanessa's taste for, like Roger, she had an ingrained distrust of the more obviously picturesque. However, as she disliked painting out of doors, she produced few landscapes, even in Provence, and it was Duncan who this year executed a brilliantly coloured view of the surrounding sun-drenched fields, filled with poppies under an ultramarine sky (Laing Art Gallery, Newcastle). When Vanessa, Duncan, Grace, Angelica and Judith Bagenal arrived at Cassis, they found Clive, Julian and Quentin already installed in rooms at Fontcreuse. Julian, very brown and sporting a thick beard, went on long solitary walks. He was quieter than usual and faintly critical of them all, expecially Clive and Quentin, perhaps grudging the latter's success with the ladies of Cassis. There were two new additions to their life-style: a smart new Citroën ('We whisk about all over the place with high respectability', Vanessa told Virginia[29]) which they shared with Colonel Teed, and a governess called Sabine de Fondeville who lived in. She relieved Vanessa of much responsibility towards Angelica and Judith, but her presence brought out Clive's love of badinage to which the young girl was incapable of responding. She seemed unable to talk of anything except the French language and cooking and before long Clive grew irritated by her presence. Even Vanessa found her wearying and decided this would be her last self-sacrifice in the cause of education.

Fortunately the terrace, protected at one end by a curved glass screen, meant that in good weather they could eat and sit out of doors. But when it rained the entire family and any visitors who were present squeezed into the small dining-room and the rattle of conversation created a pandemonium very different from the peaceful existence Vanessa had envisaged at La Bergère. Moreover as her studio-bedroom was the only sitting-room, in cold wet weather everyone crowded in there. When Quentin left, his room at Fontcreuse was immediately taken by Clive's brother Cory and the mealtime conversation at La Bergère grew still noisier, drowning the cacophony made by the nightingales, cicadas and frogs outside.

In their new car Duncan and Vanessa made a leisurely visit to the Bussys at Roquebrune. As they drove past one bay after another Vanessa fell a little into a dream, memories of Greece and Cornwall surfacing in her mind. La Souco occupies a unique position; perched on the hillside it looks out over Cap-St-Martin towards Monte Carlo. With temptation ever present before their eyes, Duncan suggested to the critical and acute Simon and to Dorothy who, as translator of André Gide, was currently emotionally and intellectually bound up with this writer, that they should visit the gaming-rooms. Though shocked they agreed, and Dorothy on their first and almost certainly last visit made vast profits, while Vanessa and Duncan gained nothing except experience. 'I was absolutely fascinated', Vanessa admitted, ' – not by the game which seemed to me too dull for words – but then I always lose – but by the players who are all obviously on the verge of suicide. I should spend all my time there if I lived nearer. The rooms have to be lit by lamps lest someone should cut the electric light and grab all the money which they all look ready to do.'[30]

On her return to Cassis among the letters waiting for her were one from Maynard and another from Julian. Maynard's brought news of the London Artists' Association's recent success (a joint R. V. Pitchforth and Raymond Coxon exhibition and an informal show of Duncan's pastels), of the forthcoming election, and of Julian's success at Cambridge where he was regarded by the fellows and dons as one of the best of his generation: 'The magazines are plastered with his poems – some not at all bad; whether Anthony Blunt (with whom he's completely and helplessly infatuated) is quite all that Julian thinks him may be found doubtful in the future – but that doesn't matter at present.'[31] Julian's letter contained the admission that he had been sleeping with Blunt. He was confident that Vanessa would not be shocked and begged her to tell no one, as if Virginia got to hear it would be tantamount to advertising the matter in *The Times*. She later recalled: 'Letter from him at Cassis telling me of his first love affair with A.B. not a very real one. The joy of reading the letter as I walked down the field path and knew he meant to tell me things. I had never expected it.'[32]

On 5 June the Woolfs arrived on their third visit to Cassis and were again so taken with the life Vanessa had created around her that they too decided to buy a villa in the area, an idea that Leonard afterwards rejected as impractical. Virginia perceived that between Vanessa and Duncan there was an 'odd intimate, yet edgy, happy free yet somehow restrained intercourse'. Her own relationship with her sister was slightly self-conscious: when Vanessa praised Julian and recounted his news, Virginia mentioned the huge sales that her *Orlando* was enjoying; to which Vanessa replied, 'I am a failure as a painter compared with you, and cant do more than pay for my models.' Despite this, Virginia's remaining impression was of Vanessa's 'overpowering supremacy'.[33]

At Cassis, even when Virginia was present, Vanessa was the focus of attention. 'Owing to Vanessa's amazing arrangements', Duncan wrote to Bunny, 'everything goes like clockwork. I admire that woman's gifts more and more – they are unrivalled.'[34] Clive was amused by her behaviour on receiving news of a figure from her past, the novelist Mrs W.K. Clifford. 'Vanessa was almost beside herself with excitement when Mrs Clifford died; in fact she was preparing to drive the Citroën into Marseilles for next day's *Times* in the hope that a correspondent would write – as of course he did. The ghoulish strain in the Stephens is very strong; in Vanessa it's almost the only definitely literary heritage – except of course her admirable prose-style.'[35] Virginia admired the reckless skill with which Vanessa handled life, creating an existence in which all could live and work happily. The established routine was that followed at Charleston: in the mornings and afternoons the artists painted while Julian retired to Angelica's hut where he wrote or read. That summer Vanessa and Duncan spent much of their time experimenting with various techniques and styles for some seven-foot-tall panels that had been commissioned by Lady Dorothy Wellesley for her dining-room. Eventually Vanessa discovered the advantages of the sponge which created a dappled effect and allowed the brown-pink underpaint to show through. Quentin, meanwhile, painted in the tower at Fontcreuse. All reappeared at meals when they were inclined to get tipsy and incoherent, Julian occasionally becoming helpless with laughter. 'One leads a purely sensual and unintellectual existence here which I at any rate find fatally easy,' Vanessa told Clive when their four-month stay neared its end. 'Everything combines to attract one's senses and put pure intellect in the shade.'[36] In August they returned to England via Paris.

Both at Cassis and in Sussex Vanessa's life had been considerably affected by the motorcar. It brought both advantages and disadvantages; it made Charleston less remote and to avoid unexpected and unwanted guests she had planted a large sign 'OUT' in the field where the track divided and led up to the house. She herself had been taught to drive by Frederick Pape, the husband of Angelica's nurse, and was rather proud of her vehicles though, as Roger observed, she drove with great *pudeur*. The first time she met him at Lewes station in her own car she parked some distance from the station entrance to avoid attracting attention to herself; which, however, she very soon did when the car stalled in the middle of the road some fifty yards from the station and where they remained until she realized that the petrol switch had not been turned on. The Charleston Bulletin got much copy out of her near disastrous meetings with numerous cars, carts, bicycles and the local bus on her short visits to Rodmell. Even once she was safely returned to Charleston there was still the difficulty of putting the car in the garage (formerly the duck shed). This required careful manœuvring and the task was usually put off until after tea. Though Vanessa became a competent driver (Duncan was always in a class of his own) she never wholly overcame what Virginia called their 'sublime ineptitude' with cars. If a strange noise was heard it was put down to ball-bearings 'wandering loose among the machinery'. When seat-belts were eventually introduced, which Duncan insisted he and Grace should use, neither could discover the release mechanism and had to drive to a garage to be unstrapped.

The visitors who arrived at Charleston in the summer of 1929 included Edward Sackville-West, Bunny, Raymond Mortimer, Frankie Birrell, Lytton, Peter Lucas and Anthony Blunt. The house continued to exert its potency so that, even if driven from the station by Julian at breakneck speed, a sense of pleasurable anticipation spread over the person arriving as the car turned down the farm track. Yet Vanessa herself was beginning to be aware that her desire to keep husband and ex-lovers all within her circle had brought about a certain loss. Despite the evident fulfilment that she evinced, there was also a constant strain of unhappiness in her life, though as yet it had not become pronounced. That August Virginia recorded in her diary that her own melancholy was much diminished 'by hearing Nessa say she was often melancholy and often envied me – a statement I thought incredible. I have spilt myself among too many stools she said (we were sitting in her bedroom before dinner).'[37]

In order to concentrate her life better she now gave up 37 Gordon Square. That autumn Angelica went off as a boarder to Lángford Grove School in Essex and Vanessa felt it no longer necessary to keep a London house. She lodged Grace in Clive's part of 50 Gordon Square and took for herself the studio next to Duncan's at 8 Fitzroy Street. After twenty-one years of looking after children she returned, Virginia observed, 'perhaps rather sadly to the life she would have liked best of all once, to be a painter on her own'.[38]

Both studios were situated at the back of 8 Fitzroy Street and were reached by passing through the dusty hallway and along a small iron and glass passageway on the first floor that connected the two buildings, the second of which opened out on to the mews behind. Beneath the studios lived an Italian, a master carver and furniture restorer called Ferro and his family with whom they were on friendly terms. Duncan's studio was the larger and more famous of the two as it had formerly belonged to Sickert and to Whistler and a reproduction of the latter's small portrait of C.E. Holloway, *The Philosopher*, hung by the fireplace and was handed on from tenant to tenant. Vanessa's studio, like Duncan's, became filled with pieces of pottery, screens and odd pieces of furniture. Her bed became a divan during the daytime, while in one corner was a small kitchen area where Grace, who came in each day, cooked the meals. Here Vanessa hoped to enjoy uninterrupted hours of work. 'Ring 3 times and remember to come in by the basement,' she told Virginia. 'Then you will find me always alone.'[39]

Thus apart from another brief visit to Paris with Duncan in October 1929, that autumn and winter she spent largely working in her new studio. Writing to Julian at Cambridge she sympathized with his temporary boredom and advised him to get to know some young women and to fall back on work. 'I don't know why I believe in work, but it is I'm sure the only real standby in life, at least if it's work one likes.'[40] She herself filled an entire sketchbook with ideas for the dust-jacket for Virginia's *A Room of One's Own* which appeared at the end of October. That autumn the Hogarth Press also began to issue the uniform edition of Virginia's novels, all of which had the same pale peacock-blue dust-jacket designed by Vanessa.

Yet 'standby' is an odd word to use of that which remained so central to her life. Compared with Virginia's unremitting dedication to her art, it has to be admitted that if children had inestimably enriched Vanessa's life, they had also dispersed her emotional and creative energies. Virginia provides us with two images of Vanessa this autumn: one is of her in her Fitzroy Street studio, 'in a great misty room, with flaring gas and unsorted plates and glasses on the floor';[41] the other is of her visiting Angelica at school. The latter is only imagined, but so beautifully judged and observed, it cannot be ignored.

> Julian has driven her over from Cambridge . . . they drive, with a map on their knees; Julian rather tense, staring through his spectacles. Some very intimate things are hinted at – of wh. I know nothing – or rather he grunts and half says things, which she understands. She is very excited, at the same time practical. Julian is excited too. They are both anxious to see Angelica. How will they see her first? She will come running down the stairs into the private room, on the left; with the Adams [sic] fireplace. And then? She will 'fly into Nessa's arms'. Nessa will hold her very tight to get the sensation of her child's body again. Julian will call her 'dear'. They will go out together into the park. Angelica will like to show off her knowledge of rules and ways and the best places to sit in; other girls will smile, and she will say 'Thats Claudia' or Annie. Thats Miss

Colly – Thats Mrs Curtis. And all the time they will be feeling the comfort and excitement of being together – of having only just broached their time together. Nessa will get at ever so many things: questions of happiness, teaching, liking, loneliness – change. They will be very proud of each other and aloof. And Julian will peer about, through his glasses, liking Nessa and Angelica better than anybody I daresay; the simple crude boy – whom I shall now never know, I daresay. For – as I am going to say to Nessa on Wednesday – you are a jealous woman, and dont want me to know your sons, dont want to take, but always to give; are afraid of the givers.[42]

If, as Virginia avers, Vanessa preferred to give rather than take, finding security in a position that made others dependent on her, then her work did perhaps become for her a 'standby', not a support but a restorative well of feeling on which she could draw, from which she too could take.

The completion of Lady Dorothy Wellesley's dining-room in November 1929 added still further to her and Duncan's growing reputations. Their patron's name, the history associated with the house (which had once belonged to William Penn, the founder of Pennsylvania) and the champagne dinner party given to celebrate the new decorations all contributed to the cachet associated with this project. 'Dottie', as Dorothy Wellesley was not ineptly nicknamed, had generously given them a free hand to do as they liked and had been locked out of the room until it was almost finished. In keeping with the William and Mary house (the dining-room was, however, a mid-Victorian extension) and its collection of Italian baroque paintings, Duncan and Vanessa had painted figurative panels that were Italianate in flavour and very much a part of the Grand Tour tradition. When seen removed from their setting (at Southampton Art Gallery, where they now belong) they appear anachronistic and difficult to reconcile with Vanessa's contemporaneous admiration for Matisse. But in their setting, in the room that Vanessa and Duncan had hung with sequined and appliquéd silk curtains, with furniture and carpets made to their own designs, a fireplace and small tables decorated with their tiles, with curved glass lights placed beneath octagonal mirrors, set into the wall at their request, the whole had a warmth of colouring and an 'iridescence' which the *Studio* magazine praised. As at Charleston, grey played a significant part, the walls being grey-green, the carpet and ceiling also grey, the latter being enlivened by a border of circles painted pale blue, green and purple. The wall paintings hung at intervals around the room, flush to the wall, and had been deliberately painted to look like statuary in arched niches. The restrained, softly glowing colours and the classical mood of the whole were largely in praise of gracious living. If the least innovatory, it was one of the most complete decorative projects they had undertaken and Vanessa was determined that they should no longer ask too small a fee for the sake of friendship or advertisement. The total cost of the room, including furnishings, came to £775 16s. 7d., of which Vanessa and Duncan received £350.

The start of the new year found Vanessa alone at Charleston. She spent part of her time sorting through Thoby's letters. She hoped that a selection might be privately printed, an idea that the Hogarth Press considered but did not pursue. She also made preparations for Angelica's eleventh birthday party which took place at 8 Fitzroy Street on 29 January. Several days passed before all traces of the party had been removed from her studio because she was simultaneously preparing for a one-artist show which opened at the Cooling Galleries, under the auspices of the London Artists' Association, on 4 February. Duncan made an advertisement poster to hang in the gallery window; Virginia wrote a short encomium for the catalogue. Twenty-seven paintings were exhibited at prices ranging from twenty to fifty guineas and they sold well, Vanessa earning some £200. John Piper praised the show in the *Nation and Athenaeum* and *The Times* critic gave it a long, if rather petulant, review. He seized on Virginia's phrase 'inviolable reticence' and complained of the artist's 'priggish' restraint, declaring that in the past she had been content to deal with obvious subjects; of the recent paintings, only two, he said, really 'nudged' the spectator. This absence of rhetoric was a quality Roger admired. In an article for *Vogue* written in 1926 he had praised her unemphatic stance, her refusal to employ sharp colours or to deepen shadows to make a picture more dramatic; 'sentimental honesty is so fundamental, so ingrained in her nature', he observed, that such tricks would never occur to her. He concluded his article:

> Her great distinction lies in her reticence and her frankness. Complete frankness of statement, but with never a hint of how she arrived at her conviction. It is with her a point of honour to leave it at that, never to explain herself, never to underline a word, never to exercise persuasion. You are left with the completest statement she can contrive, to make what you can of it or nothing at all, as the case may be. She is as full of aesthetic scrupulosity as she is free from all other anxieties.[43]

At the time of her 1930 exhibition, however, Vanessa was strung with anxiety. An American-Russian artist called George Bergen had recently arrived in England, having come to Europe from America to visit as many art collections as he could and to make his reputation as a landscape and portrait painter. He had as a patron and friend Lord Howard de Walden, whose portrait he painted and through whom he had an introduction to London society. Of Jewish descent, he had spent the first years of his life in a ghetto in Moscow, before his father moved to Philadelphia. He spoke with an American accent and his English was occasionally confused; because of this awkwardness he could sometimes remain silent in unfamiliar company. This did not prevent him from taking a delight in society, that found in both the West and East Ends of London. Though often hard up, he gave fashionable dinner parties at which he could be loquacious, argumentative and charming. His confidence, however, exceeded his experience. He would introduce Vanessa to the aristocrats and wealthy Americans he knew as the 'greatest living woman painter' – making her inwardly cringe. His susceptibility to fashion and tendency to cheapen art by treating it, at least in her eyes, as a means to an end, aroused her dislike. He was avid for specious experience and would suddenly disappear to go hop-picking in Kent and there pick up a girl for an affair. Young and handsome, with a slightly oriental cast to the shape of his eyes, he was for Duncan more exotic, less predictable than his other boy-friends. As Vanessa now realized, he presented a menacing threat to the simple humdrum existence that she and Duncan enjoyed together.

Duncan fell uncontrollably in love with George; in January he even considered taking a house in Highgate or Hampstead where they might live together. While Vanessa was at Charleston over the New Year, Duncan was seeing George in London. At first he tried to disguise the extent of his feelings by telling Vanessa that she had nothing to fear as George was addicted to both sexes and that his own feelings were probably largely paternal. But George's disloyalty was distracting and Duncan became totally obsessed with the young painter. In order to put a temporary end to his torment, Duncan persuaded Vanessa to let him take George down to Charleston after she had returned to London, and four days before Vanessa's exhibition opened they disappeared to Sussex together. There Duncan hoped to be able to assess his feelings for George with greater peace of mind. On the day Vanessa's show opened he came up to London and gave a small luncheon party for her at the Gargoyle, returning to Charleston that same day. Vanessa wrote to Duncan that evening:

> My darling Bear, I have tried very hard to write and tell you what I feel, but I can't yet. I get too involved. There's no good telling you I am sorry I was stupid today. I think I was too tired to be sensible. Somehow these last two days have been more worrying than one knew. I went to sleep in my chair after you had gone. I think – I know – we are too much for each other for things not to come right in the end. It is ignorance and uncertainty that sometimes makes it so difficult for me now. ... My dear, I don't tell you I love you, but that I know you love me and the knowledge makes me very happy. This is true in spite of all ups and downs and follies.[44]

Somehow she got through the next few days. She painted hard, from ten to four each day, sometimes from the model and in Roger's company. Duncan and George, meanwhile, sat in the studio at Charleston while outside it poured with rain. They talked little, slept and ate much, listened to records, danced and read. Duncan was convinced that George was unused to reading but once he had begun he did it, like everything else, to excess. Vanessa, meanwhile, decided to spend the weekend with Stephen Tomlin and Julia Strachey, who were now married, in order to take her mind off the pain caused by Duncan's absence.

My dear [she wrote on 7 February] you write me a very nice letter. Please don't ever be unhappy about me. As you see I am working very hard and when I work I think of nothing else. Sometimes at night – when I used to give you such bad times – I get tired and feel melancholy. I think now the only thing I really mind at the moment is the complete uncertainty – not knowing in the least how long you will be away nor what can happen afterwards. . . . I feel all future life with you must be put aside at the moment for I can't think of it with any definiteness. That's partly what makes it so different from an ordinary going away. . . . It seems now as if everything had been blotted out in vagueness. But I don't usually feel very much – I don't want to and I can generally switch off on to something else for I realize one must simply wait. . . . Duncan dear, I don't want you to come back, as far as I'm concerned, until you come back altogether. If you needn't for other reasons please don't. I think it would be more upsetting.[45]

And so she waited. And went to Stephen Tomlin's where she was dazed by his unceasing conversation and in another part of her mind was aware that Julia was unusually silent and apparently occupied with household matters. The young sculptor, despite his incessant talk, seemed lacking in vitality and Vanessa wished he would move to London where he could mix with others cleverer than himself and obtain more commissions. Returning to London, she paid a visit with Roger to Frank Dobson's studio to see his new sculptures. But by 10 February she had reached breaking-point and told Duncan she could not stand the vagueness surrounding their situation any longer. Duncan had to admit that he had not yet plucked up courage to confront George with his plans. Vanessa, in her reply, apologized for her outburst:

Today I am calmer. I don't quite know why. I think some kind of almost insanity has gone, anyhow for the time and it is a great relief. . . . But since the first few days after you went I have been getting more and more unable to deal with them [irrational feelings] and at last dreaded being alone at all. Today it's different. I was really absorbed painting this morning and the time seemed short. . . . I can't bear to think I may have forced you to talk to George when you didn't want to. . . . Duncan my dearest please forgive me for all the horrors I have made you go through. As I have said often it's being so much in the dark that prevents one from understanding and has made me so intolerable. . . . But the fact that I don't know if he's the kind of person who ever can live quietly near you and see us both and work and be happy with you makes it much harder for me.[46]

On the same day Duncan was writing a letter which crossed with Vanessa's. He asked if he might arrive back in London and see her that coming weekend. He confessed that if he had learnt anything during the last two weeks it was his need for her. As he explained: 'I have discovered the main difference between a male love affair and a female one. With a man one is really alone without being lonely, with a female that is never so because one never knows and it is always interesting, what a female thinks and feels. But occasionally one wants to be alone.'[47] Vanessa could perhaps infer from this that her future would not be as bleak as at one moment she had feared. The next development in this uneasy situation was that Vanessa joined the two men at Charleston and there they all painted, she and George undertaking a portrait of Duncan. As a guest in her house, George behaved with politeness and charm but as their relationship developed he was quick to sense her dislike and could become insolent or rude. There was a vindictive streak in his nature and once, to hurt Duncan, he made advances to Quentin in the older man's presence.

Throughout this painful month Vanessa told no one of her distress, neither Clive, Virginia, Helen Anrep nor Roger. Only after she had gone down to Charleston did she write disingenuously to Clive: 'We have been painting quietly and have had a visit from that curious painter you met at Cassis called Bergen – who is slightly inarticulate but nice and quite interesting as a painter. He turned up in London, poor and very much in want of a studio and a little peace from difficulties of various sorts in London, so we asked him here. It has been a restful interlude.'[48]

Such was the extent of Vanessa's self-control she could drop the shutters of privacy even between herself and those nearest to her, isolating herself from the people she loved. Her refusal to discuss George Bergen with others may reflect on her unwillingness to admit even to herself the fear he caused her. Then, too, there was her dislike of emotional display, of unnecessary thought being expended on issues that did not merit such consideration. Her letter to Clive, however, is not just uninformative, but plainly deceptive. One suspects it was not really Clive she was trying to deceive so much as herself.

Duncan, too, insisted on a curtain of privacy around his personal life. His emotions, however, were much nearer the surface than Vanessa's and he found it necessary to have an outlet. To Bunny, he wrote:

I have left George and Nessa in the studio. It is after supper and seems to be the first time I have been alone for weeks. ... my life for the last two months has been simply turmoil. Turmoil of love, anxiety, terror and sadness and happiness – but all at such a rate I have no particular memory of time or night as being different from day. ... I have been reading Countess Tolstoi's diary. God! What a life to lead when one is in love, and after one is married. But it puts all sorts of ideas into one's head and makes one realize how one suffers oneself and makes others suffer, and also how unnecessary perhaps it is. Doubts about love – others' love to [for] oneself are terrible. ... I know perfectly well that George loves me and I know or rather feel that something I can give him he wants as much as I want what he can give me. But why do I get into a state when he is tired and I am tired and therefore think that he has no feeling for me? And why does Nessa not believe I love her as much as ever I did? When she is unhappy I am unhappy too. ... Why does she not realize that my love for George gives me more power to love her instead of less. And when she is not here I feel too that something is wanting in my life, however happy I am alone with George.

The truth is I want them both. I want too much I suppose. Sometimes I find the tears rolling down my cheeks simply because I love both so much. That is a detestable form of self pity. But at the same time I cannot help thinking that if Nessa could see into my soul at such moments she would see that everything is all right.[49]

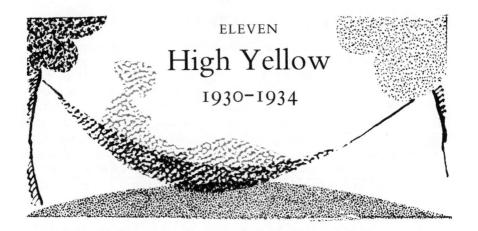

ELEVEN

High Yellow

1930-1934

In terms of books, articles and pictures, Bloomsbury's output during the interwar years was prolific. Artistic success was accompanied by increased sociability, despite their distrust of 'society', a distrust which in Vanessa's case was very deeply ingrained. They were very much a part of the London 'scene' and the extent to which they were seen and observed can be gauged from the frequency with which their names appear in memoirs of the period. With the widening of their circle of acquaintances, the term 'Bloomsbury', as has been said, degenerated in meaning. By now it was often used to suggest not the original core of friends who met on Thursday evenings but a certain manner, faintly upper-class, decidedly intellectual, often witty, slightly eccentric.

> The outlook, natural in the grand exemplars, and acquired by their followers, was one of great tolerance: surprise was never shown at any human idiosyncrasy, though an amused wonder might be expressed at the ordinary activities of mankind. The chief, most usual phrases one heard were 'ex-quisitely civilized', and 'How *simply too* extraordinary!', the first applying to some unusual human concatenation, the second to some quite common incident of burgess life, such as a man going to a railway station to meet his wife after a long absence from home. But, no less than by the sentiments themselves, the true citizens of Bloomsbury could be recognized by the voice in which they were expresseed. The tones would convey with supreme efficacy the requisite degree of paradoxical interest, surprise, incredulity.[1]

As Osbert Sitwell goes on to admit, the 'Bloomsbury' mode of speech 'spread and took captive many'. The manner became a mannerism and as such was instantly recognizable. 'Bloomsbury' now often meant no more than a certain fashionable, camp attitude. In the spring of 1935, when none of 'old' Bloomsbury were in Spain, the painter Edward Burra and Clover de Pertinez overheard in a Spanish nightclub, where nudes in diamanté jock-straps pranced across a small stage, 'a high Bloomsbury voice pipe from the row behind ... "So much beyooteh in such a sordid little place"'.[2]

Bloomsbury's exclusiveness has also been subject to exaggeration. Helen Anrep once remarked of Vanessa (admittedly often formidable and reserved) that though most of her friends had to pass through a fine sieve, others dropped into her bowl by dribbling over the side. She tolerated not only Duncan's homosexual friends but also characters from the criminal fringe around the Tottenham Court Road who occasionally found their way into his studio. She and Duncan were also on easy terms with a small number of young artists. They copied in the National Gallery with Adrian Daintrey and afterwards drank with him in a St Martin's Lane pub. They impressed Robert Medley with their commitment to painting and he found them 'very good people to cut one's teeth on as a young man, as from their conversation it was quite apparent that they were impatient of all hypocrisy.'[3] Wogan Philipps (now Lord Milford) rented a studio above Vanessa's and Duncan's at Fitzroy Street, exchanged greetings and jokes when passing, but never 'dropped in' unless invited to do so. However, when Duncan decided to execute a portrait of the highly cultivated hostess who was to become a close friend, Violet Hammersley, but was frightened to do so alone, he suggested Wogan should paint her too. For a period of about a month he was regularly in Duncan's studio; he noticed that while Duncan was very flattering about his painting, Vanessa was a much more severe critic. On one occasion while he was present Vanessa expressed regret that they did not know more artists in Chelsea and Hampstead. She did little to rectify this situation and their circle of artist-friends remained small.

Yet she was more ready to drop her reserve with painters than with other people. Around this time Frances Marshall entered Bloomsbury, becoming intimately associated with the circle around Lytton at Ham Spray. She was admired by many, especially by Clive who praised her 'gravely humorous conversation and airily competent mind' as well as her legs which were, he said, the prettiest in London. Only Vanessa, being cautious with her affections, was at first a little reserved with Frances. She was still more circumspect with the composer Dame Ethel Smyth whom Virginia now saw once a week: once a year was enough for Vanessa. She had less curiosity about people than Virginia and rather more honesty. Of this latter quality she once said, 'Perhaps I set too much store on it but I think real intimacy is impossible without it.'[4]

Clive's inconstancy also contributed to the changing scene. Now that his affair with Mary Hutchinson had ended (they were later reunited as friends), his crisp wit and natural charm sought fresh outlet. In town Clive was always impeccably dressed and fastidiously groomed; but his talents as a seducer did not rest primarily on his physical appearance: he was far more subtle and affecting. Aware of the old saying that one should flatter a beautiful woman for her brains and an intelligent woman for her beauty, Clive gave to his women friends an attentive sympathy that was rare in this period when sexual stereotypes helped determine behaviour and created invisible barriers of communication even between husband and wife. If the woman's marriage was unhappy, as in the case of Bertha Penrose, the fiery redhead Wyn Henderson or Beatrice Mayor, her need for Clive's solicitude perhaps hastened her collapse into his arms. He had a gift for giving happiness to others. He encouraged his women friends to talk and chatter, thereby raising them in their own estimation. He appeared to take them all seriously, offered advice on their reading and recommended his favourite French authors, in particular Mérimée, as well as the letters of Horace Walpole. One suspects that Clive himself strove to imitate Walpole's epistolary style in the many sprightly letters that he wrote to the opposite sex and which he expected them to keep. Their replies suggest that he gave to certain of these ladies some of their happiest experiences. When the affair ended or he was abroad, they missed the brio and attack that characterized his style. For though various in character, all these women repeated the same refrain – the desire to *talk* with him. Conversation was his *métier* for it gave him a more immediate audience than his writing. If in his books he occasionally harangues, like an orator addressing an anonymous crowd, when talking he was alert to the interests and susceptibilities of his listener; in conversation, despite his name-dropping and love of familiar stories, he could be the most entertaining and sympathetic of men.

In contrast with the passing affairs that Clive enjoyed with many women at this time, his relationship with Benita Jaeger lasted some six or seven years. When Clive met her she was living over the Étoile restaurant in Charlotte Street. There she remained, for though she sometimes lived in Clive's flat when he was away, it was his rule never to have anyone domiciled with him. (Though Clive did once propose to a French lady, Vanessa was correct in her assumption that he would never remarry as there was no woman whose company he preferred to her own; even with Mary Hutchinson he had never spent more than two weeks alone with her and on those occasions had grown edgy and bored.) Benita had been brought up in Germany and had come to England in 1926 determined to enjoy what her upbringing had not provided: Clive was both able and willing to oblige. She accompanied him on many social occasions, meeting the elegant and vivacious Christabel McLaren (later Lady Aberconway) as well as a great many of his literary friends. Though Clive encouraged Benita to chatter about the adventures she had had and the friends they both knew, they also spent a great deal of time dancing. They went to the fashionable Gargoyle in Dean Street, or Souvrani's (later Quaglino's); in Paris they danced at the Grand Écart, in Cannes at Le Bœuf sur le Toit. They travelled together extensively, at one time undertaking a six-week cruise to the West Indies. At home Benita often acted as hostess at Clive's dinner parties, for which he always hired a butler from Fortnum and Mason's. At these Benita, with her curly hair cut short on the advice of fashion expert Madge Garland, and wearing a Lanvin evening dress which plunged daringly low at the back, was bright, vivacious and eager to please.

In 1930 Clive and Benita spent six weeks at Cannes, at Madge Garland's villa in the rue d'Antibes where they frequently entertained Raymond Mortimer, Brian Guinness and John Banting who were staying near by. At other times Benita felt awkward and in the way, realizing for the first time how much of the day Clive needed to himself, to read and to write. On a subsequent visit with him to Cassis she herself started to write an autobiographical novel which Raymond Mortimer praised so highly she was encouraged to show it to Virginia whose opinion promptly terminated the project. Like others, Benita was advised on her reading by Clive. She managed the first two volumes of Froude's *History of England* and developed a liking for biographies of women. When in 1935 she saw Charles Laughton, the young James Mason and Flora Robson perform *Measure for Measure* and discovered how much she could enjoy Shakespeare, her immediate action was to ring Clive and tell him. He was pleased, but afterwards told her, 'We, of course, only read Shakespeare.' For a brief period Benita tried half-heartedly to become a painter. She had more luck with films and at Elstree and in Germany her chic appearance earned her walk-on parts, some with a few lines. When she eventually married the artist John Armstrong, Clive was upset and kept to his flat for a week. John Armstrong helped develop Benita's interest in sculpture and before long she became adept at portrait busts and heads of children. Clive, whose affection always overruled any sense of propriety when it came to reviewing his friends' work, gave her first exhibition a glowing press.

Benita and Vanessa rarely met. Clive's social life was now largely separate from that of Vanessa and Duncan, though they had many acquaintances in common. Vanessa first glimpsed Benita at a party given by Alix Strachey in Stephen Tomlin's new studio; she noted with a certain admiration that Benita's costume consisted solely of two scarves, strategically pinned and fastened at the top to her necklace. Later when she heard that this gay, humorous and *au fond* reliable young woman in Clive's life was bedridden with flu, she surprised Benita by calling at Charlotte Street to see if she was in need of anything. When they were brought together on rare social occasions they must have made a striking contrast: Benita small, pretty and fashionable; Vanessa tall, a little awkward and dressed in bizarre clothes made from stuffs bought in Italian rag markets. Vanessa rarely resorted to face powder and was the least vain of women, yet she got on well with Benita when they met. At one party given by the Kenneth Clarks, they commiserated together, finding the songs too long, the sandwiches too short.

If Benita figures rarely in Vanessa's letters of this period, a name that, for other reasons, often recurs is that of Mrs Elizabeth Curtis. She was a war widow and the headmistress of Angelica's school Langford Grove, an institution stamped with her character and initially begun by her (despite a flat in London, a son at Eton and a yacht elsewhere) in order to make ends meet. Situated in an elegant Georgian house near Maldon in Essex, the school cared more for culture than academic standards. Though a senior mistress, Miss Baggs, had been employed to give the school academic respectability, her classes were frequently interrupted by Mrs Curtis's habit of bursting in and selecting certain pupils whom she would carry off to London to see a play reviewed in the paper that morning, or to attend a concert at Cambridge or Ipswich. Equally suddenly she might decide that the whole school ought to be involved in mounting a tableau in the grounds and again the timetable was disrupted. Miss Baggs tried hard to retrieve the situation but was repeatedly flouted.

To most Mrs Curtis appeared impossibly vague, unreliable, autocratic and prone to delusions of grandeur, for her manner hinted at vast estates and inherited culture. Few of her pupils could respond to the friendship she offered. She desired to bring out their innate gifts, but her enthusiasm for play-acting often produced only forced, embarrassed performances. She wanted to civilize and catered, therefore, for an out-of-date society which believed a girl should be groomed rather than educated. Angelica, however, thrived well at this school and she became one of Mrs Curtis's favourites. Looking back on her schooldays, she has recalled 'an atmosphere of distinction, humanity and tolerance. ... There was a hint of extravagance in the air, a suggestion of fantasy which sometimes threatened our equilibrium, and which may have shocked some observers.'[5]

Mrs Curtis's unpredictable behaviour did not alarm Vanessa. On her visits to the school she was often persuaded to remain longer than she intended and, missing the last train back to London, would be obliged to stay the night. The next morning she travelled home clutching a gift from Mrs Curtis – a bouquet of greenery from the garden, large enough to fill the entire carriage. The headmistress's vagueness, love of beauty and unconventionality were entirely sympathetic to Vanessa and she remained on terms of friendship with her long after Angelica had left Langford Grove.

One friend put through Vanessa's fine sieve at this time was Maynard. Relations had been strained ever since his marriage to Lydia in 1925; now the London Artists' Association provided further grounds for disagreement. As Maynard's collection of paintings by his contemporaries reveals, he either did not have a very good eye or he often acted on principles of kindness rather than taste. In the running of the LAA he sometimes insisted on measures which Vanessa felt decreased the artistic merit of a show. In June 1930 a major row broke out between Vanessa and Maynard over a landscape exhibition in which work by LAA members mixed with that of the Old Masters. According to Raymond Coxon: 'She threatened (to Keynes) to resign if a projected show was to be titled "Constable to Coxon". Keynes gave way and Pitchforth and the other outsiders, the small clique surrounding Fry, were relegated to the floor below.'[6] Vanessa tried to be fair, as she explained to Maynard:

> Porter, Keith Baynes and I spent a long time yesterday considering whether we could alter the arrangements at Coolings so as to put some work by younger artists upstairs but we came to the conclusion in the end that nothing on the whole could be gained by the only changes we could possibly make.
>
> I think the difference of view about the hanging of the exhibition arises mostly from a difference of conception as to its whole character and aim. I believe I was responsible for the original idea – anyhow it was arranged between us by the artists' committee. We never intended to have a show consisting of works by all members and some old masters ... it was meant to be a show of a rather unusual nature likely to attract public notice and give a good start to the gallery. To do this we arranged a show of English landscapes which tried to include artists more or less representative of their time or school though not necessarily first rate themselves. ... The members whose work is shown do represent a certain school to the public which the younger members cannot yet do. In our opinion to have removed 3 works by 3 of the older members so as to include 3 by younger members would have been slightly worse for the exhibition, would have increased the difficulties of hanging and would probably have caused some ill feeling among the remaining younger members. ...
>
> We have today seen two of the artists principally concerned Pitchforth and Coxon who denied that they could have any feelings whatever of having been

unfairly treated and who seemed to understand, as perhaps only painters can be expected to do, the difficulties involved in this particular job. I only hope they can be induced to undertake the next thing of the kind themselves.

Yours,

Vanessa Bell[7]

Convinced in her views, Vanessa overrode minor considerations. She had not however quelled Coxon's resentment, for he retained the impression that she was 'bossy, resentful of new members especially the "professional" ones'. Maynard's conception of the situation, if less artistically highminded, was broader and more humane. 'Dearest Nessa', began his deliberately mild-mannered reply:

> Thank you and the others for taking so much trouble to try to satisfy me. And, as all the artists are contented with what has been done, I *am* satisfied. I don't know why, with my low ideas, I mix myself up with these high matters! – it is very foolish.
>
> But I thought and think two things (both points different from a charge of selfishness which is what you ascribe to me), namely:
>
> 1. In questions of hanging in any mixed show considerations of equity or equal treatment ought not to be too much sacrificed to the best possible appearance of the room as a whole. Such considerations really do matter.
> 2. In a body like ours it is desirable that there should be the *appearance* as well as the reality of there being no sort of discrimination or difference of treatment between the somewhat homogeneous group of older original members, who also happen to be more intimate with one another, and the other half consisting of a much less homogeneous group of younger members.[8]

Not surprisingly this letter only stirred discontent. In the row that followed Roger, who had been implicated in Maynard's criticisms, threatened to resign. The dispute, however, was abruptly forgotten when at the tea party to open the show Faith Henderson handed Maynard a newspaper containing news of the shooting of a King's College Fellow by an undergraduate. He left immediately for Cambridge and Vanessa was left to reflect, 'the truth is that Maynard interferes with things he knows nothing about, Roger takes command where he ought not to, both get furious with Angus [Davidson, now secretary of the LAA] for not doing what he ought to do and so I suppose we shall always have rows'.[9]

Vanessa's adverse opinion of Maynard was confirmed when in January 1931 he at first refused Duncan a £100 advance on his one-artist show booked for June. Maynard then agreed to the advance only on the understanding that if the LAA's funds were low in April Duncan would forgo his guaranteed salary. As Duncan was the best-selling artist within the

Association and had done much to get it off the ground, he was offended by Maynard's terms, rejected them and withdrew his agreement for the show in June. Maynard immediately climbed down and gave Duncan the advance unconditionally: Vanessa, who was now searching for a reason to break with the LAA, was disappointed of another row. To her Maynard's behaviour seemed mean and foolish. She failed to see that to him money was not just a means to an end but the medium for his creativity; he handled it with a passionate fastidiousness that to others seemed ungenerous. Even Lydia, if she wished to take two bottles of wine out of the cellar at Tilton to entertain some Russian friends, had to telegraph Maynard in London for permission to do so.

The cheerless, wineless dinners that Vanessa and Duncan were occasionally given at Tilton did not improve their relations with Maynard or Lydia who once shook her fist at the two artists from the other side of the street. Only rarely now did the two households go on expeditions together and though Tilton is only a few hundred yards from Charleston a whole summer might pass with those at one house scarcely seeing their neighbours. Maynard and Lydia did, however, remain regular attenders at Quentin's birthday parties. Vanessa and Duncan, in turn, attended Lydia's performances, either with the Camargo Ballet or at the Cambridge Arts Theatre, both ventures with which Maynard was involved. Fame, power and prestige surrounded the Keyneses' life but could not disguise the effects of age. Vanessa was surprised one day when, meeting Maynard by chance with his Rolls-Royce in Lewes, she was directed into a nearby shop and found, not the birdlike, vivacious Lydia that she had once known, but 'a very shabby dingy colourless creature rather ugly and squat and quite insignificant not even noisy, in a corner, buying very cheap ugly garden gloves'.[10]

Vanessa was herself derided as a bohemian with a private income, a West End lady imitating the style of Augustus John's women, in Wyndham Lewis's *The Apes of God*, published in 1930, in which she and Clive appear as the Jonathan Bells. There was, however, nothing self-conscious about her unfashionable dress. She aspired to neatness but often looked dowdy, and when given a Frigidaire by Virginia in 1932 was aware that she would never live up to it. She had a liking for strong colours, both in her painting and in her dress, favouring rich purples and vermilions. One year she planned Charleston garden around a scheme of reds, planting zinnias, dahlias, scabious, salpiglossis and red hollyhocks. Life at Charleston remained easy and relaxed, but within strict if unspoken terms. Vanessa, though so casually dressed, could emit a dire formality when confronted with visitors she disliked. When Raymond Mortimer arrived on a visit,

Clive told Frances Marshall: 'Raymond incurred some displeasure by paying a morning call on his friend Chips Channon who was staying at Firle Place, and is the brightest and most successful snob in either hemisphere. It was feared that his visit might provoke reprisals, but I don't think it will: Vanessa is too much dreaded.'[11]

Those who have a strong interior life often hold part of themselves back on first meeting strangers. Vanessa was no exception, but her aloofness was mixed with the arrogance of a person who knows that some things are more important than others. Nothing is more unflattering to guests anxious to succeed in social life than to discover that they are of scant interest to their hostess. But Vanessa, knowing too well the motivations that lay behind society, having been tutored in this by the unwitting George Duckworth, demanded greater honesty than polite exchange allowed. She exhibited that independence and sense of reality which are often the tokens by which artists recognize each other. Beneath her outward reserve and haughty manner lay a quick sympathy. When not blinded by matters to do with painting, she was warm, tolerant and witty. She also imposed sanity and organization on her and Duncan's unorthodox existence. 'As for Nessa and Duncan,' wrote Virginia, after a visit to Charleston in the autumn of 1930, 'I am persuaded that nothing can be now destructive of that easy relationship, because it is based on Bohemianism.'[12]

Yet there is also another level to her character which Virginia glimpsed only rarely and which for the most part was almost entirely hidden. This third layer perhaps explains more fully her superficial frigidity, for anxieties that one cannot reveal to friends, by displacement, can affect behaviour in other spheres. Beneath the casual and harmonious existence that Vanessa had created at Charleston lay the constant, nagging anxiety that her life, which centred around the activity of painting and the intimacy that she shared with Duncan, might be shattered by his removal elsewhere. The same month that Virginia commented in her diary on Vanessa's and Duncan's easy relationship, Clive was writing to Lytton:

> Duncan seems to have been pushing on his affair with this George Bergen, an east-side Jew boy from New York, now domiciled nominally in Paris. Vanessa is rather unhappy I'm afraid – but again I need hardly say I've been told nothing. I met Bergen two years ago and disliked him a good deal: he kept me walking about for two hours in the rain telling me that 'his art' was 'strong and vital' (textuellement).[13]

If others were now aware of the anxiety George caused Vanessa, she still discussed her feelings with no one except Duncan. George had proved to be a more intractable character than Angus Davidson, Peter Morris or Franzi von Haas; he was more heady, more selfish and an inveterate liar. Vanessa did not like him and found it difficult to establish easy relations. He had remarked on her 'independence' and 'self-sufficiency' when in reality, as she told Duncan, she felt weak and dependent, failings she did her best to conceal. Duncan found it easier to see the young man when Vanessa was not present. Feeling wretchedly selfish, as he admitted to Vanessa, he took George on several weekend visits to Bunny's house, Hilton Hall.

Only once did George accompany Vanessa and Duncan on their visits abroad. In October 1930 Vanessa and Quentin travelled out to Cassis, stopping at the Château d'Auppegard and Paris *en route*; Duncan and George followed, arriving in time to celebrate the *vendange*. Colonel Teed gave a feast on the terrace at Fontcreuse for all those who had helped harvest his grapes and Duncan spent the following day in bed. Nothing had changed at La Bergère except that a cane roof had been put over its small terrace and the oleander they had planted had grown into a small bush.

Vanessa had fewer visitors than usual this autumn. First to arrive were Roger and Helen in an ancient Citroën. Turning off the main road down the steep track that leads to Fontcreuse Roger nearly succeeded in over-turning the car. He drove with great concentration but occasionally accelerated when he meant to brake and resorted to the horn at every opportunity. Colonel Teed declared him none too safe; Vanessa took a calmer view, but even her omnipresent serenity was destroyed by his habit of reaching for the horn even when *she* was driving.

This visit to Cassis was not a happy one. It was overshadowed by the fact that one of Elise Anghilanti's sons had contracted a fatal disease. Vanessa drove her and the boy to a specialist in Marseilles but nothing could be done and this knowledge left them all melancholy. Her son's illness prevented Elise from working at La Bergère, and as the maid who replaced her prepared lunch but not dinner, Vanessa found herself doing more cooking than usual. Roger and Helen, though they slept at Font-creuse, ate at La Bergère, and occasionally the small house seemed too full for comfort. George remained largely silent in Roger's presence and faintly critical though he was in the end won over by the older man's charm. Soon after Roger and Helen left Quentin also departed, taking a boat from Marseilles to Naples, intending to spend some months in Italy. Left alone with Duncan and George, Vanessa cannot have found the situation easy. But all three painted hard and she would have stayed longer had not news of Clive brought her back to England.

Vanessa arrived in London shortly before Clive left for Zürich to consult a specialist at an eye clinic for he had been suffering from a disease that left him temporarily blind in one eye. Though Vanessa appeared inclined to dismiss Clive's misfortune ('She doesn't think much of it,' Virginia's diary records, 'and supposes that spectacles "which we all wear" will put it right.'[14]), it presented a serious threat, for his happiness depended upon the use of his eyes. She was however prepared to follow him out to Zürich and keep him company for he could neither read nor write; but, on the specialist's advice, he returned home and did not begin his cure until January. Vanessa instead busied herself with the Christmas show of decorative work that was to be held at Gordon Square and Clive was much comforted by friends, particularly Frances Marshall who came daily to read to him.

That winter Vanessa continued to work on a large picture which she had begun in August. 'So far', she had told Roger, 'it's entirely out of my head. Why is it that I, who am certainly an impressionist, like to paint out of my head or anyway away from nature while you, who are a pre- or post-impressionist, I suppose, want nature? It seems to me odd. I'm also painting flowers. One can't resist them.'[15] Her large picture was entitled *The Nursery*§ and when Roger saw it he was impressed: 'It's all extraordinarily gay and bright something like a Fra Angelico. I think it's one of the best things she's done.'[16] He repeated this opinion a year or so later, shortly before it was exhibited at Agnew's in June 1932, adding the hope that the Tate would buy it.★

The subject of this picture looks back to *Nursery Tea* of 1912. The main difference between the two paintings is that the more naturalistic style of the later work has allowed for more circumstantial detail. The two women are no longer anonymous, but clearly differentiated as mother and nurse, their poses and dress making apparent their different class and role; the nurse is actively engaged in holding the younger child (in a pose descended from the madonna and child theme in Renaissance art), while the more elegant mother watches with greater detachment her elder child. In another large canvas painted in 1932, *Interior with Two Women*§ Vanessa again made use of two contrasting female types, in this instance a nude model who sits resting on one side of a studio stove opposite a fully-dressed woman (presumably the painter). Here the contrast between the active

---

★ The Tate did not buy it and as Agnew's sales records contain no mention of this picture, it would appear that it went unsold. Its present whereabouts is unknown. It may have been exhibited again in 1942 with the London Group at the Leger Gallery, for 'The Nursery' by Vanessa is listed in the catalogue at a price of £65. More likely this was another painting on the same theme as two years earlier an incendiary bomb had destroyed her studio and most of the paintings in it.

and contemplative life is suggested by the poses of the two women: the model, with her frank sensuality, looks directly out at the spectator, while the painter looks down at the table beside her, as if lost in thought. Unconsciously Vanessa may here give expression to the two aspects of her nature which, because of her incomplete relationship with Duncan, she had been obliged to separate. If this hypothesis is tenable, then it is also significant that in both paintings Vanessa identified with the employer: with the mother whose detached enjoyment of her children is precisely that which she, with the help of nurses, had been able to enjoy; and with the painter contemplating the colours of the fruit on the table beside her. She is the woman who observes, and at a distance from her is the more earthy figure, more directly engaged with life.

One can only hint at the possible layers of meaning which *The Nursery* had for Vanessa. Inspired perhaps by *To the Lighthouse*, it presents a nostalgic evocation of motherhood. It creates a domestic scene in which the two groups of figures are contained within a circle that underlies the whole design. If the nurse demonstrates intimacy, the mother, in her greater stillness, suggests the remembrance of it. The toys, mapped out carefully with the picture space, suggest various types of play and may have aroused in Vanessa's mind various recollections of her own children. The child nearest the mother turns aside from her, freed by the trust established between them to play alone and discover independence. This moment of domestic intimacy, therefore, also marks the onset of separation; while celebrating motherhood, the painting is also poignantly about loss.

Vanessa herself affirmed the importance of this painting in a letter to Virginia, praising her novel *The Waves*.

> I have been for the last 3 days completely submerged in *The Waves* and am left rather gasping, out of breath choking half drowned as you might expect. I must read it again when I may hope to float more quietly, but meanwhile I'm so overcome by the beauty ... it's impossible not to tell you or give you some hint of what's been happening to me. For it's quite as real an experience as having a baby or anything else, being moved as you have succeeded in moving me. Of course, there's the personal side – the feelings you describe on what I must take to be Thoby's death. ... But that's not very important and it's accidental that I can't help such feelings coming in and giving an added meaning. Even then I know it's only because of your art that I am so moved. I think you have made one's human feelings into something less personal. If you wouldn't think me foolish I should say you *have* found the 'lullaby capable of singing him to rest'. But that's only a small bit. Mostly I am simply delighted, startled, filled with every kind of mood in turn. ...
>
> Will it seem to you absurd and conceited or will you understand at all what

I mean if I tell you that I've been working hard lately at an absurd great picture I've been painting off and on the last 2 years – and if I could only do what I want to – but I can't – it seems to me it would have some sort of analogous meaning to what you've done. How can one explain, but to me painting a floor covered with toys and keeping them all in relation to each other and the figures and the space of the floor and the light on it means something of the same sort that you seem to me to mean.[17]

This brought from Virginia the reply: 'Nobody except Leonard matters to me as you matter, and nothing would ever make up for it if you didn't like what I did ... I always feel I'm writing more for you than for anybody.'[18]

During January 1931 Vanessa wrote regularly to Clive at the Swiss eye clinic. She detailed the success of Angelica's birthday party and Duncan's new friendship with the American journalist Jimmy Sheean, to whom Clive had rented his flat. She described the Persian exhibition at Burlington House with which Roger was involved and admitted that her own response was lukewarm: the Persians' sumptuous, sensual decorative sense made their art sympathetic, but it also had an excessive refinement far removed from Vanessa's and Duncan's love of peasant simplicity.

In April she motored down to Cornwall with Angelica and one of her schoolfriends. This short holiday provided distraction from the concern dominating her correspondence with Quentin, who was now painting in a studio in the Via Margutta in Rome. The problem was an undergraduate at Girton with whom Julian was having an affair. He had told Vanessa of this development as soon as it had begun and, in March, when she visited Cambridge to watch Julian act in a Shakespeare play, she had met the young woman whom she thought plain and rather severely dressed, but intelligent and easily amused. Further acquaintance shaded Vanessa's former approval into tolerant regret but the girl would, she thought, improve when she lost her 'tiresome schoolgirl habits of thought and speech'.[19] She invited Julian and his girl-friend to dinner at her Fitzroy Street studio; Lady Wellesley and Bunny were also present and Lytton came in at the end of the meal. Lady Wellesley clashed with the young woman on sight, Bunny thought her terrible, but Lytton liked her, at least until she got up from the table and to his disappointment he discovered she wasn't a man. She visited Charleston on more than one occasion and had once lain on the studio floor dressed in black trousers, pretending to write an essay but breaking off every few minutes to ask Julian questions, trying both his and Vanessa's patience. Then, to Vanessa's consternation, Julian had proposed marriage.

Meanwhile Duncan's attention had temporarily shifted from George Bergen to Jimmy Sheean who had now taken a luxury flat in Rome where Duncan joined him at Easter. Quentin warned Vanessa (who was to follow Duncan to Rome in May) that she might find the city too sociable for her liking; Lady Ottoline was much in evidence and Jimmy Sheean threw wild and melancholy cocktail parties to which came half the royal families of Europe. When she arrived Vanessa put up at a hotel near the Via Margutta where Duncan presently joined her for he had quarrelled with Jimmy Sheean and was now more concerned with the charming and highly sensitive Edward Sackville-West, and with Peter Morris who came out on a visit with his beautiful sister Dora. But for the greater part of the day Duncan and Vanessa painted either in Quentin's studio or on the Palatine hill or in the Forum – one of the few places where Vanessa enjoyed working out of doors.

In Rome Vanessa learnt that Julian's relationship with his girl-friend had reached a crisis. She had become difficult and possessive and Julian felt obliged to go through with marriage. Though most of his male friends were against the idea, Julian twice obtained a marriage licence. It was Vanessa who finally dissuaded him. Like most Stephens, she argued, he would develop slowly over a long period of time and his feelings towards this young woman might change. Moreover if he married now he would have to give up certain opportunities and the chance of knowing people whom he would be otherwise free to meet. Then she asked him to think carefully about the character of the person he proposed marrying: she was, Vanessa said, an irrational creature, at the mercy of her emotions and therefore unable to be quite honest with herself; she lacked reasonableness. Reasoning with her own strong emotions, Vanessa argued that her chief desire was that his development should be unhindered: 'I do terribly want you to be yourself – to have freedom to grow and be whatever you have it in you to be. The one terrible thing seems to me not so much unhappiness – which is inevitable, as being thwarted, stunted, to miss opportunities and not live fully and completely as far as one can.'[20] In this way she persuasively steered him away from marriage. She was not alone in her conviction that the girl was unsuitable and could not have foreseen that this was to be the only time that Julian came remotely near wedlock. He was perfectly aware why his mother had won: 'I find it very consoling to confide in her,' he once admitted. 'Perhaps because she never does anything to shatter my self-confidence or vanity.'[21]

Vanessa and Duncan returned home from Rome the day before the opening of his exhibition at the Cooling Galleries. Looking brown and cheerful, Duncan hovered in the background while Lady Ottoline, in black dress and white hat, stood before his full-length portrait of Vanessa in fancy dress, and made a rapturous opening speech in which she compared his paintings to the music of Mozart. The approving audience included Christabel Aberconway and the Hon. Gerald (Timmy) Chichester, one of the Queen's private secretaries and a friend of George Bergen. Some three weeks after the show had opened £1,600-worth of paintings had been sold. 'I fear Duncan is in danger of too much celebrity,' Vanessa told Roger. 'We had a terrific cocktail party to wind up his show at the gallery. However, I tease him about it, but it makes no difference and most of his ladies have to walk over my corpse first – not knowing his telephone number.'22

Duncan did, however, begin to make friends in circles where Vanessa did not wish to follow. He was invited to Chatsworth by the Duchess of Devonshire and became a close friend of Violet Hammersley. Vanessa enjoyed hearing accounts of his visits to the wealthy, but herself spurned such opportunities. Clive, meanwhile, had become something of a socialite. In September 1931 he went to Venice where he was quickly caught up in three different social worlds: the sporty and bridge-playing; the cultivated and more mondain; and the ragged circle of exiled royalty, impoverished aristocrats, picture dealers and homosexuals. Much of his time he spent in the company of an American heiress from Chicago, Mary Baker, nicknamed the 'Shy Bride' because of her unwillingness to go to the altar. She was quiet in company but fond of the fast life. She danced with Clive at Martini's and dashed with him across the lagoon in her Lancia speedboat. Clive followed her and her Christian-scientist mother to Rome in the new year. 'That was a bit of old Rome,' Mary screamed over her shoulder when her car hit a pothole as she drove full tilt down the Appian Way. Her passengers rubbed their heads and recollected themselves, while Clive sat back entranced.

Vanessa was amused but sometimes slightly shocked by the evident pleasure that Clive got from fashionable society. To her such society lacked honesty and distorted feeling because it cared more for appearance than truth. It reminded her of the repression she had experienced in youth; even in its more liberated and seductive apparel, it distracted from creative effort, from that which gave her life meaning and direction. She was therefore unhappy when George Bergen again appeared in Duncan's life, for he moved in circles that previously she and Duncan had avoided. He enjoyed both high and low life, once taking Duncan on a 'beano' with the East End police force that lasted an entire weekend. Bergen thrived on caprice: he would declare that for financial reasons he had to return to America, keeping Duncan on tenterhooks fearing his imminent departure;

or he would agree to accompany Duncan to Hilton for the weekend and then at the last moment change his mind, remembering that Bunny had failed to appear at one of his parties. Uncertainty shrouded his life, disrupting Duncan's and also Vanessa's. As Duncan told Bunny, Vanessa remained 'the perfect darling', but it was impossible even for her to make George see reason.

Her personal worries were set against a background of national anxiety. The Labour Government failed to deal with the financial crisis during the summer of 1931. A National Government was formed and went to the country in the autumn. Julian and Quentin became active Labour supporters, driving canvassers to meetings in cars plastered with Labour placards. The cause of the financial crisis was complex and Vanessa's own political views were understandably modest and vague: 'I can't see how one can possibly tell which [party] is right so I keep an open mind.'[23] One evening she went with Duncan to the cinema and was surprised suddenly to see Maynard's face on the screen, his eyes blinking in the lights, his voice slightly nervous as he told his audience that everything would now be all right; the pound would not collapse, the rise in prices would be small and trade would recover. Vanessa and Clive both suffered a drop in income at this period and Clive's curt letters to Julian, attempting to curb his expenditure, betray considerable anxiety. Some attempts were made to economize but their life-styles did not noticeably alter.

There was certainly no reduction in the hospitality offered at Charleston. In the summer of 1930 George and Margaret Duckworth decided to pay a visit, much to Vanessa's surprise. 'I can't think what he will make of this establishment,' she remarked, 'though really in some ways I often think it's not unlike family life in my mother's home in the summer holiday, an odd mixture of people and all rather hurly-burly. But I expect he's forgotten how shabby and casual it all used to be and will think how the poor things have gone downhill. Quentin's hair will certainly astonish him it's simply like a bed of zinnias now and would make everyone jump.'[24] Their visit went off without a hitch, though the now elderly George Duckworth astonished Angelica by spreading his slice of rich fruit cake with a thick layer of butter.

There were a great many visitors to Charleston during these years, many of whom now arrived by their own means. On one occasion Bunny descended from the sky in an aeroplane he had bought, his arrival causing Roger to hit a gatepost with his car. Roger still continued to galvanize the occupants of Charleston with his energy and enthusiasms, while Virginia, on her visits, added an element of imaginative fantasy. When one afternoon over tea in the garden Roger offered a prize to the female who could

ROGERS' ARRIVAL

prove she was the youngest present, Virginia excelled herself as an hysterical member of the royal family with evidence that she had been born last year. On another occasion Roger's friend, the Cambridge don Goldsworthy Lowes Dickinson visited and talked at length with Julian about his dissertation on Pope. A younger generation of visitors had also begun to appear. One of Julian's guests was the painter Barbara Mackenzie-Smith who lived and worked at 117 Charlotte Street. To the young, Vanessa's quietness and dignity could make her appear aloof, and Barbara was pleased and surprised when Vanessa asked her to stay on a day or two longer than expected. The young woman had a tear in her cardigan and Vanessa, not having made any note of its colour, revealed how sharp her colour sense was when she returned from Lewes the next day with the precise shade of wool needed to mend it.

After Barbara left Julian declared that Charleston had turned grey and dismal. 'Old' Bloomsbury had arrived for a meeting of the Memoir Club and he found himself arguing with E. M. Forster on a pamphlet by T.S. Eliot on the relation between art and morality. 'It's curious how the old seem to hanker after tyrannies and absolutes,' Julian told Barbara. 'Perhaps they've got hold of something – I don't know: I doubt it'.[25] Despite political differences, tension, especially between father and sons, was happily dispersed by humour. A conversation on Gothic architecture ended with Clive's grudging admission that it had its points. 'Too many?' queried Quentin.

The year ended with sadness, with the news that Lytton was seriously ill. On 21 January 1932 he died. Vanessa, now only aware of the good that Carrington's devotion had brought, wrote:

> Dearest dearest Carrington. It's impossible not to write to you though how useless it seems. But one cannot think of Lytton without thinking of you and with all one's sorrows there is mixed the feeling of gratitude to you for having given him so much happiness. I have loved him ever since the time when Thoby died and he came and was such an inexpressible help and made one think of all the things most worth thinking of. But I know how often in those years he was depressed and gloomy and unsatisfied and how later because of you he seemed to get so much joy out of life. It is owing to you that there is nothing to regret in the past and his friends would love you for that if for nothing else.
>
> Darling creature, come before very long and talk to us, for we loved him very much, enough to understand.[26]

They exchanged photographs of Lytton and further letters. But Vanessa was all too aware how little those who had loved Lytton could do to help Carrington and on 12 March she took her own life. Two of those who suffered most after this calamity were Ralph Partridge, Carrington's husband, and Frances Marshall who had been intimately caught up in the life at Ham Spray. In order to recover from this trauma they crossed to France for a holiday and on disembarking from the Folkestone-Boulogne ferry found that Vanessa, Duncan and Angelica had also been on board. Vanessa's former reserve with Frances now gave way. In her journal Frances recorded:

> Vanessa asked us to go and see them at Cassis, pressing my arm as she did so, which touched me very much, not only because of my admiration for her but because I think of her as undemonstrative. As we walked along Duncan said that he seldom took Mothersill when going on the sea, but quite often on dry land, if he felt tired or 'a little mad' and found it 'excellent'. We saw them onto their train, followed by a porter carrying their nine very Bloomsbury-looking 'pieces'. Then we looked about for somewhere to lunch.[27]

During the early thirties Vanessa continued to seek for new outlets for her and Duncan's decorative talents. At one point she hoped that the Omega might be revived, an idea she discussed with Ambrose Heal and others. Though nothing came of this, in January 1931 she and Duncan re-entered the field of fabric design with a commission from Allan Walton. His family owned a bleach and dye works in Manchester which was run by his brother. Allan, though trained as a painter at the Slade and in Paris, had made more of a name for himself as an interior designer, with a studio in Cheyne Walk, and the decoration of Marcel Boulestin's first restaurant in Leicester Square to his credit. He rightly perceived that the modern emphasis on plain surfaces had allowed most fabric designers to lapse into either dull traditionalism or vulgar imitations of cubist patterning. To improve matters he commissioned a handful of artists to produce designs that were printed on inexpensive linen or satin-finished fabrics. According to Isabelle Anscombe, Vanessa and Duncan contributed about fifteen designs over the next few years.[28] Both resorted to figurative motifs, to flowers, birds, urns, lamps and fruit, but the end results are noticeably different, Duncan preferring an even spread of interest across the surface of the cloth, Vanessa employing more complex designs to suggest greater depth, achieving at the same time a more subtle balance between the motifs and the overall abstract design. These fabrics were then sold at the Waltons' shop in Fulham Road, through the Cooling Galleries, at Fortnum and Mason's, Dunbar Hay and at Curtis Moffat Ltd in Fitzroy Square.

Simultaneously a concatenation of events revived Vanessa's and Duncan's interest in pottery decoration. In 1931 they met Miss Phyllis Keyes who took them to a kiln in Lambeth where they experimented with colours and glazes. This gave Miss Keyes the idea of starting a kiln of her own and of using artists to help with the decoration of her pots, an idea that soon came about. Meanwhile, in the summer of 1932, Kenneth Clark decided to commission a dinner service. 'When we first frequented his [Duncan's] studio,' Lord Clark has written, 'it contained groups of rustic pottery, gathering dust, and vases of mimosa which had long since lost all the colour of life. On these unappetizing themes both Duncan and Vanessa concentrated their talents. ... In an attempt to revive his interest in decorative art we asked him and Vanessa to paint us a dinner service.'[29] The commission was aptly timed but Duncan's and Vanessa's interest had already been revived and Clark may have heard of this through their mutual friend Billy Winkworth. An aesthete and collector of Chinese and Japanese pottery, Billy Winkworth took a passionate interest in Vanessa's and Duncan's commissions, wrote long letters of advice, for a while haunted their studios and introduced them to the agent Mr Wreford at the Wedgwood showrooms at 24 Hatton Gardens. There they were shown the various services available. They disliked the modern styles and selected one not unlike the eighteenth-century moulds used by the Aubagne pottery in Provence. Next they went up to Etruria, stayed with Josiah Wedgwood and his wife, saw round the works and painted experimental designs on plain white plates. Clark left the artists free to decorate the service as they wished and found the result unexpected: there were forty-eight plates decorated with portraits of celebrated females, twelve queens, twelve writers and twelve beauties, including 'Miss 1933'. ('It ought to please the feminists,' Vanessa announced.[30]) The commission took more than a year to complete for in addition to the plates there were jugs and bowls, the whole service amounting to some 140 items. One side result was that the portrait of Queen Mary painted on one plate brought them the friendship of Lady Patricia Ramsay, the painter and granddaughter of Queen Victoria, for whom they gave a party at 8 Fitzroy Street, an occasion Grace never forgot.

Less time-consuming was the commission that followed from Messrs E. Brain and Co. of Stoke-on-Trent who made Foley china. Their Art Director, Thomas Acland Fennemore, like Walton, wanted to improve commercial products by employing artists' designs. In 1933 he commissioned various artists, including Graham Sutherland, Barbara Hepworth, John Armstrong, Albert Rutherston and others, as well as Duncan, Vanessa and the fourteen-year-old Angelica to decorate blanks which could then be mass produced. Vanessa's pattern was in yellow and purple with a slight lustre finish. The designs were produced in bone china by Foley and earthenware by Wilkinson and Co., often the same pattern being used by both. Sets were made as first editions, limited to twelve and stamped with elaborate back marks that combined a facsimile of the artist's signature, the maker's mark, copyright and date. The full range was displayed at Harrods in 1934 in an exhibition entitled 'Modern Art for the Table'. It attracted considerable press coverage and increased the sale of Harrods usual wares but commercially the experiment was a flop. However it began a whole series of artist-designed dinner sets and in 1934 Vanessa and Duncan again contributed decorations for dinner services produced by A. J. Wilkinson and Co. under Clarice Cliff's 'Bizarre' range.

Vanessa and Duncan were also two of the first artists to be employed by Jack Beddington when in 1929 he was put in charge of publicity by Shell-Mex Ltd. He commissioned paintings which could be reproduced by colour lithography as lorry bills which, with the support of the Campaign for the Preservation of Rural England, advertised incompatibles, the delights of the English countryside and the benefits of Shell petroleum. Duncan made St Ives bridge in Huntingdonshire his motif, while Vanessa chose Alfriston church in Sussex, employing a pointillist technique and a restricted range of colours.

Still more enjoyable was the opportunity to do stage design for the Camargo Society which had been formed in an attempt to fill the gap left by the death of Diaghilev. The Society had strong links with Bloomsbury because Lydia had been made choreographic director and Maynard its treasurer. In 1932 Vanessa was commissioned to design sets for *High Yellow* choreographed by (Sir) Frederick Ashton. It opened at the Savoy Theatre on 6 June and the programme contained this synopsis:

> Tropical Island. Mammy and Pappy preside over family content. Mammy's big baby obliged, by circumstances too numerous to mention, to take his leave. His elegy of departure plunges the island into general woe. But the dismay of his abandoned sweethearts (he has loved in duplicate) is dissipated at sight of two new fellows disgorged by the ship. Choreographic elation and orchestrated joy prevail.

Vanessa made a model stage to try out effects and hoped she had succeeded in proving Lydia wrong for she had said that Vanessa would not be able to make her colours hot enough. She was aware that she was not able to arrive at the light-hearted style that Duncan employed for the décor of *Le Lac des Cygnes*. Both ballets were produced together. 'Mine is quite successful I think in a very different way,' Vanessa told Roger. 'The music is jazz and there are negro dances and it's supposed to be on an island, all very hot and tropical – so I simply did sea with boats and huge tropical flowers and a striped awning and a cocktail bar and everything is as bright as possible with every sort of colour.'[31] *High Yellow*, much admired by, among others, Miss Wendy Toye, who danced in the corps de ballet, did not survive beyond the Camargo season at the Savoy and had a total of only six performances. The following year Vanessa produced the décor for another ballet by Frederick Ashton, with whom she enjoyed working, *Pomona*, and in 1934 she produced sets for *Fête Galante* in which Lydia danced to music by Ethel Smyth.

Decorative work often returned Vanessa to her painting refreshed, more able to see what needed to be done to a picture that had been causing problems. It seems that the lighter mood essential to decoration affected her painting; during the 1930s her bold handling becomes less insistent, her tonal transitions more fluent. Still lifes remained her chief subject but she also executed a number of portraits at this date, of Dorothy Wellesley's children, Frederick Ashton, Aldous Huxley, Virginia and Roger among others. According to Roger, who continued to observe and advise on her paintings, her style did not noticeably change during this period but there was a steady enrichment of her means. He told Helen Anrep: 'D. [Duncan] is giving free rein to his fancy which is all to the good. He is not really inspired by the thing seen. His vision has to come from some inner state of reflection but Vanessa is a realist. Her colour gets better and better.'[32]

In July 1931 Vanessa, Duncan and Keith Baynes, a Slade-trained painter, resigned from the London Artists' Association with which they had grown increasingly dissatisfied. They felt the need for change, knew that Duncan could get higher prices elsewhere, and approached Agnew's. This firm took them on in agreement with Lefevre's and gave them a guaranteed salary, paid in quarterly instalments and offset against sales. Maynard was furious and argued (rightly) that their departure would bring to an end the LAA. In a letter to Duncan he pointed out that over the last six years the LAA had sold £10,587-worth of his paintings. Even Vanessa, though she had not received a guarantee from the Association for some time, had to admit in her letter of resignation that she had 'no feelings but those of gratitude and friendliness' to all the guarantors.[33] Nevertheless this break with the LAA damaged still further their relationship with Maynard.

Agnew's gave them joint exhibitions which continued to link their names in the public mind. Their close working relationship was now so widely known that one journalist, writing an article on the area of Sussex around Firle, referred in passing to Vanessa as Mrs Duncan Grant. She was infuriated by this; she hated publicity of any kind and was perhaps irritated by an assumption so very far from the truth. She continued to tolerate Duncan's vagaries, throwing up her hands in mock despair with the announcement 'Duncan's gone criminal again' when he met a borstal boy on a train. His susceptibilities and generosity brought him many friends and dependants, including men like Roland Lee Warner (known as 'Tut' owing to his belief that he was Tutankhamun reincarnated) who suffered mental disorder or for other reasons hung on to the edge of life, and whom Duncan befriended and to whom he gave small sums of money in times of need. He moved as easily among the upper classes, making more friends in these circles than Vanessa. His exploits and adventures *seemed* to owe much to chance; in fact he had overwhelming charm. 'Duncan has just returned from a visit if you please – to Hilton Young,' Clive told Frances Marshall in August 1932, 'where he seems partially to have got off with a daughter of Lord Dawson of Penn – a mere boy and girl affair he calls it. His more serious attentions were directed to an empire-builder from Borneo called Bruce.'[34]

Duncan was still chiefly involved with George Bergen whose plans continued to outreach his actions. He decided to go to Paris for six months but instead went on a two-month motor tour of France with friends. 'It really has been extraordinarily nice to have Duncan in peace alone for a little,' Vanessa told Roger.[35] Her attempts to incorporate George into their lives had failed. Three years after his relationship with Duncan had begun, George still cut short his visits to Charleston and Vanessa had to beg Duncan to persuade him to stay a weekend, knowing it would keep Duncan there longer; Clive, she added as further mollification, was now amiably inclined towards George. During the summer of 1933 George continued to announce that his departure for America was imminent but as the weeks passed he remained happily in London, keeping Duncan at his side. 'It has gone on so long, one cannot help getting upset,' Vanessa, left alone at Charleston, complained to Duncan.[36] In September George did finally sail for America where he hoped to find work as a portrait painter. Duncan drove over to Southampton to see him off, arriving shortly before the boat was due to sail and finding Timmy Chichester also on the quay. George planned to return after only three months, but Duncan must have known better than to rely on this.

Throughout the summer and autumn of 1933 Vanessa was largely occupied with illness. Quentin arrived back from a visit to Spain with whoop-

The farmer Mr Stacey inspecting the pond

ing cough and in August he fell ill with pleurisy. Both were thought to be tubercular in origin and during the next three months Vanessa nursed him at Charleston. In November she flew with him to Switzerland where he recuperated in a clinic at Montana. Vanessa travelled home alone, enduring a hazardous flight. 'Nessa flying to Geneva and back and lost in fog over Paris,' Virginia wrote to Vita Sackville-West. 'Oh my God – how I hate caring for people.'[37] Vanessa herself found the experience nerve-racking and on returning to Charleston went straight to the studio where she was found, in tears, by Grace.

Generally, however, this was a period of domestic calm. The 'puddling' of the pond, which had begun to leak, constituted a major event and involved two carts and horses and six men. The advent of electricity marked the start of a more comfortable era at Charleston for no longer would guests have to take a candle to bed. Barrels of wine arrived from Cassis and had to be bottled and labelled with a linoleum cut made by Quentin. He had recently turned to sculpture and concrete heads made by him later adorned the garden walls, while in the orchard there rose his ten-foot-high sphinx-like woman made out of bricks. Vanessa observed these developments with the same amused detachment that she brought to the only article that she ever wrote for the *New Statesman and Nation* in the summer of 1933.[38] This was an unsigned review of a book by Mary Hutchinson's brother, James Strachey Barnes, *Half-a-Life*, in which he boasted of friendships with T.S. Eliot, Sacheverell Sitwell and Mark Gertler, among others, none of whose names he spelled correctly. Vanessa's light but ironic review managed to condemn him utterly with his own words. In her own social life at this time she continued to entertain informally. She gave dinner one night to Peter Morris, before his departure for Spain, and was pleased when 'a rather tattered and lugubrious figure, full of the difficulties of life'[39] wandered in. This was Helen Anrep, anxious to talk about the problems she was having with her daughter Anastasia. Vanessa had an equally relaxed attitude towards her work and, unlike Duncan who worked obsessively and incessantly, was frequently obliged to break off from what she was doing in order to attend to domestic matters. Also she now had a cat – called Marco Polo because he travelled well – and his presence in the studio, she found, made her lazier still.

She was often slightly astonished by her sons' choice of girl-friends, Quentin occasionally producing giantesses and Julian, on the whole, preferring them short and stocky. He was still based at Cambridge, at work on a thesis with which he hoped to win a fellowship, but had moved out of the town into a cottage at Elsworth. He was seeing a great deal of Frank Ramsey's widow, Lettice, who had two small children, and in order to support herself had just completed a course in photography at Regent Street Polytechnic. She lived in a house in Mortimer Road, Cambridge, and was to make her reputation as a photographer with the firm Ramsey and Muspratt, including among her sitters some of the most eminent Cambridge intellectuals. She was older than Julian and a more mature woman than his previous girl-friends. Neither of them expected too much from the affair, though Lettice did at one point complain that Julian was 'deliberately unromantic'. When in March 1932 Vanessa and Duncan went to Cambridge to see Dadie Rylands's production of *Hamlet* in early-nineteenth-century dress, they stayed with Lettice in Mortimer Road and Vanessa was photographed. She was impressed by Lettice's forthright character and invited her to Charleston. There Lettice (nicknamed 'Cabbage' by Duncan) was found lacking in finesse and tact. Though her affair with Julian ended after a period of about two years, both finding other partners, the flaw in their relationship lay less with Lettice's character than in Julian. To others Julian's friendship with men always seemed more serious than his many affairs with women, for in an old-fashioned way he tended to divide his intellectual life from his love life. As he once admitted, 'Jane Austen's really the only woman, except Nessa, whom one can have much respect for – I mean of course intellectual respect.'[40]

His choice of career was still undecided. Though he had published his first book of poems in 1930 and two years later had been included in Michael Roberts's epoch-making anthology, *New Signatures*, he had come to realize that poetry did not wholly absorb him. He seemed drawn towards an academic career, but his dissertation on Pope failed to gain him a fellowship, as did the one he subsequently wrote on 'The Good and all That', the vivid but unscholarly and aggressively provocative work, which, when it went in front of the Electors, bore the more decorous title 'Some general considerations on ethical theory, with their application to aesthetics and politics'. Leonard also rejected it when Julian submitted it to the Hogarth Press for publication.

He could not but be aware that he had much to live up to. His situation was made still more difficult by the fact that the values which his family upheld no longer had the same relevance in this more complex and political decade. To oppose the *douceur* of existence at Charleston he played Beethoven's Fifth Symphony with the volume turned up loud, to annoy Clive. 'Only hardness, strength, tragedy are endurable,' he told his friend John Lehmann. 'In fact I've had an overdose of romance and beauty. Cures: Beethoven and ten-mile walks in big boots, and the slaughter of innocent birds.'[41] He would appear in the feudal villages of Firle and Glynde, his trousers often too short, his jacket too tight, his curly hair unbrushed, an uncouth figure distributing left-wing propaganda at election time. If for others 'he could make one see things in a sane and happy way',[42] his own path seemed unclear. He admired his elders' 'hard, vigorous lucidity of mind' and 'the orderly beauty of that view of the universe',[43] but it grew increasingly hard to reconcile their belief in disinterestedness and pacifism with the rise of Fascism in Europe. On 11 November 1933 Julian took part in the anti-war demonstration at Cambridge organized by the poet John Cornford and others. He helped with a 'No More War' exhibition and drove through the streets, his car decorated like a tank and with Guy Burgess navigating at his side. Several of his friends now joined the Communist Party. Julian never did: he accepted Marx's analysis of society but not the conclusions drawn from it. The conflict in him (never satisfactorily resolved) has been described by Stansky and Abrahams: 'an emotional commitment to the past against his intellectual commitment to the future which would almost certainly mean, he thought, the end of all that he valued most'.[44]

It gave Vanessa acute delight to see Julian in Roger's company. The younger man respected the elder's scientifically-trained mind and he shared his interest in the poetry of Mallarmé and in aesthetics. It seemed to Vanessa that as her sons had grown up Roger had come to regard them as his own. In turn Julian had a touching regard for the intimacy between Roger and his mother: once when a girl-friend of his had remained in the sitting-room with Vanessa and Roger after everyone else had gone to bed, he came down and called her out. Outside the door he said, 'Didn't you know they were once lovers?', revealing his sensitivity to their need for privacy.

Now in his sixties, Roger appeared to grow younger and more vigorous daily. As a critic and lecturer he was still in constant demand, so much so that Duncan and Vanessa occasionally had the sensation he neglected them. He lectured at Queen's Hall in London each winter, on subjects related to the major winter exhibitions at the Royal Academy, as well as at the recently opened Courtauld Institute of Art. Vanessa occasionally found his lectures a little breathless, for he could tie up Sumerian and the whole of Greek art in one talk. But on the whole they were an unparalleled success, with lay and art audiences alike. Duncan, after one of Roger's lectures on English art, declared: 'I thought among other things it [the lecture] was marvellously stage-managed. After all your *désobligeances* in the first half your hymn of praise for Gainsborough reduced one to tears. It is far the fairest and most complete thing I've ever heard on Gainsborough.'[45]

Neither he nor Vanessa could find equivalent praise for Roger's paintings. Vanessa dreaded his 1931 retrospective at the Cooling Galleries, predicting a fascination, similar to that offered by Madame Tussaud's, at seeing 'all the old horrors revived'. She had first closed her mind to his paintings when she had withdrawn from him in 1913. Since then she had often found his art laboured, especially when compared with Duncan's more seductive and professional manipulation of paint. But she may also have sensed a threat in Roger's art, for his greater feeling for form undermined Duncan's decorative ease. However, her poor opinion of his paintings did not detract from her admiration of him as a critic. She still thought him one of the very few writers on art worth reading; she stayed with the aesthetic ideas that he had first put forward to justify Post-Impressionism; and she shared wholeheartedly his profound admiration for Cézanne. On his advice she also experimented with the oleoresinous Maroger medium, and used it in her portrait of Aldous Huxley which she painted in Roger's presence[§].

Five of her portraits (including one of Roger – now at King's College, Cambridge) were displayed in her one-artist exhibition which opened at Lefevre's in March 1934. Apart from these and three views of London, her subjects were mostly confined to scenes in and around Charleston and to still lifes – the subject that Roger had once praised as 'in modern times ... one of the purest expressions of aesthetic feeling'.[46] Virginia again provided a foreword in which she tried to suggest the beauty and strangeness that Vanessa found in familiar things. It was an art, she said, that took one over the boundary into a world where words have little meaning: 'And yet it is a world of glowing serenity and sober truth.' And not financially unsound, for it brought in more than any of her previous shows, earning Vanessa some £500.

Roger was in Palermo when the exhibition opened and after it had run for two weeks Vanessa wrote teasingly to him: 'You don't know how badly I've wanted you lately – *only* as a critic of course, but still that's something. ... Please my dear, do come back before my show finishes – I think it's your duty to considering that you are really responsible for me as a painter and I may go completely to the bad now if I don't get some decent criticism. You know of course how imbecile the papers are – one really can hardly even read them and not one says anything that is the slightest use to one.'[47] If Roger did catch the tail-end of this show, his comments are unrecorded. But soon after his return he went down to Charleston for a visit and afterwards told Vanessa, 'I don't think I've ever enjoyed it more – you know your atmosphere is unique and it ... seems to get better as your offspring grow up and, how fortunately, become infected with it. ... They could hardly help discovering the beauty of your way of life.'[48]

In the summer he went abroad again, driving from Dieppe to St-Rémy where he shared a house with the left-wing intellectuals and writers, Charles and Marie Mauron. On his way home he paused at the spa town Royat where he attempted to cure some trouble he was having with an artery in his leg. He had not been back in London very long before he slipped one evening on a rug and damaged his hip. An unwise decision on the part of a doctor caused him to be moved immediately into the Royal Free Hospital at Hampstead where three days later, on 9 September, he died.

Vanessa was at Monk's House when Roger's son-in-law Micu Diamand rang through with the news. She emerged from the house, told Clive and Virginia and all three sat for a while on the terrace. She was then taken back to Charleston where Clive ran to find Angelica, holding her close before he disclosed what had happened, while Vanessa in her bedroom howled uncontrollably.

News of Roger's sudden death reverberated widely. Arthur Waley and Beryl de Zoete read of it in the Tyrol; the designers McKnight Kauffer and Marion Dorn casually picked up the same edition of *The Times* in a Salzburg cafe. They and many others wrote letters of condolence to Helen Anrep, who had been living with Roger since 1929. 'He helped one use one's faculties,' Virginia told Helen, '... the most magnificent, the most loveable of all our friends. He will never die for he is the best part of our lives.'[49] The critic Alan Clutton-Brock spoke for many when he wrote: 'In many ways his mind was at once so scrupulous and so fine, so exact and so adventurous. He opened the mind of anyone who read his books, and still more of anyone who talked to him, to a multitude of new things, and to follow him was to combine the delight of discovery with that of listening to an exquisitely precise demonstration.'[50]

When Vanessa recovered from her immediate shock her thoughts turned to Helen. But their first meeting after Roger's death was evidently more than Vanessa could bear for afterwards she apologized: 'I feel nearer Roger when I'm with you. I behaved so stupidly today but I don't think I'd recovered ... for what seemed a long time I couldn't get near anyone and was so faint. But I'm all right now and it's only to explain being so feeble today. Helen dear, you know I love you very much.'[51]

That autumn Charles and Marie Mauron visited London, as had earlier been arranged, and stayed with Helen. When the time came for them to leave, Quentin and Vanessa decided to drive over to Newhaven to see them off and to bring Helen back to Charleston for a rest. Vanessa told Helen of this plan by letter, confessing also that she had spent most of the afternoon asleep in the studio with the cat in her arms. She had been dazed but not broken by Roger's death and at his funeral had become reconciled to it. No words had been spoken and those present sat in silence while music was played in a room with open doors that led on to a garden. 'I thought yesterday', Vanessa afterwards wrote to Helen, 'it was so much what Roger would have chosen. One was more conscious of the beauty of life than of anything else and it seemed enough explanation of everything. Why should one want more than that people like him and music like Bach's and such incredible loveliness as one sees all round one should exist and that one should know them. They do not really ever stop.'[52] Even so, an absence remained. 'Will one ever lose the habit of thinking one can tell him things, I wonder?' she asked.[53]

TWELVE

Between Bloomsbury and China

1935-1937

There were several projects afoot immediately after Roger's death: a memorial exhibition of his paintings was arranged at Bristol; Virginia, on the invitation of his sister Margery, began the necessary research for his biography; and his Slade lectures were prepared for publication by Helen Anrep and Kenneth Clark. Meanwhile a memento of Roger that now hung on Vanessa's wall was a small Matisse of ships in harbour which he had left her in his will.

Another project afoot, one which Roger would very much have enjoyed, was the play *Freshwater*, written by Virginia twelve years earlier and now revised for a performance in Vanessa's London studio. Taking the story of Watts, Ellen Terry and Mrs Cameron, it presented a burlesque on the Victorians' pursuit of truth and beauty. An audience of around sixty people (Vanessa estimated) crowded into her studio. Not all had a good view and several of the jokes were drowned by the laughter of Clive and his brother Cory. The climax of the play came in the third act when Ellen (played by Angelica), after having been presumed drowned, ran on stage in a white, flounced dress with blue ribbons and received roars of applause. The dress had been made by Vanessa and afterwards Duncan executed for her a pastel portrait of Angelica wearing this frock and a prettily tilted hat.[1]

This was Angelica's last year at school. It was also the year that Vanessa planned a lengthy visit to Rome. Anxious to arrive in Italy before the heat became severe, she took the sixteen-year-old Angelica away from school at Easter so that she left without having sat the School Certificate. Vanessa also made Grace, who the year previously had married Walter Higgens, housekeeper at Charleston and let it to Herbert Read and his wife. And immediately before departing for Rome she attended a dinner given in honour of the artist Ethel Walker, to whom she had sat for her portrait (Tate Gallery). Then in a chauffeur-driven car which the Harold Nicolsons had need of in Rome, she and Angelica were driven in (for them) unusual style through France, stopping for a night at Moulins and at Montélimar. From the latter Vanessa wrote to Helen:

> No wonder the French are painters. It all seems so immense and indestructible when one drives through the great spaces and everyone's life going on quite regardless of the rest of the world ... Angelica is a perfect travelling companion with very high spirits and then lapses into another existence in which I leave her alone. I suspect it looks more romantic than it is, but it's agreeable to look at. She reads Shakespeare at intervals and plays the piano in hotel drawing rooms.[2]

The next day they called on the Maurons at St-Rémy. Apprehensive of meeting them without Roger, Vanessa was surprised how easily she could talk and even joke about him with Charles and Marie. Their visit lasted longer than she intended and they subsequently arrived very late that night at Roquebrune, Vanessa, in the dark, almost falling down La Souco's steep steps. There they found Quentin who had been staying with the Bussys while he researched into the history of Monaco. He was hoping that his friend Yvonne Kapp (later to write a biography of Eleanor Marx) would help with the writing, but the project never materialized.

With Quentin, Vanessa and Angelica completed their journey. In Rome they put up temporarily at the Hotel Hassler while Vanessa looked round for a studio where they could work and live. 'I saw Vita this morning', Vanessa reported to Helen, 'looking red as beetroot – with a thick moustache – rather fine in a manly way, with a small rather mousy [sic] looking creature in tow, her sister-in-law with whom she is desperately in love.' They dined twice in the Nicolsons' company, giving Vanessa further opportunity for acute observation. 'Harold isn't a bad creature. . . . My impression is he could be led or pushed in any direction. Vita seems as masterful as Mussolini and has him in complete control.'[3] This is the only reference to Mussolini in Vanessa's letters from Rome, for as yet she did not take Fascism seriously. She could speak little Italian and was therefore somewhat cut off from the life around her. Wherever she went she seemed to carry her own world with her and before long her manner of existence had become much like that she led in London; detached, contemplative and remote from the bustle and tension of the everyday world.

Angelica, overjoyed at finding herself in Rome, walked through the streets arm in arm with Quentin, shrieking with laughter or alternatively filled with ecstasy by the sight of a church or an ancient building. She attracted much attention to herself, and the son of a well-known tenor began to sit in the hotel salon listening to her play the piano. Vanessa, meanwhile, found for herself and Angelica an enormous room at No.33 Via Margutta; it was divided in two by a curtain and had a small kitchen, water-closet and bathroom attached; it had marble floors, the minimum of furniture and cost £2 2s. a week. Duncan, when he arrived, took a studio on the top floor, and Quentin found a room near by. Before long everyone had settled down to work while Angelica took Italian lessons with a Signorina Boschetti. When the Woolfs arrived in Rome for a week, during the course of a motoring holiday through Europe, Virginia found a familiar life-style already established. 'We went rag marketing. And suddenly out sprang, to my eyes, the old triumphant Vanessa of early married days. Why? How she would bear off in full sail with Roger, Clive and me attendant. We bought pots; and a tea set, which gave her great intense potters delight more than any clothing or jewel.'[4]

As usual when abroad, Vanessa found she had more time to read. 'Her leisure, with books, is prodigious,' Virginia once complained, explaining to Ethel Smyth that Vanessa had not yet finished *Beecham and Pharaoh*: 'it reminds me of the gestation and copulation of elephants. "No, I can't say I've read more than one sentence but when I read, I read." And that's true. It'll take her six months.'[5] In Rome she buried herself in the memoirs of Mrs Humphry Ward and emerged declaring this author 'the inventor of the cinematic caption ... all dashes and notes of exclamation. I believe a fortune could be made by turning some of her works into films.'[6] During the rest of her stay in Rome Vanessa re-read all Roger's letters to herself, before giving them to Virginia for use in her biography.

At the same time she was at work on her decorations for RMS *Queen Mary*. This commission had followed shortly after the success of the music room, for which she and Duncan had designed fabrics, rugs, painted furniture and wall decorations, for an installation at the Lefevre Gallery in December 1932. The occasion had attracted notice in the press, partly because of the highly successful cocktail party given at the opening by Virginia and Vanessa. According to Cyril Connolly, 'the room vibrated to a Debussy solo on the harp, and the music, with its seasonal elegiac, seemed to blend with the surrounding patterns of the flowers and falling leaves in a rare union of intellect and imagination, colour and sound, which produced in the listener a momentary appre- hension of the life of the spirit, that lonely and un-English credo'.[7] But designing freely for a private domestic interior was a very different matter from creating murals for a public setting and both Duncan and Vanessa might have been warned of the difficulties the *Queen Mary* commission would present. Duncan had been given the task of providing three large panels to decorate the ship's main lounge; Vanessa was to produce only one painted panel for a private sitting-room. Both also had the task of designing colour schemes and patterns for carpets and stuffs. With this major commission on hand Duncan declared he needed to stay in one place and would remain in Rome until September. Vanessa intended leaving earlier in order to spend some time at Cassis on the way home, but news from Julian brought her back to England before the end of July.

For some time now Julian's public and private life had been unsettled. In 1933, anxious for change and feeling a need to assert his indepen- dence, he began to consider the possibility of employment abroad. He applied for jobs in Siam, China and Japan, at first without success. Meanwhile one girl-friend followed another. None of these relationships seem to have been very satisfactory and in one instance he was obliged to pay out £30 for an abortion. Nor did it trouble him if his women were married. With Helen Hasland, the photographer who worked under the name Helena Thornhill from Haverstock Hill, this presented little problem as she was rarely with her husband, but his affair with a biochemist proved difficult as it threatened to upset her domestic life. 'I daresay she'll find a way of managing it all,' Vanessa remarked. 'Females generally do.'[8]

The ease with which he got what he wanted did not appease his sense of failure. Then in July 1935 he was offered the post of Professor of English at the National University of Wuhan at Hankow. He wrote immediately to Vanessa, admitting that he was appalled at the thought of leaving her for three years, but that his need for change was now urgent. 'When I come back I should have got straight internally ... somehow I'm convinced that it will produce a kind of peace of mind [which] I now want above all things.'[9]

As Julian had only a month in which to prepare for his departure Vanessa hurried home in order to spend some days with him and the rest of her family at Charleston. Julian was photographed in his new clothes and when the time came for him to leave Vanessa drove him to the port. 'Nessa and I both have about the same notion of how to

The Nursery, 1930-32

Interior with Two Women, 1932

Nursery Tea, 1912

Design for a nursery, Omega workshops, 1913

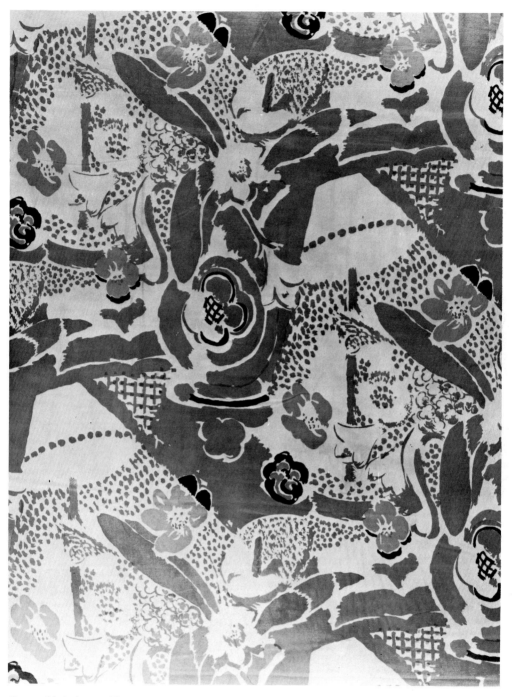

Cotton fabric designed by Vanessa Bell for Allan Walton, 1933-4

Berwick Church, showing Vanessa Bell's *Nativity*

Vanessa Bell's *Annunciation*

A corner of Angelica's bedroom at Charleston

anessa with her grandchildren Julian and Virginia Bell, 1956

/ictor Pasmore, William Coldstream, Vanessa Bell and Claude Rogers, c. 1938-9

Vanessa Bell, 1960

Portrait of Aldous Huxley, c. 1929–30

Henrietta Garnett, 1959

Vanessa Bell by Duncan Grant, 1959

The Open Door, Charleston, 1926

A corner of the dining room at Charleston, showing Jean Marchand's *La Ville*, bought by Clive Bell from the Second Post-Impressionist Exhibition

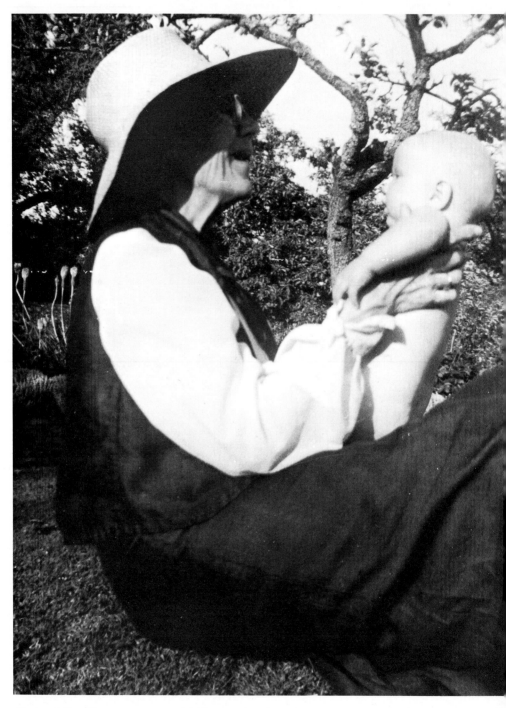

Vanessa Bell and her youngest grandchild, Cressida Bell, 1959

behave, but it isn't easy. As it happened it was her giving me some money as a present that broke me down. Then a bright, cheerful grim little drive into Lewes and Newhaven. You know, I'm almost the only person I know who has an adult relationship with their mother. It's about the most satisfactory human relationship I have, perhaps it's the only one where I've deep emotions uncomplicated by power-sadist feelings.'[10] He crossed the channel and from Paris caught a train to Marseilles where he boarded the Japanese ship, the *Fushimi Maru*.

After leaving Julian at Newhaven Vanessa drove back to Charleston partly in a dream, feeling and noticing little except the beauty of the Downs and the summer countryside. On her return Duncan was pro- tectively kind and Vanessa showed her feelings to him but not to others, not wanting to afflict Quentin and Angelica with her sense of loss. Nevertheless, Angelica was made aware that her mother 'looked on his [Julian's] departure rather in the light of a personal tragedy, an act which left her, if only temporarily, bereft and desolate'.[11] To distract her thoughts Vanessa began to transform Julian's room, tidying his books, papers and clothes in order to make space for Angelica who was to use the bedroom in his absence.

She now adopted the habit of sending Julian weekly letters written over a period of two to three days. They provided an opportunity for things to be said which in other circumstances would have been left unsaid; separation, instead of creating a rift in their relationship, licensed the expression of love and therefore may have increased Vanessa's hold on her son. 'This has been a great blessing,' she wrote to him, 'for it has made us try to tell each other what we mean to each other ... I feel so perfectly sure now that you want me to know and share things with you and what can one have more from one's children? ... How glad I am too that it didn't happen sooner, for you made such a tremendous difference to me last year when Roger died.'[12] Roger and Julian had become somehow joined in her mind and her son's departure seemed to her 'like some dim reflection of his [Roger's] death'.[13] Julian, perhaps realizing his need to compensate his mother for her loss, began composing an essay on Roger during his journey to China. He did not stick closely to his subject but often used Roger's ideas as a mere starting-point for the discussion of contemporary political theory. He completed it in January 1936 and sent it to Vanessa, knowing that his understanding of Roger would please her. 'His was a rationalism so subtle', he wrote, 'and so profound that he could cope with, and enjoy, chaos itself: that there was nothing in the universe, apparently, nor in himself, that he could not contemplate with an impartial detachment, ready to accept or reject anything on its merits. I have never known anyone so nearly the "free mind" of Spinoza's imagination.'[14]

Vanessa's distress over Julian's absence did not prevent her from enjoying an active social life. Against her better judgement she even attended a dinner given by the Palace employee Timmy Chichester to welcome the return of the dealer Duncan Macdonald from Tangier and George Bergen from America. As two days after this party Duncan arrived at Charleston alone, to join Vanessa, it would appear that Bergen no longer dominated his emotional life. More troublesome at this time was 'Tut' who had escaped from an asylum in Brighton and kept turning up either at Charleston or 8 Fitzroy Street, asking for Duncan but refusing to accept gifts of money unless he felt able to pay it back.

The most glamorous social event that autumn was the party given at Gordon Square by Charles and Elsa Laughton and at which Blooms-bury and Hollywood mixed. Vanessa, a little fearful of her shabbiness, went to please Angelica and was glad to find Bunny also present. While he carried on with a tall, beautiful and, as Vanessa thought, rather witless young lady, she made friends with the zoologist [Lord] Solly Zuckerman. That same month she herself gave a small but memorable party at Charleston at which the Woolfs, Janie Bussy, Bunny, T. S. Eliot, Duncan, Clive, Angelica, her friend Eve Younger and another were present. She had ordered eleven grouse, thinking that two sides of grouse went to one person, instead of two persons to a grouse, but this mistake proved the making of the occasion. Eliot's eyes shone at the sight of so many birds; he ate his entire (while the rest carved off half for the next day), then visibly relaxed and began to talk about himself. 'He and Bunny', Vanessa recounted to Julian, 'made a very good couple, one slow in the American and the other in the English style – and both keeping us in roars of laughter. After dinner Angelica and Eve gave us a musical entertainment in the studio which consisted of their dressing up and singing such songs as "Where are you going to my pretty maid?" with Quentin as the cow. They looked ravishing – but generally forgot their words. However everyone enjoyed it I think and Tom told us the immortal story of his party ... how, to make things go, he bought chocolates which should have been filled with sawdust but were filled with soap, and sugar lumps with india rubber fish inside which would have been all right in tea but were invisible in black coffee – and what a failure it all was.'[15]

At intervals that autumn Vanessa and Duncan painted at the nearby

Michelham Priory. Their chief concern, however, was with the *Queen Mary* decorations. During the summer they had completed their decorative panels, Vanessa's having been commissioned for a private sitting-room next to the Roman Catholic chapel. By the autumn they were in frequent contact with a Mr Leach. He visited their London studio and made arrangements for them to visit Liverpool in order to advise the Cunard Shipping Company on the choice of colours for interior decoration. Then, on the day before they were expected in Liverpool, two letters arrived, one cancelling Vanessa's contract because the Roman Catholic authorities had found her designs offensive, the other informing Duncan that certain restrictions would have to be imposed on his panels and that he would have to reduce the size of his figures. Vanessa went straight to Maynard for advice. Fortunately he knew Sir Percy Bates, Chairman of the Cunard Shipping Company, and wrote immediately to him.

> It has been suggested to her that not only is her contract now cancelled, but that she will be given some compensation less than the amount of the contract price. I imagine that the latter is not more than a suggestion which will not be persisted with. But the money side is secondary. Mrs Bell agreed to accept a low figure in relation to the time occupied, because she was interested in the work and thought the idea so admirable a one. It has also been widely published in the press that she has been engaged, and the cancellation of her contract not only takes away advantages she has been relying on, but is actually bad for her reputation.
>
> A contract with an artist is rather of a different character from any other kind of contract. Artists are at least as anxious that their work shall reach the world as that they should be paid a living wage for it. Would it not be possible to find some other room where her work could be used and enjoyed?[16]

While this letter was on its way to Sir Percy Bates, Vanessa and Duncan travelled up to Liverpool and there learnt that Cunard had been rattled by the interest the Royal Family had begun to take in the boat. The directors had suddenly realized that much of the decoration commissioned did not reflect the taste of the clientele – royalty, film-stars, business magnates – whom the ship would serve. While the American architect was absent they had decided to rid themselves of certain artists. Maynard's letter, however, made its point. Vanessa, although she now saw that commissions of this kind were doomed to failure, was re-employed, 'You will be glad to hear,' Sir Percy Bates wrote to Maynard on 7 October, 'that it has been found possible to adopt your suggestion of other work for Mrs Bell. I think you will find when next you meet her, that she is completely satisfied with her position.'[17] 'My dear Bates,' Maynard replied, 'Many thanks for your letter. I have seen Mrs Bell who is not only completely happy, but feels that she has been handsomely treated.'[18] Vanessa had been commissioned to execute another panel for the private dining-room to be used by millionaires for dinner parties. She had also received £200 compensation for her rejected panel and £150 in advance for the new one.

Soon after Vanessa's return from Liverpool the rest of her family took flight: Angelica went to Paris to stay with friends of the Bussys, François and Zoum Walter; Quentin, having established contact with T. A. Fennemore, disappeared to Staffordshire to learn about pottery production. Vanessa found herself childless in London, but hardly ever alone. Often Duncan's teatime visitors overflowed into her studio and she was frequently invited out to dinner. On more than one occasion this year she was a guest of Kenneth and Jane Clark. At the same time she absorbed in her spare moments Gerstle Mack's life of Cézanne and was struck by his solitariness and hatred of society.

The single most momentous event of each week continued to be the arrival of Julian's letter. On these mornings Duncan came through from his studio to find the toast unmade, the milk unheated. The letter would be discussed and read aloud to family and others before it was circulated among Julian's Cambridge friends. At Vanessa's request Julian was careful to describe the colours of things and the quality of light, so that she could share in the experiences he described.

Thus though living in London at a time of a general election (at which she did not vote, feeling that the Tories ought to remain in power but finding herself unable to support this party) and at the same time keeping an anxious eye on the political situation in Paris, a part of Vanessa's mind had been transposed to China. She listened to a schools radio programme on China and when the sound effects brought over the noise of crowds in Hankow she imagined herself walking the same streets looking for Julian. She read books on China, including a Chinese novel by Pearl Buck. She was observed poring over a map of China and teased for reading reports on the jute crop in *The Times*. In need of more pottery, she went with Helen Anrep to a warehouse that sold Chinese porcelain and afterwards the two women ate at a Chinese restaurant. In December all London went Chinese when a large exhibition of Chinese art opened at the Royal Academy. Vanessa visited it on more than one occasion and found her feelings were mixed. 'It seems to me as if all their instincts were for things within a very narrow range and infinitely subtle. The relief on the bronzes for instance, when kept low is amazing, so right and exquisite and always in proportion to the whole shape. Also the colours of stuffs, etc., when very sober and restrained is incredibly lovely. But when they get on to bright colours they become hideous and garish and don't seem to know how to manage them at all, as if they were all against the grain.'[19] She read none of the articles and books on Chinese art that poured from the press to coincide with the show because she felt convinced, now that Roger had died, that very little written on art was worth reading. She had just read Kenneth Clark's introduction to Roger's *Last Lectures* and found it dry and unsuggestive.

In Julian's absence she looked to others for a reflection of him; she was pleased when Bunny visited her and showed a desire to hear all Julian's news; she was glad when one of his girl-friends rang up and asked to come to tea. Afterwards Vanessa told Julian that she had enjoyed seeing his young woman but added, characteristically, that the ladies of Cambridge did not know how to make the most of their looks. On her visits to Cambridge she always enjoyed meeting Julian's friends for the conversation could again centre upon her favourite subject.

Her next letter to Julian included petals from the roses she had picked at Charleston on a brief visit to ensure that the house was ready for Duncan and his mother to occupy at Christmas. Now that Grace, her husband Walter and their new baby John lived permanently in the house, visits were made easier and more welcoming. Vanessa, Clive and Quentin went that Christmas to Seend (leaving Angelica in Paris) where on the first evening Quentin discovered that he could not get into the trousers that went with his dinner jacket. Vanessa slit them down the back as far as was decently possible but once on they looked more like black tights than trousers. They appealed to Cory for help and an old pair of Clive's were found that fitted better. Quentin arrived down a little late to dinner, as Vanessa observed, 'upset but resigned to the folly of human nature'.[20] She never worried that her sons were overweight, accepting their size as a natural, if comic, misfortune.

She sat that Christmas like an island in the ocean while Bell family life flowed around her as she wrote to Julian and Angelica. What irked Vanessa most that year was the mass of ugly, solid, expensive and mostly useless presents given and received; on Christmas day the library had looked like a bazaar. 'I am almost become a communist,' she announced. 'Really the respectable rich with their dogs and their clothes and their cars all rolling in while they eat and play tennis and become soldiers are enough to make one want to revolt. They eat and eat and eat, and they feed their dogs as carefully and their conversation about dogs beats any maternal twaddle I ever heard or else it consists of nag, nag rather like Lottie [Clive's cook] at her worst. Lorna is the worst of the lot – by far and if she is some day murdered by her children no one, not even Mrs Bell, will be surprised.'[21]

On 20 January 1936, twenty minutes after the event, Vanessa and Duncan heard on the radio that King George V had died. When they afterwards learnt that the coffin would pass through Tavistock Square, *en route* from King's Cross to Westminster Hall, they, the Woolfs, Mrs Grant and Margery Snowden who happened to be in London, crowded with others into the square garden to watch the procession. Vanessa was impressed less by the historical nature of the event than by its pageant of colour: the grey horses offset the colours of the royal standard and the flowers on the coffin, lit by the sun, while the riders' plumes added to the scene vivid touches of red.

At the end of this month she and Quentin visited Angelica in Paris. 'Oh it is nice to have a daughter again, I can't tell you how nice,' Vanessa wrote to Julian, 'I enjoy every minute of being with her, looking at her, she's so gay and lovely and full of life.'[22] They had drinks at the Deux Magots, oysters at Laborde, went on to the cinema and did not return to the Hôtel de Londres until past midnight. Angelica was very happy living with the Walters and, after an introduction from Clive, had begun to take lessons with the actress Ludmilla Pitoëff. On her return to London Vanessa began to enquire as to which acting school might best further her daughter's choice of profession. The deeply affectionate relationship between mother and daughter was one of the joys of Vanessa's life, but her son Julian perceived its drawback. He took a paternal interest in Angelica, assuming a role that Duncan did not fill, and now wrote to Vanessa warning her against unconscious possessiveness. She replied:

having a daughter ... has been in a way the most terrific experience of my life – that's to say the most penetrating, intimate, I don't know how to put it, experience. Having you was at first more absolutely thrilling and upsetting because you were the first and you entirely revolutionized existence for me, starting all the feelings and instincts that had slept all my life till then. But Angelica being my own sex – I'd never *wanted* a daughter and always imagined I'd prefer to have sons – suddenly gave me a feeling of complete intimacy with someone who had something so much in common with me fundamentally that it was like a revelation ... it was different from any relationship I'd ever experienced except perhaps at moments with my mother and with Stella – I don't think I'd ever had that peculiar thing even with Virginia. Well, that looks rather bad, doesn't it? I think I minded most horribly when she went to school first ... I felt as if a part of me had been cut off. But I didn't try to keep her, did I ... I wanted her to be independent *au fond*. For one thing I'd had a tremendous lesson as to that particular thing with my mother and Stella, who were so devoted and inseparable that Stella never had any real life of her own. [23]

Anxious that her daughter should not suffer from the kind of repression that blighted her own youth, Vanessa had adopted a liberal attitude. At school Angelica had avoided those subjects she disliked by appealing to Vanessa who had readily agreed that lacrosse and mathematics should be dropped. She was delighted by her daughter's musical gifts and in Rome arranged for her to have violin lessons with a Signor Neroni. He proved to be such a disciplinarian that Angelica returned from her first visit in tears and Vanessa instantly agreed that the lessons should cease. Yet despite her theoretical insistence on freedom, in practice her attitude towards her children was, as Julian had discerned, unconsciously possessive and con-stricting. Angelica, as the only daughter and Duncan's child (though as yet she herself did not know this), was made to feel somehow special. Her love of dressing-up had been encouraged, her beauty was constantly admired. Vanessa would go to any lengths to satisfy her whims, even standing in a boat on Charleston pond to take photographs of her daughter floating in the water in a white dress in imitation of Ophelia.

Angelica's return from Paris in March coincided with a party given by Phyllis Keyes in Clipstone Mews to celebrate the making of some pots that had been decorated by Duncan and Vanessa. The young woman arrived in a new hat trimmed with a veil, looking chic, competent and very grown up, but breaking into childish laughter when congratulated on her appearance. Only Lady Ottoline, who failed to see through the fashionable bluff, looked shocked. Angelica's appearance now often caused comment for, like Vanessa, her clothes were often made out of remnants, chosen for their colour or pattern rather than their suitability. When that summer the family attended a performance at the recently-opened Glynde-bourne, Angelica wore a crimson shawl and a red brocade dress that had formerly belonged to Vanessa, roses from the garden and red lipstick. So blinding was the effect it made her skin look green. To Vanessa's delight, as Angelica walked about all heads turned, though she did also notice that Mary Hutchinson's stare was a shade disapproving. Despite her desire to achieve normality, Angelica dressed in such a way as to confirm her eccentricity, for her garments were outside fashion, strangely combined, often bizarre. When she began that summer to attend Michel Saint-Denis's drama school, the London Theatre Studio, her fellow pupils were surprised by her gaucheness and lack of chic for there was much concerning dress and make-up that Vanessa had never taught her.

She was also ignorant of sexual matters. This again was Vanessa's fault for one curious fact about this former libertarian was that she was extremely shy of talking about sexual matters with her family. Her attitude was almost Victorian and surprisingly coy. She had so far told Angelica nothing about sex except on one occasion at the Villa Corsica in 1927. The nine-year-old Angelica had infuriated Clive by suddenly asking for information on this subject at an inopportune moment. To alleviate the situation Vanessa had taken her daughter into a separate room and at once explained all the facts which the young child promptly forgot. At seventeen Angelica was still largely ignorant on the subject of sex. Her brother Julian, again taking a paternal interest and adopting the role of a husband, advised Vanessa in one letter that it was unwise to expect her daughter to remain a virgin much longer. Therefore on the day before Angelica began drama school, she was sent by her mother to see a distinguished specialist, Dr Joan Malleson, for a talk about sex. Dr Malleson was so flabbergasted at how little this seventeen-year-old girl knew that she was able to say very little and Angelica emerged from her room almost as ignorant as when she went in.

Vanessa's attitude towards her children was both forbearing and possessive. She presented no impediments, encouraged them to follow their inclinations and yet could not disguise her voracious need of them. She suffered excessive grief when her twenty-seven-year-old son left for China, exposing her emotional dependence on him. In one letter to him she states that she would not be averse to Angelica starting an affair if she now wished. What alarmed her far more, in the case of both Julian and Angelica, was the thought of marriage.

The growing, if as yet unexpressed, sense of conflict between daughter and mother was exacerbated by the absence of any father-figure in Angelica's life. Clive pretended to fufil this role but as he lived apart from Vanessa and her family he was mostly absent; and at Charleston over the summer months it was sometimes noticeable that Angelica, as a child, had found him irritating. She preferred Duncan who as a companion always delighted her partly because he never seemed harassed by responsibilities. The pretence over Angelica's parentage allowed him to abdicate paternal duties; shortly after her return from Paris in March 1936 Duncan left for a holiday in Spain and it was Vanessa who arranged for Angelica to be auditioned for drama school.

Not until the summer of 1937 did Vanessa tell Angelica that her father was not Clive but Duncan. She took her into the garden room at Charleston and spoke in such a way that it was evident she expected an emotional scene. Angelica, however, felt little except a desire to escape from the room at the first opportunity in order to run through the fields where she could digest this information alone. As the truth had already been suggested to her by one of her school-friends, the revelation merely confirmed inchoate knowledge. She did not immediately register its traumatic implications and at first it caused no outward change: she did not broach the matter with Duncan and was advised by Vanessa not to tell Clive as he liked to think of her as his true daughter and would be upset to realize she now knew otherwise. Vanessa's disclosure, therefore, did not release Angelica from her mother's concentrated attention, from the precious atmosphere that surrounded her life. She felt a growing sense of repressed anguish, for by giving in to her every whim Vanessa forestalled freedom and condemned her daughter to a life of easy material pleasure. With hindsight Angelica has recalled: 'I was constantly striving to be thought of as somebody perfectly ordinary and I never could get through to that kind of reality ... I found it more difficult to escape from this syndrome and in the end I didn't until she died. I really didn't escape from her until I was over forty.'[24]

Vanessa's letters to Julian, meanwhile, continued to detail the main events of each week. She led a remarkably active life for one who disparaged her husband's dissipation, attending parties, dining out, going to the theatre, including performances at Maynard's recently-opened gift to Cambridge, the Arts Theatre and, like Duncan, developing a love of the cinema. A performance of Ibsen's *Rosmersholm* caused her to reflect, 'But how one enjoys a play that means as much as that. What shall I feel if I ever see Angelica acting well in such a play – too upsetting I suspect.'[25] She was equally receptive to music. ('Why is very intense beauty so upsetting?'[26] she asked, after listening to Schubert.) Among the various films that she saw, Charlie Chaplin's *Modern Times* pleased her most as she found its anti-capitalist philosophy entirely sympathetic. By contrast the film of H. G. Wells's *The Shape of Things to Come* struck her as depressing and faintly ridiculous: 'His idea of the future of the world really stops where Charlie Chaplin's begins, that is with everything reduced to hygienic machinery, the one aim of the most enlightened being to get to the moon. I suppose he once had imagination of a kind.'[27]

Freddie Ashton found her sharp, mocking humour very agreeable. Once, when seated next to her at a party, a man came up and commented that because Vanessa was dressed in lace she looked like an old cameo. Vanessa laughed in such a way as to underline both the absurdity of the remark and the man's foolishness for having made it. Only rarely did her ironic humour become sardonic, for though approaching sixty she still had an openness of mind that kept her feelings and responses fresh and, as she told Virginia, when she took her seat on the bus she still felt the youngest person present. Among friends and family, she was gay and spontaneous, still taking a delight not in social display and prestige but in the vigorous and real. During the visit to Glyndebourne to hear *Don Giovanni*, she had admired not only her daughter's appearance but also that of Marjorie Strachey:

> Gumbo looking too peculiar, drinking brandy which Kenneth [Clark] had ordered for Duncan, greatly to K's astonishment and indeed horror. In fact if you could have seen Gumbo, you wouldn't have been surprised at his taking her for some drunken troll – huge and grey and untidy, sprawling over the table and tossing off brandy.

Vanessa herself, as they sat over their picnic supper, gave an impromptu rendering of 'What shall we do with the broken tumbler', unaware of the startled head that looked out from the door which led into the singers' quarters. The family collapsed with laughter and Vanessa, taking this as a compliment to her performance, sang on until a whole troupe of singers emerged 'and I had to pull myself together and behave as a polite lady making way for them past our broken tumblers and sandwiches. Altogether it was a successful evening and the music was divine.'[28]

She was still more daring after a few glasses of champagne at a party given by Sam Courtauld for she leaned across the table and asked Lady Oxford (Margot Asquith) if she would sit for her portrait. 'Lovely Vanessa,' began the letter that arrived the very next morning, 'I'm so delighted that you and Duncan s^d. wish to paint me that I can't sleep. The trouble is that I am neither plain enough, nor pretty enough to make a *good* picture.'[29] Nevertheless she made an excellent sitter, talking incessantly about the many famous people she had known during the last sixty years, for she had been a central figure in London's social and political life. Vanessa admired her forthrightness and observed that she was not in the least a snob.

The Courtaulds' party also brought to an unhappy end the lengthy saga concerning their *Queen Mary* decorations. These had been completed at the end of January. Vanessa and Duncan had given two cocktail parties for friends in order to show the paintings before they were sent up to Glasgow to be installed in the ship. Once Duncan's three panels were in position in the main lounge the Chairman of Cunard's, Sir Percy Bates, rejected them outright. This 'floating emblem of national prestige', as the *Studio* magazine referred to the ship, boasted decorations by, among others, Anna Zinkeisen, MacDonald Gill, Bainbridge Copnall, Margot Gilbert, James Woodford, Herry Perry, Charles Pears, Kenneth Shoesmith, Rebel Stanton, all essentially lightweight artists amongst whose work Duncan's panels looked out of place. There was moreover an ideological difference for the Bloomsbury style was opposed to the materialistic and fashionable values flaunted throughout the ship. The rejection of Duncan's work, however, would not only damage his reputation but lose him the valuable advertisement which the ship's main lounge provided. He turned to Kenneth Clark, then Director of the National Gallery in London, for advice. Clark offered to send to *The Times* a letter of protest, to be signed by officials and authorities sympathetic to the case, but advised Duncan first to write a formal letter of complaint to Cunard's, demanding his panels back and some form of compensation. The press had heard that trouble was afoot and were anxious to run a story on it, but they refrained from making a fuss until Cunard's had had a chance to reply. Then everything was disrupted by Clive's article on the ship's decoration which appeared in the *Listener* and where, in his very best form, he let rip. He mocked the ship's owners for their fear of the highbrow, for their inability to leave any surface unadorned: 'The artistico-comical creeps all over the ship and proclaims the frivolous and frightened attitude to art of rich people who are not sure of themselves. The whole boat giggles from stem to stern.'[30]

This vituperative attack would have been all right had it been written by an outsider. But Clive moved in high-class circles and it was unfortunate that the person chiefly responsible for the *Queen Mary*, the Chairman of John Brown, the firm that had built the boat, was the husband of one of his erstwhile mistresses, Christabel Aberconway. Christabel, a woman of great spirit and small artistic pretensions (at a significant moment in her life she had sold her Amati violin to buy a very good fur coat), was utterly furious. She went to see Kenneth Clark and accused Clive of spitefulness. Meanwhile Cunard had refused Duncan compensation and Vanessa hoped that Clark would, as he had promised, send a letter to *The Times*. But after a three-hour session with Christabel, his views had somewhat changed. Clive's article, he argued, had been so violent that those previously willing to support Duncan's case would now refuse to sign any further protest. The matter did not end there for the *Daily Express*, of its own accord, ran an article on the rejected panels and this so terrified Cunard's they reversed their previous decision, returned Duncan his panels and paid compensation on top of his fee on the condition that he would stir up no further controversy. There the matter ended – almost. At the Courtaulds' party a couple of months later, Christabel, now considerably mollified, caught sight of Vanessa seated at a table on the other side of the garden, listening to the musical entertainment. The next moment Vanessa received an illegible note scrawled tipsily across the back of the programme. Later Christabel came over, sat at Vanessa's side and, after pouring out a torrent of resentment against Clive, expressed the hope that she and Vanessa and Duncan would remain friends. At that moment the music began again and no reply was possible, but the next day Vanessa sent her a polite note saying she too had no wish to quarrel but that Clive's views on the ship were also her own.

Vanessa had visited the *Queen Mary* in April while it had docked at Southampton. She had marvelled at its effective line in slick vulgarity and took particular dislike to the extensive reliefs, painted a sham gold or silver with metallic varnish. She found her large panel, representing a view through a window with children playing round a fountain and a huge vase of lilies on the sill, in so small a room that it could not properly be seen. She was also disappointed to find that the cabins, for which she and Duncan had chosen carpets and stuffs, had not yet been completed. The impression remained of an important commission misconceived, mishandled and disappointing in the extreme.

The *Queen Mary* affair left Vanessa critical of Kenneth Clark who she had hoped would step into the position that Roger had occupied. 'When one sees him,' she wrote of Clark to Julian, 'one of the few people who is educated about painting, one realizes more and more how much one has lost in Roger. How absolutely different it would have been to talk to him if he'd just been seeing all the pictures in America. Of course I feel it constantly and long for his help and criticism, but usually – except for Duncan, no one pretends to give any.... I suppose actually the creative critic is one of the rarest of all kinds of mind – good artists are far commoner.'[31]

After a visit to Paris with Duncan in May 1936, to see a Cézanne exhibition, Vanessa was confirmed in her opinion that this French artist was the greatest of the moderns. Her own work continued to occupy the larger part of her day. Mostly she painted direct on to canvas and when she sent Julian a batch of her drawings admitted 'I so seldom do drawings.'[32] She received no more public or private decorative commissions but that spring decorated one bedroom at Charleston, with Angelica's help, with pink and grey marbled pillars placed at intervals around the walls. Both her and Duncan's professional life had been disturbed by a disagreement with the London Group: in the winter of 1935–6 a clique, led by the artist John Cooper, had formed to oust Rupert Lee and his wife Diana Brinton-Lee from their posts as treasurer and secretary; Vanessa and Duncan had done their best to prevent this happening, raising support for the Lees among other artists at tea parties held at 8 Fitzroy Street, but by January 1936 they had been defeated. 'Evil has triumphed in the London

Group,' Vanessa told Quentin. 'Rupert Lee is dethroned. Sickert is PLG [President] ... Mrs Lee turned out, unknown female installed. We are all, D. Keith [Baynes] and I on the working committee and are considering resigning entirely and starting a new group.'[33] They did resign but no new group was founded. As it was, they still had an outlet through Agnew's and Lefevre's, though they also temporarily fell out with the latter gallery at this time over the terms of their agreement. And they were also members of the Artists International Association, founded in 1933 under the banner 'Unity of Artists for Peace, Democracy and Cultural Development'. Membership of the AIA inevitably drew Vanessa's attention to the growing threat of Fascism in Europe. She was sometimes present at AIA meetings as well as those held by Leonard, Adrian Stephen and Margery Fry to discuss ways in which anti-fascist opinion could be expressed. On these occasions Vanessa always dreaded that a vote might be taken on some issue, as the various arguments for and against always left her totally confused.

In June 1936 London woke to a surrealist invasion. The International Surrealist Exhibition, though its influence was far less wide-reaching, created a furore much like that caused by Roger's post-impressionist exhibitions.

> Duncan went to the Private View [Vanessa told Julian] and found a 10/- note lying on the floor which he tried to place on a statue so as to add to the meaning of it. Unfortunately some one, perhaps the owner perhaps not, came up and pocketed it. Then as he was going out Paul Nash came up and gave him a herring which he asked him to put outside, as he said some Philistine had attached it to a picture, but Duncan refused. Eviedently it would be easy to get up a surrealist party – in fact we think our studios are full of s.r. subjects without our troubling about it and one may find oneself one of them before one knows what's happening. [34]

She had known about Surrealism for some time and, as Roger had done, distrusted its return to story-telling. This was an aspect of art that she had so trained herself to ignore that she was often blind to a work's subject. In 1930 she had written to Quentin: 'I am most anxious to see your work. Clive hints at sur-realism – and thinks I shall disapprove – so do you apparently. But my dear child haven't you grasped the fact that the whole point of my theories, such as they are, is that I don't mind, in fact I'm not usually aware of sur-realism or romanticism or anything else?'[35]

Thus despite changes in fashion Vanessa continued to follow an independent course in life with a sense of purpose that others envied. Vanessa 'takes her own line in London life,' Virginia observed; 'refuses to be a celebrated painter; buys no clothes; sees whom she likes as she likes; and altogether leads an indomitable sensible and very sublime existence'.[36] One morning a package arrived on which £1 1s. 9d. had to be paid to cover the excess postage. Neither Vanessa nor Duncan had the required amount and the postman had to return in the afternoon. Then Vanessa discovered to her joy that the parcel contained silks sent by Julian from China. She spent all afternoon arranging them in an array of rainbow colours around the studio and afterwards put them carefully away in a drawer with a layer of paper between each. This gift was followed by a trunk-load of presents which included Chinese pottery. Julian knew exactly what would please Vanessa. His gifts also offered her a glimpse into the very different culture within which he was living. When Vanessa actually met some students from Wuhan at Margery Fry's, she reflected that Julian must be feeling a little isolated among a people so very different from himself.

Wuhan sits on the side of the Yangtse river, opposite the more commercial city of Hankow. It is the ancient capital of the Hupei province. Its university is a little outside the town, situated on a hillside overlooking a lake. The beauty of the surrounding countryside had done much to console Julian's initial homesickness. The kindness of his Dean, Professor Chen Yuan, his wife Ling Su-Hua and their charming daughter had also helped settle him in. Chen was a critic and a translator of Turgenev; Su-Hua a painter, a writer of short stories and editor of the literary page in one of the Hankow newspapers. She was also the daughter of the fourth concubine of a highly-cultured scholar and ex-mayor of Peking and was therefore able to introduce Julian, not just to westernized Chinese culture, but also to the ancient traditions of Imperial China. Charming, intelligent and artistic, Su-Hua became an invaluable friend. Julian soon developed the habit of turning up at her house in between classes, sometimes returning again in the evening, for, as Su-Hua realized, he felt a need for a family environment.[37] He was also lonely as the rest of the Chinese at the university were wary of foreigners and Julian himself did not speak the language. Su-Hua also noticed that in his conversation he made frequent reference to Vanessa, Virginia and his family. In turn she explained to him Chinese customs and he asked her advice on many matters, telling her that in her surety of judgement she was like Vanessa. When he began to give classes on Shakespeare and modern literature Su-Hua sat in to encourage him, observing that he often talked so fast that few could understand him.

In his letters home Julian detailed the circumstances of his daily life. He saw much of Su-Hua and furnished his house with her help; he began to entertain, bought a boat in which he sailed with Su-Hua, and acquired a dog. He was also candid about his homesickness and longing for Vanessa. 'Alas, dearest, I've found out more than ever how much our relationship matters to me. And we both know it.'[38] What he did not tell her was his realization that China would not solve his inner *malaise*. 'What a queer business it all is,' he wrote to Barbara Mackenzie-Smith. 'I wanted a smashing climax, and took my steps, and now after two years I've got my climax and it makes no difference. I'm not even lonely, or cut off from intellectuals. The only difference is that I lead a more reasonable life, with a job, money, and the country to walk and shoot in. The whole problem's to solve again without any exterior help or pressure. The hell, what is one to do? Look for trouble? I daresay I'll end by finding it.'[39] He was depressed by his lack of achievement, by his want of some specialized ability other than the writing of poetry (in which his interest appears to have lapsed). At the same time he was still weighed down with respect for his elders. But now removed from his background he felt able to show Vanessa a poem that he had written over a year before. Entitled 'Autobiography', it is an encomium to Bloomsbury and to his mother:

> . . . people intent
> To follow mind, feeling and sense
> Where they might lead, and, for the world, content
> To let it run along its toppling course.
> Humane, just, sensible; with no pretence
> To fame, success, or meddling with that world.
>
> And one, my best, with such a calm of mind,
> And, I have thought, with clear experience
> Of what is felt of waste, confusion, pain
> Faced with a strong sense, stubborn and plain;
> Patient and sensitive, cynic and kind.[40]

Meanwhile he taught, criticized the romantic sentiment in his students' essays and discovered that Ling Su-Hua's short stories fully justified her reputation as the Chinese Katherine Mansfield. He sent some to Vanessa in the hope that she could place them in English literary journals. (She had no success but later, in 1953, the Hogarth Press published these autobiographical short stories under the title *Ancient Melodies*, a book Vanessa read to her grandchildren.) They possessed a purity of vision that enchanted her. She wrote to Julian: 'I think painters may be specially bowled over by the Chinese as writers – they *see* everything so clearly and one isn't left in doubt about colour which to me at least makes so much difference. One seems to live in a delicious world of silvery moving colours and lights and one is aware always that the writer is aware of the looks of everything.'[41]

Julian was startled by the increasing references to politics in Vanessa's letters. A move towards appeasement had begun after Hitler sent German troops into the Rhineland in March 1936; the League of Nations invited him to negotiate a new arrangement for European security and he had responded to their invitation; but when the British Government asked for further definition of his propositions he replied with silence. Among her friends, as Vanessa recounted, opinion was divided: James and Alix Strachey refused to believe that Hitler had evil intentions; others predicted inevitable war. Clive now frequently flew into a rage when politics were discussed. Maynard, while dining at Charleston one evening, decided to give Quentin his views on what the Labour Party ought to be doing. Vanessa listened: 'I was amused by what seemed to me Maynard's typically English attitude, much cleverer of course but fundamentally the English waiting to see, hedging, non-committal attitude that foreigners mistrust so much, with a horribly clever instinct for turning things to their own advantage after behaving rather monstrously.'[42]

Though his contract at Wuhan was for three years, after only one had passed Julian began thinking of what he would do when he returned home. 'I shall have to try and get a definite political job of some kind. ... That will provide a pleasant contrast to this life, and I shall enjoy a state of excitement again. But also I should like to settle down to a country life at Charleston.'[43] He envied Quentin his involvement with the Labour Party and was amused to hear that his brother's bulk had overturned a platform at one fascist rally and had helped set up an anti-fascist meeting in its place. He was also rather bitterly aware that his future would be affected by impersonal forces. 'I believe I am working myself into a genuine enough resignation to an early death,' he had written to Janie Bussy in the spring of 1936. If granted a reprieve, his life, he reflected, would follow a sadly predictable course. 'You can't conceive how middle-aged I've grown. I shall return – I suppose in some 18 months' time – thin, bald, liverish, opinionated and *passé*. Then a last half-hearted fling – I hope Angelica will have plenty of easy-going friends by then. And finally Hitler. If I don't get liquidated or made commisar for the East I hope I shall have the pleasure of your company in 1960, editing the *Chronique Scandaleuse* of Blooms-bury.'[44]

When in June skirmishing broke out and China seemed threatened with civil war, Julian momentarily thought of applying to an English newspaper for a job as war correspondent. Instead he spent his summer vacation travelling in north China with an English geologist and one of his Chinese students, Chen Chun Yeh, who later acted as a guide to Auden and Isherwood on their visit to China in 1937 and who was to make for himself a considerable literary reputation.* He was very fond of girls and enjoyed talking to Julian about sex. They travelled up river to Yo-chow, Chungking and Szechuan, encountering various adventures. At Chengtu Julian heard of the *coup d'état* in Spain and on reaching Peking he scanned the newspapers for more details. As he immediately realized, Franco's action had created the cause that anti-fascist intellectuals in England had been waiting for. He wondered if many of his friends would fight and was eager for news from England. George Bergen, who had been staying at a seaside resort near Barcelona, had extricated himself with difficulty and returned to England with tales of corpse-lined streets. A young woman artist associated with the AIA, Felicia Browne, had been killed and Vanessa and Duncan were asked to write an introduction to her memorial exhibition. 'How desperate Spains seems,' Vanessa wrote to Julian, ' – and all else. I wish one could do anything but wait for war which is what everyone seems to be doing.'[45] To which he replied: 'Well you may be thankful I'm safe in China. I know in England I should be feeling that the only reasonable thing is to go and fight the Fascists in Spain – for even at this range I feel all the talking is pretty silly. An odd world when even you drive cars for the Labour Party.'[46]

His immediate problem on his return to Wuhan, however, concerned not politics but sex. During the previous Christmas vacation he had journeyed to Peking in order to begin an affair with the Chinese wife of one of his colleagues. Secrecy necessarily surrounded their relationship, making it more intense than perhaps Julian intended; while she fell steadily more in love, his own feelings began to cool. Vanessa, who had once told Julian how happy it made her to be informed of his affairs, received a running report. She enjoyed the intimacy and equality that his loving frankness allowed and which she did not, to the same extent, share with Quentin who was always more secretive. Julian had no hesitation in sending her his poem 'Post Coitum' or in telling her of Chen's description of Chinese prostitutes. Nor did she worry that Julian was exposing himself and his lover to considerable risk by having an affair in this rigidly conservative, small university community; her high estimation of Julian eclipsed better judgement: 'I can't believe it wouldn't be an immense gain

---

* Chen visited England in 1944 and stayed until 1949. Having earlier been recommended by Julian to John Lehmann he was immediately taken up by the literary world, his short stories published in *New Writing* and a scholarship found for him at King's College, Cambridge. During this period he paid several visits to Charleston and was painted by Duncan and Vanessa. He immediately returned to China after Chiang Kai-shek's collapse in 1949 to support the victorious revolution, only to suffer from the anti-Western xenophobia which overran the country, enduring further humiliation during the Cultural Revolution of 1966.

in one's life to fall in love with you if you would only return it enough to make some of the affair possible.'[47] But meanwhile the young wife became hysterical and jealous, for Julian had begun to flirt now and then with other women.

With Julian safely engaged in the battle of the sexes, Vanessa could continue with her life and wait for his return. 'How I envy them!' Virginia wrote of Vanessa and Duncan. 'There they sit, looking at pinks and yellows, and when Europe blazes all they do is to screw their eyes up and complain of a temporary glare in the foreground. Unfortunately politics get between one and fiction.' She was writing to Julian with her reasons for not wanting to publish his letter on Roger Fry which she thought loose and discursive ('Prose has to be so tight, if it's not to smear one with mist.'[48]). Disappointed by this, he was at the same time pleased that his second book of poems *Winter Movement* had been well reviewed in the *Times Literary Supplement*. Vanessa, on re-reading these poems, was struck by how melancholy those written in London seemed; her own preference was for those in which political ideas did not intrude. She still believed that such matter was unsuited to poetry; that art, to be whole, had to be disinterested and detached. She found she could not paint in London immediately before her departure for Charleston as she needed to feel that she had unlimited time in which to work. In London she now shared a cook called Flossie with Helen Anrep, and at Charleston, where Grace now lived permanently, employed her husband Walter as a full-time gardener so that they could grow more fruit and vegetables and, if war came, be self-sufficient. 'Oh Julian,' she wrote from Charleston, 'how often I wish I could talk to you. I feel you have a saner and larger grasp of all these things than almost anyone I know and even I now cannot help wanting badly to understand something of what is happening in the world, and most people and newspapers are simply confusing. Goodbye darling, I think of you so much here – you are essential to this place – it belongs to you and you to it.'[49]

Despite the darkening European situation, Charleston had never been gayer than it was that summer. On 30 August a small party was given at which the Bloomsbury love of skits reached its apogee. As well as the usual inhabitants of the house, Janie Bussy and Christopher Strachey were also present; the Woolfs invited over from Rodmell and the Keyneses from Tilton. Vanessa, with her usual methodicalness, had provided 'a carefully organized spread of cold pies laid out on the window sill, puddings on side tables, jellied soup, etc., all arranged so that 11 people could be helped quickly and without carving or fuss'. Virginia was in very good form and kept all the company amused, while the actors, to keep up their spirits, drank a great deal of beer. After the meal, as Vanessa's account continues, 'the Tiltonians arrived, but to our great comfort without the young Geoffrey Keynes. Margaret K [Keynes] is a stodgy worthy Darwinian, Geoffrey himself nice but rather a bore.'[50] Then the guests moved into the studio and the entertainment began.

The large room had been hung with curtains to suggest a stage and with an enormous chandelier made out of paper and blue cellophane by Quentin. The performance began with a song by Angelica's former school-friend Eve Younger who lolled across a table in Edwardian costume, taking regular swigs from a bottle of gin when she forgot her words. Next came a recitation in fast and unintelligible French by Janie Bussy, then three short solo pieces by Angelica, in one of which she played a young authoress visiting Mrs Woolf and finding her manuscript in the mouth of Leonard's marmoset. All this time Duncan had been struggling into his costume in the wings with Vanessa's help. An essential ingredient to his get-up was a fan which was nowhere to be found. Lydia stepped in with an impromptu recitation while the panic lasted and eventually the fan was found. Duncan then emerged in a simpering mask and black mantilla, a nude female figure made out of cardboard tied to his person as he pirouetted, half-concealing his private parts with his mantilla and fan.

A short play followed, written by Quentin and Janie, in which Quentin, large and shapeless in a lady's dress, hat, fur coat and lipstick (and looking very like Marjorie Strachey) showed a party of American and French ladies round Charleston in the year AD 2036. Janie acted the part of a very unpleasant French lady, more interested in the whereabouts of the w.c. than the pictures, but obliged to listen as Quentin in a falsetto voice pointed out various relics each of which was emblematic of a person in the audience (a safe represented Maynard, an escritoire Clive, etc.). When it had ended and the audience had begun to complain that there was nothing more, a knock was heard on the studio door and in walked Vanessa dressed as Lady Ottoline Morrell in a red wool wig and a hat trimmed with artichoke leaves and, in this lady's manner, spoke a few kind words to her old friends.

They returned to London in the autumn, Angelica moving out of the room she had previously rented in Charlotte Street and into one in the front part of 8 Fitzroy Street. Quentin remained behind at Charleston for he had installed a kiln in the old pumphouse and now divided his time between politics, painting (including some decorations in Rodmell village hall) and potting. Like Vanessa and Duncan, he too was a member of the AIA and heavily involved in its politics. That autumn he, Vanessa, Duncan and Angelica, at the request of Janet Vaughan, all executed posters advertising a public meeting to raise money to send medical help to Spain.

Vanessa's and Duncan's social life that autumn included a visit to Sickert and Thérèse Lessore at Broadstairs. They also saw more than usual of Bunny who was not only suffering anxiety over the book he was currently writing but also from the appalling realization that his wife had cancer. He had been cheered by a visit to Charleston that summer, also by the discovery of a Yorkshire cottage overlooking Swaledale which he rented and later bought, but he was still further pleased when in November he was invited to become a member of the Memoir Club. Simultaneously he found himself increasingly charmed by Angelica. 'I see a fair amount of your family,' he wrote to Julian, 'who are the people I am happiest with, even though they tease me. I took Angelica out the other evening, filled her with oysters until we could scarcely eat any more, and went to a film.'[51]

Though that autumn England was obsessed with the King's relationship with Mrs Simpson, the pessimism with regard to the coming of war continued to grow. At the AIA meetings political discussions came often to the fore. 'Duncan and I had to go to committee meeting at Eliz. Watson's on Wednesday,' Vanessa told Julian,

> – a com. supposed to be organizing the Int. Artists annual exhibition. I must say I seldom saw a much less competent set of people – the poor old London Groupers were far more knowing. The difficulty was not to get all the work put on to oneself – this sounds very conceited and may be only my view – but I resisted firmly. Duncan has lent them his studio for 2 meetings which I considered weak. But I see we may both inevitably be on the selecting com. for the show which will be difficult and tiresome. It's a hopeless mixture of politics and art I think – they can't be mixed.[52]

Julian's affair with the Chinese wife had meanwhile encountered disaster; they had been caught *in flagrante delicto* by the young woman's husband. As a result Julian felt obliged to resign his post, telling the university authorities that he had to return home for 'family reasons'. As he was obliged to complete the term, he could not leave Wuhan until January. To ease matters the offended husband took his wife away on a visit and while she was absent Julian had no difficulty in starting another affair with an English girl called Innes Jackson.

Meanwhile he warned Vanessa in his letters that his future would have to involve at least one of his three main interests, 'travel, politics, Spain'. He had a good knowledge of military strategy and reading the newspaper reports was made restless and impatient by the government defeats in

Spain and by England's policy of non-intervention. 'I'm tired of being an intellectual on the loose,' he told his mother. 'I want something more practicable, tiresome, and involving other people.'[53] Earlier, in 1935, he had edited *We Did Not Fight*, a collection of essays written by conscientious objectors, and had admitted in his introduction that, despite the book's emphasis on the pacifist view, there were situations that called for force. Now he came down firmly in favour of war: 'There's no longer any real hope of peace, national or international, but only a choice, between fighting and surrender.'[54] Not wanting to alarm Vanessa he at first agreed to Leonard's suggestion that he should work as an unpaid secretary for a Labour MP. Vanessa, to help fund him, found him a company directorship in a Bell family business that imported feathers from China, a job that would bring in £100 a year. It was never likely that he would have rested content with this double position, for while in China he had come to militant conclusions. 'We are confronted by an essentially tragic situation,' he had written, in his 'Open Letter to C. Day Lewis'. 'We have to abandon what is good, a free, tolerant, humane culture, and follow what is evil: violence, compulsion, cruelty. We must do this because this is the rational choice of the lesser evil, because only by doing so can we hope to avoid complete, extinguishing disaster.'[55] There was no question but that Julian was coming home with a desire to fight.

He landed at Marseilles and went straight to the Maurons at St-Rémy for he intended going from there into Spain and hoped Charles would help him. He had written to Vanessa asking her to meet him at Cassis. She had begged him to reconsider his plans and return to Charleston where they could talk alone and in peace. Mauron upheld Vanessa's pleas and on 12 March Julian arrived home. The following evening the Woolfs attended a family reunion at Charleston and Julian, dressed in Chinese robes for the occasion, distributed presents. He was thinner, more serious, ruthless even, and a little removed from his family. That evening the thought uppermost in everyone's mind was not discussed.

Looking back on this period, Vanessa felt that her son's sense of proportion and his ideas had suffered from the intellectual loneliness of his life in China. For the first time ever she experienced serious differences of opinion with him and their relationship was slightly on edge. Nevertheless the weight of family feeling dissuaded Julian from enrolling with the International Brigade and he applied instead for work with Spanish Medical Aid. There followed an interval of tension and no small anxiety. Vanessa's tendency to internalize suffering caused her to treat Angelica like a child, for at first she refrained from telling her of Julian's intended departure for Spain.

While Julian waited to hear from Spanish Medical Aid he went up to Birmingham to canvas for the Labour Party. He made a new girl-friend, Jill Rendel, whose visits to Fitzroy Street, Vanessa noticed, alternated with those of Innes Jackson. He also spent much of his time discussing the war in Spain with Yvonne Kapp, Janet Vaughan and her husband and Stephen Spender, and in between times learnt mechanics and how to drive a lorry. Aware that in Spain his life would be in danger and having just read Gibbon's autobiography, he sat down and wrote a personal memoir: it opens with a sense of satisfaction, of completeness, for his life seemed 'to have been very unusually happy, and even successful: not that I have cut much figure in the world, but in that I have had what I really wanted – except war, which I hope to see before long'.[56] He also attended a meeting of the 'Apostles' at Cambridge and surprised his audience by reading a paper in which he declared the soldier his new-found ideal.

During this lull in Julian's affairs the rest of the family continued with their own lives. Clive was temporarily entranced with a young, wealthy American who was something of an intellectual and also a painter. Quentin was continuing his research into the history of Monaco in Paris, after a brief holiday at the Pinaults' country home at Gargilesse with Angelica and her friend from drama school, Chattie Salaman. Duncan spent two weeks in Paris that spring and Vanessa joined him for five days. With Quentin, whose mission was to persuade Picasso to attend a meeting in London to raise funds for the children of Bilbao, all three visited the artist's studio. He was occupying two floors of a seventeenth-century palace in the rue des Grands-Augustins. The rooms were bare except for a single, enormous canvas – *Guernica* – which was still in progress. Vanessa, normally oblivious of subject-matter, is said to have remarked, 'C'est un peu terrible.' Duncan, writing to Bunny, described the painting as 'very fine' and then went on to give a much lengthier description of the can-can at the Bal Tabarin which they had watched in the company of Segonzac.

The date of Julian's departure was announced suddenly by Spanish Medical Aid. From his remark to Stephen Spender, that this amateurishly-directed war could be won by a great strategist, it was evident that though he was going out as an ambulance driver, his true desire was to fight. On the day he finally left he drove his ambulance down to the port at Newhaven where he was met by Vanessa who took him back to Charleston for a meal. It was a perfect summer evening but it ended in panic for when the time came to leave the car would not start. Julian sent Vanessa off to Tilton to find alternative transport but before she returned he had managed to start the car and they arrived at Newhaven in plenty of time. Apart from Vanessa, Julian had left behind a trail of distressed women. As Vanessa explained to Quentin: 'He has left Jill and Innes – neither of whom knows about the other – Jill does know about 'X' [the Chinese lady] but Innes doesn't. 'Y' knows about everyone but no one knows about her – at least I think that's the situation.'[57]

By the time Julian reached Spain the Basque and Asturian resistance in the north had collapsed. To offset this failure the Government needed to make a demonstration on the Madrid front. Their initial attack had been a partial success; Franco's front had been broken and the Government troops had advanced about ten miles into fascist territory. Julian was sent out to the 35th Division Medical Service which had just been moved from El Goloso, about ten miles from Madrid, to El Escorial, about sixty miles away. There they received news of the Government's successful capture of Brunete, and this left Julian fuming with impatience at being kept so far from the front. The next morning, however, their unit was sent to Villanueva de la Cañada where they made their headquarters in an orchard and were now in sight of battle. When there was a lull in the fighting Julian proved himself an indefatigable worker, undertaking any task that came his way, scrounging for fruit, tools and rope from the ruined shops and gardens of the bombed town. During the bombing raids they had little sleep but often worked for twelve hours at a stretch; as the other ambulance drivers grew jaded, Julian's energy seemed to increase. He enjoyed the male society in which he lived, partnered himself with Richard Rees, a former editor of the *Adelphi*, and in his letters home revealed not the slightest doubt that he had made the right decision, that at last he had got 'excitement and events'.[58]

After Julian had left for Spain Vanessa spent a few days at Charleston alone. Duncan was in Toulon, from whence he paid a brief visit to Cassis to see the Teeds and inspect La Bergère, now let to French tenants. On his return he, Vanessa and Keith Baynes had a few strenuous days finally putting together the exhibition of contemporary British art that Agnew's had asked them to select. After it opened they went down to Charleston where they were joined by Quentin and Angelica. Standing on the landing one morning, Vanessa thought she saw a figure cross Quentin's room but when she looked inside found no one there. 'It gave me such a shock,' she told Julian, ' ... but of course was some trick of light or something. I am silly enough to be glad the figure was not more like you.'[59] Meanwhile Quentin's kiln had been installed and both she and Angelica tried their hand at throwing pots.

Despite Quentin's efforts, Picasso did not appear at the Albert Hall meeting to raise money for Spain: Bloomsbury, however, was there in force. Vanessa, as she had earlier decided to do, gave ten shillings; Virginia and Leonard, having agreed to give the same as Vanessa, gave a pound each; Helen Anrep having vowed only to give two shillings gave thirty, though she could least afford it. Wogan Philipps was also present, having just returned from Spain where he had been wounded in the arm while driving an ambulance. He told Vanessa that he had just missed seeing Julian at Valencia but had heard of his safe arrival.

The sight of Wogan with his arm in a sling did little to quell Vanessa's anxiety. She could, however, do nothing but bury her feelings and continue life as before. An exhibition of her work opened at the Lefevre Gallery and was favourably reviewed in the press, her portrait of Dora Morris reproduced in colour in the *Studio* magazine. She attended a cocktail party given by the Bussys and was introduced to Matisse. Tom Eliot was also present and Vanessa asked him if he would read one of Julian's essays and consider it for publication. She herself began sending Julian letter-diaries, as she had done before, while he was in China but never far from her mind. 'I can't talk of my own want of you,' she had once written, '– yet I think very soon now it will begin to seem easier to think of you as coming rather than as having gone. But I can't say anything that's of any use, only don't forget ever how I love you.'[60]

THIRTEEN

Bitter Odds

1937–1945

Situated immediately beneath the studios at 8 Fitzroy Street was a work-shop run by a master wood-carver called Ferro. On 20 July 1937 one of his employees, George Rivers, made for Vanessa a packing-case which she filled with parcels for Julian. Later that afternoon Rivers was startled by a cry which he never forgot. It came from above. For shortly after the case had been dispatched the telephone had rung, bringing news of Julian's death.

Five days previously Julian's ambulance had been damaged by a bomb; he had immediately volunteered as a stretcher-bearer and had been put in charge of thirty men in one of the most dangerous parts on the front. Then a lorry was found to help evacuate the wounded and Julian had been given charge of it. The morning of 18 July had begun quietly and he had taken the opportunity to drive out with William (Larry) Collier (whose mother's godfather had been Sir James Stephen) and fill in the shell-holes that pitted their route to the front. While they were at work aeroplanes flew overhead and they took cover beneath the lorry where Julian's body saved Collier's life by intercepting a piece of flying shrapnel. Minutes after he had been hit he began scribbling a note to Vanessa but got no further than two or three words. He was taken back to the sanatorium and though badly wounded in the chest and suffering a severe loss of blood, he was still conscious. As often happens with lung injuries, which are normally pain-less, the wound closed again. After a blood transfusion his mind became clear; he recognized several people, spoke intermittently quite coherently and appeared not to consider himself seriously wounded. Four surgeons, two English, two Spanish, had a short consultation, and decided to operate. After the shrapnel had been removed Julian remained in a coma, spoke in

French and six hours later died. He was buried in the cemetery at Fuen-carral, about two miles north of Madrid.

On the evening of 20 July Angelica was dancing with others from her drama school in a ballet based on Goya's *Desastres de la guerra*. Duncan went to the theatre to tell her the news. Arriving back at 8 Fitzroy Street she found Vanessa in bed, her face swollen with weeping and almost unable to speak. Vanessa now suffered a complete physical breakdown, a more severe form of that momentary collapse which she had experienced after Roger's death. For a few days she felt cut off, beyond human reach. The only person whose love and persistence were at first able to touch her was Virginia. Four years later Vanessa wrote to Vita, 'I remember all those days after I heard about Julian lying in an unreal state and hearing her voice going on and on keeping life going as it seemed when otherwise it would have stopped.'[1] She was given somnifene to help her sleep and was gradually persuaded to eat. By the 29 July she was well enough to be moved to Charleston where for the next few weeks she spent her days either lying on a bed in the studio, placed in one corner near the doors which opened on to the patio, or sitting in the garden. Virginia was constantly at her side. In the loosened-up emotional state that tragedy leaves in its wake, Virginia felt able to release what for many years she had been obliged to curb and partly conceal, her ineffable love for Vanessa. 'I rather think I'm more nearly attached to you than sisters should be,' she wrote to Vanessa, on one of the rare days that she did not come over from Rodmell. 'Why is it I never stop thinking of you, even when walking in the marsh this afternoon and seeing a great snake like a sea serpent gliding among the grass? ... Lord knows I can't say what it means to me to come into the room and find you sitting there.'[2]

Like others, Virginia wondered if Vanessa would ever get over this 'perpetual wound'. 'As you say, it is much worse for Vanessa than for me,' Clive wrote to Frances Marshall, who had married Ralph Partridge in the spring of 1933. 'My life is so full of things - mostly vanities - that the hole will fill up. What I mind most is not that a particular kind of family fun and good fellowship has lost an essential ingredient for ever; but that Julian will not get all the good things out of life which I think he would have got. ... But I doubt whether the hole in Vanessa's life will be filled up ever.'[3]

Some consolation was provided by the letters of condolence. Richard Rees told Vanessa that in his opinion Julian had reached in Spain a pinnacle of existence which would have been hard to surpass, that in the face of difficulties he had remained serene and competent. But it was Maynard who sent almost the only words that Vanessa wanted to keep. He wrote an article on Julian for the *Nation*, an obituary for the King's College Annual Report and a brief personal letter: 'My dearest Nessa, A line of sympathy and love from us both on the loss of your dear and beautiful boy with his pure and honourable feelings. It was fated that he should make his protest, as he was entitled to do, with his life, and one can say nothing.'[4] At the time Vanessa could do no more than scrawl in pencil on a scrap of paper a pathetic note of thanks, but three months later she wrote at length about Julian to Maynard: 'When Julian came back from China I was aware that he had become a grown-up and completely independent human being ... he could make up his own mind and knew what he wanted to do and why. That is the only thing that in the least reconciles me to his death. I feel that he wanted, not to die – no one could have wanted that less – but to run the risks he knew he would run for reasons he judged worthwhile.'[5] By then she had received from Eddie Playfair the letter Julian had written on board ship to China and which was to be given to her if anything happened to him. In this he wrote of his feeling of responsibility in the face of 'the idiotic and infernal muddle of the world', and admitted his desire to die violently and to take risks for causes of first-rate importance.[6] Vanessa told Maynard that this letter expressed 'something very fundamental in himself which would never have changed and in which I seem to myself to share'. She continued: 'During those last three months in England, in spite of terribly difficult differences of opinion, we had an intimacy with each other greater in a way than any I have ever had with anyone else and which could only have been possible with another grown-up human being.'[7]

Once the initial wave of shock passed she began slowly to regain her strength. At first she found her mind too distracted by grief to allow her to paint. Occasionally she broke down; Grace found her weeping in the garden one day because no one realized her need to talk about Julian. Behind her collapse lay the strain of the previous winter, for she had worried about Julian ever since he had written from China, announcing his return home. After giving way in front of Duncan, she sought to reassure him: 'One can't recover very quickly. But I expect I *shall*. It's difficult now to keep interested for long at a time and when one stops [painting] one feels as if that other existence were so remote – one forgets it somehow. You are the only person I can ever behave so stupidly to my dear. It's hard on you.'[8] The greater part of her emotions she repressed; she could not even tell Virginia of her gratitude to her. Only to Vita did Vanessa confess, 'I cannot ever say how Virginia has helped me. Perhaps some day, not now, you will be able to tell her it's true.'[9] Temporarily walled in by her feelings, it was only gradually that she was able to find

release through her painting. Perhaps to encourage her, Virginia asked if
she would undertake a portrait of Clive. Vanessa replied: 'I don't think I
can paint portraits at present. It needs a special kind of effort which I don't
think that I'm capable of ... I'm only working at small things which
matter to no one by myself.'[10]

She welcomed the distraction provided by close friends and relatives,
and among her visitors that summer were her brother Adrian and Helen
Anrep, who brought the Maurons. But others were kept away for she
needed seclusion. She could not soothe herself with false sentiment and
unburdened herself fully only to one person, the girl-friend in whom
Julian had confided everything.

> I have written so many stupid letters of thanks to other people, not that I was
> not really touched often by their letters, but what can one say? – but to you
> dear 'Y' I am writing last of all because I feel that I cannot write to you without
> trying to say something of what I really feel. . . .
>
> I think there is one thing I want desperately to say to any one who will listen
> – if only I could – and that is simply that I am quite sure, reasonably and
> definitely sure, that the loss of people like Julian *is* a waste. It is not my own
> pain that makes me say it. In fact I am not really to be pitied – not on the whole.
> I never doubt for an instant that I am immensely the richer for all the feelings
> I have had and shall ever have about Julian. But I am old enough to know a
> little what he might have done and been if he had lived. I know that his life
> would have given infinite good and possibilities of good to the world which
> are now lost. . . . Fascism wants to destroy intelligence – we must not let it do
> so. The world depends upon people like Julian to help it out of its troubles later
> – and their memory will not help as their presence would. . . .
>
> I think it is a natural and very understandable pain which makes people say
> 'it was worth while – it was not a waste' – it makes it so much worse to think
> it *was*. But I feel that even greater disasters may follow if one doesn't face the
> truth.
>
> . . . he wanted desperately to go, to have this experience of war and I couldn't
> go on objecting. Everyone said then there had been no casualties in the ambul-
> ance [corps] and would be none. I didn't believe it, but I believed enough to
> make me give in. If I had not I should still have done all I could to prevent him
> from going. But I should not have been successful. Something in him, perhaps
> something like my own feeling about painting, which made him himself,
> would have been too strong, and I'm glad I didn't try.
>
> Only you see there was no willing sacrifice on my part.[11]

Vanessa first managed to smile, after receiving news of Julian's death,
while listening to Virginia, Clive, Leonard and Quentin discuss the mis-
adventures of Duncan's boy-friends. That summer, while she lay on the
day-bed in the studio, he engaged a young Irishman, a former model of

his, to build a greenhouse, and admitted to Bunny, 'I like a completely uneducated intelligent person as a companion.'[12] When later this year another of his friends got a job as a hall porter, Vanessa remarked to Quentin that 'at the moment all Duncan's protégés seem to be disposed of'.[13]

If Duncan's wandering affections drew him away from Vanessa, it had always been unlikely that he would leave her; with the loss of Julian this unlikelihood became an impossibility. Vanessa's dependence left her in a dominant position; Duncan responded with a compliant passivity. This unbalanced relationship must have both diminished certain aspects of their natures and made others more pronounced. Yet to dwell on the misfortunate or tragic aspect of their love is to occlude the very real happiness that it also created. Vanessa had once described to Julian those qualities in Duncan's character that had become indispensable to her: 'He is so incredibly full of charm, his genius as an artist seems to overflow so into his life and character, and he is so amusing too and odd and unaccountable that lots of people I think don't see clearly what to me is really his most adorable quality – his honesty – disinterestedness, absolute sincerity and simplicity of character which make one depend upon him always in difficult moments. You can imagine that our relationship hasn't always been easy but owing to him – this is true, I don't say it out of modesty – it has always come through to something better.'[14]

Once the initial shock of Julian's death had passed, nothing, perhaps, was so revivifying to Vanessa as the sight of Duncan painting, daily and assiduously. Faced on the one hand with the blank wall of death, she must also have been comforted by the potential of art to create permanence or, as Louis remarks in *The Waves*, to 'oppose to what is passing this ramrod of beaten steel'.[15] Though Duncan and Vanessa never embraced in public, not even in front of the family, their intimacy was never more clearly expressed than when both sat painting together in the studio. Quentin has recalled, 'When we were all using the same model or working jointly on some decorative project I would be in the same studio as VB and DG and if I were asked to provide an example of human serenity and perfect happiness that is where I should look for it.'[16]

By October Vanessa was well enough to spend a few days in Paris looking at pictures with Duncan, Quentin and Angelica. Helen Anrep was also staying at the Hôtel de Londres. She received a visit from her son Igor, Olivier Popham and the painter Graham Bell, all of whom were halted on the stairs by Helen in order to allow Vanessa to escape from the hotel without the bother of introductions.

That autumn Vanessa returned to her life at Fitzroy Street and was intermittently involved with the new school of painting and drawing founded that year by the artists Claude Rogers, William Coldstream, Victor Pasmore and the South-African-born Graham Bell. In April Vanessa had written to Claude Rogers offering to drum up support for the school by writing to potential patrons, among them Kenneth Clark whose financial contribution enabled Pasmore to give up his job with the London County Council. When, on the suggestion of Jane Clark, a prospectus was drawn up, Vanessa advised that it should be printed on good-quality paper. With Duncan she did all she could to help, sending out prospectuses and agreeing to act as a visiting teacher, on indefinite terms and at irregular intervals.

All four of the artists in charge of the school had come to feel that modern art, especially the extreme asceticism of recent abstract art, had lost contact with life and spoke only to a cultured élite. Coldstream and Bell had for a period stopped painting, feeling unable to see any way forward. They had both returned to their art convinced that 'the only aspect of painting that is really engrossing is the exploration of expression in paint, by actual experience, of the material world'.[17] Like Pasmore and Rogers, they grew increasingly convinced of the need for realistic painting, not the 'pseudo-realism of the Royal Academy' which relied on formulae, but a style that depended on a dedication to observation. 'Observation' became a key word at the school which declared that it made no attempt to impose a style on the students but merely to train the eye. In practice it encouraged an unemphatic, restrained realism in which the muscular bravura popularized by Duncan was noticeably absent. What is surprising about Vanessa's and Duncan's support of the school (they, with Augustus John and John Nash, agreed to act as visiting teachers) is that the method it extolled was opposed to certain Bloomsbury mannerisms, to the use of blue outlines, sensuous modelling and baroque curves. In spite of this Clive Bell, who coined the title 'Euston Road School' in 1938, confidently announced 'this [1938] is a critical moment for English painting, the most hopeful we have known for a hundred years'.[18]

Vanessa's and Duncan's part in the Euston Road School again demonstrates their willingness to associate themselves with artists who had political affiliations. Whether or not the Euston Road School's realism is seen as retrograde or revolutionary, it arose from a desire to paint in a style that could be widely understood. In 1938 it put on an exhibition at Eardley Knollys's Storran Gallery entitled 'Paintings of London' and sent private view cards to every tenth Brown, Jones and Smith in the London telephone directory. Moreover a chance passer-by, literally a man-in-the-street, was asked to open it.

Partly because of its close proximity to her studio (the school opened at 12 Fitzroy Street under the name of The School of Drawing and Painting and moved early in 1938 to 316 Euston Road) and partly because of Helen Anrep's enthusiastic support of the venture, Vanessa took considerable interest in its progress. 'The school has started and is said to be going well,' she told Quentin in October 1937. 'Most of the pupils are part-time but they have about 15 and everyone is happy and cheerful.'[19] Moreover it had models in the evening which she and Duncan could draw if they wished. They painted alongside the students, teaching by example, but did also occasionally offer criticism. In December that year Vanessa agreed to let Helen give a party in her studio in an attempt to raise money for the school.

The other project that absorbed much of her attention at this time was the collection of Julian's papers for publication. She wrote to several of his friends asking for his letters and received visits from Richard Rees, Eddie Playfair and others. Barbara Mackenzie-Smith, seeing Vanessa by chance in a shop for the first time since Julian's death, said something unequal to what she was feeling and was surprised by the quickness of Vanessa's understanding. But Angelica at this time found it impossible to speak to her mother about Julian because anything she tried to say seemed so feeble by comparison with Vanessa's evident suffering.

Vanessa turned to Quentin and to Bunny for help with the editing of Julian's letters. The latter had for some time enjoyed a prominent position in London's literary world; since the appearance of his best-seller *Lady into Fox* in 1922, he had produced a steady stream of novels, including *Pocahontas* which had become a Book Society choice. He had also become literary editor of the *New Statesman* under Kingsley Martin and in this position had given Julian books on military history to review. But as early as 1925, shortly before the appearance of his *The Sailor's Return*, he had candidly admitted to Duncan: 'I am, I'm afraid, thoroughly second rate. I find concentration fearfully difficult, and spend a lot of time botching my work; always saying to myself, Perhaps if I had a new pen, or lived in the country, or had a secretary, or dictated into a phonograph, then I should do everything perfectly – work all day long, etc., etc. All this comes from being rather parasitic on other people's brains and characters I suppose.'[20] Nevertheless Lytton thought *The Sailor's Return* good. Vanessa admired the descriptions of the coast and countryside around West Wittering which Bunny put into *No Love* in 1929 and which sold well and helped him clear his debts. Living at Hilton Hall in Huntingdonshire since 1924 he had remained a little apart from Vanessa and Duncan until the late twenties when the hospitality he had offered Julian while he was at Cambridge had reopened friendship. His wife Ray never became a part of Bloomsbury and because of her shyness and reserve was nicknamed 'the silent woman'. Vanessa once admitted: 'She terrifies me and I lose my head and power of speech when alone with her and when other people are there one tends to ignore her.'[21] The fact that she did not know Bunny's wife at all well made it easy for her to overlook Ray's feelings when Bunny began to flirt with Angelica. She was amused to discover that her daughter wrote him love letters. He continued to take her out to dinner on his visits to London and charmed her with his story-telling, his rich store of experiences and his familiarity with famous writers. Vanessa perceived how his attraction for Angelica grew but still did not take it too seriously; nor was she averse to the thought of her daughter's having a brief affair with an older man.

In December she left with Angelica for Cassis by train. They stayed at Fontcreuse because La Bergère was temporarily let. They ate dinner with Colonel Teed and Jean Campbell but otherwise led a separate existence, having a sitting-room to themselves in the tower of the small château. There, with the aid of wood fires, they allowed Christmas to pass almost unnoticed. It was six years since Vanessa had been to Cassis yet, as always, she found it encouraged a purely sensual existence. Soon they were joined by Quentin, first, and then by Duncan who had been in Paris with his mother. They made a visit to the Maurons at St-Rémy where they sat all day in the kitchen, Marie keeping up a flow of talk while she prepared delicious meals. Charles produced an introduction he had written at Vanessa's request to the book of Julian's letters and essays, and Quentin translated it, afterwards going over it again with Charles before they left.

In the tower at Fontcreuse, while snow lay on the ground outside, Vanessa worked on a dust-jacket for a novel by Edward Upward which the Hogarth Press was publishing. About this time she also created the blue and pink dust-jacket for Virginia's *Three Guineas*, basing her design entirely on the title.* When in the summer she reworked the design for the American edition Leonard declared it her most successful dust-jacket. At Cassis she also refers in one letter to work on a lithograph, which must have meant she was drawing on lithographic paper for subsequent transference to the lithographic plate or stone. Meanwhile Angelica read *Trilby*

---

* She rarely did more than this, as she admitted in a letter to John Lehmann: 'Thank you so much for the dummy. I will do my best to let you have the design soon. Until it is done I don't think I can decide about a coloured top but I will let you know then. I've not read a word of the book - I only have had the vaguest description of it and what she wants me to do from Virginia - but that has always been the case with the jackets I have done for her.' Quoted in John Lehmann's *Thrown to the Woolfs*, London, 1978, p. 27.

and in the evenings Colonel Teed recounted all the recent Cassis scandal. After Jean disappeared to bed he reminisced still more freely about life in the nineties.

Before the end of January they had returned to London. Though Vanessa found Julian's birthday on 4 February hard to bear, her attention was now chiefly occupied by Angelica. According to Bunny there was one moment at Charleston when it became obvious to all that Angelica was no longer a schoolgirl: 'Quite how far she was aware of the possibilities when she came and curled up in my lap, throwing an arm carelessly about my neck and resting her cheek against my own, I can't say. It was in the studio at Charleston where we all gathered together. Vanessa watched the scene with high amusement, throwing me occasional mocking glances. Duncan, who was probably painting, took no notice.'[22]

By early April 1938 Duncan had been forced to take notice. Formerly he and Vanessa had regarded the letters that Bunny sent Angelica as rather a joke, but now realized their seriousness when she refused to open them until after breakfast. Duncan discussed the matter with Vanessa and agreed that a mild affair between Angelica and Bunny would not be bad, so long as it did not become serious, but he was shocked when one day in London Bunny admitted that he was in danger of becoming too fond of Angelica. As Bunny was twenty-six years older than Angelica, Duncan thought the idea at first too preposterous to be taken seriously. Still he did nothing until one day an avalanche of letters for Angelica arrived from Bunny. Then, with Vanessa's agreement, he wrote to Bunny asking what his 'intentions' were, adding that he hoped they were 'honourable' as Angelica's heart was becoming touched. Both he and Vanessa were aware that the letter had a Victorian flavour, and though amused by the old-fashioned word 'intentions' they could think of nothing better.

Soon after this letter had been sent Bunny arrived at Charleston on a visit. Everyone was pleased at his coming, though he soon made it evident that he and Angelica wanted to spend much time alone. Vanessa asked Duncan to approach Bunny about their letter, to which he had not replied, and Duncan did so one evening in his bedroom, the room where Angelica had been born. Duncan recorded what happened in the same notebook into which twenty years earlier he had poured out his troubled relationship with Bunny.

> He said he would rather talk about it another time. This angered me and I said now was a good opportunity and I thought he ought to do so. He then said it was absurd was it not for me to talk about seduction and morals like a Victorian father. This I'm afraid enraged me and I told him I thought it would be a great mistake for him to start a serious affair with A just now when she was just

entering on life and that of course she would have to have a love affair soon but that I had hoped it would be with a person to some degree inexperienced and not with someone of his age. This I think touched him to the quick and he shortly after left the room saying good night to which I did not answer. I was very much agitated by the whole affair because all sorts of unnecessary emotions had suddenly welled up inside me, which I do not rightly understand even now. My heart beat very fast and I could not get to sleep for a long time. In the night I woke from a dream when Quentin came into my room his throat encircled with blood saying 'I met Angelica coming out of B's room'.

The whole thing may be of course jealousy on my part, mixed up with some curious complex/taboo about sex.[23]

The next day, speaking hardly a word, he drove Bunny to the station. Bunny warned him against interference which might affect Angelica adversely: Duncan was too enraged to reply. Soon after this Bunny wrote to Vanessa complaining of Duncan's behaviour. He admitted that his love for Angelica was mixed up with his love of Vanessa and Duncan and of the past, but he still thought it as strong, sincere and unselfish in so far as love can be. But the chief purpose of this letter was to warn Vanessa that Duncan's jealousy might hurt Angelica: 'It will do just the mischief that Julian was afraid of – producing the despair – the feeling of being sent back to the nursery – of never growing up. ... any sort of interference and suspicion and Victorian denial of freedom, however it is shown (teasing is as cruel as forbidding – or as agonized solicitude) will permanently injure her self-confidence.'[24] Vanessa accepted his warning and decided to trust in Angelica's good sense. She still felt that an affair with Bunny would do her daughter no harm. Duncan, however, knew how blindly Bunny could behave when his emotions were aroused, and feared his instability.

Vanessa felt that Bunny's love for Angelica, coming at the time of Julian's death, had helped restore her daughter's confidence in life. 'I want her happiness more than almost anything,' she told Bunny, 'and I'm simply very grateful to you for giving her so much.'[25] She knew there were risks involved but felt this was true of any relationship. She was also aware that Bunny was partly attracted to Angelica because of her likeness to Duncan, and that the situation was still more complicated because, now that George Bergen no longer wrote from America, Duncan's strongest emotional interest was Angelica.

Over the next few months Vanessa realized that Bunny was her chief access to her daughter whose confidence she had now lost. This she admitted to Bunny in August, by which time Angelica had begun to consider giving up the theatre for painting:

I've really been getting very much upset for some time Bunny – I've rather wanted to talk to you about it – because I think I get terribly on her nerves at times. No doubt mothers are apt to. But I feel sure with me its largely owing to the fact that the young *can't* understand unhappiness. ... Probably Angelica thinks me gloomy and forbidding often when I am really incapable of getting back to life. If she is tired or cross she can be very crushing and so we just remain at a long distance from each other. It makes me very unhappy. ... I told her that I knew I must have been a gloomy companion all this last year, since Julian died, that I hadn't really been able to get back to work again, which I think is the only refuge, and that I felt as if the fact that she was becoming definitely a painter might make it easier for me to do so.[26]

Having lost the intimacy which she had enjoyed with Julian, she was anxious not to lose Angelica's trust. She was aware that her grief – for her mind still constantly returned to Julian – put a barrier between herself and her daughter, and she regretted that both she and Julian had omitted to tell Angelica of his departure for Spain until the last moment. Though Bunny told Vanessa of his fear that Angelica had fallen in love with someone else while acting in a production of *Gammer Gurton's Needle* that summer, Angelica told her nothing and would remain silent if Vanessa or Quentin mentioned Bunny. 'But keep me close, please,' Vanessa implored Bunny, as if he were her lifeline to that which remained central, her joy in her children. 'Oh Quentin,' she once wrote, 'even now, please realize that you – and Angelica – can and do sometimes give me moments of exquisite happiness.'[27]

As the political situation worsened during the course of this year, Vanessa offered her service through Leonard to any worthwhile cause – 'I can read and write, even type-write, and have no pride.'[28] Julian's essays and letters were now ready for publication, but at the last moment she had to go through the proofs taking out the punctuation which John Lehmann had put in, in a misguided attempt to improve the original. She also attended a performance of Stephen Spender's play *Trial of a Judge*, despite Virginia's warning that she might find it too harrowing. And she continued to take an interest in the Euston Road School, which had collected more pupils and enough money to pay the rent on 316 Euston Road until October 1938. When Sickert lectured at the school in July, Vanessa and Duncan gave him lunch beforehand at 8 Fitzroy Street.[29] That autumn she exhibited in the Salon d'Automne in Paris where her *Garden in April* was praised in *The Scotsman*. At Charleston she still tended to confine herself in her choice of subject to the house and to the garden, which Walter Higgens anxiously overwatered that summer in preparation for the Firle flower show, at which, to his disappointment, he won only a third prize. But occasionally she did venture a little further, painting the view of a nearby barn offset by the pale, brilliant colours of summer. She was now and then entertained by the letters that Virginia produced, written by friends of Roger Fry to help her with the writing of his biography. Helen Anrep's visits to Charleston also helped remind Vanessa of Roger and the two women would sit up reminiscing till all hours of the night, irritating Clive whose bedroom was directly overhead.

But if she saw friends, she still shunned society. She refused the Bussys' annual cocktail party that year as well as another given by the Clarks, finding the effort of getting dressed for such occasions too much. She carefully protected her privacy and her working hours: Julian Morrell, daughter of Lady Ottoline, sat to Duncan for her portrait at this time and after one long session requested a light studio lunch: Vanessa, in grudging silence, produced such rough-cut sandwiches that the request was never repeated. Still more exclusive was Vanessa's attitude to the Memoir Club, which she admitted was in need of new and younger members: Julia Strachey, Janie Bussy, Pippa Strachey, Sebastian Sprott, Helen Anrep and Vita Sackville-West were all proposed at this time and all, by herself or by others, found wanting. During the anxious summer of 1938, when war seemed inevitable, the Memoir Club met at Tilton to hear Maynard read his now famous paper 'My Early Beliefs', in which he reflected on the value and limitations of the Bloomsbury attitude of mind. His painful conclusion – that rationalism, instead of enriching human nature, had impoverished it – must have perplexed Vanessa who continued to place her trust in rational thought and behaviour.

Shortly after the reading of this paper Vanessa, Duncan, Quentin and Angelica left for Cassis, crossing France while the Munich crisis was at its height. They picked up news from shopkeepers and from the groups of men who stood around street corners discussing mobilization. Vanessa had the impression that the further south they drove the closer they came to horror and calamity. She came now to depend on Quentin, for he remained cheerful, calm and sensible. 'I can't stand nowadays being separated from him [for] very long,' she told Bunny.[30] But soon after they arrived at Cassis news of the settlement came through and, though opinion was divided on Chamberlain's achievement, Vanessa gave her former acquaintance credit for starting face-to-face talks.

Once installed at La Bergère they pulled out paintings and a box of old letters left behind from their previous visits. 'It's odd to be living in this house again,' Vanessa told Virginia, 'with Elise coming as she used to. . . . Angelica was a child when we were here before – now she cooks our supper and is rather more grown up than the rest of us. I feel incredibly old – as indeed I am. But one doesn't realize it so much till one comes back to a place one hasn't been to for years.'[31] Their visit coincided with the *vendange*, and in order to capture the varied poses of the grape-pickers Vanessa and Duncan followed them about discreetly, attempting quick sketches.

She did a great deal of painting on this visit and led an anti-social life. When the others went down to Cassis, to a café or to play *boules*, she stayed at La Bergère. Most evenings found them playing poker until Quentin left for England, and then they read aloud, *Persuasion* and *Mrs Dalloway*, sitting by the wood fire and sipping brandy made on the estate. In mid November they returned home, stopping at the Maurons' *en route* and at various inns which Angelica selected for their gastronomic excellence.

There were passages in *Mrs Dalloway* that Vanessa thought had unsurpassed beauty. When in the spring of 1939 she read the short story 'The Searchlight' (later published in *A Haunted House*) she thought of illustrating it, and told Virginia: 'It seems to me lovely – only too full of suggestions for pictures almost. They leap into my mind at every turn. Your writing always does that for me to some extent, but I think this one more than usual.'[32] Virginia, who was in France and had just given Vanessa some money to pay for models, replied: 'I was all of a heap that you liked my story – the only person in the world whose opinion can help me. ... Oh how divine to see you again – it spoils my holiday, being away from you, who are the source of all joy and succulence. And kiss Angelica, and Quentin. ... And love me. And have models. And paint me a picture.'[33] She received a small painting of Quentin reading in return.

Convinced by her visit to France that she now preferred a country existence, and aware of the increasing probability of war, Vanessa made several alterations to Charleston that year. An ante-room was built in the space between the kitchen and the washhouse; the larder next to the studio was given French windows and made into a bedroom for herself; her previous bedroom was converted into a book room, with shelves running round three walls; the small attic bedroom was converted into a studio with a five-panel north-facing window; a new door (salvaged from another house) was fitted to the front porch and its brick surround made; a new sink was put into the kitchen; an old chicken-house was converted into a pottery; and finally the garden wall was mended. The chaos all this created was considerable, the dust worse, and Vanessa, confused by the new arrangement of doorways, found herself disappearing into cupboards. These alterations were timely on two scores: they prepared the house for their permanent residence during the war and they brought new life to a place now painfully associated with the past.

Vanessa was supervising these alterations when Duncan called her back to London because Angelica had fallen ill. At Bunny's insistence she had seen a Dr Richards and been sent straight into a nursing-home. It was a bad attack of cystitis which was fairly easily cured by drugs; but the anxiety and upset this small crisis caused was out of all proportion to the relative insignificance of the disease.

It began when Bunny went round to 8 Fitzroy Street to tell Duncan the news that Angelica, in severe pain, had been rushed into a nursing-home for tests. Duncan panicked, fearing Vanessa's response to this event, and in the few moments that followed Bunny felt closer to Duncan than he had been since Julian's death. Vanessa, after she had been brought to the studio by Duncan's telegram, collapsed with shock on hearing the news. Bunny went round to the nursing-home alone and sat talking with Angelica until the other two arrived. Vanessa, by then having regained her composure and apparently free from any undue emotion, chatted with Angelica about the alterations at Charleston. Before leaving they asked Bunny to dine with them that evening in her studio.

For a few minutes before the meal Bunny was alone with Vanessa and she asked him bluntly if Angelica was pregnant. Relieved to hear that she was not, she then added that if this eventuality ever occurred he must tell her at once because an abortion was easier to perform in the early stages. This appalled Bunny as her suggestion took no account of what Angelica's feelings might be, but he could not reply for at that moment Clive appeared and a jovial dinner began. Bunny was still smarting from Vanessa's words when at some point during the meal she commented how strange it was that Angelica had not let her know she had been in pain. He now blurted out that Angelica had not wanted her to know she was ill. His implication – that Angelica no longer placed her trust in her mother – wounded Vanessa and infuriated Duncan, both feeling also that Bunny had no right to make arrangements regarding Angelica without consulting them. Bunny at once left the meal, but met Vanessa the following morning at Angelica's bedside. He apologized for his behaviour the night before, but the matter did not end there. Later, after Dr Richards had confirmed that Angelica was suffering from cystitis, Vanessa suggested to her that Angelica could recuperate in her studio. Bunny immediately flared up at this suggestion and said Angelica ought not to be moved, that Vanessa could not nurse her adequately and that she would only try to get up too soon. Vanessa was furious and the next day Bunny received a terse note saying that she preferred not to have differences of opinion with him in front of Dr Richards.

The next time they met either side of Angelica's bed, all three at first sat in silence. Bunny resorted to telling a story about a cat which had jumped out of a nursing-home window after a pigeon and fallen to its death. Vanessa remarked that her cat was too sensible to do a thing like that. Bunny argued that she couldn't expect her cat to be as reasonable as herself. With deep irony Vanessa replied that *he* could not think she was flattering the cat too much to suppose it. The conversation had become so bitterly absurd that when Bunny and Angelica laughed, Vanessa also relaxed and engaged willingly in another subject.

But it had now become evident that Bunny and Angelica were severely critical of Vanessa, chiefly of her silences which hid much. Angelica did not know that Vanessa called Duncan 'Bear' in her letters and she rarely saw any physical expression of their love. Vanessa had never talked with her about Duncan's fondness for young men and had constantly protected her from subjects that might cause pain. Only in 1937, after Julian's death, had she admitted to Angelica her true parentage. She had suppressed much, acting out of kindness but causing unfortunate results. Constantly indulged, her talents praised, Angelica sometimes felt as if she had been brought up in a glass case, isolated from normality and quite deserted after Julian had departed for China and then Spain. Bunny, meanwhile, had now fallen deeply in love with her. From the spring of this year he knew that his wife's cancer had returned, but he still came often to London, having secretly taken a room in Fitzroy Street to facilitate his meetings with Angelica.

Duncan now sent Bunny a piece of his diary. In it he had recorded his fury at the other man's suggestion that Vanessa mismanaged her relationship with her daughter. In reply to this, Bunny urged both Duncan and Vanessa to talk of their feelings openly in front of Angelica; to talk of their love for each other and what they had felt when they were her age. It depended on them, he said, to break down the reserve between Angelica and her mother.

Vanessa, but not Duncan, took Bunny's advice; but once she had exposed her feelings she could not control them and became hysterical. Angelica, formerly maddened by Vanessa's silences, found this contrary display an unnerving experience and one she did not wish to repeat; it left behind, she felt, a 'fermenting wound which neither of us dared to touch'.[34]

That summer both Vanessa and Duncan sublet their studios to Basil Rocke and Victor Pasmore respectively. A good many of the canvases and belongings that over the years had collected in the studios were removed to Charleston, along with Angelica's piano and Clive's books from 50 Gordon Square. At Charleston Vanessa had difficulty in restraining her

terror as an endless procession of canvases, many of them nudes, emerged
from the two removal vans. It took five days to sort out and put away all
the books, china, cigarette cards and odds and ends. At the same time
Quentin and Grace helped Vanessa prepare her new downstairs bedroom,
furnished with, among other things, her Provençal desk, a rug designed
by Duncan, a screen decorated by him and his painting of a Spanish dancer.

These appear in the painting Vanessa executed shortly after moving into
this room[§]. The subject allows for a richly orchestrated arrangement of
warm colours – purples, dull reds, ochres and browns, cooled by touches
of green and the blue and silver highlights. The figure holding the broom
is anonymous and merely acts as a compositional link between the background wall, where a glimpse of Duncan's *Spanish Dancer* can be seen, and
the foreground chair. As in Van Gogh's painting of Gauguin's chair, the
empty chair placed next to the desk evokes awareness of its owner and of
its use. The open desk, displaying paper and pens, is prepared for the
letter-writer and its presence in her room must have reminded Vanessa of
the many letters she had sent Julian, whose absence now permeated Charleston. Her painting, though it is directed by formal considerations, is also
replete with associative values. Three years earlier Vanessa had reflected:

> But yet it seems to me always the *visual* relationship that is important in
> painting. There is a language simply of form and colour that can be as moving
> as any other and that seems to affect one quite as much as the greatest poetry of
> words. At least so it seems to me but I admit that it is very difficult to be sure
> for of course the form and colour nearly always do represent life and I suppose
> any allusions may creep in.[35]

Now that Vanessa, Duncan, Quentin and Angelica lived permanently
at Charleston and all painted, the life of the house was dominated by this
activity. Still lifes, guarded by placards saying 'Please do not touch',
inhabited corners of the rooms; on fine days the artists might take to the
garden in straw hats and, with some of the brushes and oils that abounded
at Charleston, would paint views of the flower-beds, paths, statues and
flint walls in an impressionistic idiom. Inside the house the decorated
surfaces continued to accumulate, the sensuality of these patterns and
colours stunning many visitors.

One occasional guest was the young artist Nigel Henderson who was
later to marry Judith Stephen, the daughter of Adrian and Karin, by whom
he had been informally adopted in his adolescence. He had known Julian
at Cambridge and had first been invited to Charleston for a weekend some
years before. He had been met at Lewes station by Vanessa and Angelica:

> I had only briefly met Vanessa hitherto at one or two parties in her or Duncan

Grant's studio and was a little taken aback by the figure that met my train at Lewes, and overtopping Angelica who was beside her. . . .

As I remember she wore a . . . very old and rather fatigued hat. Was she not in a polo-necked jersey, rather long, a long skirt and . . . old gym shoes? I don't remember the specifics but none of this would have raised an eyebrow on any '60s campus but was a Declaration of Independence which I found formidable, backed up by an engaging shyness and apparent unconsciousness of the bizarre figure she cut in those semi-formal times. We all crammed quite easily into the Baby Austin with Vanessa at the wheel. I was intensely nervous and shy too and I think the conversation was as stilted as the driving, in spite of the fact that I was already beginning to feel that the wonderful thing about visual artists was that they gave themselves entirely to that which was before them, were absolutely present in the here and now; and here was this impressive lady, impossible for me to read, and her beautiful daughter in the alarmingly exhilarating intimacy of a mobile hen coop.[36]

However informal the daily life and style of dress at Charleston, the underlying attitude to emotions and behaviour was anything but sloppy. 'They were very, very self-controlled,' Angelica has recalled, '. . . we were all very good-mannered with each other; we didn't step beyond certain limits, and our feelings, I think, seethed underneath and didn't come out.'[37] Vanessa, still unable to talk openly about her feelings to Angelica, welcomed Bunny's visits to Charleston but found the situation between him, herself and her daughter difficult. On one occasion Duncan was absent and to him she wrote:

> I feel somewhat detached and really don't much mind what happens – the whole thing is rather like what it used to be when one saw a nurse being foolish with one's child and had to wait till it stopped. But this evening we began to talk about pre-war days – parties in Regent Sq^{re} with the Oliviers, etc. Angelica seemed amused at first but said nothing. Then got more and more aloof and finally retired to bed seemingly in a huff while Bunny had become excited and even affectionate to me. What a strange creature she is. I can't do anything but try to take no notice.[38]

Even the imaginative effort necessary to sympathize with Angelica was momentarily impossible. 'The world is too full of pain,' Vanessa wrote to Edward Sackville-West. 'You must come to Charleston some day and see all the changes we have been making here – new studios, etc. which we now hope may just be done before the war begins, with luck.'[39]

On 3 September Britain and France declared war on Germany. Bunny was in Ireland at the time, having joined his wife and two sons for a holiday, and was called back by the Air Ministry. When he next visited Charleston, in early October, he was dressed in Flight-Lieutenant's uniform. Quentin had the year previously been rejected by the Territorials, since he had had tuberculosis, and now began work as a farm labourer for Maynard. Duncan's mother and Aunt Violet had arrived from Twickenham for safety, as Clive, with his *mauvaise langue*, describes: 'And so we have Duncan's Aunt Violet – blind in one eye, deaf in one ear, half-witted and harmless; and Duncan's mother whom I find trying. She has good qualities; but she is a Mem Sahib at heart, self-complacent, petty and esurient. She chatters incessantly and trivially about infinitely uninteresting relations and friends, and her heart bleeds for poor old Miss Horner and her six cantankerous dogs whom nobody loves. She even threw out a hint that the old vixen might be found a room here, but there Vanessa stood firm.'[40] She also stood firm on the length of their visit: when the papers declared that the Twickenham area was unlikely to be bombed, Vanessa made sure this was generally known and before long the two ladies returned home. Clive, meanwhile, was determined to keep civilization alive, and in an official capacity he sat on a British Council committee which arranged for British art to be sent abroad. He felt the world was changing radically, but in November comforted himself with six volumes of Madame de Sévigné for they enabled him to believe that certain things he cared about might survive.

They suffered no physical hardship. Vanessa had bought chickens which they kept for eggs, and with Walter Higgens as full-time gardener they grew more vegetables than usual. Grace still acted as housekeeper and was now joined by Lottie who had been Clive's cook in London. Vanessa also employed local help with the cleaning of the house, so that throughout this period there were three employees at Charleston and ample food. There was also entertainment, for at the start of the war Michal Lewis, the daughter of the concert pianist Mark Hambourg, came from Firle every Sunday and played the piano while Angelica sang. Michal was also present at the twenty-first birthday party given for Angelica that winter which Duncan thought 'a miracle of organization' on the part of Vanessa and the cook Lottie.

The war did, however, adversely affect the sales of *Julian Bell. Essays, Poems and Letters* which the Hogarth Press had published in the autumn of 1938. At first it had sold reasonably well but, despite several short favourable reviews, it had not received the attention Vanessa had hoped. It had been critically reviewed in the *London Mercury* by Janet Adam Smith who declared that Bloomsbury was incapable of dealing with human tragedy. Meanwhile Virginia's praise of *Julian Bell* left Vanessa bitterly reflecting that her sister had done little to praise Julian's writing while he lived. However, when her biography of Roger Fry appeared in July 1940, its narrative ease, restrained wit and appreciation, its tact and straightforwardness, won Vanessa's approval and helped wipe out her resentment. After finishing the typescript, she picked up a pen at midnight and sent Virginia a five-line note: 'Since Julian died I haven't been able to think of Roger. Now you have brought him back to me. Although I cannot help crying I can't thank you enough. VB.'[41]

In May 1940 Bunny took Angelica to his cottage Butts Intake at Low Row, near Richmond in Yorkshire. Two months earlier his wife had died, disseminated cancer having set in the previous November. While Ray Garnett had lived, Bunny's affair with Angelica had been kept a secret, even from Virginia. 'I ought to have telephoned you before leaving Charleston,' Angelica wrote to Virginia, ' – please forgive me for not doing so or not coming to tea but the emotional situation at Charleston got me down.'[42] It had been left to Vanessa to break the news to her sister, who was not pleased, but less shocked than expected. The fact of Angelica's living with Bunny was still to be kept within the family for Duncan worried that if news of it spread it would upset his mother. When Desmond MacCarthy and G.E. Moore visited the Woolfs in May and Vanessa went over for tea (meeting the philosopher for the first time), she told Desmond that Angelica had gone to Yorkshire but did not say with whom.

Unlike some artists, Vanessa and Duncan were relatively unaffected by war. On one of her infrequent day visits to London Vanessa arranged with the Leicester Galleries to have an exhibition in June–July 1941, having now despaired of Lefevre's. Concurrently the Tate Gallery was negotiating the acquisition of Duncan's large painting of Angelica playing the piano in the garden room. They still enjoyed the support of Kenneth Clark, then Director of the National Gallery, and on one of their visits to London in May called at his rooms in Gray's Inn. They found there Victor Pasmore as well as the Graham Sutherlands whom Vanessa invited to Charleston for a weekend. Always quick to discern when decoration had been chosen for social rather than aesthetic reasons, she remarked to Angelica: 'I was interested to see how these lovely shabby college rooms can be converted into the height of chic and *luxe*, rather horrifying to my mind. All the same I spent the next morning entirely at the studio cleaning, destroying rubbish.'[43]

Later in May Duncan travelled on a war artist's commission, to Plymouth where he found John Nash and Eric Kennington already at work. On Kennington's advice, Duncan avoided the docks, where security was very tight, and confined himself instead to the naval barracks where he made many friends. While he was away the fear of invasion increased; the

Germans had now taken Arras and Amiens and aeroplanes seemed to fly regularly over Charleston. It had become impossible to escape the depression of war, even though it also had its humorous side. Clive and Quentin enrolled with the Home Guard and, in a state not entirely sober, kept watch at night in the nearby gamekeeper's tower. Walter Higgens was also willing to join, if he could belong not to the Firle but to the Selmeston corps which met conveniently in his regular haunt, the Barley Mow. 'There is a great deal of feeling among the wives about the part the Barley Mow plays in the whole affair,' Vanessa told Duncan.[44]

It now seemed unpatriotic to keep Walter Higgens on as a full-time gardener; he found a job in the sandpits at Berwick and for the rest of the war Clive, Vanessa and Duncan looked after the garden themselves. The labour this afforded was in fact welcome, for the most dispiriting thing that year was the amount of time spent waiting for news. In June the dealers Reid and Lefevre announced they were closing at the end of July; Dunbar Hay, where Duncan and Vanessa sold needlework designs, also shut down. When bombing raids began on London, Phyllis Keyes' pottery was destroyed, as was the Woolfs' house in Tavistock Square, in which the sitting-room had been decorated by Vanessa and Duncan. Peter Quennell walked past and saw the fireplace 'now unsupported by hearth or floor, but still surrounded by a ghostly suggestion of garlands and fruit and horns of plenty'.[45] The designs were already flaking and next time he passed they had altogether vanished. In September 1940 an incendiary bomb fell on the workshop next to 8 Fitzroy Street; the fire caught Duncan's studio and spread to Vanessa's. Until the debris had been cleared no one was allowed in to assess the extent of the damage. 'Vanessa takes it very philosophically,' Duncan told his mother, 'and says she can always paint more pictures.'[46] Fortunately several of Vanessa's paintings were on exhibition, at Agnew's and elsewhere, and many of their belongings had been moved down to Charleston before the war began. When she and Duncan went in to salvage what they could (a fridge, stove, bath and some of Duncan's and Angelica's clothes) they found that very few of the paintings had survived. They received financial compensation (Duncan £1,700 and Vanessa £1,200) but this was not paid until the war ended. Clive was put out because he had occasionally used Vanessa's studio to sleep in on his visits to London and had now to resort to Claridge's.

In March 1941 Virginia fell ill. Vanessa wrote her a letter in which harsh advice on the need to rest was tempered by an admission of need: 'What shall we do when we're invaded if you are a helpless invalid – what should I have done all those last 3 years if you hadn't been able to keep me alive and cheerful. You don't know how much I depend on you.'[47] Virginia's reply was one of three suicide notes.

> You can't think how I loved your letter. But I feel that I have gone too far this time to come back again. I am certain now that I am going mad again. It is just as it was the first time, I am always hearing voices, and I know I shan't get over it now. . . .
>
> I can hardly think clearly any more. If I could I would tell you what you and the children have meant to me. I think you know.
>
> I have fought against it, but I can't any longer.[48]

On 28 March she disappeared. Her gardener Mr Bartholomew telephoned Vanessa who went to Rodmell and saw Leonard. Meanwhile Angelica, who was now living near by at Claverham with Bunny, bicycled over to Charleston and was there with Quentin when Vanessa, very calm and controlled, returned. Later that day Duncan returned from London and Vanessa and Angelica broke the news to him in the kitchen: for a brief space all three clung together in a rare moment of physical and emotional intimacy. Three weeks later Virginia's body was found in the river not far from where she had left her stick. Clive, Duncan and Quentin expected Virginia's suicide to cause Vanessa another physical collapse, but she seemed less affected than they feared; she was still able to work and garden and was more concerned for Leonard than herself. She received many letters of condolence including one from Vita Sackville-West:

> I should like you to know that (at your request) I did tell her [Virginia] what you had said about the comfort she had been to you over Julian, and I have never seen her look more pleased and also surprised. I know that your message gave her the keenest pleasure.[49]

Though at first Vanessa relived her youth through the typed and bound copies of all Virginia's early letters to Violet Dickinson which the latter now sent her, she was further cut off from her past by Virginia's death. In the months that followed a certain rigidity settled over life at Charleston. Vanessa and Duncan rarely indulged in cross-examination of each other's motives and would probably have considered any kind of public self-analysis bad form. Vanessa once told Angelica that she thought psycho-analysis was something everyone did for themselves; she doubted whether her brother Adrian, now a leading figure in the psychoanalytic field, had ever cured anyone and she was quite sure that her sister-in-law Karin never had. Though the Hogarth Press had been publishing James Strachey's translations of Freud, it is doubtful if she had read any, though *The Interpretation of Dreams* had been in her possession, for when Robert Medley asked to borrow it, Vanessa told him that Grace was reading it.

Vanessa's belief in reasonableness made her unsympathetic to any theories that placed so much importance on the unconscious, an area about which she knew, and probably wanted to know, little. Because during these years she was dragged back into life against her tendency to dwell on the past, it was as if she needed to freeze some parts of herself, to maintain certain silences, in order to make the conflict bearable. John Lehmann, visiting Charleston at this time in the company of Leonard Woolf, has left a telling description: 'Vanessa and Clive and Duncan Grant and Quentin were all there. It was strange to happen on them together like that: it increased the impression I had during the whole weekend, of visiting ghosts, of entering a dream, particularly as Vanessa was very silent, all too obviously still suffering under Julian's as well as Virginia's death. She can only have been in her early sixties at the time, but she looked much older.'[50]

In 1940 Vanessa, like Duncan, agreed to decorate a church, moved perhaps less by the Holy Spirit than by her admiration for Italian art. In 1939 both artists had joined the Society of Mural Painters and at the Society's initial exhibition, shown at the Tate, had been represented by photographs of their decorative work. It was perhaps this occasion that fired a friend of Duncan's Aunt Violet, Charles H. Reilly, a retired professor of architecture, to write to Dr G. K. A. Bell, the Bishop of Chichester, suggesting that Duncan should decorate a Sussex church. Bishop Bell responded immediately to the idea as he was keen to foster closer relations between the church and the arts. Therefore in November 1940 Duncan went to Brighton to meet him (seeing also that day a sailor he had met at Plymouth) and it was agreed that not only Duncan but also Vanessa, Quentin and Angelica should be involved in a scheme to decorate Berwick Church, some two miles from Charleston. Sir Charles Reilly and the bishop together looked round for patrons to pay for the project and found, among others, Mr Peter Jones, whose shop in Sloane Square Sir Charles Reilly had partly designed. Next an architectural adviser was thought necessary and as Edward Maufe, architect of Guildford Cathedral, disliked the idea of decorations, an alternative was found in Duncan's and Vanessa's former friend Frederick Etchells who suddenly reappeared in their lives, now a white-haired eminent architect.

Once they had enough money to proceed they had still to obtain the approval of the local church council. This was soon granted, even though the Hon. Mrs Sandilands spoke out against it. It subsequently passed the Church Advisory Committee in July 1941, but by September a group of parishioners, led by Mrs Sandilands, had begun to mount objections. Mrs Sandilands insisted that their protests should be heard at a chancellor's court. It had now become a matter of no small importance because if this lady won her case it would be difficult for Bishop Bell to encourage church decoration elsewhere. Two days before the court met in Berwick church, Bishop Bell cunningly invited all the parishioners of Berwick to a meeting in the village schoolroom to discuss the artists' designs. So much hostility was expressed at this meeting that Duncan felt it was not worth continuing, but Bishop Bell remained optimistic and assured them that Mrs Sandilands' personal objection (as yet undisclosed) was trivial. Vanessa, meanwhile, was extremely 'agitated' (a term she often used to suggest mild perturbation even though the emotion aroused might be closer to fear or terror); she was convinced that Mrs Sandilands was going to denounce her publicly as an atheist living in sin. As it turned out, Mrs Sandilands' most personal objection was easily refuted: she declared Quentin a conscientious objector which he was not. The other objections were quickly negated by representations in the artists' favour on the part of Frederick Etchells, Sir Kenneth Clark, T.A. Fennemore (now associated with the Society of Mural Painters), the artist Bertram Nicholls and the president of a local archaeological society.

'It is truly encouraging to think of you all hobnobbing with Bishops and becoming hot stuff in the sacred art line,' wrote Janie Bussy[51] from occupied Nice, where the shortage of food left her wistfully daydreaming of Charleston and the puddings she had eaten there. Had she visited Charleston in December 1941, when the decorations were well under way, she would have found angels, bishops and virgins in every room. 'The house is chaotic,' Vanessa declared, 'and all a dither with Christianity.'[52]

Once it had been decided that they should paint, not directly on to the walls of the church but on to plaster-board panels that could then be fixed into position, they had begun work in a barn lent during the summer months by Maynard, using easels for large-scale work provided by John Christie of Glyndebourne. Various people in the neighbourhood were dragooned into posing. Vanessa, in her two large decorations on either side of the aisle, a *Nativity* and *Annunciation*, made use of a local farmhand nicknamed Beckett (Stanley Standon) for one of the shepherds, as well as Grace's small son John Higgens. She also borrowed some lambs and found photographs of others in the magazine *Picture Post*. Angelica modelled for the virgin in the *Annunciation*, while her friend Chattie Salaman knelt in odd positions in chairs, simulating angels in flight for Duncan's *Christ in Glory*. He also portrayed a local soldier, sailor and airman who appear kneeling in the lower left-hand corner, while on the right are found Bishop Bell and other prelates. In the bishop's absence an old model, 'Jemima', made out of chicken wire and papier mâché and which had been used at the

Euston Road School, knelt permanently in prayer in Angelica's bedroom, dressed in the bishop's robes.

Angelica, meanwhile, had returned to Langford Grove for a term where she was employed by Mrs Curtis to teach art. Her contribution to the Berwick murals was to be a madonna on the wall opposite to the church door, but lack of time, ill health and fatigue prevented its production. From Langford Grove she wrote of her want of criticism and time to paint. Vanessa, anxious that she should not instead fall into the role of housekeeper to Bunny and his two children, thought Angelica better placed with Mrs Curtis than she might be in other jobs. 'It's so terribly difficult to paint seriously when one is responsible for other things', she wrote, 'and hasn't room and space to oneself and we females have to struggle for it all our lives one way or another. However I can't complain much at this moment for I have evolved a technique for really banning Grace and Mrs Scovell [the daily help] after the early morning for the rest of the day and am able to work quite hard.'[53]

After many sketches, the putting in and taking out of pillars in her *Annunciation*, after drastic criticism from Duncan regarding the angels' wings and pose, her two large scenes were completed along with Duncan's *Christ in Glory* and put into position in November 1942. Duncan subsequently added a large crucifixion for the end wall of the nave and four circular paintings of the seasons on the outside of the chancel screen. On the inside Quentin painted six small, rather Victorian panels representing the various sacraments, as well as the *Wise and Foolish Virgins* over the chancel arch. At a later date he added an altarpiece depicting the *Supper at Emmaus* as well as some murals over the vestry door and on the wall opposite. Finally Duncan's mother embroidered an altar cloth and Phyllis Keyes made a cross and candlesticks. Vanessa painted three panels with archangels to ornament the pulpit (destroyed by vandals in 1962 and replaced with designs of fruit and flowers by Duncan). In the summer of 1943, shortly before the decorations were consecrated, coloured bands were painted around the arches in the nave and on the chancel screen, Duncan and Vanessa overseeing this and themselves painting *trompe-l'œil* circular windows in the nave, all of which help bind the decorations to their setting. Today a visitor to Berwick church has the same shock of delighted surprise that Sir Charles Reilly felt on first seeing the results of his suggestion: 'It's like stepping out of foggy England into Italy.'[54]

Vanessa put more of herself into these paintings than into any other of her mural decorations, for she used the religious subjects as an impersonal cloak for her own feelings and experience. Her *Nativity* slowly asserts a statuesque mood, aided by the stillness of the figures, the ridges in the drapery and the repeated use of horizontals – in the ox's head, in one shepherd's arm, the line of the hills and elsewhere – which radiate up and out of the composition. Light glows, not only from the kneeling shepherd's lantern, but also from the Christ child. The Virgin, though she holds him on her lap, does not look down but straight out of the picture as if her thoughts are focused on his future sacrifice. The parallel between Mary's experience and her own cannot have escaped Vanessa. Her painting of the *Annunciation* would seem to confirm this, as the pose of the Virgin contains a deeply felt expression of resignation, of submission to the compound of joy and pain involved in maternal experience. Between the angel and the virgin is a river of blue cloth, which falls from the virgin's bent arm and leads the eye down to the narrow space between the two arches that spring up on either side. Within this thin wedge rises a vase of madonna lilies, their blooms carefully composed into an arching design. Lit from behind and edged with light, they, in Auden's phrase, 'show an affirming flame'.

Apart from the Berwick murals Vanessa continued to produce many still lifes and landscapes during the war as well as portraits of her friends. She painted Duncan, Helen Anrep and, in the year before her sister's death, had executed for Virginia a formal portrait of Leonard at his typewriter with his dog at his side (National Portrait Gallery). When Desmond MacCarthy spent a weekend at Charleston in 1943, Vanessa and Duncan both began informal portraits of him which they completed some months later when he made a second visit. Their paintings still sold, but at lower prices than before the war; in April 1942 Vanessa agreed to let the Council for the Encouragement of Music and the Arts buy a snow scene at Tilton for £15 (now in the Arts Council collection). She continued to design dust-jackets for Leonard, including one for the posthumous volume of Virginia's essays, *The Death of the Moth*, in which the loose calligraphy of her drawing jars uncomfortably with the typeset lettering. In 1943 she designed a cover for the Dutch sofa in Duncan's bedroom; its large, simple lines and patterned shapes were worked in black, brown and yellow-ochre by Ethel Grant. That year she also began a large painting entitled *The Kitchen* (Charleston Trust), showing Grace at work. Compared with the Berwick murals, it is an unsatisfactory exercise in monumentality; despite her feelings for simple mass, the spaces between objects are ugly and meaningless and every part of the canvas is worked with a dull regularity.

In the spring of 1942 Angelica and Bunny decided to marry. Though Duncan and Vanessa were warned of this fact, they were not invited to the wedding or told of its date. Vanessa had a scene with Angelica over her marriage in the garden room but afterwards concerned herself with finding a wedding present, and was anxious to effect a reconciliation. After marriage Angelica continued to visit Charleston occasionally, at weekends, but she came alone. Vanessa, however, had been less outraged by this union than some of her relations and friends who were alarmed by the twenty-six-year difference in age. Helen Anrep went so far as to predict that in the long run Bunny would suffer for allowing Angelica to fall in love with him.

Meanwhile the war continued to cause a dearth of entertainment and culture in the area around Lewes and so two elderly sisters, collectively known as 'the ladies of Miller's', determined to provide it. They had moved into Lewes from Northease Manor and taken Miller's House, the stables of which, with the help of much glass, they converted into a studio and gallery. Mrs Frances Byng Stamper and Miss Caroline Byng Lucas, or 'Bay' and 'Mouie' as they were respectively nicknamed, came from an aristocratic background, having been wards of Princess Marie-Louise and brought up in royal circles. Each week they travelled to London to spend their meagre food coupons at Fortnum and Mason's, for everything about them was of the very best, from their Ferragamo shoes to their manners. Mouie, however, tended to dress a little artily, and this, combined with their extreme gentility and lack of good looks (Mary Hutchinson declared them the ugliest women she had ever seen), made the people of Lewes laugh gently at them behind their backs.

During the war they determined to make Miller's House a cultural centre where exhibitions could be shown, lectures held, concerts performed. At one time they considered calling this venture the 'Sussex Art Centre' but this title was advisedly dropped in favour of Miller's. Both ladies were devoted to Duncan who charmed them with his manners, humour and good looks and who, because of his covert femininity, presented no threat. He, Clive and Vanessa gave their full support to the gallery and were present at its opening in July 1941. Through their influence Sir Kenneth Clark made the opening speech, while Raymond Mortimer and Joe Ackerley were asked to help with reviews. The ladies themselves, with their perfect manners, made excellent hostesses and contributed significantly to the gallery's success.

Among the more important exhibitions mounted by Miller's Gallery was one of modern sculpture, held in January 1942, to which Sir Kenneth Clark lent small bronzes by Rodin, Maillol, Degas and Henry Moore. Duncan wrote the catalogue introduction. In November 1942 Clive gave a talk illustrated with lantern slides on modern art, and two years later another on Renoir. Before the first lecture the ladies of Miller's lunched with the Charlestonians at the White Hart in Lewes, this becoming a customary routine, later continued at Shelley's Hotel. The social occasions provided by Miller's attracted Barbara Bagenal, who was now living at Rye. She appeared at a talk given by E.M. Forster and announced (to Vanessa's consternation) that a combination of pedal bicycle and a change of trains brought her easily to Glynde (the station nearest Charleston).

The ladies of Miller's were also responsible for commissioning art. They encouraged Vanessa and Duncan to do lithographs and in January 1945 included some of their work in a volume of artists' lithographs which they published. They also decided that the ancient frescos in the area should be recorded and in 1947 published – again under the imprint The Miller's Press – the book of photographs and tracings, *Twelfth-Century Paintings at Hardham and Clayton*, for which Clive wrote a lengthy introduction.

Apart from the opportunities created by Berwick church and the ladies of Miller's, the war years were noticeably short on commissions and social gaiety. In 1943 Vanessa and Duncan did, however, receive an invitation to enliven the children's restaurant at Devonshire Hill School at Tottenham. Their decorations, based on the tale of Cinderella, were unveiled in February 1944, Maynard making an opening speech and Vanessa coping on her own with the aldermen and Lord Mayor because Duncan was ill. Afterwards she spent the night in London and attended a meeting of the Memoir Club. As was the custom nowadays, they dined first at an inexpensive restaurant in Charlotte Street and afterwards collected at 46 Gordon Square to hear two or three papers read. Except for a visit to her old friend Hilton Young, now Lord Kennet, these were the only occasions during the last years of the war that Vanessa visited London.

She still depended greatly on her family and was pleased when in the spring of 1943 Quentin, after a period of work with the Political Warfare Executive in London, returned to Charleston on doctor's advice. He began work again as a farmhand for Maynard and, in the intervals, painted his altarpiece for Berwick church. Vanessa was also delighted with the news that Angelica was pregnant and began immediately to make clothes for the forthcoming child. Soon after this announcement, in April 1943, Bunny accompanied Angelica to Charleston on a reconciliatory visit. Though Duncan remained a little stiff throughout the first evening, Clive provided a great deal of noise and jollity; Bunny bumbled about trying not to show too much how glad he was to be once more within the fold, and Vanessa, in her silent fashion, emitted an emotive power that bound together all the diverse emotions and personalities.

She wrote at once when she heard of the death of Helen Anrep's favourite, Graham Bell, killed in an air crash on active service with the RAF at the age of thirty-two in 1943. Graham and his friend Anne Olivier

Popham, together with Claude and Elsie Rogers, had been staying with Helen and her children at Rodwell when the war broke out, and he and the Rogers had stayed on a few months, painting and helping her cope with two evacuees and the work of house and garden. This fresh tragedy must have seemed like an echo of Julian's death to both Vanessa and Helen, and the latter wrote: 'He was so undeveloped but I think there was a good deal to develope [sic] and he wanted so much to live. If only his divorce had been accomplished and he and Olivia [both Helen and Vanessa spelt Olivier's name thus] married it would have made a great deal of difference. ... Julian's death and now Graham's have some quality of frustration in them that makes them very hard to bear.'[55]

Shortly after this Angelica's daughter Amaryllis Virginia was born and that Christmas Charleston once again housed a small baby. On Christmas Day they dined at Tilton with Maynard, Lydia and Leonard, on turkey, plum pudding, champagne and brandy. Three days later Angelica had to go up to London with a painful tooth and Vanessa accompanied her in order to help look after the baby. Though they had bought first-class tickets, they had to stand all the way to London, which convinced Duncan that the only way to travel at holiday time was with a flask of brandy in one's pocket.

During the last year of the war soldiers arrived, camped in a nearby field and erected a searchlight run by a dynamo which thundered away at night. Those living at Charleston were now obliged to show registration cards every time they went down the farm track. However, Duncan, who forgot his on the very first day, managed to get through on charm. The soldiers proved to be very good neighbours and when the time came for them to depart a party, with songs, darts and beer, was given for them in the granary opposite Charleston. They left behind many sad faces, including that of Grace.

In June 1944 the first 'doodlebugs' or flying bombs landed in England, causing a fresh outbreak of terror. Maynard advised those at Charleston not to go to London unless it was really necessary. Duncan brought his mother and Aunt Violet to Tilton for safety, where they stayed while Maynard and Lydia were away on a visit to America. That same month, August 1944, Vanessa discovered a lump in her breast and arranged to go into a nursing-home at Hove to have a mastectomy. She told no one of this, except Quentin, until the time came for her to go into hospital. The news surprised Helen Anrep who, meeting Vanessa that summer, had thought her thin but 'serene and gay and exquisite'.[56] She was operated on that September at the same time as Quentin had his appendix removed and shortly before Bunny was operated on to cure a ruptured cartilage which was pressing on the sciatic nerve. A couple of days after her operation Duncan was immensely cheered when Vanessa began reading and complaining about the food. She was glad to get back to Charleston and to real coffee, though for some time she was in pain whenever she tried to use her arm. Charleston that autumn was a home for invalids, for while she slowly recovered strength Bunny hobbled round on a stick.

While Bunny was in hospital Barbara Bagenal came to Angelica's assistance and looked after Amaryllis for two weeks. Vanessa, who still did not enjoy Barbara's company, was again obliged to admit her usefulness. Clive, on the other hand, found her amusing and much improved; he delighted in her accounts of her husband Nick, from whom she was now separated, and her old admirer Saxon who shared a flat in Percy Street, Saxon living chiefly on buns. Clive went on a weekend visit to Barbara's house at Rye and offered to give her lunch when they were both next in town. From then until his death, Barbara made herself indispensable to Clive, driving him about, later accompanying him on visits abroad, providing him with gossip and affection. As her new role became more and more apparent, Vanessa was relieved for Clive's sake, and not a little thankful. When one day Barbara complained that a row of meters disfigured one corner of her London flat, Vanessa, of her own volition, decorated a panel which, when placed over the meters, hid them from sight.

Christmas Day 1944 began with bright sun and sparkling frost. That evening Vanessa, Clive, Duncan and the Higgens family attended a party given at Tilton by Maynard for all his employees and their families. Tables were laden with cold chicken and turkey sandwiches, cakes, ale and tea. After the meal everyone assembled in the library where beneath the Christmas tree were some forty presents, one for every guest. While in America Lydia had shopped religiously, often for eight hours a day, and had brought back not only 120 pairs of silk stockings but also a mass of useful items which were now buried in a bran tub. Duncan pulled out a lady's collar which he exchanged with Grace for a piece of soap in the shape of an orange, later changing this again for a leather belt which he very much needed. The evening ended with songs and recitations, and a performance of Little Red Riding Hood by Duncan and Clive, Duncan's wolf frightening some of the children present.

Much had been achieved during the war years, despite their confinement to a small corner of Sussex. In August 1945 Vanessa realized that, apart from her visit to the nursing-home, she had not been away from Charleston for more than two nights in six years. Things were irrevocably changed; as Vanessa had told Virginia, she could be cheerful, but she would never be happy again. At times it may have seemed as if a spectre of unhappiness stalked the low-ceilinged rooms and hung about the garden; at others as if time had stopped. Bunny, while recuperating at Charleston in the autumn of 1944, noticed that

> long-rooted habits govern behaviour and thought as unconsciously and as rigidly as at the court of Louis XIV. There is therefore a sort of spiritual crystallization. ... Conversation at meals is more like Peacock than like any other writer.[57]

But if their way of life had become static, suffering and stillness made more transparent Vanessa's integrity, as Lord Clark has recalled:

> She was not at all dogmatic, but she never relaxed her standards, and in a quiet, hesitant voice would expose false values and mixed motives. I was devoted to her, and when asked to do something questionable, I would think to myself 'What would Vanessa say?'.[58]

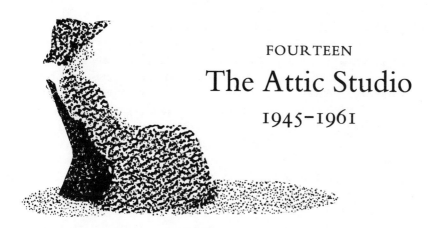

FOURTEEN

The Attic Studio
1945-1961

It pleased everyone when Angelica's second daughter, born on 15 May 1945, a week after VE-day, was named Henrietta Catherine Vanessa. Vanessa herself had suggested the name Henrietta in a letter to Angelica; Duncan had an illegitimate relative of that name of whom he was very fond – Aunt Henny, who as a child had fallen on her head from a cab in Rome and ever afterwards acted strangely; and it reminded Bunny of the American beauty Henrietta Bingham whom he had admired and who had come to London in 1922, with her friend Mina Kirstein, to be psychoanalysed. Both had enjoyed a brief acquaintance with Bloomsbury and Mina sat for her portrait to Duncan. When in 1947 she returned to London, now Mina Curtiss, *en route* to Paris where she was to undertake research for a volume of Proust's letters, she rang Charleston and asked if she might speak to Clive. He was absent, and in answer to Mina's questions Vanessa's replies were chilly and unhelpful.

Vanessa had always been exclusive. David Garnett recalled that as early as 1915 'she had developed an aristocratic characteristic which grew with the years: that of dividing the human race into two groups, those within the charmed circle of her intimates and those outside it'.[1] Yet her aloofness arose less from arrogance than reserve, coupled with a reluctance, that increased with age, to expose herself to untried situations. When among friends she continued to inspire deep affection: 'How we all loved her',[2] is the refrain of those who knew her well.

In old age, as Angelica has written, 'her movements were slow, tentative, almost enquiring, but immensely dignified'; and when, as sometimes happened after dinner at Charleston, she agreed to sing the only song she knew, the 'Old Manorial Hall', 'she stood there slightly self-conscious, noble and yet amused at herself and the ridiculous words, and we felt a genuine, if hilarious, admiration'.[3] When not the focus of attention she often appeared abstracted, as if in another world; even in social situations she seemed cocooned in her own thoughts. Her chief interests during the last years of her life were her painting and her grandchildren. In December 1946 Angelica gave birth to twins, Nerissa and Frances (Fanny) and Vanessa's almost daily letters to her daughter rattled on about nursery matters at length. In 1948, while observing her eldest granddaughter Amaryllis, she reflected how strange it was that a creature who had not existed five years before should know so much about life.

In the spring of 1945 those living at Charleston watched apprehensively the turn of political events. On 24 May, the day after Churchill resigned and a 'caretaker' government was formed to serve until the general election, Vanessa wrote to Angelica: 'Terrible political arguments go on here. I can't attend for very long and I can't see what difference lies between the sides. In any case I'm sure Mr Churchill will get in, for everyone will take Grace's view, that it wouldn't be fair to him not to elect him again after all he has done poor man. Quentin is getting rather agitated and Duncan is becoming Churchillian.'[4] Quentin had again been active on behalf of the Labour Party which, to the surprise of many when the results were announced on 26 July, won the election and began a programme of social and economic reform.

As a result Clive contemplated (never seriously) moving to South Africa. He deplored what seemed to him the collapse of civilization, the loss of elegance and style, the suppression of the first-rate. 'We live at best by BBC standards,' he asserted,[5] annoyed to find that he now had to sit on British Council committees with 'little knock-kneed socialists who draw small salaries under the guise of "expenses" and talk Lewisham culture'.[6] The shift in power discomforted him, for though he was in favour of liberty and fraternity he distrusted *égalité*.

Vanessa's opinions were always more left-wing and less clearcut than her husband's. She might not always vote at election time but she roundly declared that one thing she would never do was to vote for the conservatives. She was observant but detached. 'What a todo about the atomic bomb,' she wrote to Angelica two days after Hiroshima and the day before another bomb fell on Nagasaki. 'We discuss the possibilities a good deal as you may imagine. It's almost too nightmarish I think and I'm not sure I envy the next generation . . . I wish they'd get to the stage of labour-saving devices instead of destroying whole cities.'[7]

When it came to her own kitchen she was none too sure even about the labour-saving devices. Grace, who disliked the concrete floor in Charleston's kitchen, had difficulty at this time in overcoming Vanessa's sustained prejudice against linoleum, though an Aga was now placed in front of the old-fashioned coal range. In addition the low salary that Vanessa paid Grace, and Walter's small earnings, kept the Higgens family based at Charleston, unable to find a cottage of their own elsewhere. When Angelica's former nurse Nellie Brittain visited, boasting a husband in the police force, a son in the civil service and general prosperity, Grace was made uncomfortably aware of how restricted her circumstances were by comparison.

Vanessa, aware of Grace's dilemma, did all she could to cheer her and both employer and employee, despite Vanessa's parsimony, remained on excellent terms. It had become a relationship of mutual respect and dependence. When Grace suffered a series of headaches Vanessa made sure she saw a doctor. On her return from the surgery Grace was found in tears in the hall. In a desperate voice she announced that she had just shut a toad in the door. Vanessa hurriedly got her daily help, Mrs Stevens, to remove the corpse and then asked what the doctor had said. Grace, as she intended, had asked for new spectacles but not mentioned the headaches as she had just heard that Mrs Carter, the cook at Tilton, was going stone deaf, and thought that by comparison her headaches could not be mentioned. 'I very nearly made Grace go straight back to tell the doctor her own symptoms,' Vanessa reported. 'Of course one couldn't and I suppose Grace will just go on being Grace.'[8]

Largely because Grace remained Grace, Charleston continued to thrive; the paintwork was cleaned, cut flowers put in the rooms and delicious meals cooked. Angelica, on a visit to the house while rationing was still strict, wrote to Bunny: 'We are living marvellously well on pheasants and woodcock, fine hocks, capons, meat, rabbit, gin, beer and whiskey. The conversation is on two main topics, or perhaps I should say two chief refrains; one that the world is going to the dogs and nothing is as good as it used to be and two that the dead season of the year has now come when there is nothing to eat and will be nothing until asparagus time. . . . (They have just killed a pig and will kill another in a few weeks.)'[9]

In its style of decoration the house began to cultivate a certain prettiness. In October 1945 Vanessa and Duncan stencilled on to the pale grey walls of the garden room large, dark-grey comma shapes, each enlivened with a cascade of white flowers. The grey, white and yellow curtains, which had previously furnished the music room at the Lefevre Gallery in 1932, were hung and these helped give the room, even on a grey day, a summery feel, while at night, when the lamps are lit, the colours glow with a restrained gaiety. Likewise the dining-room was given a new coherence; the walls were painted black and then patterned with a simple pale grey geometric repeat. Its severity is mitigated by the many paintings that hang on the wall and by the curtains made out of Italian chintz.

But if the house and larder were in very good order, the garden at Charleston had grown rampant. 'This place is like the sleeping beauty's house,' Vanessa wrote, ' – the figs meet the arbutus in the Folly, fuchsias grow almost right across the doorstep, one can hardly walk down paths for the plants that get in the way – it's rather depressing.'[10] The problem was solved when 'young' Mr Stevens, as Mrs Stevens' sixty-year-old son was called, agreed to act as Vanessa's gardener, becoming as devoted to her as she to him. One improvement now undertaken was the removal of the fruit cage from one corner of the garden into the orchard. In its place a terrace was made, decorated with a mosaic of broken pottery stuck into cement and bordered with a box hedge.

The advent of peace brought visitors from France and in June 1945 Lytton Strachey's sister Dorothy Bussy, the *traductrice accréditée* of Gide, and her daughter, the painter Janie Simone Bussy, arrived at Charleston. Both had the Strachey intellect and wit. But, partly because she was an only child and very close to both her parents, Janie, despite her independent views, had never broken away from home and even in middle age still lived very much under the dominance of her mother. A certain sickliness, partly caused by living conditions in occupied France, had given a new charm to her sinuous figure and plain face. Dorothy, now rather deaf, seemed smaller and more fragile. Both were full of wartime experiences and told many amusing stories about Matisse and the writers of the Gide–Valéry school. But when the conversation turned to politics Janie could become distinctly fierce. From Sussex the two women went on to the Strachey home at 51 Gordon Square. 'It is wonderful to be in London again,' Janie wrote to Vanessa, 'but nevertheless how often do my thoughts turn back to Charleston. I don't know how I should have faced life in general and London in particular without the peace and rest of Charleston first. No words can express my happiness at being with you all again.'[11]

It was in general a time for recuperation and celebration. A peace party was held at Tilton, at which an effigy of Hitler was burned on a bonfire. When that summer, after the harvest, Quentin's employment as a farm-hand came to an end, a farewell party for his fellow labourers and their wives was given at Charleston. A goose was killed, pâté made, sausage rolls, jam tarts, cakes and sandwiches provided, as well as a barrel of beer. This last may have been the reason why one gamekeeper mistook Vanessa's painting of a dead hare for the real thing, unwittingly pointing to the degree of untroubled illusionism now found in her work, for this small incident not only amused her but gave her considerable pleasure. After the meal all those present moved into the studio where Maynard's housekeeper Ruby Weller took the lead and a seemingly endless repertoire of songs was sung. The room had been cleared for the occasion but against one beam in the ceiling leant the large *Crucifixion* which Duncan was painting for Berwick church. It was not wholly incongruous for, as Desmond MacCarthy observed, it looked as if Christ were, not crucified, but dancing.

That Christmas Maynard again threw a party for all his employees. Everyone at Charleston was invited and, with the help of Ruby Weller, they performed their own version of the popular radio programme, the Brains Trust, with Duncan acting the part of a bishop. On this occasion Maynard, who had since 1937 been suffering from angina and heart attacks, seemed well but Lydia looked exhausted. During their visit to America in the autumn of 1945, when Maynard took part in Anglo-American financial negotiations following the Bretton Woods Conference, Lydia had acted as his watchdog, insisting on rest and curtailing the demands that others made on him. Before departing Maynard had written to Vanessa: 'As you will have seen, Lydia and I are off to North America tomorrow. I hope the Memoir Club will be able to wait until we are back. But when that will be I cannot safely guess. This is the toughest mission yet, and I need your prayers.'[12] Despite all the vicissitudes of their relationship, the irritations and Vanessa's undeniable dislike of certain aspects of Maynard's character, their friendship had survived, based as it was on deep affection and respect. It was a shock therefore when, on Easter Sunday 1946, the farm manager Logan Thompson arrived at Charleston with the news that Maynard, who had taken tea at Charleston only the Thursday before, had died that morning. In the evening Vanessa and Duncan dined with Lydia at Tilton and found her calm but not unnaturally so for she had yet to realize fully what had happened. The loss of Maynard changed Vanessa's attitude to Lydia, who was now received at Charleston more regularly and with greater warmth.

Confined to Charleston throughout the greater part of the war, Vanessa and Duncan were now eager to get abroad. Duncan was the first to leave England, taking a short holiday in Copenhagen in the spring of 1946 with his mother and Aunt Daisy, the latter now blind, cantankerous and scarcely able to walk. Later that year he made a trip to Dieppe with Vanessa and the painter Edward le Bas. The town, especially on the harbour and sea front, had suffered much war damage, and their hotel, which had no hot water and very little furniture, was one of the few in operation. They found some empty rooms at the top of the hotel which they used as a studio and from where they painted views of the roof-tops. Vanessa must also have sketched in the market because eight years later she made a large subject picture out of a Dieppe fish-stall. Their painting routine was broken by culinary treats; on one occasion they dined on white wine and oysters with Ethel Sands and Nan Hudson. On another they accompanied Ethel and Nan to a nearby eighteenth-century château where the owner regaled them with tales of the destruction wrought by the Germans.* Two days later they visited the damaged Château d'Auppegard; a bomb had fallen near by, the house had been looted and German soldiers had completed the havoc. They had crudely disfigured one of Duncan's designs in the loggia and he and Vanessa spent most of the afternoon retouching their former work. Inside the château the rooms were bare and empty and in one room the ceiling had entirely collapsed. Ethel and Nan lived in only three of its rooms and declared they were now too old to restore and refurnish the house as they would like. The occasion was not, however, uncheerful; Duncan, especially, was delighted by the sight of a large pat of Normandy butter and a jug full of cream.

Edward le Bas now became their regular travelling companion. He seems to have entered their lives soon after the war, immediately becoming one of their closest friends. Sexually ambivalent, le Bas's introduction to Duncan may have come through a mutual boy-friend, the young Jamaican, Patrick Nelson, who sometimes acted as an artist's model. Le Bas later told Paul Roche that his first meeting with Vanessa had been difficult until he had made it clear that he had no intention of taking Duncan away from her. Instead he brought to their lives a welcome note of luxury, obtaining for them seats at Covent Garden, giving parties and entertaining regularly.

Le Bas was tall, bearded and had hair like an astrakhan collar. He came from a wealthy family whose fortune had been made in steel tubing. After his father's death he had inherited a third of the family business and had worked in the firm until 1932 when his mother fell mentally ill. Made deeply anxious by this, le Bas panicked and experienced a profound sense of loneliness; nervous strain caused a rash of blisters to appear on his hands and feet. He promptly resigned from the family business, which he hated, and thereafter only attended the firm's annual meeting at Claridge's, a proceeding that still made him so nervous his hand visibly shook as he

---

* Almost certainly this was the Château Miromesnil at Tourville-sur-Arques. Miss Sands and Miss Hudson were friendly with the Le Breton family who lived there, and they left Château d'Auppegard to the son Louis, a pupil of Jacques-Emile Blanche, a cousin of Henri Cartier-Bresson and an employee of the Louvre.

signed the relevant papers. In his spare time he trained as a painter at the
Royal Academy Schools, joined the Artists International Association and
made a close friend of Charles Ginner. He had begun to form a very fine
collection of twentieth-century art and even before meeting Vanessa and
Duncan had bought examples of their work. Cultivated and refined, a
perfectionist in both his dress and style of living, his most notable talent
(he was, perhaps, too selfless a person to be an outstanding artist) was his
ability to give pleasure: he had an easy, sociable manner and a gently
effervescent character; wine drunk in his presence seemed like champagne.
Even when entertaining children he knew how to turn a fairly predictable
outing into an exceptional treat.

But his passport into Vanessa's life was chiefly his deep love of painting.
He had in his collection one of her most successful still lifes, a sonorously
colourful, complex arrangement of fruit and pots, painted in 1930. His
own style was safely within the Camden Town-Bloomsbury tradition, a
high-keyed naturalism, fluent but unexceptional. Vanessa found his painting competent but restricted, and remarked of his portrait of Angelica,
painted in 1950 (and now in the Arts Council collection): 'As a painting
like all of E's work it seems to me somehow just too feeble – sympathetic
and with a good deal of charm, but not enough vision of his own.'[13]

Vanessa remained an astute, if sometimes harsh, critic, even of her
friends' work. Her familiarity with Keith Baynes did not prevent her from
seeing that one of his shows at Agnew's was 'pretty and quite empty'. She
looked with severity at the work of certain artists who had come to
maturity immediately before the 1939-45 war, in particular Graham Sutherland and John Piper, though on the whole her attitude was less forceful
to Piper than to Sutherland. When in 1951 she made her first visit to Long
Crichel, a house some eight miles from Salisbury shared jointly by Desmond Shawe-Taylor, Edward Sackville-West, Eardley Knollys and Raymond Mortimer, she found there a large collection of French and English
paintings (many of them acquired by Knollys while running the Storran
Gallery).

> The house is full of pictures, the best being a Vuillard, a Bonnard and a Pissarro,
> some other attractive ones by Pasmore, Moynihan etc., wear rather thin after
> a day or two. But the real horrors to my mind are the Graham Sutherlands and
> Pipers. They led to a terrific set to between me and Eddy. He's so intelligent
> that one can only say what one really thinks, so I abused G.S. regardless of
> politeness. ... They've got a horrible affair, large and hot and shapeless [*Red
> Landscape*, now in Southampton Art Gallery], but full according to Eddy of the
> most poetical and romantic memories of Wales. Of course in the end I am
> merely thought old and old-fashioned and incapable of appreciating the young.

But how tired one gets of most of them when one has to live with them even for a few days.[14]

What she did not mention was that her discussion with Edward Sackville-West had been for long queered by her conviction that when he spoke of 'Wales' he meant 'whales'.

Without any apparent difficulty Vanessa had slipped back into a more sociable way of life. When in Paris with Duncan and Edward le Bas in the autumn of 1947 she mixed with Segonzac, Georges Duthuit, who had married Matisse's daughter, and the artist Clairin and his wife, and was aware that certain of the younger generation were in the city – Benedict Nicolson, Philip Toynbee, Igor Anrep and Olivier Popham. But she was perhaps most happy when seated in the Luxembourg Gardens amid the flowers and falling chestnut leaves, recollecting her granddaughters as she watched the children play around a fountain.

The trio's most successful holiday during these post-war years was the trip they made to Venice in the autumn of 1948. This time Angelica was also present. They put up at the Pensione Seguso on the Zattere, avoided almost all society and, apart from the siesta, spent most of the day painting. Angelica's evident pleasure at having a break from her family delighted Vanessa. 'I hadn't really seen so much of her for years,' she told Helen Anrep, 'and it has been very nice. Edward too is extremely easy and charming, rather independent in his ways which is a good thing.'[15] Angelica, however, noticed that he was impressionable, nervous and easily taken in. He was often teased by Vanessa and Duncan who were scornful of the Royal Academy where he exhibited. But their exchange was always good-natured and they ended their days at Florian's eating ices and drinking coffee and *grappa*.

On the whole Vanessa was more willing to travel abroad than make the journey from Charleston to London. But when Helen Anrep let part of her house at Baylham in Suffolk and took a top-floor flat in Percy Street, Vanessa realized that a semblance of their former London life might be revived: 'There may be a kind of dilapidated social circle in Bloomsbury once more. How odd it would be.'[16] She herself agreed to rent a room in Marjorie Strachey's flat at 1 Taviton Street, then resigned her rights in favour of Duncan and took instead the top flat in the Strachey's house at 51 Gordon Square. For some reason – perhaps because she made too infrequent use of it – this arrangement was soon terminated. She became a member of the Cowdray Club in Cadogan Square but stayed there very rarely.

Her disinclination to leave Charleston meant that Duncan mostly visited

London alone. He still had a great many friends and dependents, among them the intellectual policeman, Harry Daley, who was also a friend of E.M. Forster, and the ex-haberdasher called 'H' who had earlier been a friend of Stephen Tomlin's. Edward le Bas remained his closest friend and to him Duncan confessed all his adventures. These did not threaten Vanessa's relationship with Duncan but the situation changed dramatically when he became familiar with the young poet Paul Roche.

They met in the summer of 1946 in Piccadilly. Duncan asked Roche if he would like to see some pictures and Don (as he was familiarly called) agreed, expecting to be taken to the cinema.[17] His bicycle was put on the roof of a taxi and they drove off to Bedford Square, where Edward le Bas was then living, to see his collection of paintings. This began Roche's education in art, for he was subsequently taken by Duncan to the Tate, the National Gallery and to various commercial galleries in the West End. At first they continued to meet at le Bas's house in Bedford Square, until Duncan arranged with Marjorie Strachey that Don should live permanently at Taviton Street, in his room, hung from floor to ceiling with his paintings and where the young man was often persuaded to pose.

Don was not quite so young as he led Duncan to believe. Nor was he in the navy. When they had first met, Don's black trousers and navy-blue shirt made Duncan ask if he was a sailor. Don did not deny it, wanting to disguise the fact that he was actually living in a London presbytery learning to do parish work. And for a short period the pretence was kept up. Duncan painted several pictures of him dressed as an able seaman (one of which was bought by Benjamin Britten, another by John Lehmann). Shortly after they met Clive remarked to Frances Partridge: 'Well, you know that Duncan has a room in Taviton Street, along with his cousin Marjorie and Mrs Enfield, but perhaps you don't know that a handsome young able-bodied seaman is often to be seen there in full uniform. I have myself seen him – with Duncan – at a performance of Carmen, and I'm bound to say he is extremely able-bodied. Please use the utmost discretion.'[18]

Vanessa, however, soon became aware that Don filled the gap in Duncan's affections left by George Bergen. (Duncan heard nothing from Bergen for several years until 1951 when a cablegram arrived at Charleston announcing that he was getting married the next day.) As with George, the age difference between Duncan and Don aroused the elder's paternal instincts. And like Bergen, there was something exotic and unpredictable about Roche. Of French descent, with some Germanic blood in his inheritance, he had been, like Duncan, brought up in India. His interest in the Greeks and Greek literature had left him with an almost narcissistic interest in physical beauty, and this, combined with his golden hair and worship of the sun gave him a bronzed glamour that had for Duncan an obvious attraction. He was also highly literate, his keen intelligence and well-modulated voice making him a fluent and sympathetic talker. Yet he would not, and perhaps could not, woo Vanessa, as le Bas had done, and made little effort to allay her apprehensions.

At first Roche took his friendship with Duncan rather nonchalantly. 'I had to tell Duncan several times at the beginning that I was not in love with *him*. He said that that was more than he could expect and that it was enough if *he* could have permission to love me. I said yes, not yet realizing the staggering humility of the request. What I was never able to *tell* him in later years, though I tried to show it by looking after him, was that I came to love him more intensely than I have ever loved anyone.'[19] When Duncan began making weekly visits to London, to draw and paint Don, he would remark enigmatically that 'certain people' made his visits difficult. 'If only certain people could understand,' he would remark. When pressed by Don to explain who these 'certain people' were, he blurted out: 'Vanessa has never got over Julian's death . . . she never used to be like this.' When Don asked whether Vanessa made a scene, Duncan replied, 'Oh no, no. Nothing like that . . . but it is all very powerfully felt. And I can't bear to do anything that hurts her.'[20]

Vanessa did make an effort to befriend Roche. She visited Taviton Street on several occasions and Don modelled for both her and Duncan. She was kind and considerate, but also hesitant and uneasy. It obviously pained her to see Don doing things for Duncan, shopping and cooking and being so completely at home in this *pied-à-terre*. The domestic intimacy he enjoyed with Duncan had the direct effect of sharpening Vanessa's isolation. According to Roche, Duncan constantly asked him to visit Charleston and even live there permanently with him and Vanessa. Roche had the impression that Vanessa was steeling herself to accept him, but he never took up the invitation and rarely visited Charleston while she was alive. He nevertheless remained a dominant figure in Duncan's life until 1954, when, with Clarissa whom he was to marry, he left for America to take up a teaching post at Smith College, Massachusetts. He returned to England at Duncan's request after Vanessa died and thereafter spent long periods as his companion, looking after him in his final illness at his house in Aldermaston.

Roche has recalled that Vanessa was never unkind to him, but that she accepted his presence with a sad, yearning smile and a hidden sigh. Scarcely any mention of him appears in her letters to Angelica and Quentin and what suffering she endured was inward and unexpressed. Her chronic unhappiness inevitably left its mark. 'Self-denigration and timidity became a habit,' Angelica has recalled, 'expressed outwardly in drab, unstylish clothes, a shrinking from society and the constant reiteration that Duncan's work was so infinitely better than her own.'[21] Denied intimacy with his deepest feelings, she withdrew more profoundly into herself.

In December 1948 Duncan wrote Vanessa a letter which discloses his split loyalties – his deep love and affection for Vanessa, and his obsession with Roche.

Darling Nessa, I am writing you a letter – everyone else has gone to bed and the wind is howling outside – because I sometimes feel it is so very difficult to talk to you, I mean about the things that occupy our thoughts now. I cannot bear to think that you are unhappy about me. When I see that you are unhappy I simply do not know what to say or do. It makes me feel terribly guilty, a feeling that perhaps I ought to be more used to because I suppose I have made several people unhappy, long ago. ... I would like to try to explain to you a little of what I feel ... in writing I can say things which I should find very difficult to say to you in words. The first thing I want to say is, that I think you do not understand at all how much I love you, and Angelica. I never *say* so – it is quite out of my power. I try to show it sometimes by what I do, and by suggestion. But I don't think that it is much understood. As for Angelica, she is so much occupied by family life and so on that I don't think it necessary to say much, but with you, I always thought you knew and know, and when I find that you do not know apparently, it leaves me without words, and I feel quite helpless. And then I never can express to you my admiration for you as a painter and as an artist. You always laugh at me when I try to say what I think and make out that I am trying to be nice to you. But that is very far from the truth. I have the very highest opinion possible to have of you as an artist. I often and especially if you are away or I can see a picture of yours away from you, feel that here is an artist quite different from me and quite of another order. How silly people are not to be able to distinguish.

I suppose you may be wondering why I am writing all this well it is partly to explain that I find it so difficult to make you believe what I say. And also of course because I never seem to be able to talk to you about my feelings for other people, at least I mean about Don. One of the reasons I feel it difficult is because I think you may be hard on him. I don't mind in the least if you don't like him. For one thing he has no place in my heart that can possibly be compared to what you mean to me. I absolutely rely on you for everything. You do everything for me, and I never can do anything for you which distresses me. But Don, for one, is a quite different thing. I love him, but surely one can love a good many people? I do not think that Don is in love with me, though he does love me. Is not that a possible state of affairs? I have been lately through rather a bad time with him, through no fault of his, nor of mine, but I think now we understand each other a good deal. But I am very slow to get to know

337

people.

When we were in Venice I had a letter from Don from Brussels where he went first sending me a diary which I had asked him to write. In it he wrote an account of going to bed with a girl which I did mind in a silly sort of way. I had told him of course on his holiday he must feel perfectly free to do as he liked, and which I really meant. But somehow from the diary I got the impression that he was happy to be away from me and do as he liked. He is by nature a purely normal young man and I want him to do as he wants. But it made me unhappy to think he was glad to be away from me. . . . In spite of all this I do not think that I have ever been so happy as when I was in Venice with you, Angelica and Edward. There was a sort of background of unhappiness for a little, but not so bad after all, because Don wrote to me every day almost, and I really did believe nothing mattered between us, except our love for one another, very unequal possibly, but he wanted my love and I was quite ready to give him mine. He always wanted to know why I couldn't spend my holiday with him and although I would have liked this, I could never wish to give up our painting holiday and all that it meant to us and at last convinced him that I could not give that up. But I think that he was sad about it, and always said he had so few holidays and that we were so little together, that he could not understand why I should not give up a little time to him.

It is true I only see him for little bits. You think that he is free with my time to come and see me, but that is not true. He has one day off in the week and can sometimes come round for an hour or two otherwise. I often think you must wonder how we spend our time together. Well, he is always severe with me for wasting time. And sets me down to draw or paint nearly all day and always after supper. He reads to me if I can give him a pose in which he can do it, or sometimes we have the wireless on. We never go out. I sometimes suggest a movie or a theatre – but he thinks that a waste of time, and I am really quite happy not doing anything like that or seeing anybody, except Margery who comes occasionally and begs to read her latest poem or asks us to cook her a meal. Is this, my dear, very painful to you? It literally is a quite good description of how we spend our time. I will stop now . . . I think that even you will agree that Don is very understanding of me and my unfortunate disposition. If he loves me, it is only because he can perhaps help me, and therefore you too. Yr loving D.[22]

'In spite of all the terrible things that happen how much one still has to lose.' This reflection of Vanessa's was sent to Julian's Chinese friend Ling Su-Hua in a letter written in July 1939. Ever since Su-Hua had read of Julian's death in a Chinese newspaper, she had corresponded with Vanessa, the two women freely exchanging a sympathy made possible by their fondness for Julian. When in the winter of 1946–7 Su-Hua arrived in

England, Vanessa went to meet her in St John's Wood where Su-Hua's husband, Professor Chen, was already established. Afterwards Vanessa wrote:

> You must not blame yourself for breaking down with me – I understood so well. It has been very strange after knowing you intimately for so many years by letter to see you at last, and I seemed to be in an unreal world where I could hardly tell what I felt. I have had for so long now to make up my mind to life without Julian and to try all the same to get something from it – and I think that at first your presence made me feel again how much I wanted him.[23]

Vanessa arranged for Su-Hua to have English lessons with Margery Strachey; she gave her an introduction to Arthur Waley and invited her down to Charleston. Su-Hua arrived, painted some of Quentin's pots in a Chinese style and produced a small book in which she asked Vanessa and Duncan to paint a picture in miniature. Turning its pages, Vanessa was astonished to find a work signed Roger Fry, which the poet Shu on a visit to England had obtained for Su-Hua.

In 1947 the magnolia grandiflora, which they had planted some twenty years before at the front of the house, flowered for the first time. 'It was as usual heavenly to be at Charleston again,' wrote Janie Bussy after one visit. 'How extraordinary that there should be such an unchanged spot in the world still.'[24] This year also saw the publication of Quentin's first book, *On Human Finery*, which he read to Janie Bussy in manuscript in order to have her advice, and also dedicated to her. According to fashion specialists, this witty, erudite book remains one of the few books worth reading on this much underrated subject. But its success at the time did not compare with that enjoyed two years later by Dorothy Bussy's *Olivia*, published anonymously, which ran into six impressions within the first ten months. The book was dedicated to the memory of Virginia and two years after it appeared Dorothy wrote to Vanessa: 'The other day, looking through letters which I had kept (about *Olivia*) I came across yours, and the tears unexpectedly and irresistibly came to my eyes. You say you put it on the shelf where you keep your Virginias. Nothing could touch me more.'[25]

Though Vanessa read Ruskin's autobiography *Praeterita* at this time, it is not known what she thought of it. Her literary judgements were often closely related to her understanding of painting: when reading Thackeray she felt 'some curious ease and flow of writing which makes me indifferent to his sentimentality and other failings – I don't mind them more than I do the same qualities in Raphael ... perhaps it's true he's not able to make his characters completely real and solid – but I forget that and am only aware of some quality of imagination, often of visual imagination, anyhow it has almost the effect on me of free, big painting but I cannot analyse it'.[26]

She continued to distrust 'literary' content in painting, even though traces of sentimentality could now be found in her paintings of children. In December 1945 she had visited the important Picasso and Matisse exhibition held at the Victoria and Albert Museum, and had left feeling critical of the former's paintings. She admired Picasso's vitality and his use of design and colour, but certain of his paintings seemed to her 'to insist on some literary or dramatic intention which to my mind generally upsets the rest and doesn't seem to be part of the whole'.[27] It was, therefore, Matisse's 'astonishing inventions' which for her carried the show.

In her own painting Vanessa now sought a tighter and more exacting degree of finish. In her easel paintings she had begun to use smaller brushes and in her portraits she often built up the modelling of the face with minute touches of colour. Her move into a more high-keyed colour range had first been noticed by Kenneth Clark at her one-artist show at the Lefevre Gallery in May 1937. Clark had visited the show six times in order to be able to give her his criticisms; he told her that he detected in her work some of the adverse effects of middle age. At the time Duncan had been affronted by Clark's suggestions and to combat them had told Vanessa, 'I date the assurance of yr. later work from the time of your Roman visit and it seems to have gone on ever since.'[28] Rarely did Duncan and Vanessa give each other any objective criticism other than immediate practical advice – suggesting a touch of vermilion here or a vertical feature there. As Vanessa withdrew more and more into herself her large-scale group portraits grew strangely awkward and devoid of feeling. But in her small paintings, generally richer and more concentrated than those of the previous two decades, there is a release of lyrical delight in the observation of the everyday world, in the fall of light on cloth, bowl or fruit or in the burst of colour created by a bunch of flowers against a dark wall.

In May 1946 Vanessa's and Duncan's interest in decorative work was stimulated afresh when Miller's art gallery in Lewes put on an Omega exhibition which was opened by Leigh Ashton of the Victoria and Albert Museum. They again toyed with the idea of reviving the Omega, visited a wallpaper factory in Islington and consulted Ambrose Heal and Jack Beddington (now in charge of the decoration of all Lyons teashops) for advice. However nothing further came of this suggestion. They continued to decorate some of Quentin's pots and made tiles for table tops, but most of their decorative work at this time was done for themselves or for friends.

The chief outlet for their paintings was the London Group (which they had rejoined) and the Lefevre Gallery where Duncan Macdonald generally kept two or three of their paintings on his walls. They now sat willingly on the London Group's selection jury, where they hoped to influence the vote with regard to Angelica's paintings, but invariably they were lunching with Edward le Bas at the crucial moment. They enjoyed belonging to an artistic society and were amused by its proceedings.

> We left them in full swing at nearly 6 [wrote Vanessa after one meeting] but were saved from collapse by the wonderful tea produced by Mrs Seabrooke, a very stout and good-natured Dutch lady who gave about 30 people tea and sandwiches with cress and some sort of fish filling and very good cakes. I ate all I could get. Everyone was quite wild and no one attempted to do anything according to rules. Pasmore got wilder and wilder till he looked exactly like a monkey with hair flying in all directions and beard also. What it all amounted to I don't know but we enjoyed it very much in spite of the incredible slowness of everything.[29]

Both she and Duncan continued to hold aloof from the Royal Academy, though by now the difference between the two exhibiting venues was slight.

Duncan spent Christmas 1947 in London, travelling each day to Twickenham where his ninety-year-old mother was dying. On one occasion he took a day off to accompany Vanessa to an exhibition at the Tate and to lunch with her and the ladies of Auppegard at a restaurant in the King's Road. Immediately after lunch Duncan went to the nearest telephone box and learnt from his Aunt Violet that his mother had died. 'It seemed strange standing in a crowded post office with people coming and going and hearing this news,' Vanessa commented.[30] In May 1948 her brother Adrian died, and though they had never been close, even less so since his marriage, she must have felt a wrench with her past. At the same time she drew closer to her grandchildren. 'What a blessing they exist,' she admitted to Angelica, 'and what an incredible difference such small creatures make to life. They're so full of it, it seems to spill over all round.'[31]

The two eldest, Amaryllis and Henrietta, were often sent on visits to Charleston. Once, while returning them by train to Hilton, Vanessa had a slight accident:

> Having lifted the children carefully on to the train which seemed an unusually long way from the platform I plunged myself into the gap between the two – and suddenly found myself up almost to my waist in an abyss. It was really rather a horrible sensation, but a kind and active porter fished me out and though I'm still bruised I was really none the worse.[32]

Her detachment from events, even from her own physical misfortunes, enabled her to exaggerate their comic aspect.

I had such a horribly creepy sensation the other night. As I was sitting as usual after dinner I suddenly became vaguely aware of something – hardly enough to be sure of it – yet something – under the jacket I had on – at my back – creeping up to my shoulder ... it got more and more definite till at last I thought it couldn't be only imagination. I got up and went into my room thinking I might have to strip, when there could be no doubt – something was running or flying or scrambling up under my jacket. Just as I was going to tear off my jacket the creature darted up into my hair into my hair net! I tore that off and flung it to the floor with a little wriggling object thank goodness inside it. I then sought male aid from next door and the creature was seen to be a field mouse, which darted out into the room and was lost for ever.[33]

To amuse others she also exaggerated her ineptitude. But though apparently cocooned in vagueness, her mind in fact remained sharp and penetrating. The artist Robert Medley occasionally accompanied her on shopping expeditions and has recalled how, dressed in a shabby coat and hat and looking odd but infinitely distinguished, she would enter a shop and look helpless, thereby attracting the attention of the assistants. 'I'm looking for some stuffs,' she would vaguely murmur in answer to their questions; but once she found what she wanted her manner instantly changed and she was in complete charge of the situation.

On the other hand, it has to be admitted that she could read her way half through a copy of *The Times* before realizing it was two years out of date. But if she remained detached from world events, she was not indifferent to them. Her lack of interest in politics grew largely out of her distrust of political rhetoric; in 1950 she voted Labour because the candidate seemed to her honest and straightforward. She also disliked the fanfare of publicity and when a *Sunday Times* photographer arrived at Charleston he was given tea and cake but allowed to take no pictures. 'Vanessa's strength lay in her closeness to reality, to the everyday world,' her daughter has written.[34] She continued to run the house with great efficiency and the minimum of fuss; while she ruled, local tradesmen did not dare refuse to deliver. When Clive visited America in January 1950, where he opened the famous Cone Collection at Baltimore Museum of Art, Vanessa herself spring-cleaned his sitting-room, dusting every book and shelf and putting out of sight his gun-cleaning rags and mousetraps.

While Clive was away, news arrived of his sister-in-law's death. 'The Bell family as usual have filled me with astonishment,' Vanessa told Leonard. 'Cory wrote to Quentin, Clive being in America, and filled the first part of his letter with apologies for not having sent some port which he had promised – Violet had been ill he said and he hadn't had much time. Then on the next page 'in fact she died this morning' but still the port *would* come. In fact I hear it's at the station so no doubt Bell common sense has triumphed as usual. . . . Do you remember when they ordered a coffin for Dorothy in case she should be so perverse as to die at the weekend? Of course she was much too sensible to do so though apparently at the last gasp.'[35]

If Bell common sense had not failed, neither had Vanessa's dislike of Christianity. When the morning service came on the air, she was unusually brisk in her move to switch off the wireless. 'God is not allowed in the studio,' she firmly told her grandchildren who nevertheless did their best to reintroduce religion into the house by singing hymns in their bedroom at the top of their voices. Her granddaughter, Henrietta, has recalled:

When we stayed at Charleston, Amaryllis and I were always made to sit as models. Breakfast over, we walked down the length of the passages to get to Duncan's studio. We were not altogether willing models and both of us charged our grandparents sixpence for each hour that we endured. We were seldom painted in our ordinary clothes. In her bedroom, next to Duncan's studio, Nessa kept a huge painted cupboard which was filled with a fantastic assortment of coloured silks, discarded dresses and moth-eaten tapestries in which we were variously draped. I remember there was a vermilion hat, like the head-dress of a Venetian Doge, which was excruciatingly itchy for me to wear. Generally, Nessa sat down to paint. Her easel was infinitely more spindly, more rickety than Duncan's. She sat behind it, mixing the colours on her palette, glancing first at one and then at the portrait, gently stabbing the canvas so that, posing somewhat uneasily and swathed in remnants on the model's throne, one could see the back of her canvas quiver from the impressions she made on it. The glances she sent to one across the room were extraordinarily intimate and reassuring; an observant nod, an amused smile in order to encourage one to keep still.[36]

While they painted Vanessa and Duncan told stories about the figures in their past. The children became familiar with intimate details concerning such semi-mythical creatures as George Duckworth, Julia Stephen and Virginia. Often they listened to music on the radio, in particular to Beethoven, Mozart, Debussy and Ravel. Sometimes Amaryllis read aloud while they posed. They were all addicted to the novels of Charlotte M. Yonge, relishing the death scenes which made them both cry and laugh. 'Nessa would laugh too,' Henrietta recollected; 'a strangely mellow cackle; the amused hoot of a barn owl.' When these sessions ended the children would stretch out on the rug on the studio floor, in front of the pither stove and would munch digestive biscuits as they all listened to Mrs Dale's Diary. 'After each episode ended to the twinkling tones of its signature tune we would all speculate and elaborate wildly upon the curious lives of

Mrs Maggs, Mrs Dale and her scandalous sister Sally, dwelling as they did in Virginia Water.'

Vanessa's granddaughter goes on to describe how the midday meal usually consisted of ham, baked potatoes, pickled walnuts and dressed salad, followed by pudding.

> Whilst Nessa and Duncan and Clive sipped their coffee, Nessa gave us *canards*. The duck, a lump of white sugar, would be sent for a sail in a silver teaspoon boat across the dark waters of the black coffee within her painted blue cup. And then, very gently, the silver boat capsized. The snow-white duck became stained with the brown liquid and then Vanessa would lift the spoon as far as she could reach to our gaping mouths and we swiftly gobbled up the ducks.

In 1950 Vanessa and Duncan were invited to submit to the '60 Paintings for '51' exhibition, sponsored by the Arts Council to coincide with the 1951 Festival of Britain. In an attempt to stimulate the artists involved it was stipulated that every painting included in the show had to measure at least 45" by 60". Canvas and paints were supplied free of charge. The problem confronting all the artists involved was the discovery of a subject suited to such large-scale production and to the 'public patrons' who the Arts Council hoped would buy the paintings. In 1946 Duncan and Vanessa had executed nine-foot-high figurative panels for the 'Britain can make it' exhibition, but these had been merely decorative works, whereas the paintings for the 1951 exhibition were intended not to ornament an architectural site but to exist in their own right. While work was in progress, Vanessa wrote to Angelica:

> Duncan is I hope going to use a very rakish affair he did a long time ago, meant for a theatrical scene, with lots of fantastic figures, a knight on a prancing horse in the middle and architecture round, all extremely gay and lively and the sort of thing that no one else would do. ... Mine is very sober by comparison, simply figures at the drawing room window which is open on the garden with sun outside – all very *terre à terre* but then I'm interested in *terre à terre* subjects and encourage myself by thinking that many good artists have been. Certainly Velasquez was better when he didn't leave the earth.[37]

The result was Duncan's *The Arrival of the Italian Comedy* and Vanessa's *The Garden Room* both of which were marked down by [Sir] Colin Anderson, who had helped select the artists for the show, as 'pathetic'. However his comments on most of the paintings exhibited were equally damning and the show as a whole was not a success. 'Art without faith,' wrote *The Studio*.[38] Vanessa herself agreed. Even the much praised *Interior in Paddington* by Lucian Freud she thought 'conspicuously horrible'.

The view through the French windows in the garden room at Charleston was a scene Vanessa had often repeated. In her 1951 *The Garden Room* it is the figures that give the picture an additional layer of meaning. It is possible to regard this picture, like Virginia's *The Waves*, as a dialectic confrontation between past, present and future. It was in this room that Vanessa had told Angelica that Duncan was her father; it was here that mother and daughter had a painful scene over Angelica's marriage; it was here that Vanessa learnt from an ashen-faced Leonard that Virginia's body had been found. For Vanessa, the room was imbued with memories that would have made her aware of time passing. When the painting was complete she told Angelica: 'Anyhow there you are, looking at yourself at 3 yrs old with Amaryllis in attendance and an unknown female outside.'[39] Dissatisfied with the final painting, she repainted the seated figure on the left after the picture was returned unsold from the exhibition; like Duncan's huge canvas, it was then relegated to Charleston attic.

One person who had posed for the seated figure before it became recognizably Angelica was Olivier Popham to whom Vanessa had recently been introduced at a party given by Helen Anrep. Because Helen had always stressed Vanessa's shyness and desire for privacy, Olivier was surprised to meet with such ease and amiability. It was, in fact, Vanessa who now promoted Olivier's acquaintance with Quentin by inviting her to visit Charleston. 'Next weekend we have Olivia,' Vanessa had written in May 1950, 'as to whom I'm rather curious as I hardly know her.'[40] But she had known Olivier's mother, Brynhild Olivier, who had married A.E. Popham, Keeper of Prints and Drawings at the British Museum. Olivier had herself trained as an art historian at the Courtauld Institute, been employed as a civil servant during the war and was now working for the Arts Council of Great Britain. She quickly became Quentin's most regular companion. Vanessa found her the most sympathetic of his female friends and the one most willing to sit and be painted. She paid two or three visits to Charleston, and by the summer of 1951, shortly before Quentin and Olivier went on holiday in Italy with Claude and Elsie Rogers, Vanessa wrote to Angelica:

> Q. is obviously very much in love with her (in fact he has told me so, but this is *for you alone*). I think she's a good deal in love too – but what will happen I don't know. I suppose on their travels they may come to some definite arrangement – at present she has to work all the week and Q dashes up to London during the week and sometimes stays there for weekends. I think she's very nice and obviously very intelligent and beautiful – and she seems to like being

here and gets on well with all of us. . . . In any case she's far the nicest young woman I have ever known Q to be attracted by and I think he's very happy.[41]

In February 1952 they married and Vanessa gave Olivier a pendant that had belonged to Virginia. In April Quentin accepted a lectureship in Art Education at King's College, Newcastle, and when they set up house there in the autumn Vanessa and Duncan took over Olivier's flat at 26a Canonbury Square in Islington. 'On the whole I'm against marriage,' Vanessa told Helen Anrep, 'though as yet it seems all right with our young people. They're the right age . . . so I hope for the best and especially am delighted at the prospect of more grandchildren.'[42]

By now biographers and historians were already beginning to encroach on their lives. Roy Harrod had begun his biography of Maynard Keynes and paid his first visit to Charleston in December 1948. In May 1950 Noël Annan arrived for the weekend, in connection with his study of Leslie Stephen's contribution to the history of ideas. He surprised Vanessa by not behaving like other dons she had known; instead of producing long, pregnant silences, he chattered away all evening and caused her no strain. She gave him all the help she could, but when a Miss Busen began making enquiries about Bloomsbury and the Friday Club, Vanessa made herself unavailable and said she was 'wandering indefinitely in France'. When Aileen Pippett wrote saying that the time had come for a biography of Virginia, Vanessa's immediate instinct was to reply that in her opinion it had not. She did however meet Miss Pippett, who stressed the need for accuracy in a biography and then made the gaffe of referring to Virginia's mother as 'Lady Stephen': Vanessa was rather crushing. The author then went ahead and published *The Moth and The Star: A Biography of Virginia Woolf* in 1955, quoting from letters in Vita Sackville-West's possession without obtaining permission from the copyright owner, Leonard. He at first threatened to stop the book altogether, relented and agreed to its publication, but in America only. At the same time Bunny was working on the second volume of his autobiography, *The Flowers of the Forest*, which dealt with their life at Wissett and the early years at Charleston. Vanessa rather dreaded it and forbade Bunny to quote one of her letters describing her first visit to Garsington. She disliked exposing their private lives, but she did agree to read parts of her memoir on Virginia's childhood in a radio programme on her sister which went out in August 1956.

Vanessa was equally distrustful of 'society' and, though often a part of it, made little or no gesture towards it. While most of Sir Kenneth Clark's guests arrived at his cocktail parties in large limousines, Vanessa and Duncan appeared dripping wet, having lost their way in the rain while walking from the tube. Once at Charleston a car drove up and out stepped a man and his wife who lived in a nearby manor and who had decided to pay a 'call'. After some stilted conversation they produced their card and expressed the wish that the call would be returned: Vanessa despaired and considered putting up another 'OUT' sign at the end of the track leading up to the house. She shared Flaubert's belief that 'honours are dishonourable' and once declared that if ever Clive accepted a knighthood she would have nothing more to do with him. He replied that he would do no such thing, but if offered a peerage he'd take his chances.

In spite of the advantage of Olivier's flat in Canonbury Square, Vanessa led an increasingly circumscribed, domestic existence, surrounded by her immediate family and intimate friends. It was as if the emotional effort needed to involve herself in the interests of others was now too great. Nevertheless there were often guests at Charleston: Desmond Shawe-Taylor and Edward Sackville-West lunched there before attending performances at Glyndebourne; Helen Anrep, Angus Davidson, Edward le Bas and Marjorie Strachey came infrequently; and the artists Eardley Knollys, Roger de Grey, Kenneth Martin, and John Napper, among others, were invited to visit. Clive still effervesced in company and brought up good wine from the cellar. At mealtimes, while the conversation grew witty, frequently at the expense of other people, Vanessa was often the most silent; she seemed abstracted, as if her mind were occupied still with the painting on which she was working. Visitors felt mindful of their talk in her presence, and the exchange, even between the regular inmates of Charleston, was always good-mannered. The combination of manners and reserve made it sometimes difficult to assess what she was feeling. Now and then, however, she would hoot with laughter at one of Duncan's more ribald jokes; but for Milo Keynes it was an anxious moment when his aunt, Lydia, reported Quentin's remark that her bottled plums looked like 'pickled balls'. A silence followed. Then Vanessa's deep, slow voice murmured, 'I see what he means.'

To the organization of domestic matters she brought a unique combination of liberty and order. Her days were so well organized that after she had given the orders for the day she retired to the studio until the bell rang at one o'clock for lunch. It rang again at five for tea, and again at eight for dinner. Apart from the occasional making of scones, she was largely divorced from the practical matters of daily life over which she nevertheless had total command. Just by being there, Duncan later recalled, she made life at Charleston 'different, more sensible'.[43] Edward le Bas thought her influence curbed Duncan's drinking. Her housekeeping was careful, almost parsimonious, and when in London she never took taxis until rheumatism in her knees made it difficult for her to get on and off buses. Her life was measured, ordered but nothing was done according to rule: once when her granddaughter Henrietta complained of the free-flowing hair which Bunny liked his daughters to wear, Vanessa took her the next day into Lewes to have it bobbed, feeling it right that the young girl should rebel. She continued to adore her two eldest grandchildren, but particularly Amaryllis with whom she felt a special affinity, perhaps because she occasionally caught on the child's face a look of penetrating insight and understanding.

In her professional life Vanessa now found that positions of authority were conferred upon her. She sat on the jury for the Prix de Rome awards in 1953. That same year she, Duncan, Robin Darwin and Dame Laura Knight judged a student competition sponsored by the Bowater Paper Company; it earned her £10, expenses and lunch at the Dorchester Hotel. Her most important contribution in an official capacity was the work that she did for the Edwin Austin Abbey Memorial Trust Fund for Mural Painting. She joined its committee in 1949 and did not resign until 1959, by which time she found it difficult to travel to London. The Fund had been established in 1931 with an endowment of almost £80,000, but due to legalities and the onset of war, its operation had been delayed. It now publicized its role by sending a letter to *The Times* (2 May 1952) advertising its desire to find authorities willing to commission murals in public buildings. Thirty-one replies were received. Of these, only twelve commissions were considered suitable at the next committee meeting, the minutes of which were signed by Vanessa.

One of these commissions involved the decoration of the Russell Chantry, dedicated to St Blaise, in Lincoln Cathedral. A competition was held to decide the choice of artist and there were fifty-five applicants. The winner was Duncan, and during 1955-9 he produced two large scenes, *The Good Shepherd Ministers to his Flock* and *The Wool Staple in Medieval Lincoln,* as well as a roundel with the head of the saint for a side wall. Vanessa did at one point admit that she sat on this committee in order to get jobs for her friends, but her work for this Trust Fund was more disinterested than this suggests. She was instrumental in obtaining for the young John Napper, an artist previously unknown to her, the commission to decorate the vestibule of the Whitechapel Art Gallery with murals (now destroyed) based on T.S. Eliot's *Four Quartets* for a thousand guineas. With the other members of the committee she helped bring to fruition murals in the New Council House, Bristol (by Tom Monnington and John Armstrong), the Students' Union, University of London (by Gilbert Spencer and Clive Gardiner) and St Philip's Church at Hove (by Augustus

Munn). She herself now received very few decorative commissions, though she did execute some tile paintings for the stairwell in the King's College, Cambridge, Garden Hostel annexe, at the request of its architect Paul Hyslop. They are variations upon a theme, flowers in a vase framed by curtains. Their large simplicity and assured control of space, shape and colour mark a momentary return to her earlier, post-impressionist style.

Meanwhile the Omega had entered the annals of history, receiving mention in John Rothenstein's *Modern English Painters*. In connection with his first volume in this series, Rothenstein had visited Charleston in order to gain information for his chapter on Duncan. 'He threatens to do the same by me,' Vanessa told Angelica, 'but I dislike him so much that I could hardly be polite.'[44] The immediate cause of her intense dislike had been Rothenstein's remark, inadvertently made at lunch, that Titian could not draw. Vanessa said nothing but she directed at him a stare of such fury and utter contempt that he visibly cowered and momentarily lost his social aplomb. Almost certainly her withering look fuelled Rothenstein's dislike of Bloomsbury, which he strenuously attacked in his chapter on Wyndham Lewis. He accused its members of untiringly advertising each other's work and of going out of their way to denounce young painters and writers who showed themselves to be independent: 'If such independence was allied to gifts of an order to provoke rivalry, then so much the worse for the artists. And bad for them it *was*, for there was nothing in the way of slander and intrigue to which certain of the "Bloomsburys" were not willing to descend. I rarely knew hatreds pursued with so much malevolence over so many years; against them neither age nor misfortune offered the slightest protection.'[45]

What is baffling to the historian of Bloomsbury is the scant documentary evidence to prove this vehement assertion, which has been often repeated, notably in recent years by Jeffrey Meyers in *The Enemy. A Biography of Wyndham Lewis* (1980). The chief offender with regard to the two main criticisms – that Bloomsbury overpraised themselves and wrecked the reputations of others – was Clive Bell. His references to Vanessa and Duncan in his exhibition reviews do make embarrassing reading; and on more than one occasion he slated the art of Wyndham Lewis with what seems like a personal vindictiveness. But Roger Fry had written as extensively on Mark Gertler and John Nash as on Vanessa's art and had done much to encourage younger artists, as did Vanessa and Duncan through their association with the LAA, the London Group and the Euston Road School. Rothenstein had been influenced by Wyndham Lewis who, since 1913 when his 'Round Robin' letter attacking the Omega had met with an infuriating silence, had persistently railed at Bloomsbury in his articles and books. His earlier grievance had become mixed with paranoia and his deep-seated hatred of homosexuality and privilege. But his verbal stabs were for the most part ignored and there is no evidence among the letters and articles written by Bloomsbury of any conspiratorial methods or malevolent hatreds pursued over many years. Lewis had attacked Bloomsbury with aggressive verbosity, and Rothenstein, like others since, had repeated his claims without substantiating them. After Rothenstein's book appeared Duncan felt obliged to send a letter of protest: Rothenstein sent back a note saying that he was just leaving for America and had no time to reply; and though he has since on more than one occasion been asked to justify his accusations, he has not done so. 'What a little worm he is,' was Vanessa's final comment.[46]

During the early 1950s Vanessa's life followed an established routine that was both satisfying and happy: she painted; she travelled abroad; she made occasional visits to London. She rarely mentioned Don Roche in her letters and seems to have largely ignored his existence. To all appearances she was deeply contented, active, often amused and obsessed with everything that had to do with her family. After the war Bunny had returned to Hilton Hall and Vanessa stayed there on several occasions. As a guest in someone else's house, she could be difficult and complained to Angelica that the coffee was not as she liked it. But she adored her grandchildren, was fascinated by all their doings and pleased if they produced a drawing or painting. In her letters to them she entered fully into a child's world. She also admitted that on the whole she now preferred children to adults. She was, therefore, delighted by the birth of Quentin and Olivier's son, Julian, in October 1952.

Now in her seventies, she was still shy, an essentially private person not always capable of rising to public occasions. When the Royal Academy gave a dinner for the Royal Family and invited Duncan and Vanessa to the party held afterwards in the galleries, Vanessa declined the invitation.

> I simply couldn't face it. Edward [le Bas] asked us to dine at Claridges and go with him and his sister and I knew she'd be in her grand Molyneux dress (she was) and that not only have I no evening dress or shoes or gloves or coat but that I'd have to have my hair done – and altogether one has to feel a good deal stronger than I did to go to such things.[47]

She nevertheless listened avidly to the description that Duncan brought back and passed on a detailed account to Angelica.

She was happiest at Charleston largely because she was surrounded by colours that she liked. When 'young' Mr Stevens undertook to decorate certain rooms, she herself mixed the colours, finding shop-sold house paint always too strong in hue. When she visited Clive's brother Cory she was revolted by the stodgy hideous colours that everywhere afflicted the eye. At Charleston not only did the colours of the objects and decorations in every room form an harmonious whole, but from her desk by the French window in her bedroom she looked on to the garden which in summer boasted a mass of roses, carnations, lilies and sweet peas.

In the summer of 1951 she read of Colonel Teed's death in *The Times* and remarked that it seemed 'to bring to an end all that curious Cassis existence'.[48] As it was she had no wish to return as Clive, on a brief visit in 1949, had brought back reports of huge motorways, modern hotels and Marseilles trippers. Instead she and Duncan toured France by car in 1950 and on two occasions (1949 and 1952) stayed at Lucca in Italy, the austerity of this town satisfying a certain astringency in her nature.

These trips abroad provided a refreshing supply of new subjects to paint. At home her choice could become repetitive for she never tired of flower pieces, still lifes (often set against a patterned cloth) and garden scenes. Only occasionally did she venture into the surrounding landscape, painting the fields at Tilton, Michelham Priory, Newhaven or Brighton beach. Even her portraits were now mostly confined to members of the family and close friends. A new outlet for these paintings was found at this time in the Royal West of England Academy at Bristol which was currently attracting an interesting range of young artists, including Bryan Wynter, Edward Middleditch, Anthony Fry and Mary Fedden. Duncan and Vanessa began sending to this in 1952, becoming members in 1953 and 1954 respectively. As the RWEA had a legacy which was used to buy members' work, several paintings by Vanessa and Duncan entered its collection over the next few years.

In May 1953 Vanessa, with Duncan, made her first visit to Newcastle to stay with Quentin and Olivier and to see her new grandson. She found them absorbed into university life which she regarded with a certain distrust, though she enjoyed meeting again Julia Strachey who had married Lawrence Gowing, at one time a student of the Euston Road School and now Professor of Fine Art. One day Quentin drove Vanessa and Duncan to Durham which Vanessa declared the most beautiful of cathedral towns. On another occasion she borrowed Quentin's car in order to shop in the centre of Newcastle: unable to find where she had parked it, she was obliged to return home on the bus. From Newcastle she and Duncan went on to Edinburgh where he regretted the scarcity of kilts and she bought Edinburgh rock for her grandchildren. There they dined with Colin and Clodagh Mackenzie, friends of Ralph and Frances Partridge, whose elegant house in Heriot Row was filled with paintings. Two of them happened to be by Vanessa and on being shown one of these she stared at it for several minutes with evident distaste, eventually remarking, 'I never remember painting that!'

Though Vanessa did make at least one other visit to Newcastle, she was not attracted to the north and instead Quentin developed the habit of bringing his family to Charleston for the greater part of the long vacation. This began in the summer of 1953. Clive, finding himself once again domiciled in the same house as a very small child, observed the very different conditions that mothers with children now faced, unassisted by the various servants that Vanessa had been able to employ. Also this summer Vanessa was afflicted by her first severe bout of rheumatism in her knees. In June, therefore, she chose to watch the Coronation, not in the streets, but on Edward le Bas's television, while they ate cold chicken and plovers' eggs and drank the Queen's health in champagne.

By the following March Vanessa was well enough to travel by herself to Roquebrune to stay with the Simon Bussys, Duncan having gone to Ireland on the invitation of the Duchess of Devonshire. Vanessa was pleased to find herself once again at the villa set on the hillside overlooking the sweep of the bay. Its garden was already full of roses as well as the forever ripening lemons and oranges. The house, too, she found sympathetic, with its many books and pictures and the recent addition of Gide's deathmask. 'Only I don't think people realize how much solitude painters want,' she wrote to Angelica. 'They seem rather surprised if one vanishes for an hour or two. Not that I've done much here.'[49] She did, however, make a trip to Antibes to see Picasso's pottery and to Vence to see the chapel decorated by Matisse. The former she liked more than she had expected, but the latter she found disappointing; the large line drawings on the white tiles seemed to her a failure and she disliked the colours in the stained glass windows. Dorothy Bussy, who accompanied her, could not get over her horror that Matisse, who admitted to no Christian beliefs, had accepted the commission. With Dorothy and Janie, Vanessa returned to Paris but no sooner had they arrived in the city than news reached them of Simon's stroke. Mother and daughter returned immediately to Roquebrune and shortly afterwards Vanessa learnt of Simon's death.

Over the years Vanessa's and Duncan's 'sublime ineptitude' with cars had remained unchanged. Duncan always looked startled by the noise of the engine and seemed uncertain whether the car would move forwards, backwards or sideways. 'Duncan, *do* be careful,' Vanessa would repeatedly murmur, not unadvisedly. Nevertheless in the spring of 1955 they safely steered their way across France to Asolo in Italy where they rented a house belonging to the Marchesa Fossi. It was called 'La Mura', being partly built into the ancient wall of the town, and had old wooden beams, solid walls and large rooms; upstairs one with windows on three sides made a perfect studio. Two women were employed to look after the house, and Vanessa and Duncan arrived to find the beds already made and the shopping done. Still more important, the place offered Vanessa many subjects to paint: 'Of course the light is so amazing, everything is colour and definite and exciting.'[50]

Soon after they settled in they were joined by Edward le Bas and Eardley Knollys. The latter had recently taken up painting and hoped to learn much from Duncan and Vanessa during the course of the holiday. He quickly perceived that though they talked a great deal about painting in general, they rarely discussed each other's; it was just possible to make a passing remark on Duncan's paintings, but Vanessa froze any discussion of her own. Knollys also noticed that Duncan painted a little too readily, putting up his easel in front of any motif without much forethought; and that Vanessa regarded everything he did as good.

They did a little sight-seeing. One visit took them to the Villa Maser where Vanessa admired the Veronese frescos; another trip to Venice enabled her to revise her opinions on Tintoretto in the Scuola di San Rocco: she now concluded that his *Crucifixion* was one of the greatest pictures in the world. Her companions, meanwhile, remarked on her meticulous housekeeping and her accounting for every expenditure, a habit that her father had instilled in her. She wanted to buy a coffee percolator and went to great lengths to find the right shape, size and price. Though le Bas kept saying that one could easily be acquired at Harrods, she insisted that it had to be bought abroad. He and Knollys were equally surprised at her dread of society; when they invited Freya Stark, who lived opposite, and one of her guests in for a drink, Vanessa was unable to paint at all that day, though when evening came and the guests arrived she relaxed and enjoyed their company.

On their drive back through France Duncan and Vanessa stopped at Alizay, outside Rouen, to visit Amaryllis who was staying with a family in order to learn French. They took her for lunch in a nearby restaurant and afterwards sat in a boat on a river eating cherries. Duncan fell asleep while the other two talked, Amaryllis gradually releasing all her anxieties and unhappiness, caused less by the family than by her extreme shyness: she longed for cheese, but as she had refused it on her first evening was never offered any; she was afraid to speak French and therefore rarely talked to anyone and feared that her mouth was shrinking. Vanessa did what she could to put things right when they returned that evening.

While at Asolo Vanessa had heard that Saxon Sydney-Turner was moving into an old people's home. That summer she gave up 26a Canonbury Square and moved back to Bloomsbury, into Saxon's former flat at 28 Percy Street. Closer to shops, picture galleries and friends (Helen Anrep had a flat on the other side of the street), it was more suited to their needs, but had first to be thoroughly cleaned and whitewashed as Saxon's life had sadly deteriorated and been made impecunious by his addiction to betting. When a number of his friends got up enough money to buy him a television and radio combined, Vanessa illuminated for him a sheet with all the names of the subscribers. In the autumn of 1955 she and Duncan moved into the new flat and soon after received news of the birth of Quentin's and Olivier's daughter, Virginia.

The Percy Street flat remained a *pied-à-terre*. Vanessa's life was still centred at Charleston where in the mornings she was often the first to arrive down to breakfast. She would drink a cup of coffee, sprinkle her buttered toast with salt and then have the first of the three cigarettes which she allowed herself a day. She would gaze abstractedly out of the window, engage a little in conversation with the others, give Grace her orders and then disappear to her studio, situated at the top of the house with its view out across the valley to the Weald, the distant horizons amplifying her detachment. At four she would descend from her studio and, if guests were present, go into the kitchen and make scones. If her grandchildren were staying they would watch as she took off her rings and rubbed the very minimum of butter into the flour with her long fingers. During this period, apart from two Italianate concrete pots made by Quentin for the gateposts, the house did not greatly change. But to the visitor its qualities never seemed to tire or fade but always gave a shock of unexpected pleasure. It had also a unique smell, a compound of turpentine, toast, apples and cut flowers.

The paintings in the house, on the walls, in the racks or left unstretched, continued to accumulate. In February 1956 the Adams Gallery in London gave Vanessa an exhibition which sold well. When Angelica praised the show, Vanessa was touched, admitting that it mattered more to her that her children should think her paintings good than anyone. She had no conception of the public and exhibitions were never her goal: she painted primarily for herself. The initial impulse began with something seen – light on the garden path, reflections in glass or polished wood, a colour chord created by the juxtaposition of fruit with bowl and cloth. As she painted, the intense concentration needed to translate visual impressions into pictorial facts carried her, as she once said, 'into a world quite remote from one's human one.'[51] She brooded over paintings, as Virginia observed, for refreshment because they occupied the timeless realm of the imagination and therefore opposed the endless drift of life. Only in this other world could she become reconciled to the fact of Julian's death. Her often small, serene late still lifes draw their strength not only from a lifetime's experience of painting but also from the fact that they were set against this appalling and undiminishing sense of loss.

Despite the inner richness of experience that she now brought to her work, she still looked with interest at the paintings of others. She was generally critical of the young and still felt a particular dislike for the work of Graham Sutherland, whose reputation was now at its height. On a visit to the Whitechapel Art Gallery in May 1956, however, she was impressed by the work of Nicolas de Staël, of whom she had not previously heard. She missed seeing the American art exhibition at the Tate Gallery in 1956 where one room was devoted to Abstract Expressionism, nor did she see its follow-up, the 1959 exhibition devoted entirely to this large-scale abstract art, but she was aware of the excitement it caused. 'I couldn't go to the American show unluckily,' she wrote to Angelica in 1959, 'which didn't sound to me as though I should like it as much as you did. The only one I've seen was Jackson Pollock whom I didn't really think very good. But I suppose one will see them one day. I cannot somehow believe they are really a nation of painters though I think they are writers.'[52]

In March 1956, on the suggestion of John Piper, Duncan was asked to design sets for John Blow's opera *Venus and Adonis*, performed that summer by the English Opera Group at the Aldeburgh Festival. On the day of the first night Duncan and Vanessa lunched at the Red House, the home of the composer Benjamin Britten and the singer Peter Pears. Vanessa not only admired the collection of paintings that hung in the house but also her host: 'Britten himself is obviously very intelligent and interested in all kinds of things besides music. Also I liked his elder sister, a funny little ugly creature who doesn't live with him but seemed devoted to him.'[53] They met the artist Mary Potter who lived in a studio built in the garden of the Red House, and on their next visit, in 1959, went all over her home looking at her paintings. The following year their visit was returned: Potter, Britten and Pears had decided to forgo a holiday abroad in favour of Sussex and Surrey. As Britten felt a little apprehensive of meeting Clive Bell, the three friends had a drink in a pub before arriving at Charleston. Duncan and Vanessa were waiting in the porch when their guests finally arrived, and greeted them with the apology that Clive was away. More drinks were gladly accepted and the five of them went in to lunch. Afterwards the guests sat in the garden and announced their intention of spending some nights in Brighton, horrifying Vanessa with the thought of its pier, band, candyfloss and crowds.

To her friends Vanessa seemed to live a little outside time: the length of her skirts did not vary according to fashion; she had developed a fondness for scarves and shawls and still wore her hair pulled back either side of her narrow head into a bun. In a late self-portrait, painted in 1958, she looked at herself with unflinching severity[S]. The unbroken outlines of each form enfold the sitter. The still design increases the fixity of her stare. She observes herself dispassionately and without comment. Shorn of self-pity, the residuum of suffering this portrait expresses is contained, as if made manageable through restraint. The confrontation, however, is not only with herself, or the spectator, but ultimately with the approach of death.

In 1952 Desmond MacCarthy died. A year later his wife Molly, having a few months earlier declared that she, like the garden produce, was 'nearly over', also died. In 1956 Vanessa visited Nan Hudson on her deathbed in a nursing-home in Kilburn and found her raving about Napoleon, convinced she was back at her home in Normandy. When in August 1957 one of Duncan's former boy-friends Peter Morris returned to England, having been out of the country for almost twenty years, Vanessa felt as if he had come back from the dead. Instead of the former rich young man there now appeared a silver-haired, rather poor, anxious gentleman, still, however, generous, charming and affectionate. He had brought with him the daughter of a friend in an attempt to distract her from an affair with an undesirable young man. He and the girl joined Vanessa and Duncan that October in Venice, where a small group of their friends gathered: Raymond Mortimer, Eardley Knollys, Barbara Bagenal and Clive. Vanessa still found it hard to tolerate Barbara. 'She didn't actually dance on the Bridge of Sighs, as some expected,' she commented acidly to Angelica, 'but she tripped it merrily on the Zattere, she talked endlessly and with emphasis, and eventually Clive most wickedly asked me and Duncan and Peter who were going for a pleasant day's outing to Torcello and Burano, to take her with us, in her presence. So there was no escaping it.'[54]

The following year Grace followed in her footsteps and made her first visit to Venice, in the company of her friends Ruby Weller and Mrs Harland. Duncan completed his Lincoln Cathedral decorations, which naturally won Vanessa's approval: 'I think they looked lovely, most brilliant, glowing colour, with a wonderful view of Lincoln and the Italian shops with wool, and Olivia, Angelica, Julian and I looking on at the handsome young men.'[55] At the same time she was delighted to discover that her granddaughter Nerissa, one of Angelica's twins, had gifts as a painter. The following year Quentin was offered the post of senior lecturer in art at the University of Leeds (and two years later was given a Chair), and in April 1959, before their move, his and Olivier's second daughter, Cressida, was born. Clive also seemed to prosper (though he complained it now took him two hours to get up in the mornings) and on his annual visit to France visited Picasso at his house outside Cannes and dined with Somerset Maugham.

Towards the end of 1958 preparations began for Duncan's Tate Gallery retrospective which opened the following April. Martin Butlin and Dennis Farr arrived at Charleston to discuss the selection, lunched at the round table in the dining-room and afterwards made a courtesy call to Lydia at Tilton.

> I remember seeing a Picasso drawing [Denis Farr has recalled] fluttering on the mantelpiece in the warm air currents thrown up by a blazing log fire. I expected it to fall into the flames any moment but Lady Keynes seemed totally oblivious of any danger.

When the show opened the rheumatism in Vanessa's knees prevented her from attending the private view. But a few days later she went round the show with Clive and was given tea in the Rex Whistler restaurant by Butlin and Farr, as the latter goes on to describe:

> We both felt such babes entertaining these two pillars of Bloomsbury ... and I remember her warning me not to take David Garnett's stories about Bloomsbury too seriously. ... She said he had a very fertile imagination! The Bells seemed to me to be very reticent and, if I am not imagining things in retrospect, somewhat tense.[56]

On this occasion Vanessa probably feared seeing Rothenstein (then Director of the Tate). She blamed him for the selection which she thought 'idiotic' and the retrospective, despite its prestigious venue, did nothing to lessen her antipathy towards him. E.M. Forster was also unsatisfied: 'The Duncan Grant show was a disappointment, too big and ill chosen, none of Ben's [Benjamin Britten's] sailors or of Harry Daley [the policeman].'[57]

Vanessa was also aware at this date that Janie Bussy was somewhat less than happy. For some time she had regretted the demands made upon Janie by her fast-ageing mother and her Strachey aunts. On one occasion Vanessa caught sight of Janie shopping in Marchmont Street and thought her quite changed, stouter and looking more decidedly French. 'I must say I often think females are downtrodden even now,' she wrote to Angelica. 'If Janie were a son no one would ever have expected her to do anything but paint – and the poor creature hasn't children to make any of it worthwhile. She can only have real freedom after all her relations have died it seems.'[58] Clive also saw what Janie suffered: 'She bears up nobly; but one can't lead the life she has to lead without showing it. Pain will be paid quite as much as pleasure [sic]. She can't face taking Dorothy back to Roquebrune and seems not quite to know what is to happen to La Suco [Souco] this winter. She has offered it to Vanessa and Duncan; but they procrastinate. Someone she feels must live there to prevent the roof falling in.'[59]

The reason they havered over taking La Souco for the winter was Vanessa's poor health. Early in 1959 she had contracted bronchial pleurisy which left her in a frail condition. She resigned from the Edwin Austin Abbey Memorial Trust Fund and shrank from making visits to London. Instead she began a large group portrait of Angelica and her four daughters, Amaryllis, Henrietta, Nerissa and Fanny, striving again for a monumental design. The result was a strange pastiche of an eighteenth-century conversation piece. The figures appear expressionless, doll-like and wooden. There is a curious absence of any real feeling and instead a substitute, morbid sentimentality. Nevertheless this painting was sent this year to the Royal West of England Academy's annual exhibition and, at £300, the most expensive picture in the show, went unsold.

By January 1960 Vanessa had recovered her strength enough to travel to Roquebrune by train with Duncan and Grace. At La Souco they were assisted by a woman who came each day to do the shopping and housework. Nevertheless the holiday began a little gloomily and Vanessa, like the stray cat that haunted the villa, did not wish to leave the house and garden. They looked through Simon Bussy's paintings which Janie had put in order in the studio, and waited for the garden to burst into flower. Among the many books in the house Vanessa found a volume of Thackeray's letters and papers, which she fell upon, hoping to encounter her Aunt Anny as she read. She also painted, and in December 1960 *The Garden Window, Roquebrune* hung at the Royal West of England Academy.

When Clive and Barbara Bagenal arrived at nearby Menton, where they put up in an hotel, they thought the inhabitants of La Souco seemed dismal. 'Duncan would enjoy himself immensely and would dearly like to join us in little restaurants and make acquaintance with our acquaintances. But V. seems to have no idea of going beyond the garden; and Duncan can't very well leave her alone – we can't very well invite him alone either. Later Angelica and Edward le Bas are coming out – perhaps Peter Morris too – then the situation will become easier.'[60] It became clear that Vanessa was losing her grip on practical matters, which had always been her concern. This worried Duncan and his usual serenity was replaced by a cantankerous grumpiness. The arrival of Peter Morris, then Angelica, improved matters. The latter hired a car and this enabled them all to go out 'on the motif' or in to Menton to dine with Clive and Barbara in small restaurants. Vanessa enjoyed these outings, but remained quiet and passive. Early in March Angelica returned to her family and Clive wrote to Frances Partridge: 'Her stay at Le Suco [La Souco] was a great pleasure to everyone. She took complete charge of the establishment and effected change for the better in every department: hired a car and drove it admirably (Duncan now drives it less skilfully so far as I can judge): went off for a day's shopping in Ventimiglia market with Barbara and Grace – a great success – gave extensive orders for desirables and much needed comestibles and appliances: rang up several veterinary surgeons ... in fact made things hum and attracted numerous admirers.'[61]

Not long after Angelica left, Vanessa began to think about returning home. 'This is an odd place,' she wrote. 'I like it in a way very much and yet I don't think I want to stay here very long or come often. Everything in the house is simply falling to pieces and after a bit it rather gets on one's nerves. The lights go out, the chairs seem to be going to fall to pieces in a day or two, the cats increase. I am becoming aware of ghosts.'[62] Towards the end of March a spell of fine weather set in. They sat out on the terrace, overlooking the sea and the curve of the shore which was obliterated from sight when a mountain mist descended. They picked the oranges and sent a boxful to Janie. Edward le Bas arrived and stayed a few days, and Clive and Barbara paid regular visits. 'Clive and B. came to their usual Sunday lunch,' Vanessa wrote, 'and I was greeted in the garden by a spectacular rush from B. jumping down the garden path flinging herself into my arms and shrieking out some hectic remark about her feelings on the occasion – oh God – that woman will drive me mad if I have to see much of her.'[63] Barbara's imminence strengthened Vanessa's resolve to leave and in early April, after pausing two nights in Paris *en route*, she returned home.

As soon as was possible they arranged to see Janie in order to give her news of La Souco. The day before they were due to meet, Marjorie Strachey rang up: Janie had been found dead in the bathroom at 51 Gordon Square. An inquest was held; the verdict was accidental death caused by an old-fashioned gas water-heater which had not been regularly cleaned. The whole event was devastating to everyone concerned. Janie's two aunts, Pippa and Marjorie Strachey, never forgot the kindness shown them by Vanessa and Duncan, who turned up unexpectedly at 51 Gordon Square with a hot meal. Dorothy Bussy, too senile to realize what had happened, was moved into a nursing-home where she died a couple of weeks later. 'If only it could have happened before',[64] Vanessa remarked, bitterly reflecting on the restricting circumstances that had thwarted the last part of Janie's life. Though very different in character and intelligence, Janie had recently turned for solace and friendship to Barbara Bagenal, and she was hard hit by this tragedy. She and Clive had received the news at Lydd airport, as Clive recounts: 'For a few moments Barbara collapsed in the custom's house. . . . The shock was hardly surprising, seeing that Janie had become her closest friend. They were in constant correspondence and B. was bringing back all sorts of little presents for her.'[65] Though two more deaths occurred in May, those of Douglas Davidson and Dora Morris, neither caused such a sense of loss, for Janie's distinctive personality, her astute mind, caustic humour and love of painting had caused both Clive and Vanessa to regard her with ever-increasing affection.

One tale of the past with which Vanessa regaled her grandchildren was that concerning her great-grandmother, Adeline de l'Etang, eldest daughter of the Chevalier de l'Etang, whose likeness had been recorded in a miniature which Julia Stephen had often worn as a locket. According to Vanessa, Adeline could speak no English at all except for one sentence – 'If you don't like it you must lump it.'

It was a philosophy that Vanessa had trained herself to observe but one she did not always impart to others. As with Angelica, she would attend to most of the whims of her grandchildren, making dolls' clothes, entering their childhood world of fantasy, sharing the pretence that the dolls pined of love or suffered terrible fevers; occasionally she would jab them in the arm with her darning needle to inoculate them against further misfortunes. 'As we grew older,' Henrietta has recalled,

> Amaryllis and I were sometimes allowed to stay up for dinner instead of being given an early supper. On these occasions we both paraded in extravagant and fantastic evening dress concocted from curtains, lengths of Omega cloth, Vanessa's nightdresses, feathers, flowers and finery borrowed from her jewel boxes. Then we pretended that we were grand ladies. Duchesses, courtesans and curate's daughters. We flirted outrageously with Duncan and with Clive. On one occasion we went so far as to have a double wedding. Amaryllis married Clive, I married Duncan. This curious wedding party took place one sunny afternoon and it was held in the piazza by the small fish pond beneath the apple tree. Nessa officiated as high priestess. Then we all had tea.
>
> They were delightful evenings. Our childish follies were entered into and bettered by the company we kept. For Clive was a witty and erudite conversationalist of great charm and intelligence. Duncan was an enchanting and eccentric individual. Nessa loved them both. She gazed from one to another with her beautiful blue-grey eyes and let the smoke drift slowly from the gauloise which she took with her after dinner coffee. At certain intervals she

would murmur 'How absurd'.[66]

Detached, amused, surrounded by those she loved and still able to take pleasure in a career that had directed and enriched her life; an elderly woman who had survived the tragic death of her son and distress over her daughter's marriage, emerging from this fearful period securely and affectionately married, in all but name, to the person with whom she had chosen to share her life. These are reasons enough to explain the serenity reflected in her paintings and letters. But they do not account for the sense of isolation and poignant sadness found in the photographs and portraits of Vanessa in old age.

Over the years she had sat to Duncan on many occasions. His most formal portrait of her is that painted in 1942 and now in the Tate Gallery. Dressed in a long cloak, seated on an upright chair and framed by swags of drapery, she looks straight out at the spectator with stern, regal aloofness. Given her longstanding intimacy with Duncan, it is a curiously external likeness, contrived, stiff, repelling. By comparison, the portrait he painted of her in 1959 is more harmoniously arranged; folds of material lap round her in curves that echo those in the sofa behind. The frontality is also modified by the decision to show her gaze averted. She sits brooding within herself, her personality withdrawn; even the artist is shut out by the melancholy that surrounds her[§]. It presents the person with whom Angelica had for some time found it difficult to communicate freely, to whom Duncan was obliged to write on the rare occasions that he strove to break through the barriers of privacy surrounding their intimate yet separate lives. It portrays a woman who when young, as Virginia had observed, had contained 'volcanoes underneath her sedate manner';[67] who had found in painting the philosopher's stone to transmute suffering into serenity, but in so doing had become walled up in her own feelings, isolated by her reserve and left profoundly alone.

In the autumn of 1960 she visited London because the Picasso exhibition at the Tate Gallery was an event that others knew she would enjoy. For the most part Charleston had now become her entire world. 'Yesterday Leonard and Morgan [E.M. Forster] came to lunch and seemed to enjoy themselves,' she wrote to Angelica in September. 'Duncan is painting, I am sitting in my room with the door open between us. The garden is full of Red Admirals and birds and apples.'[68] That winter she never left the house. She heard of Ralph Partridge's death and immediately wrote an affectionate note to Frances. Clive also wrote, urging Frances to join him and Barbara at Menton in the new year. After his departure, Vanessa and Duncan were alone at Charleston. Edward le Bas, possibly sensing a loss of motivation, persuaded the Adams brothers to give Vanessa another show.

They began negotiations and Vanessa responded with hesitant vagueness. 'I feel very incompetent nowadays,' she admitted to Angelica. 'As I can't drive I can do nothing if left to myself. I have seen no one for ages.'[69] Even her grandchildren were either too distant or too occupied with their own lives to visit. When Henrietta telephoned Charleston and announced that she was taking part in one of Bertrand Russell's peace marches, Vanessa was thrown into confused alarm and wrote anxiously to Angelica for further explanation. Real concern was caused by news of Clive. While looking at a church in Menton in the company of his friend Raymond Mortimer, he had fallen down some steps and broken his leg. As Frances Partridge was confined to her hotel room with flu, Barbara Bagenal was left to cope with Clive's misfortune unaided. Fortunately Kenneth Clark was staying near by and he arranged for Clive to be flown home. He went straight into the London Clinic. Duncan visited him there, but Vanessa was not strong enough to make the journey to town. Instead she comforted herself with the thought that he would soon be recuperating in Charleston garden.

In March Duncan and Vanessa finished *Mansfield Park* which they had been reading aloud to each other. The fine weather brought out the daffodils and crocuses. 'I haven't been to London for ages and really don't much want to go – it seems so silly when it's so lovely here,' Vanessa wrote to Angelica, enclosing with her letter a cheque for £50 which she had mistakenly dated 1956.[70] The mild spring perhaps seemed warmer than it really was because on 4 April Vanessa fell suddenly ill with bronchitis. Her north-facing bedroom, with its French windows opposite the bed, was cold in temperature if warm with the colours of her and Duncan's paintings, his screen and rug. Grace tried repeatedly to put hot water bottles into her bed but frequently found them on the floor. She was struck by Vanessa's remoteness, by the fact that after more than forty years in her employment she seemed unknowable. On the day that she had fallen ill Quentin had arrived at Charleston on a pre-arranged visit with his small son. As Vanessa's condition was evidently serious, he took Julian up to London early on the morning of 7 April and left him with his Popham grandfather. He returned to Charleston just before 11.30 a.m., when Vanessa's heart gave out and she died without pain.[71] Shortly afterwards Angelica arrived, having been telephoned, too late, earlier that morning. In the London Clinic, Clive received the news from Barbara, and wept for the wife he had never ceased to love.

Five days later, on 12 April, Duncan, Quentin, Angelica and Grace accompanied Vanessa's coffin to Firle churchyard where, without any form of service, she was buried. Later a plain, black tombstone was erected, giving only her name and dates. Its starkness is a reminder of her innate solitariness. For even amid company at Charleston, when surrounded by a sensuous concord of line, form and colour, she emitted a remarkable contained and containing power; it translated an essentially tragic love into a lasting, creative union; it caused Virginia to liken Vanessa to 'a bowl of golden water which brims but never overflows'.[72]

Notes

The whereabouts of manuscript material is indicated at the end of each note. Certain holders of manuscripts are referred to by the following abbreviations:

QB – Quentin Bell
AVG – Angelica Garnett
HC – Henrietta Couper
FP – Frances Partridge
AP – Anrep Papers (in a private collection)
BL – British Library, Manuscript Department
KCC – King's College, Cambridge
Berg – Berg Collection, New York Public Library
Sussex – University of Sussex Library
Texas – Humanities Research Center, the University of Texas at Austin

The reference to papers at King's College, Cambridge, does not in every instance point to the original document but to copies of the originals made while the Charleston Papers were in their care. On 21 July 1980 the Charleston Papers were sold at Sotheby's in London and are now dispersed. A large number were bought by the Tate Gallery and are now in its Archive Department, but at the time of writing (1982) had not been fully catalogued.

In every instance the references to Virginia Woolf's edited letters and diaries are abbreviated; e.g., Woolf, *Letters*, vol. I, p. 174, and the full title of each volume given in the bibliography.

Chapter 1: Always the Eldest
1879–1895

1 Vanessa Stephen to M. Snowden, no date [March 1903]: KCC. According to William Rothenstein, Watts said his painting, entitled *The Parasite*, represented 'the undisciplined art of the day slowly sapping the life of a centuries-old artistic inheritance'. *Men and Memories*, vol. I (Rose and Crown Library Edition, 1934), p. 207. The painting belongs to the Watts Gallery, Compton, Guildford.

2 Vanessa Stephen to M. Snowden, 11 January 1905: KCC.

3 Woolf, *Letters*, vol. I, p. 174.

4 Vanessa to Clive Bell [? June 1915]: KCC.

5 Georgiana Burne-Jones, *Memorials of Edward Burne-Jones*, vol. I, 1904, p. 159.

6 du Maurier, Daphne (ed.), *The Young George du Maurier*, 1951, p. 112.

7 John Ruskin, *The Winnington Letters*, ed. Van Akin Burd, 1969, p. 150.

8 *Memorials of Edward Burne-Jones*, vol. I, p. 188.

9 Quoted in Brian Hill, *Julia Margaret Cameron. A Victorian Family Photograph*, 1973, p. 83.

10 Quoted in Frederic Maitland, *The Life of Sir Leslie Stephen*, 1906, p. 335.

11 *Sir Leslie Stephen's Mausoleum Book*, introd. Alan Bell, 1977, p. 35.

12 Leslie to Julia Stephen, 22 March 1887: Berg.

13 Vanessa Bell, *Notes on Virginia's Childhood*, ed. R.J. Schaubeck Jr, 1974, unpaginated.

14 Virginia Woolf, *Moments of Being*, 1976 p. 29.

15 Ibid., p. 30.

16 Leslie to Julia Stephen, 13 April 1884: Berg.

17 Same to same, 12 July 1890: Berg.

18 Same to same, 27 July 1893: Berg.

19 *Notes on Virginia's Childhood*.

20 *Moments of Being*, pp. 28, 29.

21 Noël Annan, *Leslie Stephen, His Thought & Character in Relation to his Time*, 1951, pp. 100–101.

22 Sir Henry Newbolt, *My World as in My Time*, 1932, p. 177.

23 Vanessa Bell to Virginia Woolf, 11 May 1927: Berg.

24 *Selected Letters of Henry James*, ed. Leon Edel, 1955, p. 149.

Chapter 2: Mrs Young's Evening Dress 1895–1904

1 William Rothenstein, *Men and Memories*, abr. and ed. Mary Lago, 1978, p. 141.

2 Ibid., p. 60.

3 For information on Ebenezer Cooke I am indebted to an unpublished thesis by A.E. Richardson (University of Newcastle, 1971).

4 L. Stephen to J. Duckworth, 18 July 1877: Berg.

5 See Quentin Bell, *Virginia Woolf*, 1972 vol. I, pp. 42–4.

6 Vanessa to Virginia Stephen, 8 September 1904: Berg.

7 *Moments of Being*, p. 96.

8 Ibid., p. 96.

9 Ibid., p. 46.

10 Vanessa to Thoby Stephen, 16 March [1897]: KCC.

11 Vanessa Bell, Memoir II: AVG.

12 Virginia Stephen, Hyde Park Gate Diary, 1897 (June 13): Berg.

13 L. Stephen to C.E. Norton, 25 July 1897: Harvard University Library.

14 Woolf, *Diaries*, vol. I, p. 69.

15 Violet Dickinson, 'Notes on the Stephen Family': The Library, Longleat House.

16 *Moments of Being*, p. 54.

17 Vanessa Bell, Memoir III: AVG.

18 Cynthia Asquith, *Remember and Be Glad*, 1952, p. 64.

19 Vanessa Bell, Memoir II.

20 Vanessa Bell, Memoir III.

21 *Moments of Being*, p. 149

22 Interview with Mrs Gilbert Russell, 27 September 1980.

23 Hyde Park Gate Diary, 1903 (July 15): Berg.

24 Maitland, *The Life of Sir Leslie Stephen*, p. 439.

25 L. Stephen to C.E. Norton, 31 December 1900: Harvard University Library.

26 *Moments of Being*, p. 59.

27 Ibid., p. 122.

28 Ibid., p. 119.

29 'Notes on the Stephen Family'.

30 Woolf, *Diaries*, vol. III, p. 255.

31 The portrait of Leslie Stephen was sold at Sotheby's on 21 July 1980, and that of Elizabeth Hills, daughter of Eustace Hills, belongs to Walter Aylen. As the child was born in November 1900 and appears to be around eighteen months old, the picture can be dated to the early summer of 1902.

32 Vanessa Bell to Virginia Woolf, 11 May [1927]: Berg.

33 Vanessa Stephen to M. Snowden, 4 January [1902?]: KCC.

34 Quoted in Evan Charteris, *John Sargent*, 1927, p. 188.

35 Vanessa Bell, Memoir VI: AVG.

36 Ibid.

37 Ibid.

38 *Moments of Being*, p. 126.

39. Vanessa Stephen to C. Bell, 10 September 1902: KCC.

40 *Moments of Being*, p. 124.

41 Vanessa Bell, Memoir III.

42 Quoted in Winifred Gerin, *Anne Thackeray Ritchie*, 1981, p. 287.

Chapter 3: Changing Places 1904–1906

1 Vanessa Stephen to M. Snowden, [9 April 1904]: KCC.

2 Ibid.

3 Same to same, 3 May 1904: KCC.

4 Vanessa Stephen to C. Bell, 11 May 1904: KCC.

5 Vanessa Bell, Memoir III: AVG.

6 Vanessa to Virginia Stephen, 8 September 1904: Berg.

7 Same to same, [? 30 October 1904]: Berg.

8 Same to same, 31 October [1904]: Berg.

9 *Moments of Being*, pp. 162, 163.

10 Vanessa Bell, Memoir III.

11 L. Strachey to L. Woolf, 21 December 1904: Texas.

12 Quentin Bell, *Bloomsbury*, 1968 (Omega edn 1974), p. 13.

13 Vanessa Bell, Memoir IV: AVG.

14 David Garnett, *The Flowers of the Forest*, 1955 p. 23.

15 'Letter to a Lady', *Ad Familiares*, The Pelican Press, October 1917 (privately printed).

16 'Mrs Raven-Hill' (essay written for the Memoir Club): Trinity College Library, Cambridge.

17 Quoted in Michael Holroyd's *Lytton Strachey: a biography* (London. Penguin rev. edn 1979), p. 139.

18 C. Bell to L. Strachey, 9 August 1908: BL.

19 Vanessa Bell, Memoir IV.

20 C. Bell to L. Strachey, [20 July 1905]: BL.

21 Vanessa Stephen to M. Vaughan, 25 March [1905]: KCC.

22 Vanessa Stephen to M. Snowden [14 August 1905]: KCC.

23 Vanessa to Virginia Stephen, 7 December 1904: Berg.

24 Richard Shone, 'The Friday Club', *Burlington Magazine*, May 1975, vol. CXVII, no. 866, p. 279.

25 Woolf, *Letters*, vol. I, p. 201.

26 Ibid., p. 213.

27 Sir Charles Petrie, *Scenes of Edwardian Life*, 1965, p. 43.

28 Vanessa to Virginia Stephen [15 April 1906]: Berg.

29 Vanessa Stephen to C. Bell [2 November, 1906]: KCC.

30 Same to same, [8 November 1906]: KCC.

31 C. Bell to S. Sydney-Turner, 16 November [1906]: KCC.

32 *Moments of Being*, p. 170.

33 M. Snowden to C. Bell, 30 November 1906: KCC.

34 Vanessa Bell to M. Vaughan, 11 December [1906]: KCC.

35 Vanessa to Virginia Stephen, 14 December [1906]: Berg.

Chapter 4: Mr and Mrs Clive Bell
1907–1909

1 Quoted in Quentin Bell's *Virginia Woolf*, vol. II, p. 6.

2 Vanessa Bell to Virginia Stephen, 22 March [1907]: Berg.

3 *Moments of Being*, p. 170.

4 M. Keynes to D. Grant, 2 August 1910. Quoted Quentin Bell, *Virginia Woolf*, vol. I, p. 124.

5 Vanessa Bell to D. Carrington, 25 January [1932]: Texas.

6 Vanessa Bell, Memoir IV: AVG.

7 Leonard Woolf, *Beginning Again*, 1964, p. 23.

8 G.E. Moore, *Principia Ethica*, 1903, p. 189.

9 *Beginning Again*, p. 75.

10 Raymond Williams, 'The Significance of "Bloomsbury" as a Social and Cultural Group', *Keynes and the Bloomsbury Group*, ed. D. Crabtree and A.P. Thirlwall 1980, p. 59.

11 Vanessa Bell to Virginia Stephen, 2 September [1909]: Berg.

12 Same to same, [3 August 1907]: Berg.

13 Same to same, [13 August (?) 1907]: Berg.

14 Same to same, [20 August 1907]: Berg.

15 Ibid.

16 Notebook dated July 1937 on Julian Bell: KCC.

17 Vanessa Bell to M. Vaughan, February 17 [1907]: KCC.

18 Vanessa Bell to Virginia Stephen, [21 April 1908]: Berg.

19 The description of life at Hyde Park Gate is published as 'Reminiscences' in *Moments of Being*.

20 Vanessa Bell to Virginia Stephen, 20 April [1908]: Berg.

21 Same to same, [19 April 1908]: Berg.

22 Ibid.

23 C. Bell to Virginia Stephen, 18 April 1908: Sussex.

24 Vanessa Bell to Virginia Stephen, 20 April [1908]: Berg.

25 Quentin Bell, *Virginia Woolf*, vol. I, p. 133.

26 Vanessa Bell to Virginia Stephen, 4 May [1908]: Berg.

27 Woolf, *Letters*, vol. I, p. 329.

28 C. Bell to Virginia Stephen, 7 May 1908: Sussex.

29 Woolf, *Letters*, vol. III, p. 172.

30 Ibid., I, p. 255.

31 C. Bell to Virginia Stephen, 30 July 1908: Sussex.

32 Same to same, 7 August 1908: Sussex.

33 Same to same, 3 August 1908: Sussex.

34 Vanessa Bell to Virginia Stephen [30 July 1908]: Berg.

35 Same to same, [11 August 1908]: Berg.

36 Vanessa Bell to L. Strachey, 27 August [1908]: BL.

37 Vanessa Bell to Virginia Stephen, [21 August 1908]: Berg.

38 Vanessa Bell to M. Snowden, 7 October [1908]: KCC.

39 C. Bell to Virginia Stephen, 30 December 1908: Sussex.

40 Vanessa to Clive Bell, 31 December [1909]: KCC.

41 J.M. Keynes to D. Grant, 14 February 1909: BL.

42 The portrait no longer exists. It did not remain with the Corsini family, was possibly never completed and is probably destroyed.

43 Vanessa Bell to Virginia Woolf, 16 May [1909]: Berg.
44 Vanessa to Clive Bell, no date [December 1909?]: KCC.
45 R. Gathorne-Hardy (ed.), *Ottoline: The Early Years*, 1963, p. 197.
46 Vanessa Bell to M. Snowden, 7 October [1908]: KCC.
47 C. Bell to Virginia Stephen, 25 December 1909: Sussex.
48 C. Bell to L. Strachey, 22 October 1909: BL.

Chapter 5: Petticoats over Windmills 1910-1912
1 Vanessa Bell, Memoir VI: AVG.
2 H. Head to R. Fry, 14 November 1910: KCC.
3 Memoir VI.
4 Vanessa Bell to Virginia Stephen, 27 July 1910: Berg.
5 Vanessa Bell to M. Vaughan, 5 June [1910]: KCC.
6 Vanessa to Clive Bell, 25 June [1910]: KCC.
7 Vanessa Bell to Virginia Stephen, 24 June [1910]: Berg.
8 M. Keynes to D. Grant, 15 November 1910: BL.
9 Vanessa to Clive Bell, [23 June 1910]: KCC.
10 Vanessa Bell to Virginia Stephen, 20 July [1910]: Berg.
11 Vanessa to Clive Bell, 30 August [1910]: KCC.
12 Vanessa Bell to Virginia Stephen, 12 October [1910]: Berg.
13 D. MacCarthy to O. Morrell, no date: Texas.
14 Memoir VI.
15 Ibid.
16 Ibid.
17 Clive Bell, *Old Friends*, 1956, p. 64.
18 Memoir VI.
19 Vanessa Bell to Virginia Stephen, 6 April [1911]: Berg.
20 C. Bell to Virginia Stephen, 13 April 1911: Sussex.
21 Memoir VI.
22 C. Bell to Virginia Stephen, [3 April 1911]: Sussex.
23 Same to same, [?12 January 1911]: Sussex.
24 Vanessa Bell to Virginia Stephen [2 June 1911]: Berg.
25 Memoir VI.
26 Vanessa Bell to L. Strachey, 9 August 1911: BL.
27 Vanessa Bell to R. Fry, 23 June [1911]: KCC.
28 Same to same, [3 July 1911]: KCC.
29 Ibid.
30 *Old Friends*, p. 64.
31 O. Sitwell, *Noble Essences*, 1950, p. 166.
32 Vanessa Bell to R. Fry, [6 July 1911]: KCC.
33 Roger Fry, 'The Salons and Van Dougen [sic]', *Nation*, 24 June 1911, pp. 463-4.
34 Vanessa Bell to R. Fry, 27 September [1911]: KCC.
35 Vanessa to Clive Bell, 23 October [1911]: KCC.
36 Ibid.
37 Michael Holroyd, contributing to 'A Boom in Bloomsbury', BBC Radio 4, 3 August 1982.
38 Vanessa Bell to R. Fry, 23 November [1911]: KCC.
39 Ibid., no date [1911]: KCC.
40 Vanessa to Clive Bell, [16 January 1912]: KCC.
41 Ibid.
42 Vanessa Bell to R. Fry, 18 January [1912]: KCC.
43 Vanessa Bell to Virginia Stephen, 13 January [1912]: KCC.

44 *The Flowers of the Forest*, pp. 102, 103.
45 Vanessa Bell to R. Fry, 5 June [1912]: KCC.
46 Ibid., no date [June 1912]: KCC.

Chapter 6: Asheham 1912–1914

1 Vanessa to Clive Bell, 17 August [1912]: KCC.
2 Vanessa Bell to Virginia Woolf, 14 August [1912]: Berg.
3 Vanessa Bell to R. Fry, no date [Spring 1912]: KCC.
4 Vanessa to Clive Bell, 20 August [1912]: KCC.
5 Vanessa Bell to Virginia Woolf, 18 September [1912]: Berg.
6 Vanessa to Clive Bell, 20 August [1913]: KCC.
7 D. Grant to Virginia Woolf, 23 September 1912: Sussex.
8 R. Fry to Vanessa Bell, 15 September 1912: KCC.
9 *Beginning Again*, p. 27.
10 Vanessa Bell to R. Fry, 28 December [1913?]: KCC.
11 Same to same, no date [Spring 1912]: KCC.
12 Same to same, 11 September [1912]: KCC.
13 Vanessa Bell to L. Woolf, 21 September [1912]: Sussex.
14 D. Grant to J.M. Keynes, 28 September 1912: BL.
15 *Morning Advertiser*, 4 October 1912.
16 *Star*, 3 February 1913.
17 *Observer*, 27 October 1912.
18 *Nation*, 24 June 1911.
19 Roger Fry in the *Nation*, 20 April 1912.
20 Catalogue introduction to the Second Post-Impressionist Exhibition. Reprinted in Roger Fry, *Vision and Design*, 1920.
21 Vanessa Bell to R. Fry, 2 November [1912?]: KCC.
22 Angelica Garnett, 'Life at Charleston': MS lecture notes: AVG.
23 Interview with Sarah Whitfield 1970 or 1971. Tape in Tate Gallery Archives.
24 Vanessa Bell to Virginia Woolf, 6 February [1913]: Berg.
25 Angelica Garnett, introduction to *Duncan Grant: Works on Paper*, catalogue to an exhibition held at the Anthony d'Offay Gallery, 25 Nov. – 18 Dec. 1981.
26 Vanessa Bell to R. Fry, 7 January [1912]: KCC.
27 Vanessa Bell to Virginia Woolf, 3 May [1913]: Berg.
28 Vanessa Bell to R. Fry, 6 February [1913]: KCC.
29 Vanessa Bell to J.M. Keynes, 16 April [1914]: KCC.
30 Vanessa Bell to Virginia Woolf, [17 August 1913]: Berg.
31 Woolf, *Letters*, vol. II, p. 292.
32 Vanessa Bell to R. Fry, no date [1912–13]: KCC.
33 Simon Watney, *English Post-Impressionism*, 1980, p. 100.
34 Vanessa Bell to L. Woolf, 22 January [1913]: Sussex.
35 *Pall Mall Gazette*, 8 January 1914.
36 D. Grant to J.M. Keynes, no date [22 January 1914]: BL.
37 Vanessa Bell to D. Grant, no date [1914]: HC.
38 Ibid., 14 January [1914]: HC.
39 Vanessa to Clive Bell, no date [August 1914]: KCC.
40 Conversation with Paul Roche.
41 Conversation with Richard Shone.
42 Vanessa Bell to R. Fry, 8 April [1913]: KCC.
43 R. Fry to H. Anrep, no date: AP.

44 Vanessa to Clive Bell, no date [April/May 1914]: KCC.

45 Woolf, *Letters*, vol. I, p. 475.

46 *Moments of Being*, p. 30.

47 Vanessa to Clive Bell, 25 June 1910: KCC.

48 Vanessa Bell, Memoir IV: AVG.

49 Vanessa Bell to R. Fry, 20 August [1914]: KCC.

50 R. Fry to Vanessa Bell, 15 June [1914?]: KCC.

51 Same to same, 21 September 1914: KCC.

52 Same to same, no date [? August 1914]: KCC.

53 Vanessa Bell to R. Fry, 17 September [1914]: KCC.

Chapter 7: Granite and Rainbow 1914–1916

1 Geoffrey Keynes, *The Gates of Memory*, 1981, p. 89.

2 Quoted in Holroyd, *Lytton Strachey* (Penguin rev. edn), p. 297.

3 BBC radio programme, 'Recollections of the Bloomsbury Group' by Marjorie Strachey, Light programme, 27 August 1962.

4 Woolf, *Diaries*, vol. I, p. 288.

5 Bell, *Virginia Woolf*, vol. I, p. 170.

6 David Garnett's diary 1914–15: Richard Garnett.

7 David Garnett, unpublished essay on Vanessa Bell originally intended for inclusion in his *Great Friends* (1978): Richard Garnett.

8 Ibid.

9 Angelica Garnett, introduction to *Duncan Grant: Works on Paper*, catalogue to an exhibition held at the Anthony d'Offay Gallery, 15 Nov.– 18 Dec. 1981.

10 D. Grant, quoted in David Garnett's *The Flowers of the Forest*, p. 129.

11 Vanessa Bell to R. Fry, [? March 1915]: KCC.

12 Vanessa Bell to H. Young, 15 April [1915]: University of Cambridge Library.

13 Vanessa Bell to Virginia Woolf, [?27 March 1915]: Berg.

14 Vanessa to Clive Bell [?25 March 1915]: KCC.

15 Vanessa Bell to D. Garnett, 12 April 1915: HC.

16 Vanessa Bell to Virginia Stephen, [24 March 1914]: Berg.

17 Vanessa Bell to D. Garnett [25 August 1915]: HC.

18 Vanessa to Clive Bell [28 April 1915]: KCC.

19 Vanessa Bell to R. Fry, 2 May [1915]: KCC.

20 D. Grant to D. Garnett [6 May 1915]: HC.

21 Woolf, *Letters*, vol. II, p. 111.

22 R. Fry to Vanessa Bell, 27 February 1915: KCC.

23 Same to same, 11 April 1915: KCC.

24 Vanessa Bell to R. Fry, 25 June [1915]: KCC.

25 Vanessa to Clive Bell, 22 June [1915]: KCC.

26 Vanessa Bell to D. Garnett, 12 July 1915: HC.

27 Same to same, 24 July 1915: HC.

28 Vanessa Bell to D. Garnett, 1 August [1915]: HC.

29 Vanessa Bell to R. Fry, 2 July [1915]: KCC.

30 Vanessa Bell to Maynard Keynes, [Autumn 1915]: KCC.

31 Vanessa Bell to R. Fry [1915]: KCC.

32 See note 7.

33 Adrian Daintrey, *I Must Say*, 1963, p. 124.

34 Vanessa Bell to L. Strachey, 27 April [1916]: BL.

35 Vanessa Bell to Virginia Woolf, [22 August 1915]: Berg.

36 Vanessa Bell to D. Garnett, 22 September 1915: HC.

37 D. Grant to D. Garnett, 5 November 1915: HC.

38 Vanessa to Clive Bell, [Spring 1916]: KCC.

39 Vanessa Bell to R. Fry, [Spring 1916]: KCC.

40 Vanessa Bell to L. Strachey, 27 April [1916]: BL.

41 Quoted Michael Holroyd, *Lytton Strachey*, 1978, p. 657.

42 Vanessa Bell to R. Fry, [early Summer 1916]: KCC.

43 Vanessa Bell to R. Fry [? June 1916]: KCC.

44 Woolf, *Letters*, vol. II, p. 108.

45 Quoted in R. Fry to H. Anrep, 8 April 1925: AP.

46 Woolf, *Letters*, vol. II, p. 400.

47 Ibid., vol. III, pp. 498–9.

48 Vanessa Bell to R. Fry, Summer 1916: KCC.

49 Ibid.

50 Vanessa Bell to M. Keynes, 27 August [1916]: KCC.

51 Vanessa Bell to D. Grant [18 September 1916]: BL.

52 D. Garnett to L. Strachey [September 1916]: BL.

53 Vanessa Bell to R. Fry, [October 1916]: KCC.

Chapter 8: One Among Three 1916–1918

1 At the time of writing (1982) Charleston is being repaired and restored by the Charleston Trust which publishes a regular newsletter detailing its progress.

2 Milo Keynes (ed.), *Essays on John Maynard Keynes*, 1975, p. 3.

3 Paul Levy, 'The Bloomsbury Group', ibid., p. 69.

4 J.M. Keynes to Vanessa Bell, 21 August 1916: KCC.

5 Woolf, *Letters*, vol. II, p. 149.

6 Ibid., pp. 147–8.

7 Letter to the author, July 1982.

8 Vanessa Bell to R. Fry, [September 1917]: KCC.

9 R. Fry to Vanessa Bell, 16 September 1917: KCC.

10 Vanessa Bell to Virginia Woolf, [23 July 1917]: Berg.

11 Same to same, 3 July [1918]: Berg.

12 Vanessa Bell to Virginia Woolf, 13 February [1918]: Berg.

13 Same to same, [?19 December 1918]: Berg.

14 Same to same, [?4 April 1918]: Berg.

15 Vanessa Bell to R. Fry, 3 July [1917]: KCC.

16 Woolf, *Letters*, vol. II, p. 337.

17 Vanessa Bell to Virginia Woolf, 13 February [1918]: Berg.

18 Ibid., [13 January 1918]: Berg.

19 Vanessa Bell to Virginia Woolf, 13 February [1918]: Berg.

20 David Garnett, unpublished essay on Vanessa Bell originally intended for inclusion in *Great Friends* (1978): Richard Garnett.

21 David Garnett's diary for 1918: Richard Garnett.

22 Watney, *English Post-Impressionism*, p. 103.

23 Duncan Grant's 1918 diary: HC.

24 Vanessa Bell to R. Fry, [August 1918]: KCC.

25 Woolf, *Letters*, vol. II, pp. 232–3.

26 D. Grant to M. Keynes, [July 1918]: BL.

27 Vanessa Bell to R. Fry, [?18 December 1918]: KCC.

28 D. Garnett to L. Strachey, Christmas Day 1918: BL.

29 David Garnett's 1919 diary: HC.

Chapter 9: At Home and Abroad 1919–1926

1 Vanessa Bell, Memoir IV: AVG.

2 Woolf, *Letters*, vol. II, p. 128.

3 Leonard Woolf, *Downhill All the Way*, 1967, p. 115.

4 Vanessa Bell to M. Vaughan, 10 March [1920]: KCC.

5 Same to same, 16 March [1920]: KCC.

6 Woolf, *Letters*, vol. III, pp. 220-1.

7 Ibid., II, p. 332.

8 Vanessa Bell to Virginia Woolf, 13 May [1919]: Berg.

9 J.M. Keynes to Vanessa Bell, 16 March 1919: KCC.

10 Same to same, 3 June 1919: KCC.

11 Vanessa Bell to R. Fry, 29 October [1919]: KCC.

12 Same to same, 29 April [1920]: KCC.

13 Ibid.

14 Same to same, 17 May [1920]: KCC.

15 Lytton to James Strachey, 10 September 1920: BL.

16 D. Grant to D. Garnett, 17 April 1921: KCC.

17 Vanessa Bell to D. Grant, [3 August 1921]: KCC.

18 This and subsequent quotations are taken from copies of the Charleston Bulletin (later the New Bulletin) in the possession of Quentin Bell.

19 Vanessa to Clive Bell, [?23 October 1921]: KCC.

20 Vanessa Bell, notebook on Julian's life, written 1937: KCC.

21 Woolf, *Diaries*, vol. II, p. 159.

22 Vanessa Bell to R. Fry, 2 March [1922]: KCC.

23 Vanessa Bell to J.M. Keynes, 4 February [1922]: KCC.

24 J.M. Keynes to Vanessa Bell, 22 December 1921: KCC.

25 J.M. Keynes to Vanessa Bell, 20 May 1922: KCC.

26 L. Lopokova to J.M. Keynes [11 April 1922]: KCC.

27 Same to same, [27 October 1922]: KCC.

28 Vanessa Bell to J.M. Keynes, 1 January 1922: KCC.

29 Vanessa Bell to J.M. Keynes [no date]: KCC.

30 Woolf, *Diaries*, vol. II, p. 195.

31 *New Statesman*, 5 May 1923.

32 *The Times*, 24 April 1923.

33 Vanessa Bell to D. Grant, 21 April [1923]: HC.

34 Same to same, [July 1923]: HC.

35 Same to same, 11 June [1923]: HC.

36 Same to same, [April 1923]: HC.

37 Woolf, *Diaries*, vol. II, p. 299.

38 Woolf, *Letters*, vol. III, p. 97.

39 L. Lopokova to J.M. Keynes [21 May 1922]: KCC.

40 R. Fry to H. Anrep, [1925]: AP.

41 Same to same, 5 August [1925]: AP.

42 Leighton Park lecture (typescript): AVG.

43 Woolf, *Letters*, vol. III, p. 209.

44 Woolf, *Diaries*, vol. III, p. 33.

45 Woolf, *Letters*, vol. III, p. 270-1.

46 C. Bell to Virginia Woolf, 6 April 1926: Sussex.

47 R. Fry to H. Anrep, 15 August 1926: AP.

Chapter 10: Charleston in France 1927–1930

1 Letter to the author [September 1981].

2 *Nation and Athenaeum*, 15 February 1930.

3 *Nation*, 9 June 1923.

4 F. Henderson to C. Bell, 4 April 1927: KCC.

5 D. Grant to Vanessa Bell, 7 January 1927: KCC.

6 Leslie Stephen, *Swift*, 1882, p. 134.

7 Vanessa Bell to D. Grant, [10 January 1927]: KCC.

8 Woolf, *Diaries*, vol. III, p. 124.

9 Vanessa Bell to R. Fry, [January 1927]: KCC.

10 Vanessa Bell to Virginia Woolf, 5 February [1927]: Berg.

11 Vanessa to Quentin Bell, 5 February [1930]: QB.

12 Vanessa Bell to Virginia Woolf, 17 March [1928]: Berg.

13 Woolf, *Letters*, vol. III, pp. 340–1.

14 Vanessa Bell to Virginia Woolf, 23 April [1927]: Berg.

15 D. Grant to D. Garnett, 6 May 1929: HC.

16 Vanessa Bell to R. Fry, 3 April [1927]: KCC.

17 Vanessa Bell to Virginia Woolf, 3 May [1927]: Berg.

18 Ibid., 11 May [1927]: Berg.

19 Vanesssa Bell to R. Fry [July? 1927]: CP.

20 Vanessa Bell to Virginia Woolf, 22 February [1927]: Berg.

21 Woolf, *Letters*, vol. III, p. 391.

22 Vanessa Bell to D. Grant, 11 October [1927]: HC.

23 Vanessa Bell to R. Fry, 4 May [1928]: KCC.

24 Vanessa Bell to Virginia Woolf, 9 March [1928]: Berg.

25 Woolf, *Diaries*, vol. III, pp. 186–7.

26 Virginia Woolf, *To the Lighthouse*, 1927, p. 232.

27 Vanessa to Julian Bell, no date: QB.

28 Vanessa Bell to R. Fry, 22 January [1929]: KCC.

29 Vanessa Bell to Virginia Woolf, 29 April [1929]: Berg.

30 Ibid., 24 May [1929]: Berg.

31 J.M. Keynes to Vanessa Bell, 24 May 1929: KCC.

32 Vanessa Bell, notebook on Julian's life, written 1937: KCC.

33 Woolf, *Diaries*, vol. III, pp. 232–3.

34 D. Grant to D. Garnett, 2 June 1929: HC.

35 C. Bell to F. Partridge, 30 April 1929: FP.

36 Vanessa to Clive Bell [late July 1929]: KCC.

37 Woolf, *Diaries*, vol. III, pp. 242–3.

38 Ibid., p. 255.

39 Vanessa Bell to Virginia Woolf, 29 April [1929]: Berg.

40 Vanessa to Julian Bell, 15 October [1929]: QB.

41 Woolf, *Diaries*, vol. III, p. 260.

42 Ibid., pp. 261–2.

43 *Vogue*, early February 1926.

44 Vanessa Bell to D. Grant, [4 February 1930]: HC.

45 Same to same, 7 February [1930]: HC.

46 Same to same, 13 February [1930]: HC.

47 D. Grant to Vanessa Bell, [13 February 1930]: KCC.

48 Vanessa to Clive Bell, 4 March [1930]: KCC.

49 D. Grant to D. Garnett, 2 March 1930: HC.

Chapter 11: High Yellow
1930–1934

1 Osbert Sitwell, *Laughter in the Next Room*, 1949, p. 17.

2 William Chappell (ed.), *Edward Burra. A Painter Remembered by His Friends*, 1982, p. 79.

3 Robert Medley, in conversation with the author, 23 January 1981.

4 Vanessa Bell to R. Fry, 2 October [1932]: KCC.

5 Angelica Garnett, introduction to *Elizabeth Curtis: Poems*, published by

the Elizabeth Curtis Memorial Fund, 1970.

6 Raymond Coxon to the author [Summer 1981].

7 Vanessa Bell to J.M. Keynes, 31 May [1930]: KCC.

8 J.M. Keynes to Vanessa Bell, 2 June 1930: KCC.

9 Vanessa to Clive Bell, 15 June [1930]: KCC.

10 Vanessa Bell to D. Grant, 7 August [1931?]: HC.

11 C. Bell to F. Marshall, 6 August 1930: FP.

12 Woolf, *Diaries*, vol. III, p. 316.

13 C. Bell to L. Strachey, 6 September 1930: BL.

14 Woolf, *Diaries*, vol. III, p. 328.

15 Vanessa Bell to R. Fry, 15 August [1930]: KCC.

16 R. Bell to H. Anrep, no date [1930]: KCC.

17 Vanessa Bell to Virginia Woolf, [October 1931]: Berg.

18 Woolf, *Letters*, vol. IV, p. 390.

19 Vanessa to Clive Bell, 15 June [1930]: KCC.

20 Vanessa to Julian Bell, 5 May [1931]: QB.

21 Peter Stansky and William Abrahams, *Journey to the Frontier*, 1966, p. 98.

22 Vanessa Bell to R. Fry, [? July 1931]: KCC.

23 Same to same, 20 October [1931]: KCC.

24 Vanessa Bell to R. Fry, 29 September [1930]: KCC.

25 J. Bell to B. Mackenzie-Smith, no date: the author.

26 Vanessa Bell to D. Carrington, 25 January [1932]: Texas.

27 Frances Partridge, *Memories*, 1981, p. 214.

28 Isabelle Anscombe, *The Omega and After*, 1981, p. 133.

29 Kenneth Clark, *Another Part of the Wood*, 1974, pp. 247–8.

30 Vanessa Bell to R. Fry, 2 October [1932]: KCC.

31 Same to same, [12 June 1932]: KCC. A sketch for her backdrop design was exhibited at Davis and Long, New York, in April–May 1981 in *Vanessa Bell: A Retrospective Exhibition*, no. 43.

32 R. Fry to H. Anrep, 19 August 1931: AP.

33 Vanessa Bell to J.M. Keynes, 28 July 1931: KCC.

34 C. Bell to F. Partridge, 16 August 1932: FP.

35 Vanessa Bell to R. Fry, 18 June [1932]: KCC.

36 Vanessa Bell to D. Grant, [1933]: HC.

37 Woolf, *Letters*, vol. V, p. 243.

38 *New Statesman and Nation*, 24 June 1933.

39 Vanessa Bell to D. Grant [31 July 1934]: DG Papers.

40 Stansky and Abrahams, *Journey to the Frontier*, p. 58.

41 Ibid., p. 68.

42 Barbara Morrison (née Mackenzie-Smith) to the author, 19 July 1981.

43 Stansky and Abrahams, op. cit., p. 93.

44. Ibid., p. 126.

45 D. Grant to R. Fry, no date [1933 or 1934]: KCC.

46 *Burlington Magazine*, 1929, vol. LIV, p. 58.

47 Vanessa Bell to R. Fry, 18 March [1934]: KCC.

48 R. Fry to Vanessa Bell, 19 April 1934: KCC.

49 Virginia Woolf to H. Anrep, [September 1934], unpublished: AP.

50 A. Clutton-Brock to H. Anrep, [September 1934]: AP.

51 Vanessa Bell to H. Anrep, [September 1934]: AP.
52 Same to same, [14 September 1934]: AP.
53 Ibid.

Chapter 12: Between Bloomsbury and China 1935-1937

1 Reproduced in Richard Shone's *Bloomsbury Portraits*, 1976, p. 213.
2 Vanessa Bell to H. Anrep, 19 April [1935]: AP.
3 Two undated letters, Vanessa Bell to H. Anrep [1935]: AP.
4 Woolf, *Diaries*, vol. IV, p. 314.
5 Ibid., p. 399.
6 Vanessa Bell to Virginia Woolf, 14 June [1935]: Berg.
7 *The Architectural Review*, February 1933, quoted in Shone, op. cit., p. 239.
8 Vanessa to Quentin Bell, 3 April [1935]: QB.
9 Quoted in Stansky and Abrahams, *Journey to the Frontier*, pp. 250-51.
10 Ibid., p. 252.
11 Angelica Garnett, *The Web of Kindness* (forthcoming publication).
12 Vanessa to Julian Bell, 18 September [1935]: QB.
13 Same to same, 1 November [1935]: QB.
14 Quentin Bell (ed.), *Julian Bell. Essays, Poems and Letters*, 1938, p. 261.
15 Vanessa to Julian Bell, 24 September [1935]: QB.
16 J.M. Keynes to Sir Percy Bates, 25 September 1935 (carbon copy): KCC.
17 Sir Percy Bates to J.M. Keynes, 7 October 1935: KCC.
18 J.M. Keynes to Sir Percy Bates, 9 October 1935 (carbon copy): KCC.

19 Vanessa to Julian Bell, 15 December [1935]: QB.
20 Same to same, 26 December [1935]: QB.
21 Vanessa Bell to Virginia Woolf, 29 December [1935]: Berg.
22 Vanessa to Julian Bell, 1 February [1936]: QB.
23 Same to same, 9 May [1936]: QB.
24 'Angelica Garnett and her leaving Charleston', Southern Television programme, 1979.
25 Vanessa to Julian Bell, 11 March [1936]: QB.
26 Same to same, 13 February [1936]: QB.
27 Same to same, 11 March [1936]: QB.
28 Same to same, 5 July [1936]: QB.
29 M. Oxford to Vanessa Bell, 16 July 1936: KCC.
30 *Listener*, 8 April 1936.
31 Vanessa to Julian Bell, 13 December [1935]: KCC.
32 Same to same, 2 January [1936]: QB.
33 Vanessa to Quentin Bell, 21 January [1936]: QB.
34 Vanessa to Julian Bell, 13 June [1936]: QB.
35 Vanessa to Quentin Bell, 1 July [1930]: QB.
36 Woolf, *Letters*, vol. VI, p. 20.
37. Conversation with Ling Su-Hua, 13 May 1982.
38 *Julian Bell*, p. 44.
39 J. Bell to B. Mackenzie-Smith, 16-18 November [1935]: the author.
40 *Julian Bell*, pp. 228-9.
41 Vanessa to Julian Bell, 5 June [1936]: QB.
42 Same to same, 15 August [1936]: QB.
43 *Julian Bell*, pp. 132-3.
44 Ibid., pp. 111-12.
45 Vanessa to Julian Bell, 22 July [1936]: QB.

46 *Julian Bell*, p. 156.

47 Vanessa to Julian Bell, 25 April [1936]: QB.

48 Virginia Woolf to J. Bell, 20 June 1936 (unpublished): KCC.

49 Vanessa to Julian Bell, 29 March [1936]: QB.

50 Same to same, 5 September [1936]: QB.

51 D. Garnett to J. Bell, [October 1936]: KCC.

52 Vanessa to Julian Bell, 19 December [1936]: QB.

53 *Julian Bell*, p. 180.

54 Ibid., p. 165.

55 Ibid., p. 324.

56 Ibid., p. 10.

57 Vanessa to Quentin Bell, 8 June [1937]: QB.

58 *Julian Bell*, p. 193.

59 Vanessa to Julian Bell, 20 June [1937]: QB.

60 Same to same, 31 May [1936]: QB.

Chapter 13: Bitter Odds 1937–1945

1   Vanessa Bell to V. Sackville-West, 2 April [1941]: Nigel Nicolson.

2   Woolf, *Letters*, vol. VI, pp. 158–9.

3   C. Bell to F. Partridge, 30 July 1937: FP.

4   J.M. Keynes to Vanessa Bell, 22 July [1937]: KCC.

5   Vanessa Bell to J.M. Keynes, 30 November 1937: KCC.

6   The complete letter is found in Quentin Bell (ed.) *Julian Bell. Essays, Poems and Letters*, pp. 197–8.

7   Vanessa Bell to J.M. Keynes, 30 November 1937: KCC.

8   Vanessa Bell to D. Grant, 5 August [1937?]: HC.

9   Vanessa Bell to V. Sackville-West, 16 August [1937]: Berg.

10 Vanessa Bell to Virginia Woolf, 9 September [1937]: Nigel Nicolson.

11 Vanessa Bell to 'Y', 24 August [1937]: private collection.

12 D. Grant to D. Garnett, [13 August 1937]: HC.

13 Vanessa to Quentin Bell, 9 November [1937]: QB.

14 Vanessa to Julian Bell, 7 March [1937]: QB.

15 Virginia Woolf, *The Waves*, 1931, p. 102.

16 Q. Bell to the author, 24 August 1982.

17 W. Coldstream and G. Bell 'A Plan for Artists' *c.* 1935, quoted in full in an appendix to Nicholas Serota's unpublished thesis 'Realism and the Euston Road School', May 1968, University of Cambridge.

18 *New Statesman*, 5 November 1938.

19 Vanessa to Quentin Bell, 19 October [1937]: QB.

20 D. Garnett to D. Grant, 2 March [1925]: HC.

21 Vanessa to Quentin Bell, 29 November [1935]: QB.

22 David Garnett, *The Familiar Faces*, 1962, p. 165.

23 Duncan Grant's diary, 18 April [1938]: HC.

24 D. Garnett to Vanessa Bell, [16 April 1938]: HC.

25 Vanessa Bell to D. Garnett, 20 April 1938: HC.

26 Ibid., 25 August 1938: HC.

27 Vanessa to Quentin Bell, no date [Autumn 1938?]: QB.

28 Vanessa Bell to Virginia Woolf, 17 March [1938]: Berg.

29 For an account of the lunch and lecture see Richard Shone, 'Duncan Grant on a Sickert lecture', *Burlington Magazine*, November 1981, vol. CXXIII, no. 943, pp. 671–2.

30 Vanessa Bell to D. Garnett, 16 October 1938: HC.

31 Vanessa Bell to Virginia Woolf, no date [late September 1938]: Berg.

32 Ibid., 31 May [1939]: Berg.

33 Virginia Woolf to Vanessa Bell [5 June 1939]: KCC (previously unpublished).

34 Angelica Garnett, *The Web of Kindness* (forthcoming publication).

35 Vanessa to Julian Bell, 25 January [1936]: QB.

36 Nigel Henderson to the author, 17 September 1982.

37 'Angelica Garnett and her leaving Charleston', Southern Television programme, 1979.

38 Vanessa Bell to D. Grant [28 July 1939]: HC.

39 Vanessa Bell to E. Sackville-West, 14 July [1939]: Berg.

40 C. Bell to F. Partridge, 12 September 1939: FP.

41 Vanessa Bell to Virginia Woolf [13 March 1940]: Berg.

42 Angelica Bell to Virginia Woolf, no date [May 1940]: Sussex.

43 Vanessa to Angelica Bell, 11 May [1940]: AVG.

44 Vanessa Bell to D. Grant, no date [May/June? 1940]: HC.

45 Peter Quennell, *The Sign of the Fish*, 1960, p. 73.

46. Duncan to Ethel Grant, 26 September 1940: HC.

47 Vanessa Bell to Virginia Woolf, 20 March [1941]: Sussex.

48 Woolf, *Letters*, vol. VI, p. 485.

49 V. Sackville-West to Vanessa Bell, 31 March 1941: KCC.

50 John Lehmann, *Thrown to the Woolfs*, 1978, pp. 112–13.

51 J. Bussy to Vanessa Bell, 18 February 1941: KCC.

52 Vanessa to Angelica Bell [24 November 1941]: AVG.

53 Ibid.

54 Quoted in Richard Shone's comprehensive account of the commission in *The Berwick Church Paintings*, published by the Towner Art Gallery, Eastbourne, July 1969, unpaginated.

55 H. Anrep to Vanessa Bell, 12 September 1943: KCC.

56 Ibid., no date [October 1944]: KCC.

57 David Garnett, *The White-Garnett Letters*, 1968, p. 178.

58 Kenneth Clark, *Another Part of the Wood*, 1974, pp. 248–9.

Chapter 14: The Attic Studio 1945–1961

1 David Garnett, *The Flowers of the Forest*, p. 26.

2 Lord Milford (Wogan Philipps) to the author, 19 September 1982.

3 Angelica Garnett, *The Web of Kindness* (forthcoming publication).

4 Vanessa Bell to Angelica Garnett, 24 May [1945]: AVG.

5 C. Bell to F. Partridge, 11 August 1946: FP.

6 Same to same, 27 November 1947: FP.

7 Vanessa Bell to Angelica Garnett, 8 August [1945]: AVG.

8 Same to same, 12 June [1949]: AVG.

9 Angelica to David Garnett, no date (*c.* 1945–6): HC.

10 Vanessa Bell to Angelica Garnett, 25 August [1945?]: AVG.

11 J. Bussy to Vanessa Bell, 26 June 1945: KCC.

12 J.M. Keynes to Vanessa Bell, 26 August 1945: Marshall Library, University of Cambridge.

13 Vanessa Bell to Angelica Garnett, 4 May 1950: AVG.

14 Ibid., 31 October [1951]: AVG.

15 Vanessa Bell to H. Anrep,
20 September [1948]: AP.

16 Vanessa Bell to Angelica Garnett,
11 June [1945]: AVG.

17 This, and much else concerning their
relationship, is recalled in Paul Roche's
With Duncan Grant in Southern Turkey,
1982.

18 C. Bell to F. Partridge, 20 December
1947: FP.

19 P. Roche to the author, 5 May 1982.

20 Ibid.

21 Angelica Garnett, *The Web of Kindness*
(forthcoming publication).

22 D. Grant to Vanessa Bell, 6 December
1948: KCC.

23 Vanessa Bell to Ling Su-Hua, 4 July
1939 and 14 January [1947]: both letters
in the possession of Ling Su-Hua.

24 J. Bussy to Vanessa Bell, 29 May 1947:
KCC.

25 D. Bussy to Vanessa Bell, 3 January
1951: KCC.

26 Vanessa Bell to Angelica Garnett,
14 October [1946?]: AVG.

27 Same to same, 15 December [1945]:
AVG.

28 D. Grant to Vanessa Bell, 6 June 1937:
KCC.

29 Vanessa Bell to Angelica Garnett,
10 March [1946]: AVG.

30 Same to same, 7 January [1948]: AVG.

31 Same to same, 5 May [1948]: AVG.

32 Same to same, 18 April 1949: AVG.

33 Same to same, 23 July [1949]: AVG.

34 Angelica Garnett in *Recollections of
Virginia Woolf*, ed. Joan Russell Noble,
1972, p. 104.

35 Vanessa Bell to L. Woolf, 26 January
1950: Sussex.

36 'Visits to Charleston: Portrait of
Vanessa Bell', unpublished memoir:
HC.

37 Vanessa Bell to Angelica Garnett,
26 March [1950]: AVG.

38 *The Studio*, August 1951. Quoted in
James Hamilton's *25 from '51. 25
Paintings from the Festival of Britain*,
catalogue to an exhibition held in
Sheffield and Birmingham, 1978.

39 Vanessa Bell to Angelica Garnett,
11 February [1951]: AVG.

40 Same to same, 30 May [1950]: AVG.

41 Same to same, 23 August [1951]: AVG.

42 Vanessa Bell to H. Anrep, 5 March
[1952]: AP.

43 Interview with Robert McDonald of
Canadian Broadcasting at Charleston,
31 August 1976: typescript in Tate
Gallery archives.

44 Vanessa Bell to Angelica Garnett,
23 August [1951]: AVG.

45 John Rothenstein, *Modern English
Painters*, 1952, pp. 14-15.

46 Vanessa Bell to Angelica Garnett,
3 October [1952]: AVG.

47 Same to same, 17 February [1951]:
AVG.

48 Same to same, 29 July [1951]: AVG.

49 Vanessa Bell to Angelica Garnett,
10 May [1954]: AVG.

50 Vanessa Bell to Angelica Garnett,
3 May [1955]: AVG.

51 Vanessa to Julian Bell, 17 October
[1936]: QB.

52 Vanessa Bell to Angelica Garnett,
1 April [1959]: AVG.

53 Ibid., 19 June [1956]: AVG.

54 Vanessa Bell to Angelica Garnett,
16 October [1957]: QB.

55 Vanessa to Quentin Bell, 12 October
[1958]: QB.

56 D. Farr to the author, 6 May 1982.

57 E.M. Forster to R.J. Buckingham,
[12 May 1959]: KCC.

58 Vanessa Bell to Angelica Garnett,
[6 September 1954]: KCC.

59 C. Bell to F. Partridge, 12 November 1959: FP.

60 Ibid., 25 January 1960: FP.

61 Ibid., 14 March 1960: FP.

62 Vanessa Bell to Angelica Garnett, 13 March [1960]: AVG.

63 Ibid., 24 March [1960]: AVG.

64 Ibid., 2 May [1960]: AVG.

65 C. Bell to F. Partridge, 2 May 1960: FP.

66 See note 36.

67 Woolf, *Letters*, vol. I, p. 31.

68 Vanessa Bell to Angelica Garnett, 27 September [1960]: AVG.

69 Same to same, 22 February [1961]: AVG.

70 Same to same, 6 March [1961]: AVG.

71 The story that Quentin told Duncan shortly before the end came, 'Tell her that you love her' (see Roche, *With Duncan Grant in Southern Turkey*, p. 21) is unfounded.

72 Woolf, *Letters*, vol. III, p. 363.

Select Bibliography

Anscombe, Isabelle, *Omega and After* (London: Thames and Hudson, 1981)

Askwith, Betty, *Two Victorian Families* (London: Chatto and Windus, 1971)

Asquith, Cynthia, *Remember and Be Glad* (London: James Barrie, 1952)

Bell, Alan (ed.), *Sir Leslie Stephen's Mausoleum Book* (Oxford: Clarendon Press, 1977)

Bell, Clive, *Art* (London: Chatto and Windus, 1914)

    Civilization (London: Chatto and Windus, 1928)

    Old Friends. Personal Recollections (London: Chatto and Windus, 1956)

Bell, Quentin (ed.), *Julian Bell. Essays, Poems and Letters* (London: Hogarth Press, 1938)

    Roger Fry, An Inaugural Lecture (University of Leeds, 1964)

    'The Omega Revisited', *Listener*, 30 January 1964, pp. 201 ff.

    and Stephen Chaplin. 'The Ideal Home Rumpus', *Apollo*, October 1964, Vol. 80, pp. 284–91

    and Stephen Chaplin. 'Reply with Rejoinder'. *Apollo*, January 1966, Vol. 83, p. 75

    Bloomsbury (London: Weidenfeld and Nicolson, 1968)

    Virginia Woolf: A Biography. Volume One: Virginia Stephen 1882–1912 (London: Hogarth Press, 1972)

    Virginia Woolf: A Biography. Volume Two: Mrs Woolf 1912–1941 (London: Hogarth Press, 1972)

Bell, Vanessa, *Notes on Virginia's Childhood*, ed. R.J. Schaubeck (New York: Frank Hallman 1974)

Boyd, Elizabeth French, *Bloomsbury Heritage. Their Mothers and Aunts* (London: Hamish Hamilton, 1976)

Brenan, Gerald, *South from Granada* (London: Hamish Hamilton, 1957)

Brown, Oliver, *Exhibition. The Memoirs of Oliver Brown* (London: Evelyn Adams and Mackay, 1968)

Burne-Jones, Georgiana, *Memorials of Edward Burne-Jones*, 2 vols. (London: Macmillan, 1904)

Cecil, Viscount Cecil of Chelwood, *All the Way* (London: Hodder and Stoughton, 1949)

Chesterton, G.K., *G.F. Watts* (London: Duckworth, 1904)

Clark, Kenneth, *Another Part of the Wood* (London: John Murray, 1974)

    The Other Half (London: John Murray, 1977)

Cork, Richard, *Vorticism and Abstract Art in the First Machine Age. Volume One: Origins and Development* (London: Gordon Fraser, 1975)

Crabtree, Derek and A.P. Thirlwall (eds.), *Keynes and the Bloomsbury Group* (London: Macmillan 1980)

Curtiss, Mina, *Other People's Letters* (London: Macmillan, 1978)

Daintrey, Adrian, *I Must Say* (London: Chatto and Windus, 1963)

Dangerfield, George, *The Strange Death of Liberal England 1910-1914* (London: Constable, 1936)

Darroch, Sandra Jobson, *Ottoline. A Life of Lady Ottoline Morrell* (London: Chatto and Windus, 1976)

Dunlop, Ian, *The Shock of the New: Seven Historic Exhibitions of Modern Art* (London: Weidenfeld and Nicolson, 1972)

Fielding, Daphne, *The Rainbow Picnic: A Portrait of Iris Tree* (London: Eyre Methuen, 1974)

Fry, Roger, *Vision and Design* (London: Chatto and Windus, 1920)
  Duncan Grant (London: Hogarth Press, 1923)
  Transformations (London: Chatto and Windus, 1926)
  Cézanne (London: Hogarth Press, 1927)
  Last Lectures (Cambridge University Press, 1939)

Fuller, Hester Thackeray and Violet Hammersley, *Thackeray's Daughter: Some Recollections of Anne Thackeray Ritchie* (Dublin: Euphorion Books, 1951)

Furbank, P.N., *E.M. Forster: A Life. Volume One: The Growth of a Novelist (1879-1914)* (London: Secker and Warburg, 1977)
  E.M. Forster: A Life. Volume Two: Polycrates' Ring (1914-1970) (London: Secker and Warburg, 1977)

Furse, Katherine, *Hearts and Pomegranates: The Story of Forty-Five Years 1875 to 1920* (London: Peter Davies, 1940)

Garland, Madge, *The Indecisive Decade* (London: Macdonald, 1968)

Garnett, Angelica, 'Duncan Grant' in *Duncan Grant (1885-1978): Works on Paper* (catalogue to exhibition held at the Anthony d'Offay Gallery, 25 November to 18 December 1981)

Garnett, David, *The Golden Echo* (London: Chatto and Windus, 1954)
  The Flowers of the Forest (London: Chatto and Windus, 1955)
  The Familiar Faces (London: Chatto and Windus, 1962)
  Great Friends (London: Macmillan, 1979)

Gathorne-Hardy, Robert (ed.), *The Early Memoirs of Lady Ottoline Morrell* (London: Faber and Faber, 1963)
  Ottoline at Garsington. Memoirs of Lady Ottoline Morrell 1915-1918 (London: Faber and Faber, 1974)

Gerin, Winifred, *Anne Thackeray Ritchie: A Biography* (Oxford University Press, 1981)

Gillespie, Diane Filby, 'Vanessa Bell, Virginia Woolf and Duncan Grant: Conversation with Angelica Garnett', *Modernist Studies. Literature and Culture 1920-1940*, vol. 3, 1979, pp. 151-8

Grosskurth, Phyllis, *John Addington Symonds: A Biography* (London: Longmans, 1964)

Gunn, Peter, *Vernon Lee* (London: Oxford University Press, 1964)

Hamnett, Nina, *Laughing Torso: Reminiscences* (London: Constable, 1932)

Harrod, Roy, *The Life of John Maynard Keynes* (London: Macmillan, 1951)

Heilbrun, Carolyn G., *The Garnett Family* (London: George Allen and Unwin, 1961)

Hill, Brian, *Julia Margaret Cameron: A Victorian Family Portrait* (London: Peter Owen, 1973)

Holroyd, Michael, *Lytton Strachey: The Unknown Years 1880-1910* (London: Heinemann, 1967)

    Lytton Strachey: The Years of Achievement 1910-1932 (London: Heinemann, 1978)

    Augustus John: The Years of Innocence (London: Heinemann, 1974)

    Augustus John. Volume Two. The Years of Experience (London: Heinemann, 1975)

Johnstone, J.K., *The Bloomsbury Group* (London: Secker and Warburg, 1954)

Keynes, John Maynard, *Two Memoirs* (London: Macmillan, 1949)

Keynes, Milo (ed.), *Essays on John Maynard Keynes* (Cambridge University Press, 1975)

Lago, Mary M. (ed.), *William Rothenstein. Men and Memories* (London: Chatto and Windus, 1978)

Lees-Milne, James, *Harold Nicolson. A Biography, 1886-1929* (volume I) (London: Chatto and Windus, 1980)

Lehmann, John, *The Whispering Gallery. Autobiography I* (London: Longmans, 1955)

    Thrown to the Woolfs (London: Weidenfeld and Nicolson, 1978)

Levy, Paul, *Moore. G.E. Moore and the Cambridge Apostles* (London: Weidenfeld and Nicolson, 1979)

Lilly, Marjorie, *Sickert. The Painter and his Circle* (London: Elek Books, 1971)

Love, Jean O., *Virginia Woolf. Sources of Madness and Art* (London: University of California Press, 1977)

MacCarthy, Desmond, 'The Art-Quake of 1910', *Listener*, 1 February 1945

    Memories (London: MacGibbon and Kee, 1953)

Maitland, Frederic William, *The Life and Letters of Leslie Stephen* (London: Duckworth, 1906)

Meyers, Jeffrey, *The Enemy. A Biography of Wyndham Lewis* (London: Routledge and Kegan Paul, 1980)

Moore, G.E. *Principia Ethica* (Cambridge University Press, 1903)

Morphet, Richard, 'The Significance of Charleston', *Apollo*, November 1967, Vol. XXXVI, No. 69, pp. 342-5

Morphet, Richard, 'The Art of Vanessa Bell', *Vanessa Bell: Paintings and Drawings*, catalogue to exhibition held at the Anthony d'Offay Gallery 20 November to 12 December 1973

Nash, Paul, *Outline: An Autobiography and other Writings* (London: Faber and Faber, 1949)

Partridge, Frances, *A Pacifist's War* (London: Hogarth Press, 1978)

    Memories (London: Victor Gollancz, 1981)

Petrie, Sir Charles Alexander, *Scenes from Edwardian Life* (London: Eyre and Spottiswoode, 1965)

Poole, Roger, *The Unknown Virginia Woolf* (Cambridge University Press, 1978)

Ritchie, Hester (ed.), *Letters of Anne Thackeray Ritchie* (London: John Murray, 1926)

Roche, Paul, *With Duncan Grant in Southern Turkey* (London: Honeyglen, 1982)

Rosenbaum, S.P. (ed.), *The Bloomsbury Group: A Collection of Memories: Commentary and Criticism* (London: Croom Helm, 1975)

Rothenstein, John, *Modern English Painters. Volume One: Sickert to Grant* (London: Eyre and Spottiswoode, 1952)

Shone, Richard, *The Berwick Church Paintings* (Eastbourne: The Towner Art Gallery, 1969)

'The Friday Club', *Burlington Magazine*, May 1975 Vol. CXVII, No. 866, pp. 279-84

Bloomsbury Portraits (Oxford: Phaidon Press, 1976)

'Introduction' in *Duncan Grant designer*, catalogue to exhibition held at the Bluecoat Gallery, Liverpool and at Brighton Museum, 1 February to 13 April 1980

'Vanessa Bell', *Vanessa Bell 1879-1961: A Retrospective Exhibition* held at Davis and Long, New York, 18 April to 24 May 1980

Sitwell, Osbert, *Laughter in the Next Room* (London: Macmillan, 1949)

Spalding, Frances, *Roger Fry: Art and Life* (London: Elek/Granada, 1980)

Spater, George and Ian Parsons, *A Marriage of True Minds: An Intimate Portrait of Leonard and Virginia Woolf* (London: Jonathan Cape and Hogarth Press, 1977)

Spender, Stephen, *World within World* (London: Hamish Hamilton, 1951)

Stansky, Peter and Abrahams, William, *Journey to the Frontier: A Biography of Julian Bell and John Cornford* (London: Constable, 1973)

Strachey, Barbara, *Remarkable Relations: The Story of the Pearsall Smith Family* (London: Victor Gollancz, 1980)

Su Hua, *Ancient Melodies* (London: Hogarth Press, 1953)

Sutton, Denys (ed.), *Letters of Roger Fry* (2 vols.) (London: Chatto and Windus, 1972)

Todd, Dorothy and Raymond Mortimer, *The New Interior Decoration* (London: Batsford, 1929)

Trombley, Stephen, *All that Summer She was Mad: Virginia Woolf and her Doctors* (London: Junction Books, 1981)

Watney, Simon, *English Post-Impressionism* (London: Studio Vista, 1980)

Wees, William C., *Vorticism and the English Avant-Garde* (Manchester and Toronto: Manchester University Press)

Woolf, Leonard, *The Wise Virgins. A Story of Words, Opinions and a Few Emotions* (London: Edward Arnold, 1914)

Beginning Again. An Autobiography of the Years 1911-1918 (London: Hogarth Press, 1964)

Downhill All the Way. An Autobiography of the Years 1919-1939 (London: Hogarth Press, 1967)

Woolf, Virginia, *Roger Fry: A Biography* (London: Hogarth Press, 1940)

Moments of Being. Unpublished Autobiographical Writings, edited by Jeanne Schulkind (Sussex: The University Press 1976)

The Flight of the Mind. The Letters of Virginia Woolf, Vol. I: 1888-1912, edited by Nigel Nicolson (London: Hogarth Press, 1975)

The Question of Things Happening. The Letters of Virginia Woolf, Vol. II: 1912-1922, edited by Nigel Nicolson (London: Hogarth Press, 1976)

A Change of Perspective. The Letters of Virginia Woolf, Vol. III: 1923-1928, edited by Nigel Nicolson (London: Hogarth Press, 1977)

A Reflection of the Other Person. The Letters of Virginia Woolf, Vol. IV: 1929–1931, edited by Nigel Nicolson (London: Hogarth Press, 1978)

The Sickle Side of The Moon. The Letters of Virginia Woolf, Vol. V: 1932–1935, edited by Nigel Nicolson (London: Hogarth Press, 1979)

Leave the Letters Till We're Dead. The Letters of Virginia Woolf, Vol. VI: 1936–1941, edited by Nigel Nicolson (London: Hogarth Press, 1980)

The Diary of Virginia Woolf, Vol. I: 1915–1919, edited by Anne Olivier Bell (London: Hogarth Press, 1976)

The Diary of Virginia Woolf, Vol. II: 1920–1924, edited by Anne Olivier Bell (London: Hogarth Press, 1978)

The Diary of Virginia Woolf, Vol. III: 1925–1930, edited by Anne Olivier Bell (London: Hogarth Press, 1980)

The Diary of Virginia Woolf, Vol. IV: 1931–1935, edited by Anne Olivier Bell (London: Hogarth Press, 1982)

Zink, David D., *Leslie Stephen* (New York: Twayne Publishers, 1972)

Index